Critical Essays on
James Baldwin

Critical Essays on James Baldwin

Fred L. Standley
Nancy V. Burt

G. K. Hall & Co. • Boston, Massachusetts

Library of Congress Cataloging in Publication Data

Standley, Fred L.
  Critical essays on James Baldwin.

  (Critical essays on American literature)
  Includes index.
  1. Baldwin, James, 1924–   —Criticism and
interpretation. I. Burt, Nancy V. II. Title.
III. Series.
PS3552.A45Z88 1988   818'.5409   88–1802
ISBN 0–8161–8879–3

This publication is printed on permanent durable acid-free paper
MANUFACTURED IN THE UNITED STATES OF AMERICA

CRITICAL ESSAYS ON AMERICAN LITERATURE

This series seeks to anthologize the most important criticism on a wide variety of topics and writers in American literature. Our readers will find in various volumes not only a generous selection of reprinted articles and reviews but original essays, bibliographies, manuscript sections, and other materials brought to public attention for the first time. This volume is a collection of reviews and essays tracing the critical reputation of James Baldwin. It contains a balanced historical record of critical reaction to one of the most important writers in American literature. The book contains both a sizable gathering of early reviews and a broad selection of more modern scholarship, including an interview with Baldwin, a section of general essays exploring his career, and two sections devoted to his fiction and drama. Among noted early reviewers are Langston Hughes, Julian Mayfield, Leslie A. Fiedler, Granville Hicks, Joyce Carol Oates, and Stephen Spender. Among the authors of reprinted articles are Houston A. Baker, Jr., Trudier Harris, Jocelyn Whitehead Jackson, and Roger Whitlow. In addition to an important introduction which presents an overview of Baldwin's career and of scholarly reactions to it, there are also three original essays commissioned specifically for publication in this volume, new studies by Sondra A. O'Neale, Fred L. Standley, and Yoshinobu Hakutani. We are confident that this book will make a permanent and significant contribution to American literary study.

JAMES NAGEL, GENERAL EDITOR

Northeastern University

CONTENTS

INTRODUCTION

James Baldwin's permanent niche in the pantheon of American men and women of letters now seems assured. During four decades of work in a broad spectrum of genres, Baldwin earned an international reputation and "retains a place in an extremely select group: that composed of the few genuinely indispensable American writers."[1] During the last quarter of a century "his intensely personal art" "achieved an extraordinary popular appeal which has made him one of the most widely read black writers"; for example, *Nobody Knows My Name* (1961), a collection of essays, sold over two million copies, and *The Fire Next Time* (1963), an extended personal essay, sold a million.[2]

From his early book reviews in *New Leader* in 1947 to his latest collection, *The Price of the Ticket: Collected Non-Fiction 1948–1985* (1985), and his volume of poetry, *Jimmy's Blues* (1985), Baldwin's works have never lacked an audience, although they have been alternately extolled and denigrated by the critics—black and white alike. Indeed, the rationale for such a medley of public response appears readily discernible, for throughout his corpus

> there echoes in prophetic tone and moral concern, in intense language and poignant sincerity, a passionate and perceptive exploration of a broad spectrum of themes: the indivisibility of the private life and the public life; the intertwining of power and love in the universal scheme of things and in the structures of society; the misplaced priorities in the value systems of the United States; the historical significance and the potential explosiveness of the continuing racial crisis at home and in the third world; the essential need of the individual to develop sexual and psychological consciousness and identity; and the special responsibility of the artist to promote and contribute to the evolution of the individual and the society. Each of these thematic emphases is consistent with his perspective that only two options are open to all "writers, black or white—to be immoral and uphold the *status quo* or to be moral and try to change the world."[3]

1

In these four decades of literary work, Baldwin published twenty-two books, including six novels, two dramas, eight volumes of essays, one edition of short stories, two series of dialogues, a scenario, a children's book, and a collection of poetry; additionally, he produced innumerable shorter pieces—articles, interviews, recordings, and discussions. Similarly, the criticism elicited by the volume and magnitude of this literary output has also been constant and prodigious, thereby attesting to the interest generated by this contemporary man of letters. For those individuals interested, then, in the life and works of James Baldwin, substantial secondary sources exist that provide references, reviews, commentaries, analyses, and interpretations of the man, the mission, and the results. To that end a survey of the principal sources for the study of Baldwin can be valuable in contributing to the overall assessment of his achievements as well as providing the background and context for the articles and reviews in this present volume.

BIBLIOGRAPHIES AND ANTHOLOGIES

Four bibliographical sources are especially helpful in pursuing studies in Baldwin. Therman B. O'Daniel's "James Baldwin: A Classified Bibliography," which appeared in his edited volume entitled *James Baldwin: A Critical Evaluation* (1977), is an initially useful listing of books, articles, and other works by Baldwin as well as a rather extensive but still selective listing of secondary sources about the author.[4] The bibliography by Carolyn Wedin Sylvander in her *James Baldwin* (1980) is quite serviceable, also, but comprises only primary sources—book, reviews, articles, interviews, and discussions—some of which supplement O'Daniel.[5] The essay entitled "James Baldwin" by Daryl Dance (1978) is a significant, albeit necessarily selective, annotated bibliography of primary works and secondary sources; the latter includes biographical data, manuscript materials, criticism of specific works, general studies, personal criticism, and a sketch of future needs for scholarship to treat.[6] However, the most comprehensive bibliography to date remains *James Baldwin: A Reference Guide* (1980) by Fred L. Standley and Nancy V. Standley; it is a comprehensive annotated study of all works about him dating from 1953 to 1977, with a few items from 1978. The work employs a methodology that "involved a combination of quotation and paraphrase in an effort to construct an annotation in the format of précis or abstract that would reflect the writer's own points of emphasis and evaluation."[7] Moreover, the book provides an extensive list of primary sources, including novels, dramas, essays, short stories, dialogues, scenario, essays, reviews, letters, debates, discussions, short story excerpts, interviews, recordings, and films.

An examination of the bibliographies demonstrates unmistakably the abundance of critical commentary and reviews as well as other data about Baldwin, both by defenders and detractors. Thus far, some three dozen or so of the myriad sources have been anthologized and made more accessible in these edited volumes: Donald Gibson, *Five Black Writers* (1970),[8] Keneth Kinnamon, *James Baldwin: A Collection of Critical Essays* (1974),[9] and Therman O'Daniel, *James Baldwin: A Critical Evaluation* (1977).[10] Gibson's volume contains four early essays on Baldwin as well as others on Richard Wright, Ralph Ellison, Langston Hughes, and Leroi Jones, plus an introduction. Kinnamon's collection of thirteen essays, reviews, a chronology of dates, and a highly selective bibliography offers a broader and more representative approach to Baldwin's diverse concerns. The editor's rationale insists that "a proper understanding of Baldwin and his work must take into account a complicated amalgam of psychological and social elements sometimes thought to be antithetical";[11] such a viewpoint includes biographical data; a summation of recurrent themes—a confrontation with reality, a quest for love, a writer's social responsibility, a regard for sexual and personal identity, etc.; and comments about the innumerable opinions of Baldwin's work.

O'Daniel's edition consists of nearly two dozen items grouped under such headings as "Raps and Dialogues"; accordingly, while some of these materials had already been published earlier in *CLA Journal, Phylon, Black World,* and *Negro American Literature Forum,* more than half were new contributions for this collection and thus a new departure in Baldwin studies. The volume also contains "James Baldwin: A Classified Bibliography," the most complete list of works by and about the author in print to that time.

A judicious investigation of the table of contents of the three anthologies and a cursory inspection of the larger bibliographical inventory of secondary titles lead almost inevitably to some generalizations about Baldwin scholarship and criticism. In the first decade—the fifties—the principal responses to him were in the form of reviews and of commentary on him as spokesman for his race, with little attention afforded the literary artistry. The sixties witnessed not only the continuation of extensive book reviews but also a decided change of emphasis to the author's role as a civil rights advocate as well as an increasing attention to the artistic achievement in literature. The third decade—the seventies—saw the prolongation of interest by the reviewers, an attenuation of interest in his participation in the civil rights movement, a definite enlargement in the consideration given to his literary and aesthetic accomplishments, and an overall estimation of his place as a contemporary man of letters. The decade of the eighties has been characterized by the continuing of the concerns of the previous ten years but also by an acceleration in the

critical evaluation of Baldwin's literary stature and a greater attention
to his understanding of and embodiment of politics, economics, psychology, music, religion, and aesthetics.

THE FIFTIES

During the 1950s the responses occurred in the form of book
reviews and analysis of the author as spokesman for his race, with
only slight acknowledgment of Baldwin's literary artistry. Richard
Barksdale considered Baldwin's first novel, *Go Tell It on the Mountain*
(1953), a religious novel concerned with ethical values and patterns
of conduct rather than race relations;[12] and Granville Hicks also
regarded it as a promising first novel treating morality and religion,
not protest.[13] However, Anthony West described it as "humorless"
and seriously lacking in penetration when compared to Ellison's *Invisible Man* with its rich comic invention relative to religion and to
Dostoyevski's *The Brothers Karamazov* with its "broad farce effects
treating religious behavior."[14] And Steven Marcus contended that *Go
Tell It* treated the problem of personal identity for the urban black
in the North and that Baldwin tried to define precisely what it is
like.[15]

Notes of a Native Son (1955) evoked a considerable, but mixed
response. Langston Hughes labeled it as "pungent commentary" on
certain phases of contemporary American life—Harlem, the protest
novel, Jews, and blacks, among others, presented by an essayist who
is thought-provoking, tantalizing, irritating, abusing, and amusing."[16]
J. Saunders Redding viewed the book as concerned with "the same
question of identity that burdened" *Go Tell It,* but that some of the
essays were irrelevant to the question and others argued in a non-
sensical way that the black American is "by the nature of his being
and his experience disqualified to find and even unlicensed to seek
his identity in the very environment which he helped to create."
Redding further asserted that if Baldwin could settle his own question
of identity, he would become "either a contributor to the magazines
not intended for ladies from Dubuque, or one of the best writers of
his generation."[17]

Neither of these books created a stir comparable to that of
Giovanni's Room (1956). Whereas the reviewer in *Crisis* saw the
book as treating "the scabrous subject of homosexual love" in scenes
resembling "the brutal world of Jean Gênet,"[18] the writer for *New
Republic* declared it the best American novel on homosexuality which,
though "a painful novel," did not deal "cheaply or too simply" with
its subject.[19] Leslie Fiedler affirmed that it was Baldwin's attempt to
be more than just a black writer since it dealt neither with blacks

nor black problems per se; instead it was a book about "the loss of the last American innocence" in Europe.[20]

As the recipient of a Ford Foundation grant in 1959, along with Saul Bellow, e. e. cummings, Bernard Malamud, and Theodore Roethke, Baldwin was touted as among those whose "talents give promise of major contributions to their artistic development and to contemporary American art."[21] Simultaneously, Norman Mailer proclaimed in *Advertisements for Myself* (1959) that *Notes* and *Giovanni's Room* possessed a "sense of moral nuance" and courage, but both were "sprayed with perfume" and by them Baldwin was "doomed to be minor."[22]

THE SIXTIES

The decade of the sixties witnessed the publication by Baldwin of no less than eight books—three volumes of essays, two novels, two dramas, and a collection of short stories. It was also in this period that he became more personally active in the civil rights movement and more outspoken publicly in his account of what it was like to grow up black in America. Furthermore, the first book about Baldwin was written in this period—*The Furious Passage of James Baldwin* (1966) by Fern Marja Eckman—which described him as the "dark man" who rubbed salt in the "wounds of the nation's conscience" and had "an accusing finger thrust in the face of white America." Eckman's extensive personal accounts, based on taped interviews, is the single most important source of autobiographical and biographical data not otherwise available. The book recognized clearly Baldwin's dual role as creative artist and participant in the civil rights revolution.[23]

The essay collection entitled *Nobody Knows My Names* (1961) elicited further praise for the author. Irving Howe argued that the personal essay form of the book presented the author's own protest—nonpolitical in character and spoken as anguish, not revolt—about living under the stigma of skin color;[24] and Julian Mayfield suggested in "A Love Affair with the United States" (1961) that Baldwin grappled honestly and irreverently with the problems of race relations as a "native artist seriously concerned with the fate" of his country.[25]

The appearance in 1962 of his third novel *Another Country* sparked a heated controversy. The popular weeklies tended to denigrate the novel as a failure in which the author tried to "unburden" his feeling about racism and homosexuality via an inadequate narrative frame, wooden dialogue, and intensive sermonic recollections of stereotypical characters.[26] In contrast, Granville Hicks described it in the *Saturday Review* as "one of the most powerful novels of our time" and "shaped with vigorous care" by a "skilled craftsman"; for Hicks the novel's power lay in the presentation of the complexities of love and the terrifying forces of hate among both blacks and whites.[27] Similarly, Norman Podhoretz advocated in "In Defense of a Maltreated Best Seller" that the book embodied a "remorseless insistence" on a "cruel truth" and would ultimately be seen as the work in which "the superb intelligence of Baldwin the essayist became fully available to Baldwin the novelist."[28] Still another important essay about the novel was "The Phrase Unbearably Repeated," by Eugenia Collier, which acknowledged that it contained something "offensive" for everyone but also concentrated on seeing the conjunction between its brutality and violence and its tenderness as a "hurting compassion." Collier stressed that the book was not about race or sex but "the individual's lonely and futile quest for love" reinforced by the author's use of blues as a medium for revealing the victimizing of personal and social forces that the individual cannot control.[29]

One of the true high points in Baldwin's career as a writer came with the publication of *The Fire Next Time* (1963). That book sold almost a million copies and has remained a favorite among readers and critics alike, although it has also elicited a mixture of opinions. F. W. Dupee contended in "James Baldwin and the 'Man' " that in earlier works the author had expressed "a condition of spirit" in formal prose with a syntax suggesting an ideal prose; however, in *The Fire* prophecy had been exchanged for criticism and exhortation for analysis and that the subjects covered lack definition and specificity except for the "cruel paradoxes" of black life, the failures of Christianity, and the relations between blacks and Jews.[30] In stark contrast to that assessment, poet and critic Stephen Spender claimed that *The Fire* represented Baldwin as the "voice of an American consciousness (conscience) which is not Negro" and as a writer without color but with "mind and feelings as they are realized in words." His real contributions as an American writer consisted in his "imagination using words which know no class nor color bars" to "express what one knows to be true."[31]

The critical reception of the volume of photographs by Richard Avedon with text by Baldwin entitled *Nothing Personal* (1964) was primarily negative; generally speaking, the text was regarded as irrelevant, dishonest, hasty overstatement presented in a contorted grammar, a "compendium of beautifully phrased clichés, pompous pronouncements and . . . outrageous generalizations."[32] Fortunately for Baldwin, however, *Blues for Mister Charlie* (1964) also was brought out that year, and in spite of adverse reactions, helped to add another dimension to his emerging reputation, namely, that of dramatist. Tom Driver's essay "The Review That Was Too True to be Published" resulted in the *Negro Digest* bringing out what *Reporter* refused to print; in it Driver praised *Blues* for its acting, production, and content. He argued persuasively that Baldwin stepped outside the usual context of the racial struggle as a constitutional question of civil rights to show racial strife as rooted in the separate ways people experience life with "the difference symbolized in their sexuality." For Driver what the play offended was not the reality down South (for example, in the accurate portrayal of small-town Southern whites) but "the social (hence aesthetic) myths up North"; the drama was a call to action whose social significance lay in what is revealed about fear: "Those who cannot risk when they are afraid . . . will be made impotent by their fear."[33] Subsequently, Waters Turpin also lauded the play, despite its having been frequently labeled as badly written, because it combined the authenticity of nightmare and the blues into "an expressionistic outcry that captures the distilled agony of this racially tormented, mid-twentieth-century America."[34]

Still another facet of Baldwin's literary talent was revealed in 1965 by the volume of short stories called *Going to Meet the Man*. The reviewer for the *New Republic* identified the blues tradition as central to the volume and presenting the reader with a series of problematic conditions with no resolutions, for example, urban desolation and spurious religiosity; but the author's greatest strength was described as endowing "his experience, his feelings, with universal significance."[35] Individual stories in the collection have also received special attention: John Hagopian acknowledged the accomplishments of Baldwin and saw "This Morning, This Evening, So Soon" as one of the most important short stories since World War II, not because of its thematic focus on the black taking his rightful place in society but because of its structure and its "I" narrator "who focuses on public life and society."[36] Later praise of "Previous Condition" concentrated on the story's "alienated and invisible man in miniature" predating Ellison's novel by four years and also revealing the plight of the "black-artist-intellectual."[37] John Reilly later applauded "Sonny's Blues" as the best expression of Baldwin's leading theme—the discovery of identity; the bases of the story and its relationship to the general purpose of his writing were analyzed in terms of the use of the "blues as a key metaphor" with "its combination of personal and social significance in a lyric encounter with history."[38] Keith Byerman has presented the case for "Sonny's Blues" as Baldwin's best short story, and indeed it has been anthologized frequently in the last ten years. Byerman sees the story as a study of the nature and relationship of art and language in which the author adopts a stratagem of falsification whereby the chief character and the story itself suggest "a message of order and a community of understanding" while both covertly question "through form, allusion, and ambiguity" the adequacy of such a relationship between life and art. The author uses the artifice of narration as necessary for the story and message but implies the inherent limitation of such as being "a perfect metaphor for life itself."[39]

A second drama, *The Amen Corner*, was published in 1968, though its initial performances had occurred some three years earlier. Harold Clurman, writing for the *Nation*, admitted the play's blemishes and limitations but also praised its contact with reality and its genuineness, "its sure feeling for race, place and universality of sentiment" and its "folk material unadorned and undoctored."[40] Ten years later director Carlton Molette continued to praise *The Amen Corner* for its embodiment of "the rhythms of the Afro-American church" as a "means of eliciting a sense of community or belonging" because it is about love that transcends "the petty bickering, the jealousies, the family fights."[41] And Darwin Turner had posited in 1977 that the dilemma of the black writer was embodied in Baldwin's two works: whether to direct himself "to a white audience—to entertain them, or to educate them about black people"—or to direct himself "to a black audience—to educate them to awareness of their needs." For Turner *Blues* was in the protest tradition and written for a white audience, while *Amen Corner*, artistically superior in both theme and characterization, "seems more clearly designed as a drama written about black experience for a black audience."[42]

As the sixties drew to a close, Baldwin's fourth novel—*Tell Me How Long the Train's Been Gone* (1968)—was published and almost immediately panned by the critics. Two representative voices were those presented respectively in *Harper's* and the *New York Times Book Review*. In the former Irving Howe saw *Tell Me* as a "remarkably bad novel, signalling the collapse of a writer of some distinction" who seemed "to have lost respect for the novel as a form" and to prefer the "clichés of soap opera." Among the delimiting features of the book, he listed a loss of "exactness of diction," a deceit manifest "through rhetorical inflation and hysteria," the use of "postures of militancy and declarations of racial metaphysics," and a "compulsive use of obscenities."[43] In the latter novelist Mario Puzo described the novel as "simpleminded" and "one dimensional" with "mostly cardboard characters"; with a "polemical" rather than a "narrative" tone as well as a "theatrical . . . predictable form," the book seemed like a "soap opera." He also asserted that it was time for Baldwin to "forget the black revolution and start worrying about himself as an artist who is the ultimate revolution."[44]

An important dimension of the attention elicited by Baldwin's works during the period under discussion was the increased number of secondary analyses and interpretations devoted not to the review of a specific book but to the variety of emphases inherent to the works, to the techniques used in them, and to Baldwin's stature as a writer. For example, in "Baldwin and the Problem of Being," George Kent discussed the fiction as relying on "Negro folk tradition," that is, blues, jazz, spirituals, and folk literature, as well as on "experimental practioneers of modernistic fiction, with special emphasis on Henry James." Baldwin's moral vision was seen as being concerned with men and women as they relate to good and evil and to society; in this view human nature is confronted by love and involvement, and in the process of development, an individual achieves "functional being." The fiction, therefore, is not in the tradition of the protest novel but instead is "preoccupied with sex and love as instruments in the achievement of full being."[45] Likewise, Charles Newman specified the author's literary antecedents in "The Lesson of the Master: Henry James and James Baldwin." He focused not on the color of characters as the cause of their suffering just as money was not the cause of suffering for James's characters; rather the problem for both was more universal—the quest for identity, the "reflective burden of Western Man." Thus, Baldwin uses the black man to show the white man what he himself is and thereby "his artistic achievements mesh with his historical circumstances" in a "genuinely visible revolution."[46]

Relatedly, Charlotte Alexander postulated that in Baldwin's fiction physical intimacy was a means to "emotional fulfillment," but that the experience brings risk and the "stink" of reality to the individual. The quest for love necessarily involves intimacy which results in a loss of innocence. The male characters, paradoxically, are repelled by intimacy, for any of several reasons, and avoid commitment to "legitimate" heterosexual relationships. Thus, Alexander concluded, there are only "mothers or whores (the ideal or the shattered ideal)" in the fiction, and Baldwin's characters always "seem groping from an immense loneliness" in search of love.[47] Eldridge Cleaver carried his line of thought further by declaring there was something disturbing in Baldwin, namely, a "grueling, agonizing, total hatred of the blacks particularly of himself" and a "shameful, fanatical, fawning . . . love of whites" that cannot be found in any black. This signifies a quirk in the author's vision that corresponds to his relationship to blacks and masculinity; thus, Baldwin venerates Andre Gide, repudiates the manliness of Norman Mailer's *The White Negro,* slanders his black protagonist Rufus in *Another Country,* and stabs Richard Wright in the back by his critique of him.[48]

In a similar vein John Lash affirmed Baldwin's position as a "major contemporary writer" who was also "a surprisingly devout and hopefully persuasive religionist." While denouncing Christianity, Baldwin nevertheless has sought in both the title and content of his works "a value system that can transfigure the self"; and this value system can be found in "a modern cult of phallicism, the fear and admiration and worship of the male sex organ." His novels, especially, reveal this "current religious faith," although Baldwin cannot recognize his own rejection of religion even if that religion is phallicism.[49]

Cleaver's view of Baldwin's attack on Wright as novelist points to a controversy that has yet to be fully resolved—the relationship between Baldwin and Wright. Maurice Charney described it as "James Baldwin's Quarrel with Richard Wright" and summarized Baldwin's contention in "Everybody's Protest Novel" (1949) as Wright's failure in *Native Son* to "deal with man in his wholeness and complexity" by creating Bigger Thomas and other characters who embodied "stereotypes with carefully defined social roles." Hence, the novel was seen by Baldwin as a failure as social protest, for it gave the impression that the black "has no real society and tradition about which one can write"; thus, Wright's response was the feeling he had been "betrayed by his spiritual son."[50] Irving Howe also took up the fight. He argued in "Black Boys and Native Sons" that whatever Baldwin intended by his expressed hope for an aesthetic that could portray black life "with greater richness and affection," and for becoming more than "merely a Negro or, even a Negro writer" in his polemic against the "school of naturalistic protest fiction," his own fiction and nonfiction, embodied elements of protest and a narrative voice of anger. While acknowledging Baldwin "as one of the two or three greatest essayists this country has ever produced," Howe also believed that Baldwin had evaded "through rhetorical sweep, the genuinely difficult issue of the relationship between social experience and literature."[51]

Ralph Ellison was incensed by Howe's analysis of Baldwin and the association of himself with Baldwin as being "guilty of filial betrayal" toward Wright; he countered in "The World and the Jug" that Howe's restrictive "sociological vision of society" failed to understand that neither social nor political segregation could fetter "the level of imagination" which could be hindered only by "individual aspiration, insight, energy and will." For Ellison, as in the case of Baldwin, Wright's Bigger Thomas was not the "final image of Negro personality."[52] Howe's rejoinder to this view in "The Writer and the Critic: An Exchange" included *ad hominem* attacks on Ellison and the observation that "plight and protest are inseparable from Negro experience, not the whole of it." He also reiterated that notwithstanding Baldwin's claims for something more than Wright's protest as principal emphasis, his own strongest specific works reached "heights of passionate exhortation."[53] The most complete account of the personal and literary relationships between Baldwin and Wright as well as the most extensive study of the interpretations of that relationship can be found in Fred Standley's " 'Farther and Farther Apart:' Richard Wright and James Baldwin." There the fundamental difference between the two authors is traced to their contrasting aesthetic positions about "protest literature" and how Bigger Thomas represents the embodiment of that difference.[54]

What eventually emerged, then, in the sixties was a common view of Baldwin, admittedly a controversial figure, as an author who would last. The most generous of his apologists would unhesitatingly proffer, as did Colin MacInnes in "Dark Angel: The Writings of James Baldwin," that even a century later his works would continue to be discussed because his style was "classic" and his theme "one of the most relevant" since the days of the Greeks: a "life-death-passion-honour-beauty-horror" theme. Thus, a perusal of his works would demonstrate that he was a "premonitory prophet, . . . a soothsayer, a bardic voice falling on deaf and delighted ears." His best work, the essays, possessed "a natural dignity, a sadly acid wit, and an enormous . . . humanity."[55] Accordingly, Robert Bone could state unequivocally in *The Negro Novel in America:* "The most important Negro writer to emerge during the last decade is, of course, James Baldwin. His publications . . . have had a stunning impact on our cultural life. His political role as a leading spokesman of the Negro revolt has been scarcely less effective. Awards and honors, wealth and success have crowned his career, and Baldwin has become a national celebrity."[56]

THE SEVENTIES

As in the sixties, so also in the seventies, Baldwin published another eight books—two dialogues, two volumes of essays, two novels, a scenario, and a children's book. Again, the responses to Baldwin and his works were varied: reviewers continued to demonstrate interest in him because of his reputation, though abatement of the civil rights movement resulted in a shift of attention from Baldwin's role therein. A more deliberate assessment of his overall literary and aesthetic accomplishments began to emerge as did discussion of his place in the pantheon of American letters.

An arranged and prolonged conversation of seven hours between Margaret Mead and Baldwin was recorded in 1970 and the transcript was published the following year as *A Rap on Race.* Reactions to the book were generally favorable and tended to focus on the exchange of perspectives, since the work offered "no solutions, no comfort, no ending to the sufferings of what men experience in race relations in America."[57] Kenneth Zahorski described the book as possessing "dynamism, clarity, incisiveness and a considerable number of memorable lines," as well as a misleading title; the exchange of ideas ranged far beyond race and included marriage, the judicial system, the influence of Christianity, the impact of nuclear power, American materialism, and the search for identity. Although occasionally containing "notes of optimism," the book expressed "a profoundly personal perspective" of Baldwin pervaded by "an aura of frustration, bitterness, despair, and anguish."[58] Two years later another transcript of a conversation appeared as *A Dialogue*—the result of a television encounter between Baldwin and poet Nikki Giovanni. While often viewed as an endeavor by two black writers a generation apart to bridge the gap on a number of topics, it also was thought to contain numerous fragments and unexplained comments. Some reviewers saw Baldwin as stressing the black man's machismo masking as self-respect and raging at the emasculating "black mama" and Giovanni as emphasizing a revolutionary impatience for change, a rage at the jiving black hustler," and a demand that black men stop evading their responsibilities toward women and children.[59] On the other hand, A. Russell Brooks in "Power and Morality as Imperatives for Nikki Giovanni and James Baldwin" later contended that *A Dialogue* sets forth the transition of the former from a "supporter of black revolution to harbinger of black love" in her works but that "the Baldwin of 1973 is, by and large, the Baldwin of 1953" who had "never advocated power for blacks except as it should lead to control of their own image and of their future."[60]

An ambitious undertaking by Baldwin as playwright resulted in the completion in 1972 of *One Day, When I Was Lost,* a scenario based on Alex Haley's *The Autobiography of Malcolm X.* This screenplay adaptation was not particularly well-received; in fact one respondent labeled it "no substitute for the original."[61] In "Baldwin's Unfulfilled Obligation" Patsy Brewington Perry pinpointed three reasons for the failure of Baldwin's effort to present the complex nature and stature of Malcolm X as man and leader: (1) the author's inordinate emphasis on violence in the United States, (2) his "transformations of important persons and events," and (3) his undercutting of both the achievements and potential contributions of Malcolm.[62]

The first volume of essays in the decade came out in 1972 as *No Name in the Street.* Benjamin DeMott lauded the author unhesitatingly in "James Baldwin on the Sixties: Acts and Revelations" as belonging in "an extremely select group: that composed of the few indispensable American writers"; he saw the book as "a reconstruction" of the writer's "activities and states of mind during the Sixties" and, therefore, it functioned as "a public voice of rage or frustration or denunciation or grief." The book was really a miscellany of fragments in the form of reports, comments, and glimpses—unified by discursive and historically oriented ruminations on black-white relationships.[63] Mel Watkins in "The Fire Next Time This Time" recalled that when Baldwin had first emerged as essayist, "the civil rights movement was barely ambulatory"; and his "passions, honesty and persuasiveness" contributed greatly to "free the impasse in the racial discourse." Consequently, his essay style set a literary precedent that ultimately produced the "New Journalism" of *No Name* as "a memoir, a chronicle of and commentary" on the civil rights movement.[64] Finally, Yoshinobu Hakutani argued that the artistry of *No Name* consisted in its role as "a successful satire against man" with a "vast and prophetic implication" for the American scene, namely, further exposure of "the falsehood to which Americans try to cling"—white supremacy at home and abroad. While this conception of supremacy no longer has any validity, Baldwin's personal attitude of positing further hope as a possibility for America had become at best ambiguous.[65] Still another excursion into the essay form was *The Devil Finds Work* (1976) in which Baldwin provided his personal reactions to American film and revealed as much of himself as he did about specific movies; in this "cinema of my mind" the author attempts to challenge some primary, and often unvoiced, assumptions of American society and culture. Orde Coombs declared in his analysis that the book does not call for rejoicing because "it brings forth . . . pain" and "teems with a passion that is all reflex, and an anger that is unfocused and almost cynical."[66] Conversely, others proposed that the book offered "genuine insights" with "disturbing urgency" about the evolution of American films from the 1930s through the 1970s, especially in the superficial views of cinematic reality offered and the manipulative strategies directed toward the public, for example, in the distorted and mythical images of blacks.[67]

The last three books produced by Baldwin in the seventies were two novels and a children's book. *If Beale Street Could Talk* came out in 1974, again with varied reactions. John Aldridge considered the novel "pretentious and cloying with goodwill and loving kindness and humble fortitude and generalized honorableness," and, therefore, a fantasy in which black Harlem characters live in an urban ghetto that can only be regarded as "idyllic."[68] Joyce Carol Oates, in contrast, indicated that while the novel reflected in part the "turbulence" of the times, its most significant dimension was as "a quite moving and very traditional celebration of love" not only between a man and a woman but also among family members.[69] Five years later Baldwin brought out *Just Above My Head* (1979), his most ambitious piece of fiction to date. In "Blues for Mr. Baldwin" Darryl Pinckney pointed out that it repeated "many of Baldwin's obsessions"—the church, Harlem, homosexuality, and social and political outrage, but that it also dropped the earlier view of homosexuality as "symbolic of a liberated condition" and embraced instead a sentimental view of the family that is "hardly convincing." With its "forced polemical tone," the novel was no more than "a conversion to simplicities that so fine a mind as Baldwin's cannot embrace without grave loss."[70] Eleanor Traylor has enthusiastically presented a contrary analysis of the novel in "I Hear Music in the Air." For her the story is a mythic movement of narrative with implications about three new "tale tellers"—Wright, Ellison, and Baldwin. Its theme is "the terrifying journey of the possibilities and failures of love" which is also "the dramatic center of the blues-gospel narrative mode" already used in a variety of ways in the author's previous fiction and nonfiction and which "essentially sketches one tale or one theme." Thus, the latest work, for Traylor, was "a gospel tale in the blues mode" whose "beauty is achieved by an opposition of contraries arranged not merely by an elegance of words, but of moods, of scenes, of chords, of mighty beats. The tale begins with death but celebrates a life. It laments a loss, yet it sings a love song. It is both a dirge and a hymn. It is simultaneously a blues moan and a gospel shout. Its scheme of ironies evokes the sublimity of the songs of the elders, lines of which begin each of the five sections" of the book. "It summons, once again, a tale told consistently for twenty-six years by a narrator whose features are etched among the splendid in twentieth century global literature."[71] *Little Man, Little Man: A Story of Childhood* (1976), Baldwin's third fictional composition of the decade, has left its readers pondering whether it is a children's book for adults or an adult story for children.[72] The virtue of the book is a masterful blend of black English and children's talk; however, the lack of "intensity and focus" prevents it from accomplishing what such works as Henry Roth's *Call It Sleep* and Harper Lee's *To Kill a Mockingbird* did, for each of them, "a child's story for adults," attains "a change in the perception of adult reality."[73]

Concomitant with the literary output during this era was the spate of secondary materials devoted to explaining the man and explicating the works. Donald B. Gibson's *Five Black Writers* (1976), as mentioned earlier, opened the decade with the first collected pieces about Baldwin. In his introduction Gibson claimed that the author was better as essayist than novelist but then traced in the fiction a movement "from the purely individual toward the social"; he also noticed a convergence between the fiction and essays as to political and moral content, especially in such points as the nature of the human condition, the definition of American society, the personal acceptance of responsibility, and an underlying social concern.[74] An intriguing essay "James Baldwin 1924—" (1979) by Keneth Kinnamon affirmed that Baldwin's "interrelated treatment of psychological and social issues derives so directly from his personal history" that a study of his biography is necessary to a consideration of his literary career. From such a study "the terrain of Baldwin's imagination" is derived as encompassing "four main sectors: church, self, city, and race" whose boundaries are not clearly defined but are, nevertheless, "general areas" in which to explore his literary achieve-

ment. That literary accomplishment is a record of "expanding perspectives," especially in the personal essay, which often enlarges the
topic presented to "global dimensions" and thereby enhances the
author's reputation as being among the contemporary masters in that
genre.[75] Works of a similar nature that appeared later, and which
have already been cited, included the bibliography of Daryl C. Dance
and the anthologies edited by Kinnamon and Therman O'Daniel,
respectively.[76]

Still another response was the more detailed attention given to
Baldwin as literary artist and craftsman. Fred L. Standley in "James
Baldwin: The Artist as Incorrigible Disturber of the Peace" analyzed
that role as an outgrowth of the author's belief that "the public life
and the private life are an indivisible whole" and that the artist must
"present the existential knowledge of experience to man" by means
of a personal perspective "pervaded by an ethical vision and historical
orientation that includes concern for his own generation and his
descendants." This involved "the discovery and the rejection of
illusion and delusion about oneself," including the recognition of love
as the means for "overcoming the existential abyss between oneself
and another person" and the defining of humanness as a direct "attack
upon the philosophy of naturalistic determinism."[77] Similarly, Calvin
Hernton's "Blood of the Lamb" saw Baldwin "in the class with Camus,
Sartre." He was "the categorical head of the newly emerging young
. . . Existential Negroes"; his concerns were "love, torture, agony
and forgiveness" as he wrote about "the blood of the lamb, sin, and
redemption."[78] Furthermore, Houston A. Baker, Jr., in "The Embattled Craftsman: An Essay on James Baldwin" (1977), argued that
the author's "quest" or journey had been "circular, beginning and
ending with the black urban masses" while his expression had been
reflective: "an engaged black voice," though a voice with differing
emphases in the various works. Hence, the early novel *Go Tell It
On the Mountain* revealed the writer as an embattled craftsman
struggling for a sensibility wherein to present a "black cultural tradition"; yet a late work such as *If Beale Street Could Talk* embodied
the concept of family and those actions inherent to "a genuine concern
for one another," as well as males who were positive characters.
Therefore, in Baldwin could be detected a craftsman portraying a
tortured but inexorable evolution toward a new life.[79]

Additional studies ranged across a spectrum of topics related both
to more generalized interpretations and to specific genres and works.
For example, Jacqueline E. Orsagh analyzed Baldwin's female characters in the fiction as being "extraordinarily strong, dynamic, and,
even more importantly, interesting" as well as being individuals who
"act and are not condemned for doing so." These features, for her,
helped to contrast that fiction to the "well-accepted fact that there

have been few, if any, well-developed and believable women characters in English and American literature."[80] Shirley Anne Williams
suggested in "The Black Musician: The Black Hero as Light Bearer"
that music in the author's work is more than metaphor; indeed, the
musician becomes "an archetypal figure whose referent is black lives,
black experience and black death." The musician, thus, is a kind of
hope for "making it in America" as well as the bitter mockery of
never making it well enough to escape the dangers of being black.
He becomes "the living symbol of alienation from the past and hence
from self and the rhythmical link with the mysterious ancestral past."[81]
Following the same motif of confronting one's past, Daryl C. Dance
established in "You Can't Go Home Again: James Baldwin and the
South" that neither the black African experience nor the wandering
in Europe could provide the solution to that "inescapable dilemma
of the Black American—the lack of a sense of positive self-identity."
In Baldwin's case, she said, he had to make an "odyssey to the South"
to be able to "appreciate the positive results of these beginnings."
Yet the trip to the South, a "going home," threatened him with the
real loss of manhood; consequently, having found his roots there, he
also realized that he "cannot go home again," for it could signify
extinction.[82]

   Two other facets of Baldwin were explored for the first time in
this period by Craig Werner's "The Economic Evolution of James
Baldwin" and Donald B. Gibson's "James Baldwin: The Political
Anatomy of Space." Werner argued in 1979 that "a comprehensive
secularization has been taking place" in the works of Baldwin and
that "in the economic dimension" as well as in the political and social
facets, the author had been "de-emphasizing purely spiritual approaches to problems" and had "adopted a perspective stressing social
action in the face of an oppressive environment." With primary stress
on analysis of the fiction, Werner suggests that each novel contributes
to "a constantly refined critique of the American economic system"
and points toward "a general direction for future action." The novels
thus portray the author "as ever more willing to deal directly with
the institutional basis of the problems"; yet, they retain "a strong
spiritual undercurrent which helps raise them to the level of poetry"
even while the "comprehensive secularization" is underway.[83] In a
contrasting manner Gibson concluded that Baldwin's "ability to express the innermost, deepest longings of his psyche" is both his
strength and his weakness because "his analysis of his own personal
needs is indistinguishable in his mind from his analysis of the world
and its society." For Gibson there is an explicit change between
Baldwin's earlier emphasis on love and personal regard for another—
"inner space"—and the later concern about "public space" in "determining the nature, character and quality of human experience";

however, Baldwin has retained in both his fiction and essays primary assumptions that are "highly subjective reflections of personal need and desire." It is not surprising, then, that his social analysis is limited in scope and conservative, with no overt solution offered in politics; while his morally based rhetoric confronts society, he does not question the basic operations of society, especially its uses of power, for that "would unsettle too many things that have been thus far settled."[84]

Several critical items continued to treat the significance of Baldwin's first novel, *Go Tell It on the Mountain.* Michel Fabre saw the basic purpose of the book as having been a kind of prophetic fulfillment that the black adolescent son, John, would grow up to be a preacher just like his father. Complications, such as the prevention of reciprocal love by "holiness standing opposed to happiness" rather than by "divine ordinance," are self-evident. The novel juxtaposed father figures—unknown father, mythical or real/legitimate father, putative father—with sons—natural, born of adultery, adopted, prodigal. The novel was, then, a "fictionalized account" of the author's life and an attempt "to free himself" and to prove himself as a writer "worthy before Wright."[85] Seeing the theme of the novel as the "ritual symbolization" of a youth's initiation into manhood via the "psychological step from dependence to a sense of self," Shirley S. Allen pointed out the use of biblical allusion and Christian ritual for the symbolic expression of the Freudian "psychic realities" that Baldwin desired the reader to experience. The religious symbolism keeps the reader aware of the "universal elements" in the book and, by means of such symbolic identification, Baldwin presents the problem of being a "victim of persecution out of a particular racial situation in twentieth-century United States and places it in a larger historical and religious context."[86] Also, in another essay Allen demonstrated how the same novel incorporates three uses of irony: in the narrator's diction, in statement and action, and in voice as a character. The ultimate irony, however, consists in the story's validation of those tenets of that Christian faith professed by the characters even when such faith is misinterpreted by their own lives.[87]

Two other novels received attention worth noting also. In an interpretation of *If Beale Street Could Talk,* Trudier Harris saw "The Eye as Weapon"; she posited that "if the eye is indeed the light to the soul," then Baldwin "lays many of his characters bare" in the novel. From her perspective the author conveys "his belief in black community and spirituality" through the interactions among characters by means of "voice, body language and eye contact." Eye contact, both casual and intense, is especially important, for by it the people in the novel "reveal many of their subconscious thoughts and feelings"; it is a means of "real and symbolic confrontation, be it for purposes of communion, seduction or conquest." Whatever forms the confrontation may take, "the idea of transformation" is central to all of them, that is, "of coverting people to a different point of view, of change of mind or change of attitude." Hence, *Beale Street* as novel presents the black family and love relationships among those who realize "they are just folks who love each other and who are committed to the welfare of those whom they love."[88] In stark contrast to that view stands the contention of William Edward Farrison in "If Baldwin's Train Has Not Gone" that both *Beale Street* and *Tell Me How Long the Train's Been Gone* are seriously flawed. The former was seen as having no clear relation between the title and narrative, no characters capable to eliciting high regard from readers, and weakly motivated actions for most of the characters. The latter was castigated as lacking in insight, resourcefulness, and human vitality as well as being permeated by "phallus-consciousness" and a plethora of sexual acts. Unless Baldwin could regain his devotion to the "art of fiction" as exemplified in *Go Tell It on the Mountain,* Farrison ventured that he would never "reach the greatest heights of distinction."[89]

The short stories "Going to Meet the Man" and "Sonny's Blues" also generated critical commentary. Roger Whitlow noted that the relationship between race and sexuality has long been described and explained in American literature, and he placed the former story in that tradition as one of "the finest" interpretations of how "sexual stimulation and subsequent gratification . . . can be achieved through racial brutality." The problem for Jesse, white Southern deputy sheriff, in the story is male impotence; he is transformed only by "psychological assimilation with blackness" and by thus forcing his wife to respond to him in that mode, a form of sexual pleasure he cannot achieve in any other way and a complement thus to his effort to dominate all blacks.[90] In her analysis Arthenia Bates Millican saw the same story as using "fire" as a symbol of frustration for the protagonist, Jesse, from his boyhood to manhood. Doomed to the acceptance of the burden of his heritage, namely, the perpetuation of Southern white superiority, the protagonist is prevented by frustration "from priming the depths of his own personality."[91] The essay "Style, Form and Content in the Short Fiction of James Baldwin" by Harry L. Jones advocates that the stories written between 1948 and 1965 "contain in microcosm the universe that later manifests itself" in the major works; the stories are for Baldwin "a means of imposing his ideological positions on the nature and purposes of fiction." Most of the stories lack "the kind of cyclical structures that make for good narrative art"; but, "Sonny's Blues" is the "most perfectly realized story" as judged by the criteria for aesthetic wholeness.[92]

Baldwin's achievements as essayist were the subject of several noteworthy studies in the late seventies, each of which was a contribution to the further development of his reputation in that genre. Jocelyn Whitehead Jackson isolated the phenomenon of "the quest for personal and artistic identity" in the early essays. She maintained that the artistic, religious and sexual crises in the writer's personal life gave "rise to a single-minded dedication to the search for discovery of the self"; therefore, being aware of "the triple burden of Black, artist, and bisexual in an American environment inimical to each," Baldwin informed his essays "with an irony that intensifies his search."[93] Approaching the author from a different perspective, A. Russell Brooks endeavored to point out Baldwin's self-designated role of "poet-prophet" who probed "for sources, causes and roots" in the race problem in America. Only by getting Americans to confront the complexities of history—past and present—could there be any hope "to change the Western assumptions" and make a "larger civilization."[94]

Two other studies tended to emphasize the larger dimensions of Baldwin's talents as essayist. Nick Aaron Ford stressed the dominant theme of Baldwin as "what it means to be black in a nation and world dominated by 'white' power in social, political, religious, artistic, and ethical matters." For Ford the best work was *The Fire Next Time*: "a beautiful book, a challenging book, a powerful book . . . a profoundly philosophical book." The stylistic combination of first-person narration, vivid imagery, personal examples, and general truths caused Ford to describe the essays as "unstructured, instinctive, and emotional utterance often unsupported by rational safeguards." The appeal of Baldwin's works was never intended to be done through "logic and rationality" but rather by means of "pragmatism and prophecy" whereby he provoked "humane thought" and announced "eternal truths" in order to raise in the reader "spiritual or philosophical contemplation."[95] Similarly, Hobart Jarrett proclaimed Baldwin a "great writer" directed to the essay "by choice, by talent, by calling." Three efforts underlay Jarrett's considerations of Baldwin: first, an overview of his conception of the writer performing a "special mission"; second, a list of recurring motifs—hatred for his father; concern about religion, Christianity, and the church; and the significance of being black in a white denominated world; and third, the exploring of techniques and faults—self-projection, insights, contradictions, discovery of the South symbolism, etc. Many of the essays have contributed significantly to the social changes that occurred in the United States and thereby remain "major interpretations of our era."[96]

The final group of critical postures about Baldwin in the seventies consists of a half-dozen books. W. J. Weatherby's *Squaring Off: Mailer vs. Baldwin* (1977) is a helpful and realistic, reportorial view of both writers as well as a record of their myriad escapades, adventures, interrelations, and opinions for the years 1959 to 1976 by one who knew both of them personally. He relates clearly their views on such subjects as power and poverty, blacks and whites, competition and conformity, artistry and social action, friends and acquaintances. Weatherby's thesis argued that the two writers are "reverse sides of the same coin, representative figures of the sixties, when blacks and whites were struggling creatively to understand each other."[97] Likewise, Karin Moller produced a thematically oriented work in *The Theme of Identity in the Essays of James Baldwin: An Interpretation* (1975). Moller specified the theme of identity as the most pervasive one in his work and involving the major issues of race, nationality, sexuality, art, and morality. Baldwin's methodology involves both a "dialectic quality" and a "lyrical affirmation" in order to establish "the existence of polarities and incompatibilities of all kinds" which can lead to the discovery of synthesis. His quest for identity thus became an effort to dramatize his personal situation as an Afro-American and "to render it universally intelligible by infusing physical reality and concrete facts with myth and metaphysics."[98] In a still more highly specialized way, Georges Michel Sarotte treated Baldwin's works within the context of three varieties of homosexual desire: homoeroticism, homosexuality, and homogenitalism. Sarotte found Baldwin to be incapable of identifying with a white or black "who is only heterosexual, or with a homosexual who is exclusively homosexual." Thus, his novels vacillate between the extremes of "settling accounts with the white race—since he feels that they are what has forced him to hate himself—and his homosexual life for the white man, with whom he desperately tries to identify."[99]

Each of the other three book length studies was an endeavor to examine with care the entirety of the writer's accomplishments and to provide a judgment about him. *James Baldwin: A Critical Study* (1973) by Stanley Macebuh argues that a major shift occurred in Baldwin's perspective of life, namely, from life envisioned "as a matter of private myth-making to one in which public action had become all important." Accordingly, for Macebuh the author's works were a record of his fashioning out of his private history and the social and political upheavals of the time a public voice, both dignified and terrifying, by which to express "his moral disgust and passionate fury" in an era of moral ambiguity. Consequently, he had attained "a place in the history of American letters that few so far can claim in this century." The book is especially rewarding in the emphasis on Baldwin's view of man "as a theological rather than a political animal" and on his struggle with theological terror and apocalyptic dread. Ultimately, the shift in Baldwin's work from a *homo theologicus* that insists on spiritual realities and apocryphal dreads to an overt concern with "the socio-political ambience of man's life" constitutes the author's "blueprint for a new world."[100]

Peter Bruck offered a somewhat disparaging assessment of Baldwin's career in 1975 by splitting his works into parts: essays and fiction. As essayist Baldwin was interpreted as having three goals: to specify his stand in the politics of the race conflict, to stress the validity of a love ethic, and to continue "the wedding of the two races." As novelist he tended toward the presentation of heroes who suffer from their racial plight and are unable to determine their own lives. He thinks that Baldwin had never written for a black audience but rather to correct the racial ignorance of the white readers; he was not, therefore, a black writer but one who wrote for the ruling class as "a universal minority writer."[101] Louis Hill Pratt presented in 1978 an evaluation that runs explicitly counter to that of Bruck. Pratt's ostensible goal was to explore Baldwin's literary art so as to delineate the broader concerns than merely "white versus black," namely, "the universal concepts of freedom versus slavery, liberation versus oppression, reality versus illusion, identity versus darkness, confusion, and chaos." In a fine chapter on the essay as used by Baldwin, Pratt acknowledged the sociological dimension but also explores the artistic achievement in use of language, style, and techniques. Pratt suggests the essay is "his major contribution to American letters." In the survey of scholarship about Baldwin, Pratt concluded that "the narrow context of sociology" as the basis for judgment of his work had been scrapped by critics who had moved toward an evaluation that stressed "the consummate artistic skill which transcends the social value of his artistry."[102]

THE EIGHTIES

Within the eighties neither the creative productivity by Baldwin nor the critical response to it has abated. For example, in 1985 three additional books by the writer appeared in print. *The Evidence of Things Not Seen* is simultaneously a kind of meditation and a polemic generated by the infamous series of child murders in Atlanta in late 1979 and the early 1980s and commissioned originally by *Playboy* magazine. Using the series of murders and the arrest of Wayne Williams as points of reference, Baldwin roamed over a diverse group of topics pertaining to the general conditions of American society in the present decade; and he gave special stress to an issue that had been of long standing concern—the problem of being black in predominantly white America. While documentary evidence and facts are intermingled with analytical thought and speculative judgments, his most serious indictment was focused on that long beloved concept of the American Dream as "the final manifestation of the European/

Western/Christian dominance." A few hints of faint praise surfaced about the work, but the principal response was definitely negative. Jonathan Yardley attacked the book unhesitatingly in the *Washington Post* as "a piece of nonsense in the literal meaning of the word: it makes no sense at all . . . an effort that leads Baldwin into wild, and wildly irrelevant, speculations." He goes on to describe it as "a pathetic embarrassment" and "certainly it is embarrassing to read." The most damaging comment, moreover, centers on this conclusion by the reviewer: "if the writer who once warned us against hatred has not transformed himself into a racist, he is certainly putting on a good imitation of one."[103]

A slender edition of nineteen poems also came out in the same year, *Jimmy's Blues: Selected Poems,* and is Baldwin's only volume of published verse. For the reader already familiar with the numerous moods and emphases in the earlier works of fiction, drama, and nonfiction, there are no surprises in this volume. Again, a predominant consideration is the notion of what it means to be black in white America. The poetic diction is somewhat deceptively simple as it embodies direct statement but also emotions and feelings that are acute and intense and wrapped in irony. This book is further evidence of the inherent toughness and commitment also underlying the earlier works. In general the reviewers have largely ignored the volume.

The large and handsomely packaged edition entitled *The Price of the Ticket: Collected Non-Fiction 1948–1985* was the third book published in 1985. A compilation of fifty-one essays previously published, the work had the advantage of containing some twenty-five items that had not been collected in book form and were therefore frequently difficult to locate. More importantly, the volume was introduced by an autobiographical excursion that is revelatory and confessional of the author's life and insightful about his personal principles and philosophy. Some reactions to the anthology have been quite caustic; for example, one reviewer agrees that the collection displays "Baldwin in all his guises," but that it also sets forth "quite unwittingly" the "painful evidence" that since *The Fire Next Time* in 1963 the author's "skills have steadily deteriorated." For this reviewer "the preacher has taken over from the writer" and for two decades "his rhetoric has grown steadily more bombastic, grandiloquent and predictable, while the humor, sensitivity and self-mockery of the early essays have virtually disappeared."[104] Julius Lester corroborated the limitations in the volume while also confirming the strengths of Baldwin in his reply to the book titled "Some Tickets are Better: The Mixed Achievement of James Baldwin." For Lester the nearly four decades of essays reveal the writer as a "tremendously eloquent humanist" and "a hard-edged, uninviting, and terrifying one." For the first fifteen years he was a black writer "pleading the cause of humanity" and exhibiting "his ability to weave the deeply autobiographical with the political and social." In subsequent works to *The Fire Next Time* though, Lester argues that gradually "a black vision of the world has slowly gained precedence over his humanistic one" and a propensity for "cosmic generalizations" is discernible. Lester admires the many prose pieces because "read as a body, the essays of James Baldwin are a sustaining act of love and faith of which America has not been worthy." Nevertheless, he raises serious questions about the later works of Baldwin and "laments the absence of the growth we would want for that person—and ourselves"; the latter essays, he concludes, are frequently "an imitation" and "a continuation of principles Baldwin taught us to despise."[105]

Early in this introduction the decade of the eighties was depicted as a "continuing of the concerns of the previous ten years but also [marked] by an acceleration in the critical evaluation of Baldwin's literary stature and a greater attention to his understanding of and embodiment of politics, economics, psychology, music, religion, and aesthetics." Two individual books that have received further consideration recently are *Go Tell It On the Mountain* and *No Name in the Street,* yet in each instance the purpose was to suggest a broader context. In "Religion as the Indirect Method of Indictment," Fred L. Standley summarizes several ways in which *Go Tell It,* replete with ecclesiastical, doctrinal, and scriptural matters, has been interpreted religiously, but he then insists that the book embodies a more substantive cultural concept of which religion is merely a component. Drawing upon the broader cultural context of the "down home" lifestyle, Standley analyzes the narrative lines of the novel and their inherent ironical rendering of sociopolitical condemnation of both blacks and whites for the condition of society and their ways of dealing with it. Religion provides the technique for "indirect communication" via a novel in 1953—in the midst of an era saturated by a religious "cult of serenity" as exhibited in *Peace of Mind, Peace of Soul, Peace with God,* and *The Power of Positive Thinking.*[106] Similarly, Yoshinobu Hakutani has dissected the artistry inherent to *No Name* and presented it as "a successful satire against man" in "James Baldwin's Image of the Sixties." Showing the work to have been a departure from the earlier books of essays that expressed a theory of identity and love, Hakutani posits *No Name* as a "sustained examination of the falsehood to which Americans try to cling"; the severity of the vision is underpinned by a "calmness," perhaps even "a sense of resignation." For Hakutani the implications of the book are "vast and prophetic" given what has occurred in the world since its original publication, thereby fulfilling Baldwin's assertion that "it is no longer important to be white—thank heaven—the white face is no longer invested with the power of the world." The ambiguous conclusion of the book focuses on whether the answer to society's ills is militancy based on hatred and social activism. Baldwin leaves the question unanswered but uses an imagery that might allow for some inference of hope.[107]

Baldwin as dramatist also claimed a degree of attention recently as a result of his being included in the volumes entitled *Twentieth Century American Dramatists.* His stature as playwright is presented as still problematical, with a range of opinions extending from the idea that "the dramatic form is not a congenial one" for him to the position that his remarkable success as a playwright is based on his ability to accomplish a "collaborative working relationship" through "his trust of and reliance upon many other artists." *Blues for Mister Charlie* is viewed as a complex drama, using the dual settings of Whitetown (the courthouse) and Blacktown (the church) to relate several stories and explore several ideas simultaneously. The conclusion exhibits the bankruptcy of white liberalism and the conjoining of "the Bible and the gun" in the pulpit "like the pilgrims of old" in the person of the Reverend Meridian Henry. *The Amen Corner* is a drama that ignores relations between blacks and whites and stresses instead the necessity for love in the black family and community; it also derides the theological conception of the church that emphasizes only a God of wrath. Thus, the centrality of love and compassion are ultimately embodied in the conversion of Sister Margaret Alexander to the realization that "it's an awful thing to think about, the way love never dies."[108]

Thus far in the eighties at least six critical essays of a general nature deserve scrutiny, for each of them represents an effort to treat the larger context and significance of Baldwin. C. W. E. Bigsby describes his own work in "The Divided Mind of James Baldwin" as less a detailed critical analysis than "an account of a career and a mind instructively divided, a sensibility drawn in opposing directions." On the one side, he has been drawn toward the position of faith in the moral responsibility of the individual and the possibility of social change; thus, "at the heart of his work, beneath the level of contingent event and social determinant, an unexamined confidence in the possibility of action and the recovery of ethical purpose" have been manifested over and over. Running counter to and beside this phenomenon throughout his work has been "a secular belief in the authenticating power of the self"; in short, "the self resists the peripheral role which seems its social fate, and the primary agent in this resistance is the imagination." The communicative act involved in art thus becomes a paradigm of a desired social interaction, while the individual's imposition of order, implied by the creative act, becomes "a model for a coherence which is generated by the sensibility and not imposed by social fiat." It is not surprising, then, that virtually all of Baldwin's protagonists are artists of some kind and that the "demonstrable logic of revolt" creates "an autonomous self" by means first of the rejecting of the authority of the father, then of white society, and finally of God. For Baldwin's fictional characters, the question of identity is accordingly ever present because "the usual stratagems of definition now fail." Consequently, history, memory, and belief are at odds with the drive for self-creation and the need for personal alliances that can deny the reality of all boundaries; the characters, therefore, adopt an ambiguous stance with regard to time and declare their "right to define process and resist versions of historical progress which threaten to subordinate them to an alien logic." By using the language and imagery of the Old Testament, he undermines his insight about "present history as present reality" and the effort to establish social responsibility because the diction of sin and guilt on the lips of the Old Testament prophet "denies the efficacy of New Testament grace" or any other active principle: "The writer who wishes to establish a racial indictment is thus inhibited from dramatizing the need for racial reconciliation which is a conviction he holds with equal force. . . . The deficiency is an intellectual one."[109]

Louis H. Pratt has pointed out that whether "Baldwin the writer or Baldwin the critic" is examined, "the value system which influences his analysis remain the same." Pratt traces that value system to some twenty-nine book reviews in 1947–49; chief among several points to be discovered there is the aesthetic principle that "literature is a political vehicle whose analysis and evaluation should be based upon the overt and covert assumptions which it makes about society." Pratt then delineates six assumptions that inform Baldwin's critical evaluations of the works of others and that also inform his own literature. Many of the issues raised by Baldwin in those early reviews ultimately found expression in his own novels, plays, and essays as "writer/prophet."[110]

In a comparable manner Marlene Mosher draws upon the significance of the blues to isolate and expound upon Baldwin's use of "the black American blues" as "a natural vehicle in which to express his ideas." Traditionally, the blues singer articulated a mood of suffering—deprivation, racism, poverty, injustice, infidelity, oppression, etc.—and provided "a degree of transcendence over the troubles of this world." Baldwin, too, typically functions in that way: "he honestly looks at the horribleness of a situation, but he does *not* give up," and "this theme of surviving despite tremendous odds is persistent" in his fiction, drama, and essays. The means of surviving for blacks in white America requires both honesty and creativity; and Baldwin, "though writing in nonsong form, usually writes 'blues.' " As he said early on, the writing of "plays, poetry and short stories" constitutes "an act of love. . . . It seemed a way to save myself and a way to save my family. It came out of despair. And it seemed the only way to another world."[111]

Again stating the commonly held view of the "search for self-identity" as one of his central themes, Emmanuel S. Nelson has suggested that Baldwin's vision of "otherness and community is closely related to and dependent upon his vision of self." Frequently individuals are unable to confront the "darker" sides of their human nature, and hence personal and collective failures result; this point is vividly presented in *Blues for Mister Charlie* as well as other works. This failure to confront the darker impulses of the soul has two implications: it robs the individual of genuine identity because of the denial of part of being human; and it incapacitates the individual for satisfactory "interpersonal and communal experience." All of Baldwin's works, as interpreted by Nelson, posit the validity of the effort to "achieve a genuine sense of self only through one's identification with the humanity within all men and women"; his works thus "constitute a magnificent assertion of the oneness of the human spirit that unites the family of mankind."[112]

The same motif of the search for identity is also central to Sondra A. O'Neale's "Fathers, Gods, and Religion: Perceptions of Christianity and Ethnic Faith in James Baldwin." She reasons that "a close critical and theological exegesis of Baldwin's writings" shows undeniably "that more than the heritage of any other Black American writer, Baldwin's works illustrate the schizophrenia of the Black American experience with Christianity." For blacks need a "clear distinction between Christianity as they knew it to be and Christianity as it was practiced in the white world"; obviously such cognizance demonstrates clearly "the thematic ambiguity between possibilities of individual faith in and societal practice of Christianity as a religious system." O'Neale refers back and forth among the various works to emphasize that "Baldwin should be seen as the last Black American writer to exploit as a major theme the Black man's relationship with Christianity." Moreover, "he will be seen as the first Black American writer to distance himself from the lone enduring Black institution, the Black Church, not by its notable absence . . . but by his overtly persistent portrayal of its lack of authentic Christian commitment." She further maintains that by this stance and by his advocacy of "homosexuality as an acceptable form of human love," Baldwin "opened the floodgate for contemporary anti-Christian, non-Biblically based Black American literature." Although his own works question "Divine existence while still courting its fond allegiance . . . his boldness invited younger writers to complete the schism between Black art and Black faith." Nevertheless, Baldwin himself has not yet fully abandoned belief in "that unseen spiritual truth."[113]

Still another essay worthy of perusal is the long piece on Baldwin in *The Concise Dictionary of American Literary Biography*. The author weaves together the complex strands of biographical context and critical interpretation of works to offer a relatively succinct overview of the man and the literary artist. After an expository account of his theory of art, each of the major works in novel, drama, essay, and poetry is examined and interpreted. After four decades of work and a secure place in the mainstream of American literature, Baldwin's totality of endeavor toward the expounding of "the black experience for its universal dimensions" has been fully recognized.[114]

As complement to those six essays a final group of studies in the eighties consists of three books. The first, *James Baldwin: A Reference Guide* (1980), has been described above. It is to date the most comprehensive bibliography about Baldwin for 1953–77. Another book, *James Baldwin* (1980), by Carolyn Wedin Sylvander, though briefly alluded to earlier, deserves further consideration; it appeared as part of the Modern Literature Series published by Ungar. The volume is a good overview of the author: it provides a biographical summary, an aesthetic perspective, an analysis of specific works, a list of critical sources, and a bibliography. Sylvander emphasizes the key to Baldwin's belief system as "his concept and use of History" and suggests that "students of cultural and social history would do well to listen very closely to this exceedingly articulate witness." She gives considerably more weight to explication and interpretation of the fiction than to the essays; the chapter on *Just Above My Head* is an early exegesis of that novel and sees its significance as the manner in which it "repeats, expands, and resolves many of the ideas, questions and conflicts that surface throughout his published works." She quotes from a Baldwin interview to buttress her argument that with this novel some of his principal "themes have been taken to resolution." As Baldwin said: "What I've really been feeling is that I've come full circle. From *Go Tell It on the Mountain* to *Just Above My Head* sums up something of my experience—it's difficult to articulate—that sets me free to go someplace else."[115]

The latest critical book is *Black Women in the Fiction of James Baldwin* (1985), by Trudier Harris, a pioneer work on a subject that had received scant attention previously. Aware both of the limited treatment of Baldwin in general and of the role of black women in his fiction, Harris examines the fiction carefully to explicate the nature of the roles women play and the significance of their characters for Baldwin as author. In general she sees a progression in Baldwin's use of women in his fiction. At first they are conceptually limited figures as measured by standards drawn from the fundamentalist church; as such they view themselves as wives, mothers, sisters, and lovers. Any failure in one of the roles generates guilt and the expectation of being damned. However, a shift occurs as the female figures come to believe that the church offers neither meaning nor comfort; and the author tends to withhold his prior exercise of moral strictures. This enables him to allow women greater freedom of action and complexity of personality in later works until the woman who separates from the church experiences both greater freedom from guilt and more profound contentment. Nevertheless, "no woman is ultimately so acceptable to Baldwin that she is to be viewed as equal to the prominent male characters . . . they are in a supportive, serving position in relation to the males and the male images in their lives." This is a provocative and stimulating study; it will be read for years to come.[116]

RATIONALE FOR THIS EDITION

This survey of some of the principal sources for the study of Baldwin, together with the evolving nature of Baldwin criticism, should clarify the larger context in terms of which this volume is to be understood. This book has been designed to exemplify the evolution of scholarly developments and trends in Baldwin criticism and scholarship during approximately the last decade and a half. Consequently, the format comprehends four main sections: general essays, essays on fiction, essays on nonfiction, and essays on drama. Within each category an attempt has been made to avoid the reprinting of essays that have already been anthologized and to solicit by commission some original essays that cover differing aspects of Baldwin's accomplishments. Taken together, these essays not only represent an easily recognizable gamut of the author's interests and concerns but attest also to the author's current literary stature. While it is true that some of James Baldwin's books have not received the same critical attention as in previously published collections of essays, it is equally the case that his total achievements have received here a more balanced examination and objective evaluation (in terms of fundamental conceptions, presuppositions, and implications) than previously available.

Florida State University   FRED L. STANDLEY
Florida A. & M. University   NANCY V. BURT

Notes

1. Benjamin De Mott, "James Baldwin and the Sixties: Acts and Revelations," *Saturday Review*, 27 May 1972, 66.

2. Louis Pratt, *James Baldwin* (Boston: Twayne, 1978), 9.

3. Fred L. Standley and Nancy V. Standley, *James Baldwin: A Reference Guide* (Boston: G. K. Hall, 1980), ix.

4. Therman O'Daniel, ed., *James Baldwin: A Critical Evaluation* (Washington: Howard University Press, 1977), 243–61.

5. Carolyn Wedin Sylvander, *James Baldwin* (New York: Ungar, 1980), 163–71.

6. Daryl Dance, "James Baldwin," in *Black American Writers: Bibliographical Essays*, ed. Thomas Inge (New York: St. Martin's, 1978), 73–120.

7. Standley and Standley, *James Baldwin*, ix.

8. Donald Gibson, ed., *Five Black Writers: Essays on Wright, Ellison, Baldwin, Hughes, Leroi Jones* (New York: New York University Press, 1970).

9. Keneth Kinnamon, ed., *James Baldwin: A Collection of Critical Essays* (Englewood Cliffs, N.J.: Prentice-Hall, 1974).

10. O'Daniel, *Critical Evaluation.*

11. Kinnamon, *Critical Essays*, 1–8.

12. Richard K. Barksdale, "Temple of the Temple Fire Baptised," *Phylon* 14 (1953):326–27; reprinted below.

13. Granville Hicks, "James Baldwin's Promising First Novel," *New Leader* 36 (1 June 1953):21–22.

14. Anthony West, "Books: Sorry Lives," *New Yorker* 19 (20 June 1953):93.

15. Steven Marcus, "The American Negro in Search of Identity," *Commentary* 16 (November 1953):456–63.

16. Langston Hughes, "From Harlem to Paris," *New York Times Book Review*, 26 February 1956, 26; reprinted in Kinnamon, *Critical Essays*, 9–10, and in this volume.

17. J. Saunders Redding, "James Baldwin Miscellany," *New York Herald Tribune Book Review*, 26 February 1956, 4.

18. James W. Ivy, "The Fairie Queenes," *Crisis* 64 (February 1957):123.

19. William Esty, "The Cities of the Plain," *New Republic* 135 (17 December 1956):26.

20. Leslie A. Fiedler, "A Homosexual Dilemma," *New Leader* 39 (10 December 1956):17–17; reprinted below.

21. "Ford Fund Gives Writers $150,000," *New York Times*, 16 February 1959, 31.

22. Norman Mailer, *Advertisements for Myself* (New York: Putnam, 1959), 471–72.

23. Fern Marja Eckman, *The Furious Passage of James Baldwin* (New York: M. Evans, 1966).

24. Irving Howe, "A Protest of His Own," *New York Times Book Review*, 2 July 1961, 4.

25. Julian Mayfield, "A Love Affair with the United States," *New Republic* 145 (7 August 1961), 25.

26. "New York Cacophony," *Time*, 29 June 1962, 76.

27. Granville Hicks, "Outcasts in a Caldron of Hate," *Saturday Review* 45 (7 July 1962):91–92; reprinted in Gibson, *Five Black Writers*, 143–47.

28. Norman Podhoretz, "In Defense of a Maltreated Best Seller," *Show* 2 (October 1962): 91–92.

29. Eugenia W. Collier, "The Phrase Unbearably Repeated," *Phylon* 25 (Fall 1964):288–96; reprinted in O'Daniel *Critical Evaluation*, 38–46.

30. F. W. Dupee, "James Baldwin and the 'Man,' " *New York Review of Books* 1 (February 1963):1–2; reprinted in Kinnamon, *Critical Essays*, 11–15.

31. Stephen Spender, "James Baldwin: Voice of a Revolution," *Partisan Review* 30 (Summer 1963):256–60; reprinted below.

32. Robert Brustein, "Everybody Knows My Name," *New York Review of Books* 3 (17 December 1964):10–11; see also Margaret Cooley, "Social Science," *Library Journal* 89 (15 December 1964):4925.

33. Tom F. Driver, *"Blues for Mister Charlie:* The Review That Was Too True to Be Published," *Negro Digest* 13 (September 1964):34–40; reprinted below.

34. Waters E. Turpin, "A Note on *Blues for Mister Charlie,"* in *Critical Evaluation,* ed. O'Daniel, 195–98.

35. Joseph Featherstone, *"Blues for Mister Baldwin,"* New Republic 153 (27 November 1965):34–36; reprinted below.

36. John V. Hagopian, "James Baldwin: The Black and the Red-White and Blue," *College Language Association Journal* 7 (December 1963):133–40; reprinted in Gibson, *Five Black Writers,* 159–66, and O'Daniel, *Critical Evaluation,* 38–46.

37. Sam Bluefarb, "James Baldwin's 'Previous Condition': A Problem of Identification," *Negro American Literature Forum* 3 (Spring 1969):26–29; reprinted in O'Daniel, *Critical Evaluation,* 151–55.

38. John M. Reilly, " 'Sonny's Blues': James Baldwin's Image of Black Community," *Negro American Literature Forum* 4 (July 1970):56–60; reprinted in O'Daniel, *Critical Evaluation,* 163–69, and Kinnamon, *Critical Essays,* 139–46.

39. Keith E. Byerman, "Words and Music: Narrative Ambiguity in 'Sonny's Blues,' " *Studies in Short Fiction* 19 (1982):367–72; reprinted below.

40. Harold Clurman, "The Amen Corner," *Nation* 200 (10 May 1965):514–15; reprinted below.

41. Carlton W. Molette, "James Baldwin as Playwright," in *Critical Evaluation,* ed. O'Daniel, 1983–84.

42. Darwin T. Turner, "James Baldwin in the Dilemma of the Black Dramatist," in *Critical Evaluation,* ed. O'Daniel, 189–94.

43. Irving Howe, "At Ease in Apocalypse," *Harper's* 237 (September 1968):94–100; reprinted in Kinnamon, *Critical Essays,* 96–108.

44. Mario Puzo, "His Cardboard Lovers," *New York Times Book Review,* 23 June 1968, 5; reprinted below.

45. George E. Kent, "Baldwin and the Problem of Being," *College Language Association Journal* 7 (March 1964):202–14; reprinted in Gibson, *Five Black Writers,* 148–58, Kinnamon, *Critical Essays,* 16–27, and O'Daniel, *Critical Evaluation,* 19–29.

46. Charles Newman, "The Lesson of the Master: Henry James and James Baldwin," *Yale Review* 56 (October 1966):45–59; reprinted in Kinnamon, *Critical Essays,* 52–65.

47. Charlotte Alexander, "The 'Stink' of Reality: Mothers and Whores in James Baldwin's Fiction," *Literature and Psychology* 18, no. 1 (1968):9–26; reprinted in Kinnamon, *Critical Essays,* 77–95.

48. Eldridge Cleaver, "Notes on a Native Son," *Ramparts* 5 (June 1966):51–56; reprinted in his *Soul on Ice* (New York: McGraw-Hill, 1968), 97–111, and in Kinnamon, *Critical Essays,* 66–76.

49. John Lash, "Baldwin Beside Himself: A Study in Modern Phallicism," *College Language Association Journal* 8 (December 1964):132–40; reprinted in O'Daniel, *Critical Evaluation,* 47–55.

50. Maurice Charney, "James Baldwin's Quarrel with Richard Wright," *American Quarterly* 15 (Spring 1963):65–75.

51. Irving Howe, "Black Boys and Native Sons," *Dissent* 10 (Autumn 1963):353–68.

52. Ralph Ellison, "The World and the Jug," *New Leader* 46 (9 December 1963):22–26.

53. Irving Howe, "The Writer and the Critic: An Exchange: A Reply to Ralph Ellison," *New Leader* 47 (3 February 1963):12–14.

54. Fred L. Standley, ". . . 'Farther and Farther Apart': Richard Wright and James Baldwin," in *Critical Essays on Richard Wright*, ed. Yoshinobu Hakutani (Boston: G. K. Hall, 1982), 91–106.

55. Colin MacInnes, "Dark Angel: The Writings of James Baldwin," *Encounter* 21 (August 1963):22–33; reprinted in Gibson, *Five Black Writers*, 199–42.

56. Robert Bone, "The Novels of James Baldwin," *Tri-Quarterly* 2 (Winter 1965):3–20.

57. "Black Talks to White," *Times Literary Supplement*, 20 August 1971; 1000.

58. Kenneth Zahorski, "Margaret Mead and James Baldwin: *A Rap on Race*," *College Language Association Journal* 14 (June 1972):470–73; reprinted in O'Daniel, *Critical Evaluation*, 199–204.

59. "A Dialogue," *Library Journal* 98 (1 March 1973):771; and "A Dialogue," *Publishers Weekly* 203 (18 June 1973):68.

60. A. Russell Brooks, "Power and Morality as Imperatives for Nikki Giovanni and James Baldwin: A View of *A Dialogue*," in *Critical Evaluation*, ed. O'Daniel, 205–9.

61. Bruce Cook, *"One Day When I Was Lost," Commonweal* 99 (12 October 1973):47.

62. Patsy Brewington Perry, *"One Day When I Was Lost*: Baldwin's Unfulfilled Obligation," in *Critical Evaluation*, ed. O'Daniel, 213–27.

63. DeMott, "James Baldwin," 63–66.

64. Mel Watkins, "The Fire Next Time This Time," *New York Times Book Review*, 28 May 1972; 17–18; reprinted below.

65. Yoshinobu Hakutani, *"No Name in the Street*: James Baldwin's Image of America in the Sixties," in this volume.

66. Orde Coombs, *"The Devil Finds Work," New York Times Book Review*, 2 May 1976, 6–7.

67. Claude Reed, *"The Devil Finds Work," Unique*, 1976, 32.

68. John Aldridge, "The Fire Next Time?," *Saturday Review*, 15 June 1974, 24–25.

69. Joyce Carol Oates, "A Quite Moving and Very Traditional Celebration of Love: *If Beale Street Could Talk, The New York Times Book Review* 26 May 1974, 1–2; reprinted below.

70. Darryl Pinckney, "Blues for Mr. Baldwin," *New York Times Book Review*, 6 December 1979, 32–33; reprinted below.

71. Eleanor Traylor, "I Hear Music in the Air: James Baldwin's 'Just Above My Head,' " *First World* 2, no. 3 (1979):40–43; reprinted below.

72. Ann S. Haskell, "Baldwin: Harlem on His Mind," *Book World*, 11 September 77, E6.

73. Julius Lester, "Children's Books," *New York Times Book Review*, 4 September 1977, 22.

74. Gibson, *Five Black Writers*, xix–xxiii.

75. Keneth Kinnamon, "James Baldwin 1924–," in Leonard Unger, ed. *Jane Adams*

to *Sidney Lanier*. Supplement I to *American Writers: A Collection of Literary Biographies* (New York: Scribners, 1979), 47–71.

76. Dance, "James Baldwin"; Kinnamon, *Critical Essays;* and O'Daniel, *Critical Evaluation.*

77. Fred L. Standley, "James Baldwin: The Artist as Incorrigible Disturber of the Peace," *Southern Humanities Review* 4 (Winter 1970):18–30; reprinted below.

78. Calvin C. Hernton, "Blood of the Lamb," in *White Papers for White Americans* (New York: Doubleday, 1970), 105–21.

79. Houston A. Baker, Jr., "The Embattled Craftsman: An Essay on James Baldwin," *Journal of African-Afro-American Affairs* 1, no. 1 (1977):28–51; reprinted below.

80. Jacqueline E. Orsagh, "Baldwin's Female Characters—A Step Forward?," in *Critical Evaluation,* ed. O'Daniel, 56–68.

81. Shirley Ann Williams, "The Black Musician: The Black Hero as Light Bearer," in *Give Birth to Brightness* (New York: Dial 1973), 145–66; reprinted in Kinnamon, *Critical Essays,* 147–54.

82. Daryl C. Dance, "You Can't Go Home Again: James Baldwin and the South," *College Language Association Journal* 18 (September 1974):81–90; reprinted below.

83. Craig Werner, "The Economic Evolution of James Baldwin," *College Language Association Journal* 33 (1979):12–31; reprinted below.

84. Donald B. Gibson, "James Baldwin: The Political Anatomy of Space," in *Critical Evaluation,* ed. O'Daniel, 3–18.

85. Michel Fabre, "Pères et Fils dans *Go Tell It on the Mountain* de James Baldwin," *Etudes Anglaises* 23 (1970):47–61; reprinted in English translation in Kinnamon, *Critical Essays,* 120–38.

86. Shirley S. Allen, "Religious Symbolism and Psychic Reality in Baldwin's *Go Tell It on the Mountain,*" *College Language Association Journal* 19 (December 1975):173–99; reprinted below.

87. Shirley S. Allen, "The Ironic Voice of Baldwin's *Go Tell It on the Mountain,*" in *Critical Evaluation,* ed. O'Daniel, 30–37.

88. Trudier Harris, "The Eye as Weapon in *If Beale Street Could Talk,*" *MELUS* 5, no. 3 (1978):54–66; reprinted below.

89. William Edward Farrison, "If Baldwin's Train Has Not Gone," in *Critical Evaluation,* ed. O'Daniel, 69–81.

90. Roger Whitlow, "Baldwin's *Going to Meet the Man:* Racial Brutality and Sexual Gratification," *American Imago* 34, no. 4 (1977):351–56; reprinted below.

91. Arthenia Bates Millican, "Fire as the Symbol of a Leadening Existence in *Going to Meet the Man,*" in *Critical Evaluation,* ed. O'Daniel, 170–80.

92. Harry L. Jones, "Style, Form and Content in the Short Fiction of James Baldwin," in *Critical Evaluation,* ed. O'Daniel, 143–50.

93. Jocelyn Whitehead Jackson, "The Problem of Identity in Selected Early Essays of James Baldwin," *Journal of the Interdenominational Theological Center* 6 (1978):1–15; reprinted below.

94. A. Russell Brooks, "James Baldwin as Poet-Prophet," in *Critical Evaluation,* ed. O'Daniel, 126–34.

95. Nick Aaron Ford, "The Evolution of James Baldwin as Essayist," in *Critical Evaluation,* ed. O'Daniel, 85–104.

96. Hobart Jarrett, "From a Region in My Mind: The Essays of James Baldwin," in *Critical Evaluation,* ed. O'Daniel, 105–25.

97. W. J. Weatherby, *Squaring Off: Mailer vs. Baldwin* (New York: Mason/Charter, 1977), 1–217.

98. Karin Moller, *The Theme of Identity in the Essays of James Baldwin: An Interpretation* (Göteborg, Sweden: Acta Universitatis Göthoburgensis, 1975) 1–189.

99. George Michel Sarotte, *Like a Brother, Like a Lover: Male Homosexuality in the American Novel and Theater from Herman Melville to James Baldwin,* trans. Richard Miller (New York: Anchor/Doubleday, 1978), 27–29, 54–60, 96–103.

100. Stanley Macebuh, *James Baldwin: A Critical Study* (New York: Okpaku, 1973).

101. Peter Bruck, *Von der "Store-front Church" zum "American Dream: James Baldwin und der Amerikanische Rassenkonflikt* (Amsterdam: Grunnen, 1975).

102. Louis Hill Pratt, *James Baldwin* (Boston: Twayne, 1978).

103. Jonathan Yardley, "The Writer and the Preacher," *Washington Post Book World,* 27 October 1985; 3–4; reprinted below.

104. Ibid., 4.

105. Julius Lester, "Some Tickets Are Better: The Mixed Achievement of James Baldwin," *Dissent* 33 (1986):189–92, 214; reprinted below.

106. Fred L. Standley, "*Go Tell It On the Mountain:* Religion as the Indirect Method of Indictment," in this volume.

107. Hakutani, "*No Name in the Street.*"

108. Fred L. Standley, "James Baldwin as Dramatist," in *Twentieth Century American Dramatist,* vol. 7, ed. John MacNicholas (Detroit: Gale Research, 1981), 45–48; reprinted below.

109. C. W. E. Bigsby, "The Divided Mind of James Baldwin," *Journal of American Studies* 14, no. 2 (1980):325–42; reprinted below.

110. Louis H. Pratt, "The Political Significance of James Baldwin's Early Criticism," *Middle Atlantic Writers Association Review* 1, nos. 2–3 (1982):46–49; reprinted below.

111. Marlene Mosher, "James Baldwin's Blues," *College Language Association Journal* 26 (1982):112–24; reprinted below.

112. Emmanuel S. Nelson, "James Baldwin's Vision of Otherness and Community," *MELUS* 10, no. 2 (1983):27–31; reprinted below.

113. Sondra O'Neale, "Fathers, Gods, and Religion: Perceptions of Christianity and Ethnic Faith in James Baldwin," in this volume.

114. Fred L. Standley, "James Baldwin," in *Concise Dictionary of American Literary Biography* (Detroit: Gale Research, 1987), 40–59.

115. Sylvander, *James Baldwin.*

116. Trudier Harris, *Black Women in the Fiction of James Baldwin* (Knoxville: University of Tennessee Press, 1985).

Interview

James Baldwin: Looking towards the Eighties
Kalamu ya Salaam°

James Baldwin, like an old testament prophet whose insistent voice refuses to fall silent, has been one of this country's most persistent witnesses. He is a witness in that he testifies to everything he thinks and feels as we move through the minefields of love/hate, Black/white, rich/poor relationships in twentieth century America.

His complex prose style has often been favorably compared to the King James version of the Bible (primarily the fire and brimstone old testament). Although books such as *The Fire Next Time* have earned Baldwin a reputation for being a harsh critic, James Baldwin is actually most concerned with the problems and possibilities of finding and holding love.

While he has not found it easy to live and work in this country, Baldwin continues to prolifically produce novels and essays. Most often he writes from a small town in France, but on occasions he has sent work to us from Turkey. The important thing is that he is not running away but rather searching out a rock, a desk, a stone tablet from which he can find the needed moments of silence and rest out of which will come rushing full force another letter, or a new nerve-jangling essay, or perhaps a huge and rich novel (such as his latest *Just Above My Head* which some critics think is his best since his first novel *Go Tell It On The Mountain*).

Having crossed the half-century mark, he is no longer an angry young man; he is an elder. He is a seer who has seen much. There is much we can learn from the visions he has, visions which have been tempered by a long time coming.

James Baldwin, a witness, a writer, a Black survivor: listen, he speaks and it is life-song he is singing.

Now that you are back in this country, do you plan to stay?

°Reprinted from the *Black Collegian* 10 (1979):105–6, 108, 110, by permission of the journal.

35

Baldwin: I'll be here for a while. I'm sort of a commuter.

Why do you choose to commute?

Baldwin: I'm not sure I chose it. I went to Paris a long time ago, didn't stay away as long as people thought I had. I came back home in 1967 and was based here until 1969. Since then I have been more or less commuting because it's very hard for me to write here.

What makes it difficult to write?

Baldwin: Well, there are so many other demands which have to be met. There is no way to sit in an ivory tower.

During the sixties there were a number of people who attempted to say what the role of the writer was. I remember a quote of yours which said that the "role of the writer is to write." Do you still think that quote encapsules what should be the role of the writer?

Baldwin: The role of the writer *is* to write, but this is a cryptic statement. What I meant is that a writer doesn't dance. His function is very particular and so is his responsibility. After all, to write, if taken seriously, is to be subversive. To disturb the peace.

Why do you say that?

Baldwin: "What it is" must be examined. Reality is very strange. It's not as simple as people think it is. People are not as simple as they would like to think they are. Societies are exceedingly complex and are changing all of the time, and so are we changing all of the time. Since to write implies an investigation of all these things, the only way that I can sum it up is to say that the role of the writer is to write.

In essence then, the role of the writer is to point out how things got the way they are and how. . . .

Baldwin: . . . how they can continue and change.

You're teaching at Bowling Green College now. Have you taught school before?

Baldwin: No. I'm doing a writer's seminar which is a catch-all term that means whatever you make of it.

For a very long time until Martin died, I was operating as a public speaker in the context of the civil rights movement. And when Martin died, something happened to me and something happened to many people. It took a while for me and for many people to pull ourselves back together. Then I had to find another way to discharge what I considered to be my responsibility. I've been working on college campuses and in prisons; which is why I don't bring my typewriter across the ocean.

The responsibility on the other side of the ocean is to be a writer in the sense of a craftsperson who puts words on the page. The responsibility on this side is what?

Baldwin: On this side my responsibility is, well, it's very difficult to answer that because it involves being available, it involves being visible, it involves being vulnerable, it involves my concept of my responsibility to people coming after me and to people who came before me. . . .

To, in a sense, tell their story, so that others can understand from whence they came.

Baldwin: Yes. I consider myself to be a witness.

On one side of the ocean you can write about what you have witnessed, and on this side of the ocean you bear witness to that which you would write about.

Baldwin: That puts it about as well as it can be put.

Looking at our current situation, in your opinion, what are some of the key themes that need to be expressed?

Baldwin: That is so vast.

I understand that it is vast, but, for example, after fifty-four and going into the sixties, it was critical that people understand the necessity of the civil rights struggle. Do you think there is anything that has a similar cutting edge for us today?

Baldwin: I think that what you've called the civil rights movement, although it is an acceptable term, well, it might clarify matters if one thought of it as, in fact, a slave insurrection. When one thinks of it in that way, in the first place, one is prevented from descending into despair. On one level the civil rights movement was betrayed, but on a much more important level, we all learned something tremendous out of that effort and out of the betrayal something important about ourselves.

What are some of the things we learned about ourselves?

Baldwin: That the people who call themselves "white," I must put it that way, well, as Malcolm X said, "white is a state of mind." The implications of that statement are enormous because it finally means that the people who call themselves white have really invented something which is not true. The key to this is European power which is a very complex thing and which involves the history of the church. White people invented Black people to protect themselves against something which frightened them.

Which was?

Baldwin: I don't know. Life, I guess. All the legends about Black people are very revealing. They are all created by white people: "Aunt Jemima," "Uncle Tom," "Topsy," the Black stud, the nigger whore. Those descriptions, which are labeled legends, do not describe Black people at all.

They describe the creator.

Baldwin: That's right. Whatever you describe to another person is also a revelation of who you are and who you think you are. You can not describe anything without betraying your point of view, your aspirations, your fears, your hopes. Everything.

As you pointed out earlier, if white is a state of mind, then there are many of us who have a Black legacy but who also can be very much white.

Baldwin: Yes, you can not tell a Black man by the color of his skin.

Let's talk about that betrayal of civil rights. In your opinion, who did the betraying and how was it done?

Baldwin: It was inevitable from the moment it started. From the moment it started, we came up against a tremendous political and economic machinery which was not going to dismantle itself. The attempt was made by some very well meaning people, I'm not putting down or condemning Black people, but finally, these estates could find no way to accommodate this discontent and no way to respond to it. All of the civil rights acts passed during that time, including the supreme court decision outlawing segregation in school, were all gestures attempting to ameliorate something which could not be ameliorated without a profound change in the state and that profound change in the state involves an absolutely unthinkable revision of the American identity.

Drawing that out then, there are some of us who believe that the present state of the entertainment arts is in fact a true reflection of what those who think they are white would like to believe about those whose faces are Black?

Baldwin: Precisely. That is why there are only minstrel shows on Broadway now. And white people flock to them in droves to be reassured of their legends, to be reassured of their state, their identities. That's the brutal truth and the bottom line.

So, how do you assess the seventies? The civil rights period and the sixties brought our struggle to a point of sharpness, so much so, that it was unthinkable to believe that we didn't have to struggle.

Baldwin: But of course. Out of that something was clarified for us and, even more importantly, for our children.

Which was what?

Baldwin: That one was no longer at the mercy of white imagination. I was born fifty-five years ago. In a sense I was born in the nightmare of the white man's mind. All of my growing up and all my early youth was first that discovery and then the bloody struggle to get out of that mind, to destroy that frame of reference for myself and for those coming after me. I'm the oldest of nine children; this is very important. I know that my great-nieces and great-nephews are living in a different world than the world in which I was born. They can not imagine the world which produced me, but I've seen the world for which they are going to be responsible.

So although they can't imagine the world that produced you, you understand the world which produced them and understand still the state which remains to be dealt with?

Baldwin: Precisely. And I trust them to do it. We have so far. There's no reason to despair now.

When you say we have so far, how does that correlate with your assessment that the civil rights struggle was betrayed?

Baldwin: The civil rights struggle was betrayed and the people who betrayed it were responsible for that betrayal. We are not.

If I understand you correctly, you are suggesting that although there was a betrayal of the civil rights struggle, there was also a profound impact whose shock waves are still being felt. In fact, although the state may have not toppled at the first blow, it is still tottering and the winds are still blowing.

Baldwin: Oh yes. In fact, the winds are getting stronger because it is not only this particular state, it is the whole western world.

You are obviously very hopeful about the eighties.

Baldwin: Yes, but that doesn't mean it's going to be easy. But I'm far from being in despair. We cannot afford despair. We have too many children. Despair is a luxury only white men can afford.

You mentioned the church. In your new novel you suggest that the church has proven not to have been the redemptive force. . . .

Baldwin: This is something very complex. It depends. When I said the church, I was thinking about the overall, two thousand year history of the Christian church, one of the results of which was the enslavement of Black people. On the other hand, what happened here in America to Black people who were given the church and nothing else, who were given the bible and the cross under the shadow of the loaded gun, and who did something with it absolutely unprecedented which astounds Black people to this day. Finally, everything in Black history comes out of the church.

Given that the church, in the classical sense of church, was both an offer we could not refuse and also has not fulfilled its role as a redemptive force for our people, but at the same time, at the juncture where our people took the church, it did serve as a bridge cross troubled water. . . .

Baldwin: Yes it did. The essential religion of Black people comes out of something which is not Europe. When Black people talk about true religion, they're "speaking in tongues" practically. It would not be understood in Rome.

If you believe that the church is the foundation for our people. . . .

Baldwin: It was how we forged our identity.

What do you see for the generations who are here and who are to come, who have no sense of church?

Baldwin: This is an enormous question. In the first place, I'm not absolutely certain that they have no sense of church, although I hear you very well. I know what you mean when you say that. I don't know if one can divest one's self of one's inheritance so easily. I would go so far as to say it's not possible. Things are changing all of the time. The form changes but the substance remains.

What do you think about the current group of students?

Baldwin: People are very critical and very despairing of the young. But I can only say that in my own experience, and admittedly it's limited, and even admitting I'm in somewhat of a special situation, I must say that my experience in all these years on campus has given me a great deal of hope. Kids ask real questions. I begin to suspect that, in fact, the elders who are so despairing of the young are actually despairing of themselves. Kids ask real questions, very hard questions. Those questions imply a judgement of the man of whom you're asking the question. All you can do is be as open as possible and as truthful as possible and don't ever try to lie to the kids.

You know in the early sixties, if someone had come along and judged the then current crop of students in the Black colleges, they might have felt the same way some people feel about students today.

Baldwin: Of course, and I must repeat myself, that's a luxury one can't afford. I've dealt with junkies, lost girls, exprisoners, people ruined by bitterness before they were eighteen years old, ok. But that's not all there is to that.

What would you note about the prison experiences?

Baldwin: The candor of the prisoners, their knowledge, and I'm not being romantic about prisoners. People get lost. But, I've encountered very few prisoners, and of course this is not a Gallup poll, but I've encountered very few people who did not really understand their situation.

The college situation sets up the type of environment that leads to questioning and the prison situation sets up the type of environment that leads automatically to reflection, whether or not you want that.

Baldwin: Yeah, you could put it that way. The college situation is exceedingly difficult. The Black kid in college, no matter how we cut it, risks paranoia, risks schizophrenia because there is no way for this society to prepare them for the same future that the white boy is prepared for.

The real meaning of the word progress in the American vocabulary, for the most, and there are exceptions to this rule, but for the most part when they say progress they're talking about how quickly a Black kid can become white. That's what they mean by progress. Well I don't want my nephew to grow up to be like Ronald Reagan, or Richard Nixon, or Jimmy Carter.

Let's discuss the relationship, the understanding, the reality of sex and sexual relations in our people's lives. On one level our relationships have been vulgarized. . . .

Baldwin: In the lives of Black people—everyone overlooks this and it's a very simple fact—love has been so terribly menaced. It's dangerous to be in love, I suppose, anytime, anywhere. But it's absolutely dangerous to be in love if you're a slave because nothing belongs to you, not your woman, not your child, not your man. The fact that we have held on to each other in the teeth of such a monstrous obscenity, if we could do that, well I'm not worried about the future.

So you would think that the so-called sexual revolution that's going on. . . .

Baldwin: What do you mean "sexual revolution"?

What I'm basically asking is for a commentary on the current situation.

Baldwin: All I can tell you is that, as regards for example gay liberation, I'm very glad that it seems to be easier for a boy to admit that he's in love with a boy, or for a girl to admit that she's in love with a girl, instead of, as happened in my generation, you had kids going on the needle because they were afraid that they might want to go to bed with someone of the same sex. That's part of the sexual paranoia of the United States and really of the western world.

Homophobia.

Baldwin: A kind of homophobia, but it's . . .

Actually it's life-phobia.

Baldwin: Yeah, that's what it is.

Afraid of someone who is living.

Baldwin: Everybody's journey is individual. You don't know with whom you're going to fall in love. No one has a right to make your choice for you, or to penalize you for being in love. In a sense, I think they've put themselves in prison.

That's what you meant in your story about the sheriff who could not love his wife ("Going To Meet The Man")?

Baldwin: That's right. He was going to meet the man!

Yeah, he was going to meet the man, and everytime they meet men or women they try to kill them.

Baldwin: Exactly.

There is a technological revolution happening. Do you think there is a future for writing within this revolution?

Baldwin: The technological revolution, or rather the technological situation, I am not as worried about it as some other people are. First of all, it depends entirely on the continued validity and power of the western world. I don't think it is in our power to eliminate human beings. And although it may seem at this moment that the television has rendered everyone illiterate and blind, the world can not afford it. When you talk about writing today, you're talking about the European concept of writing, you're talking about the European concept of art. That concept, I assure you, has had its day. There will be different things written in the future, coming out of a different past, and creating another reality. We are the future.

Thank you very much James Baldwin the witness and James Baldwin the writer. We encourage both of you to continue.

Baldwin: Thank you very much and keep the faith.

General Essays

James Baldwin: The Artist as Incorrigible Disturber of the Peace

Fred L. Standley°

Although opinions about James Baldwin vary greatly, a typical view of him, expressed in a popular news weekly, discloses "two James Baldwins, equally passionate, at times equally gifted. One is the racial rhetorician, the polished pamphleteer, the literate prophet . . . [whose] preachments remain intensely articulate, painfully—and plainly—relevant. The other James Baldwin is the questing novelist, the private man loaded down with personal problems that he must defeat—or be defeated by. This is the Baldwin who . . . as a fictioneer . . . is in great danger of becoming drearily irrelevant."[1] This judgment reflects a widespread opinion which until recently tended to denigrate Baldwin as an author and to emphasize his role as a leader in the Negro struggle for civil rights. Such a view has never been accurate in evaluating Baldwin and fails to consider his own conception of himself, as given in an interview two years ago: "I have never stopped fighting for civil rights, but I must do my work or I'll be of no use to anyone."[2] Furthermore, a quick survey of significant books dealing with contemporary social, economic and political issues relative to black Americans reveals almost no mention of Baldwin. No essays by or about him, for example, can be found in *The Negro American,* edited by Talcott Parsons and Kenneth B. Clark (Boston, 1966), or in *Negro Protest Thought in the Twentieth Century,* edited by Francis L. Broderick and August Meier (Indianapolis, 1965). But in numerous books devoted to recent American literature Baldwin is consistently accorded a place as a writer of fiction and essays.[3]

This is not to deny that Baldwin has been an outspoken activist in the struggle for social, economic and political justice for the black minority in American society; rather it is to affirm that the exercise of such communal responsibility was consonant with Baldwin's view of himself as a man of letters and not merely an adjunct to that

°Reprinted from *Southern Humanities Review* 4, no. 1 (1970):18–30, by permission of the author and the journal.

vocation. As he himself phrased the proposition: "the liberation of this country . . . depends on whether or not we are able to make a real confrontation with our history . . . [which] has been criminally falsified by white, Anglo-Saxon Americans, who now find themselves prisoners of their own falsehoods and myths. . . . Two options [are] open to all writers, black or white—to be immoral and uphold the *status quo* or to be moral and try to change the world."[4] While some critics now openly acknowledge that Baldwin is "undoubtedly the best known Negro writer in America today" . . . and "a serious artist," they continue to stress his role as civil rights leader and conclude that: "If the two roles are not mutually exclusive, they are really not compatible either, and they have forced him to become a dual personality: both a fiery prophet of the racial apocalypse and a sensitive explorer of man's inmost nature."[5]

There is a specious logic in this approach to Baldwin, which centers upon the dichotomy of his life and literature; for that is definitely not his own view. Instead, "his endeavor is to show us— even to the point of hallucination—that the public life and the private life are an indivisible whole, that society cannot exist half slave and half free."[6] Careful examination of his thought and his work will reveal that Baldwin's concept of art and of himself as literary artist cannot readily be divorced from his concept of art as involving protest. Both have been vigorously set forth in his controversy with Richard Wright, as well as in his novels.

As a man of letters Baldwin is characterized by a passionate devotion to his vocation. "I consider that I have many responsibilities," he said, "but none greater than this: To last, as Hemingway says, and get my work done. I want to be an honest man and a good writer."[7] To fulfill this ambition he recognizes that "the artist . . . cannot allow any consideration to supersede his responsibility to reveal all that he can possibly discover concerning the mystery of the human being",[8] and that "the business of the writer . . . [is] . . . to examine attitudes, to go beneath the surface, to tap the source."[9] For Baldwin this means that the role of the artist is to present the existential knowledge of experience to man: "the states of birth, suffering, love and death are extreme states—extreme, universal, and inescapable. We all know this, but we would rather not know it. The artist is present to correct the delusions to which we fall prey in our attempts to avoid this knowledge."[10] Only when the artist discovers and expresses it, can there be an adequate perspective of man for our technological era, a perspective in which man is not "merely a member of a society or a Group or a deplorable conundrum to be explained by Science . . . [but] something resolutely indefinable, unpredictable." Only when the artist faces, explores, and strives to reveal "the disquieting complexity of ourselves," can he hope to find "the power that will free us from ourselves."[11]

For Baldwin the effort "to go beneath the surface" and thereby to define man emerges from the artist's openness to and awareness of experience—experience which appears to the ordinary man both fragmented and chaotic. "One writes out of one thing only—one's own experience. Everything depends on how relentlessly one forces from this experience the last drop, sweet or bitter, it can possibly give. This is the only real concern of the artist, to recreate out of the disorder of life that order which is art."[12] In discharging that task Baldwin thinks that the artist is dedicated to a special vocation whose value never dissipates.[13]

Thus, it is clear that in Baldwin's conception of art and of himself as literary artist, this "special function" involves both personal and social responsibility. His personal responsibility implies a duty to avoid the unexamined life and self-delusion; "his subject is himself and the world and it requires every ounce of stamina he can summon to attempt to look on himself and the world as they are."[14] The writer is also "responsible to and for—in any case, always for—the social order"; however, the exercise of this responsibility does not mean that he must become a mayor or a social worker. Rather, the writer's task must be pervaded by an ethical vision and historical orientation that includes concern for his own generation and his descendants.[15]

How then should the creative writer deal with the problem of protest literature—especially if he is black? In current discussions of the protest theme in twentieth century American literature written by Negroes, there is a general inclination to dwell on the novel as being basically a sociological treatise. C. M. Hughes, for example, stated boldly in: *The Negro Novelists: A Discussion of the Writings of American Negro Novelists, 1940–1950* that "Protest literature by category deals with sociology since it propagates the idea of change in American social conditions."[16] A similar idea was expressed by Saunders Redding in his harshly critical estimate of Baldwin's essay "Everybody's Protest Novel":

> . . . ostensibly a criticism of Harriet Beecher Stowe's *Uncle Tom's Cabin,* it was actually a glitteringly written, envy-motivated, and stupid attack on protest fiction in general and contemporary Negro writers in particular. Baldwin should have known better. He should have realized that all good fiction, from *Pilgrim's Progress* to *Tom Jones* and *Swann's Way,* is protest fiction. All of it is *against* something, even when it is not *for* something else. The writing of novels is not solely a "cultural" (artistic-aesthetic) activity. The novel serves a social function as well. Indeed, unless it does serve a social function, it is worthless as art.[17]

It is precisely this kind of attitude that Baldwin was combatting when he said in that essay—"literature and sociology are not one and the same"; a view which is also shared by Ralph Ellison in his statement that "people who want to write sociology should not write a novel."[18] The point to be emphasized is that while Baldwin rejects the notion of "protest" literature as espoused by Hughes and Redding, he does not reject the notion of protest literature.

In his essay "The Creative Dilemma" Baldwin described the artist as an "incorrigible disturber of the peace" with whom "all societies have battled. I doubt that future societies will get on with him any better."[19] One might well ask "why is this so?" Because, said Baldwin, "the entire purpose of society is to create a bulwark against the inner and outer chaos, in order to make life bearable and to keep the human alive. And it is absolutely inevitable that when a tradition has been evolved, whatever the tradition is, the people, in general, will suppose it to have existed from before the beginning of time and will be most unwilling and indeed unable to conceive of any changes in it."[20] In Baldwin's opinion, although society assumes its own stability, the artist "knows there is nothing stable under heaven. One cannot possibly build a school, teach a child, or drive a car without taking some things for granted. The artist cannot and must not take anything for granted, but must drive to the heart of every answer and expose the question the answer hides."[21] Therefore, the writer's peculiar nature as artist imposes on him a constant condition of "warring" with his society, "for its sake and for his own."[22] In the United States the exercise of such responsibility by the artist is, in Baldwin's view, "dangerous" and requires "sweat and terror" of the artist. "This is because the nature of the society isolates its artists so severely for their vision; penalizes them mercilessly for their vision and endeavor; and the American form of recognition, fame and money, can be the most devastating penalty of all. This is not the artist's fault, though I think that the artist will have to take the lead in changing this state of affairs."[23] Specifically, American society seems determined to prohibit the artist's vision of human experience "in which one discovers that life is tragic, and therefore unutterably beautiful."[24] Yet this vision rests upon the validity of paradox as a category of explanation, and "American, now, this country devoted to the death of paradox— . . . may, therefore, be put to death by one."[25] What must be asserted repeatedly, though "societies never know it," is that "the war of an artist with his society is a lover's war, and he does it at his best, what lovers do, which is to reveal the beloved to himself and, with that revelation, to make freedom real."[26]

Consequently, for Baldwin the novel must be more than a sociological treatise or a political tract or a black power polemic. True, the novel will have social, political and economic presuppositions and implications. However, as in syllogistic logic so in aesthetics, the whole is greater than the sum of its parts, and what informs the novel in the most significant way is the artist's vision of mankind, in all of its baffling and enigmatic complexity, a vision which, said Ralph Ellison, "has always defined itself *against* the negatives thrown by society and the universe."[27] This signifies "protest" not in the sense of merely concern for and dedication to a cause or movement characterized primarily by temporality: "for the conquest of the physical world is not man's only duty. He is also enjoined to conquer the great wilderness of himself. The precise role of the artist, then, is to illuminate that darkness, blaze roads through that vast forest so that we will not, in our doing, lose sight of its purpose, which is, after all, to make the world a more human dwelling place."[28]

Within the context of his concepts of the artist and social protest, Baldwin's attitudes toward Richard Wright and *Native Son* (1940) throw an illuminating light on his concern for the black artist in America. In three essays particularly ["Everybody's Protest Novel" (1949), "Many Thousands Gone" (1955), and "Alas, Poor Richard" (1962)][29] Baldwin openly acknowledges his affection for Wright, who in spite of working "during a bewildering and demoralizing era in Western history," became for him "the greatest black writer in the world" and a "spiritual" father. "I had made my pilgrimage to meet him because he was the greatest black writer in the world for me. In *Uncle Tom's Children,* in *Native Son,* and above all, in *Black Boy,* I found expressed, for the first time in my life, the sorrow, the rage, and the murderous bitterness which was eating up my life and the lives of those around me. His work was an immense liberation and revelation for me. He became my ally, and my witness, and alas! my father."[30] However, according to Baldwin the anticipated relationship between the fledgling and the idol could not be sustained because of "the deep and irreconcilable differences" between their points of view.[31] He felt that two major points, related but distinguishable, were responsible for the rupture: first, Wright's contention that Baldwin had "betrayed him and not only him but American Negroes by attacking the idea of protest literature;" and second, Baldwin's contention that Wright became unable to accept "my right to my own vision, my right, as his equal, to disagree with him."[32]

In the essay "Everybody's Protest Novel" Baldwin analyzed the idea of the novel as protest literature (i.e. " 'problem' literature when written by whites, 'protest' literature when written by Negroes"),[33] and saw *Native Son* in that tradition. His thesis was that "since literature and sociology are not one and the same, it is impossible to discuss them as if they were."[34] The protest novel, according to Baldwin, has become "an accepted and comforting aspect of the

American scene" because it satisfies the passion for "categorization, life fitted into pegs"; so that "whatever unsettling questions are raised are evanescent, titilating; remote, for this has nothing to do with us, it is safely ensconced in the social arena, where indeed, it has nothing to do with anyone, so that finally we receive a very definite thrill of virtue from the fact that we are reading such a book at all." The result is that the so-called lofty purpose of the protest novel is forfeited, and it becomes "a mirror of our confusion, dishonesty, panic. . . . They are fantasies, connecting nowhere with reality, sentimental. . . ." And, the aim of the protest novel, therefore, becomes "to reduce all Americans to the compulsive, bloodless dimensions of a guy named Joe," as was the aim of "the zeal of those alabaster missionaries to Africa to cover the nakedness of the natives, to hurry them into the pallid arms of Jesus and thence into slavery."[35]

In the second essay "Many Thousands Gone," Baldwin praised *Native Son* as "the most powerful and celebrated statement we have yet had of what it means to be a Negro in America";[36] yet, he also declared that the protagonist Bigger "is Uncle Tom's descendant, flesh of his flesh, so exactly opposite a portrait that, when the books are placed together, it seems that the contemporary Negro novelist and the dead New England woman are locked together in a deadly, timeless battle; the one uttering merciless exhortations, the other shouting curses."[37] Thus, while Wright became the eloquent spokesman for the "New Negro," recording his rage in an era of inequities, he "also nevertheless recorded, as no Negro before him had ever done, that fantasy Americans hold in their minds when they speak of the Negro: that fantastic and fearful image which we have lived with since the first slave fell beneath the lash."[38]

Although Wright's intention was to confront us with this "monster (Bigger Thomas) created by the American republic" and to make us share his experience and to feel pity and horror at his inevitable doom, Baldwin asserted that Bigger, having no "discernible relationship to himself, to his own life, to his own people, nor to any other people," also had no force as a social unit or social symbol; he had significance only "as the incarnation of a myth."[39] For Baldwin, then, Wright's book, while representing a significant contribution by a Negro to the American literary tradition, also contributed to the continuation of that belief that

> in Negro life there exists no tradition, no field of manners, no possibility of ritual or intercourse, such as may, for example, sustain the Jew even after he has left his father's house. But the fact is not that the Negro has no tradition but that there has as yet arrived no sensibility sufficiently profound and tough to make this tradition articulate. For a tradition expresses, after all, nothing more than the long and painful experience of a people; it comes out of the battle

wages to maintain their integrity or, to put it more simply, out of their struggle to survive.[40]

Consistently adhering to the idea that the reality of man, whether black or white, is more than a social reality and that the artist is strangled who deals with man only in social terms, Baldwin has characterized Richard Wright as an "illustrious victim" of "the war in the breast between blackness and whiteness," a war which denies "both the heights and depths of our nature, takes, and has taken, visibly and invisibly as many white lives as black ones."[41]

Clearly, Baldwin believes that his own vision was a threat to Wright's "system of reality" and offended him, "always, it turned out, in the same way: by failing to take his word for all of the things he imagined, or had been led to believe, his word could cover."[42] In recent years, however, Baldwin has asserted that Wright, when he died, "was acquiring a new tone, a less uncertain esthetic distance, and a new depth," and that in some of his later work "Wright's unrelentingly bleak landscape was not merely that of the Deep South, or of Chicago, but that of the world, of the human heart."[43]

Thus far in his own literary career Baldwin has written four novels—*Go Tell It on the Mountain* (1953), *Giovanni's Room* (1956), *Another Country* (1962), and *Tell Me How Long the Train's Been Gone* (1968)—and these have elicited a variety of judgments, favorable and otherwise, of his importance as a writer of fiction. According to Irving Howe, Baldwin desired to show in his fiction "the Negro world in its diversity and richness, not as a mere spectre of protest"; to show it as "a living culture of men and women who, even when deprived, share in the emotions and desires of common humanity; . . . to evoke something of the distinctiveness of Negro life in America, as evidence of its worth, moral tenacity and right to self-acceptance." Nevertheless, because of the great gap between his aims and achievement Howe thinks Baldwin has yet to "register a major success."[44] While praising Baldwin's integrity as an essayist, Saunders Redding has derided him as a novelist who subscribes to the white man's view of the Negro reality and who functions only within the white man's structure of thought and myth, thereby avoiding the very special truths that Negroes know better than anyone else and thus misrepresenting the reality Negroes live in.[45] In a similar manner Robert A. Bone acknowledges Baldwin as "the most important Negro writer to emerge during the last decade," his publications having made "a stunning impact on our cultural life"; yet Bone also concludes that Baldwin is an uneven writer whose accomplishment in the novel is open to dispute, since his only "impressive achievement" in the genre is *Go Tell It on the Mountain*.[46] Even Norman Mailer, long a close friend of Baldwin, accuses him of being "too charming a writer to be major" and to genteel to tell off his writers in four letter words: hence, "one itches at times to take a hammer to his detachment, smash the perfumed dome of his ego, and reduce him to what must be one of the most tortured and magical nerves of our time."[47]

Although space is too limited here for detailed analyses of Baldwin's novels, reference to some of their general and recurring characteristics and motifs may at least modify these grudging tributes. First, one must be aware that Baldwin's novels deal with the impact on the individual of the conditions of urban life and society. He treats not the rural and natural setting but the grime and the gutter, the anonymity and impersonality, the confinement and isolation indigenous to the modern metropolis, especially in its impact upon those within the lower socio-economic stratum. Consider, for example, the opening scene from *Another Country:*

> He was facing Seventh Avenue, at Times Square. It was past midnight and he had been sitting in the movies . . . since two o'clock in the afternoon. He was so tired. . . . He was hungry, his mouth felt filthy . . . and he was broke. And he had nowhere to go.

> The Avenue was quiet, too, most of its bright lights out. . . . A sign advertised the chewing gum which would help one to relax and keep smiling. A hotel's enormous neon name challenged the starless sky. The great buildings, unlit, blunt like the phallus or sharp like the spear guarded the city that never slept.

> Beneath them Rufus walked, one of the fallen—for the weight of this city was murderous—one of those who had been crushed on the day, which was every day, these towers fell. Entirely alone, and dying of it, he was part of an unprecedented multitude.[48]

Second, the protagonist in the Baldwin novel is best described as "a rebel-victim." According to Ihab Hassan, he is "the central and controlling image of recent fiction"; both "an actor but also a sufferer. Almost always he is an outsider, an initiate never confirmed in his initiation, an anarchist and a clown, a Faust and Christ compounded in grotesque and in ironic measures. The poles of crime and sainthood define the range of his particular fate, which in his character." While this rebel-victim assumes many forms in contemporary fiction, in that of Baldwin, he is "the Negro in search of the eternal, elusive identity."[49] This quest for identity is indispensable in Baldwin's novels because the problem is serious in America (though it is not confined only to the black man), and the failure to undergo the experience is indicative of a fatal weakness which destroys man. Recording his own sojourn in Europe, Baldwin wrote:

I didn't meet anyone in that world who didn't suffer from the very same affliction that all the people I had fled from suffered from and that was that they didn't know who they were. They wanted to be something that they were not. And very shortly I didn't know who I was, either. I could not be certain whether I was really rich or really poor, really black or really white, really male or really female, really talented or a fraud, really strong or merely stubborn. In short I had become an American. I had stepped into, I had walked right into, as I inevitably had to do, the bottomless confusion which is both public and private, of the American confusion.[50]

In the novels the quest for identity always involves the discovery and the rejection of illusion and delusion about oneself, encountering and fighting "all the dragons of the inner life: alienation, abandonment, isolation and solitariness."[51] However, in Baldwin's view there can be no self-perception apart from or outside of the context of interpersonal relations. In order to define oneself, a person has to be willing to reveal his interior being; "in order to have a conversation with someone you have to reveal yourself."[52] For Baldwin the motivating force and the means for overcoming the existential abyss between oneself and another person is love—love which is "so desperately sought and so cunningly avoided." "What is the nature of such love? Love takes off the masks we fear we cannot live without and know we cannot live within. I use the word 'love' here not merely in the personal sense but as a state of being, or a state of grace—not in the infantile American sense of being happy but in the tough and universal sense of quest and daring and growth."[53] Love in this sense is no spiritual entity or metaphysical concept abstracted from physical embodiment; rather it signifies the ultimate concern for man's relationship with man within all of the vicissitudes and vagaries of human experience: "Whites coupled with Negroes, heterosexual men coupled with homosexuals, homosexuals coupled with women, none of it involving casual lust or the suggestion of neurotic perversity, and all of it accompanies by the most serious emotions and resulting in the most intense attachments."[54]

Love, for Baldwin, embodies the only redemptive power capable of aiding man in defining his humanness; and love is "the force and mystery that so many have extolled and so many have cursed, but which no one has ever really understood or ever really been able to control."[55] In short, what Baldwin seems to be saying in these novels is that the only significant realities are individuals, whether black or white, and love, whether homosexual or heterosexual; that these individuals pursue love; and "that anything which is permitted to interfere with the free operation of this fact is evil and should be done away with."[56] This emphasis in the novels is thus consistent with his assertion in the essays that "if the concept of God has any validity or use, it can only be to make us larger, freer and more loving. If God cannot do this, then it is time we got rid of him."

A third important consideration of Baldwin's novels is the burden of responsibility he places on the characters for fashioning their own destiny, no matter how awesome the forces arrayed against them. This endeavor ought to be praised for it is a forthright and fundamental attack upon the philosophy of naturalistic determinism. The "undoctrinaire comprehensiveness"[57] of Baldwin's view may seem frank, militant and even cruel; the vision of experience he expressed may seem bizarre and grotesque; it may seem to be only the emotion of rage and of shame. However, I think it is "not without an element of sweet spiritual generosity." "For implicit in it is the idea that everyone carried his own burden, that every burden is ultimately as heavy as every other and that a man is either brave enough or strong enough to stand up straight under the weight on his back or he isn't; and if he isn't he will pay the price and no one else has the right to judge him harshly; and if enough people are found to be lacking in enough bravery or enough strength, then there must be something wrong with the conditions they are being forced to endure and the values these conditions have bred."[58] In spite of the fact that the art of his novels frequently appears to be propagandistic, weakened by flaws of literary technique, there are fundamental values informing it which give that art a maturity of insight not readily apparent to those who see in the novels merely hatred, violence, vulgarity, and promiscuity. The question of whether Baldwin's novels are any more successful than those of Wright in executing his own understanding of what "protest" signifies in fiction remains a moot one. What seems more important than this question is that Baldwin recognizes the distinction between sociology and aesthetics (as does Ralph Ellison) and that he is thus among those writers described by Hubert Hill in *Anger, and Beyond* (1966)—Negro writers for whom "simple protest and anger are not enough."[59]

Notes

1. "Milk Run," *Time*, 91 (June 7, 1968), 104.

2. "James Baldwin Breaks His Silence," *Atlas*, XIII (March 1967), 47–49.

3. See for example *How We Live: Contemporary Life in Contemporary Fiction*, edited by Penny Chapin Hills and L. Rust Hills (New York, 1968); *Dark Symphony: Negro Literature in America*, edited by James A. Emanuel and Theodore L. Gross (New York, 1968); and *Contemporaries* by Alfred Kazin (Boston, 1962).

4. Hoyt Fuller, "Reverberations from a Writer's Conference," *African Forum*, I (Fall 1965), 79.

5. Howard Harper, Jr. *Desperate Faith: A Study of Bellow, Salinger, Mailer, Baldwin and Updike* (Chapel Hill, 1967), p. 138.

6. John Rees Moore, "An Embarrassment of Riches," *The Hollins Critic,* 2 (December, 1965), 12.

7. James Baldwin, "Autobiographical Notes," *Notes of a Native Son* (New York, 1964), p. 6.

8. James Baldwin, "The Creative Dilemma," *Saturday Review,* February 8, 1964, p. 15.

9. "Autobiographical Notes," p. 3.

10. "The Creative Dilemma," p. 15.

11. Baldwin, "Everybody's Protest Novel," *Notes of a Native Son,* p. 11.

12. "Autobiographical Notes," p. 5.

13. James Baldwin, "The Male Prisoner," *Nobody Knows My Name* (New York, 1964), pp. 125-6. "The importance of a writer is continuous . . . his importance, I think, is that he is here to describe things which other people are too busy to describe. It's a function, let's face it, it's a special function. There's no democracy on this level. It's a very difficult thing to do, it's a very special thing to do and people who do it cannot by that token do many other things."

14. Baldwin, "The Discovery of What It Means to Be an American," *Nobody Knows My Name,* p. 12.

15. Baldwin, "The Black Boy Looks at the White Boy," *Nobody Knows My Name,* p. 188.

16. James D. Graham, "Negro Protest in America, 1900–1955: A Bibliographical Guide," *South Atlantic Quarterly,* LXVII (Winter, 1968), 105.

17. Saunders Redding, "Since Richard Wright," *African Forum,* I (Spring, 1965), 21–23.

18. Graham, p. 105.

19. "The Creative Dilemma," p. 15.

20. *Ibid.*

21. *Ibid.,* pp. 15, 58.

22. *Ibid.,* p. 15.

23. James Baldwin, "Sidney Poitier," *Look,* 32 (July 23, 1968), p. 56.

24. "The Creative Dilemma," p. 58.

25. "Everybody's Protest Novel," p. 16.

26. "The Creative Dilemma," p. 58.

27. Ralph Ellison, "A Very Stern Discipline: An Interview," *Harper's Magazine,* 234 (March, 1967), 84.

28. "The Creative Dilemma," p. 15.

29. The first two essays are in *Notes of a Native Son* and the third is in *Nobody Knows My Name.* Irving Howe, *A World More Attractive* (New York, 1963), pp. 98–122; see also, Miles Jackson, "Significant Belles Letters by and about Negroes Published in 1964," *Phylon,* XXVI (1965), 216–227. The essay, "Black Boys and Native Sons," by Irving Howe treating Baldwin's view of Wright will not be discussed since it fails to consider several statements made by Baldwin in "Alas, Poor Richard." Howe criticized Baldwin and Ellison as "phonies" who rejected the protest novel and pretended to be "mere American writers trying to react to something of the pluralism of their predicament."

30. "Alas, Poor Richard," *Notes of a Native Son,* pp. 147, 151.

31. *Ibid.,* p. 152.

32. *Ibid.,* pp. 156, 159.

33. "Many Thousands Gone," *Notes of a Native Son,* p. 23.

34. "Everybody's Protest Novel," p. 14.

35. *Ibid.,* pp. 14–15.

36. "Many Thousands Gone," p. 17.

37. "Everybody's Protest Novel," p. 17.

38. "Many Thousands Gone," p. 26.

39. *Ibid.,* pp. 26–27.

40. *Ibid.,* p. 28.

41. "Alas, Poor Richard," p. 170.

42. *Ibid.,* p. 161.

43. *Ibid.,* p. 149.

44. Howe, p. 110.

45. Redding, pp. 21–23.

46. Robert A. Bone, "The Novels of James Baldwin," in Seymour L. Gross and John Edward Hardy, eds. *Images of the Negro in American Literature* (Chicago, 1966), pp. 265–268.

47. Norman Mailer, *Advertisements of Myself* (New York, 1959), pp. 93–94.

48. *Another Country* (New York, 1963), pp. 9–10.

49. Ihab Hassan, "The Character of Post-War Fiction in America," in Richard Kostelanetz, ed. *Contemporary Literature* (New York, 1964), p. 39–41.

50. "Notes for a Hypothetical Novel," *Nobody Knows My Name,* pp. 122–123.

51. Stanley Romaine Hopper, "The Problem of Moral Isolation in Contemporary Literature," *Spiritual Problems in Contemporary Literature* (New York, 1957), p. 153.

52. "Notes for a Hypothetical Novel," p. 124.

53. "The Male Prison," *Notes of a Native Son,* p. 128.

54. Norman Podhoretz, "In Defense of a Maltreated Best Seller," in Kostelanetz, p. 234.

55. "The Creative Dilemma," p. 15.

56. Podhoretz, p. 235.

57. Jesse Bier, "Recent American Literature: The Great Debate," *Bucknell Review,* XIV (1966), 99.

58. Podhoretz, p. 236.

59. Hubert Hill, ed. *Anger, and Beyond* (New York, 1966), p. XXI–XXII.

You Can't Go Home Again: James Baldwin and the South   Daryl C. Dance*

James Baldwin, like innumerable other Black artists, has found that in his efforts to express the plight of the Black man in America,

*Reprinted from *CLA Journal* 18 (1974):81–90, by permission of the author and the journal.

he has been forced to deal over and over again with that inescapable dilemma of the Black American—the lack of sense of a positive self-identity. Time after time in his writings he has shown an awareness of the fact that identity contains, as Erik Erikson so accurately indicates, "a complementarity of past and future both in the individual and in society."[1] Baldwin wrote in "Many Thousands Gone," "We cannot escape our origins, however hard we try, those origins which contain the key—could we but find it—to all that we later become."[2] And again he notes in *A Rap on Race*, "If history were the past, history wouldn't matter. History is the present, the present. You and I are history."[3] He has his narrator in "Sonny's Blues" state this same idea:

> Sonny's fingers filled the air with life, his life. But that life contained so many others. And Sonny went all the way back. . . . He had made it his: that long line, of which we knew only Mama and Daddy. And he was giving it back, as everything must be given back, so that, passing through death, it can live forever. I saw my mother's face again, and felt, for the first time, how the stones of the road she had walked on must have bruised her feet. I saw the moonlit road where my father's brother died.[4]

In his research for his roots the American Negro quite naturally turns to Africa. And yet for many Black Americans, the separation from their African homeland and many aspects of its culture was so complete that Africa remains a far-off, remote land from which they are irretrievably estranged. Author John Williams has noted, "I have been to Africa and know that it is not my home. America is."[5] And Chester Himes asserts, "The American Negro . . . is an American; the face may be the face of Africa, but the heart has the beat of Wall Street."[6] Having visited Africa Langston Hughes wrote, "I was only an American Negro—who loved the surface of Africa and the rhythms of Africa—but I was not African."[7] Saunders Redding had noted that Richard Wright went to Africa "seeking again a place, a home, and came away from there knowing that he had not found it."[8] Despite the fact that from time to time Baldwin avers that his past takes him back to Africa, that past is so remote that he is completely lost when asked to look backwards to his origins in Africa, as he notes in this account of a conversation which he had with a Black Jamaican:

> [He] asked me where I was from, and I said I was born in New York. He said, "Yes, but where are you from? I did not know what he meant, "Where did you come from before that?" he explained. I said, "My mother was born in Maryland . . . [and] My father was born in New Orleans." He said, "Yes, but where are you from?" Then I began to get it; very dimly, because now I was lost. And he

said, "Where are you from in Africa?" I said, "Well I don't know," and he was furious with me.[9]

Baldwin has on other occasions noted the distance between the Black African experience and the Black American experience. He writes in "Encounter on the Seine":

> The African before him [the Black American] has endured privation, injustice, medieval cruelty; but the African has not yet endured the utter alienation of himself from his people and his past. His mother did not sing "Sometimes I Feel Like a Motherless Child," and he has not, all his life long, ached for acceptance in a culture which pronounced straight hair and white skin the only acceptable beauty.
>
> They face each other, the Negro and the African, over a gulf of three hundred years—an alienation too vast to be conquered in an evening's good will. . . .[10]

James Baldwin has continued his quest for identity abroad—specifically in France. But despite the positive aspects of his experience abroad, he consistently speaks of it as a temporary escape, which reminds him more than anything else that he is, above all, an American and that France will never be his home. Speaking of his experience in France, he writes in his "Notes" for *The Amen Corner,* "I had escaped. but I had not escaped myself . . . [France] was not really my home. I might live there forever and it would never be my home."[11]

In France Baldwin becomes as sentimental about his loneliness for Black America as W. E. B. Du Bois' Matthew Towns, of whom Du Bois had written, "What would he not give to clasp a dark hand now, to hear a soft, Southern roll of speech, to kiss a brown cheek? To see warm, brown, crinkly hair and laughing eyes."[12] In like manner Baldwin has asserted, ". . . no Frenchman or Frenchwoman could meet me with the speed and fire of some black boys and girls whom I remembered and whom I missed."[13] Again he notes, "I missed Harlem Sunday mornings and fried chicken and biscuits, I missed the music, I missed the style—that style possessed by no other people in this world. I missed the way the dark face closes, the way dark eyes watch, and the way, when a dark face opens, a light seems to go on everywhere . . . [I] missed the life which had produced me and nourished me and paid for me."[14]

Thus, no matter how much he must suffer in America, no matter how much he fears and hates the situation into which he is cast in this country, no matter how much he dreads the trip back, Baldwin realizes that he, like all of his characters who go abroad, must return to America. His Leo Proudhammer, for example, acknowledges, "I was part of these people [Americans], no matter how bitterly I judged them. I would never be able to leave this country. I could only leave it briefly, like a drowning man coming up for air."[15] And Baldwin himself recognizes after two years in Paris, and seven years before his return, that the American Negro living abroad *will* "one day . . . face his home again."[16] Further, as he points out in the "Introduction" to *Nobody Knows My Name,* he discovered during his last years in Europe that he had to find the answer to the question of who he was, and that in order to do that he had to leave Europe, which was his haven, and face America, which was his home.

Thus, after nine years in Paris, Baldwin returned to America, realizing: "It was only here, after all, that I would be able to find out what my journey had meant to me, or what it had made of me."[17] But after arriving in New York, Baldwin had yet another journey to make in quest of his roots, perhaps the most important of all his journeys and certainly the most awesome—he had to make his odyssey to the South.

It is important to note here that from slavery through the present century, Black literature, folk tales and songs have portrayed characters who view the North as an Eden, a heaven to which they aspire to escape from the South, which they equate with hell. And though many of these characters find that the North is indeed no paradise, the South remains associated with hell, a place to which no one would ever return. Something of the general attitude is recaptured in the joke concerning a Negro who moved to Cleveland from the South and was faced with a multitude of problems, such as scarcity of jobs, high rents, and others. He prayed to God, asking Him what to do. The answer was, "Go South again, my child," and the suppliant replied, "Lord, I can't go back south . . . unless it is your will to lead me there. Will *you* go with me?" And the Lord answered, "Yes, as far as Cincinnati."[18]

James Baldwin feared his first trip to the South as much as the speaker in the joke feared to return. He had terrifying nightmares about his proposed journey, and once he reached the South, he later declared, "I felt as though I had wandered into Hell."[19] Commenting upon a white man who directed him to the colored entrance in a restaurant, he notes, "he was, indeed, being as kind as can be expected from a guide in hell."[20] Looking back on his trip, he observes, "I doubt that I really knew much about terror before I went South."[21]

But if James Baldwin was ever to find his origins and thereby the key to his own identity, to paraphrase his own words, he had to make that journey to the South, for there—not in Africa— was where it all began for him. Noting that Haitians have been said to be able to trace their ancestry back to African kings, he comments, "but any American Negro wishing to go back so far will find his journey through time abruptly arrested by the signature on the bill of sale which served as the entrance paper for his ancestor. . . . The identity of the American Negro comes out of this extreme situation. . . ."[22] Later he asserts, "I have to talk out of my beginnings, and I did begin here auctioned like a mule. . . ."[23] It is only when he finally makes his odyssey to the South that he is able to appreciate the positive results of these beginnings—the strength and beauty of the people who have suffered slavery and the most degrading social and economic persecution; it is only then that he is able to appreciate the real possibility for creativity inherent in suffering and tragedy. . . . It is then that he can write:

> This past, the Negro's past, of rope, fire, torture, castration, infan-ticide, rape, death and humiliation, fear by day and night, fear as deep as the marrow of the bone; . . . this past, this endless struggle to achieve and reveal and confirm a human identity, human authority, yet contains, for all its horror, something very beautiful. I do not mean to be sentimental about suffering—enough is certainly as good as a feast—but people who cannot suffer can never grow up, can never discover who they are. That man who is forced each day to snatch his manhood, his identity, out of the fire of human cruelty that rages to destroy it knows . . . something about himself and human life that no school . . . can teach.[24]

Of his trip to the South Baldwin asserts, "Something began, for me, tremendous. I met some of the noblest, most beautiful people a man can hope to meet, and I saw some beautiful and some terrible things."[25] He found that there was no word to describe so many of the Black men he met in the South except "heroic."[26] He found, in other words, that in the midst of, despite *and* because of, the horror, tragedy and suffering, out of his painful experience and struggle to survive, the Southern Negro has maintained a strength, a purity, a nobility, an integrity, and a sense of identity that can represent the salvation of the race.

Not only does he feel a sense of awe at the Southern Black man, but also the beauty of the Southern countryside—which again is associated with tragedy in his mind. He writes: "There was more than enough to fascinate. In the Deep South . . . there is the great, vast, brooding, welcoming and bloodstained land, beautiful enough to astonish and break the heart."[27] Indeed the love of the physical beauty of the Southland that Baldwin suggests here reflects the paradox of the Negro's flight north. Despite the Northern immigrant's attacks on the South and his usual refusal to return, he frequently recalls the beauty of the land with a sentimentalism and romanticism that one feels in recalling home. Such are the accounts of the physical beauty of the South to be found in W. E. B. Du Bois, Jean Toomer, Richard Wright, and John Williams, to name a few. Further many Black authors have their fictional characters who flee to the North recall certain aspects of their days in the South with deep nostalgia. And for most, the South remains *home.*

And thus it is that having searched all over the world for his roots, James Baldwin, who until he was thirty-three had "never seen the landscape of what Negroes sometimes call the Old Country,"[28] finds his home at last. He writes: "I was very glad I had come South . . . I felt very much at home among the dark people who lived where I, if so much had not been disrupted, would logically have been born. I felt, beneath everything, a profound acceptance, an unfamiliar peace, almost as though, after despairing and debilitating journeys, I had, at last, come home."[29]

But the sense of peace that Baldwin suggests is not to last long and he finds that having found his home, he has also found that one can't go home again, for he could never learn to once more make the adjustments that a Black man must make to live in the South—and by extension in America. Thus he says:

> I wasn't sorry I'd come—I was never, in fact, ever to be sorry about that, and until the day I die, I will always consider myself among the greatly privileged because, however inadequately, I was there. But I could see that the difficulties were not going to be where I had confidently placed them—in others—but in me. I was far from certain that I was equipped to get through a single day down here, and if I could not so equip myself then I would be a menace to all that others were trying to do. . . .[30]

His trip South so unnerved Baldwin that when he returned to New York, he collapsed, evidently suffering neurasthenia, or what he described as a paralysis resulting from retrospective terror.[31] A similar reaction is experienced by his character Caleb Proudhammer when he returns from a horrifying experience in the South. Transformed into a lonely, sad, thin, beaten, hysterical man, unable to talk with his brother, he spends his nights in terrifying paroxysms, trembling, his breast heaving, the bitter tears gushing from his eyes, recalling that nightmare: "Oh, what they did to me, Oh what they did to me."[32] The narrator of Baldwin's short story. "This Morning, This Evening, So Soon," undergoes a similar reaction when he returns South to his mother's funeral. Even Richard Henry, a Baldwin character who was born and raised in the South, finds that once having left, he can't go home again either. Like the doomed Willie of Frank Yerby's "The Homecoming" and the Black violinist of Langston Hughes's "Home," Richard has forgotten how to do things the way they had to be done "down home." As Parnell comments, "After all, he had lived in the north a long time. He wasn't used to the way we do things down here."[33]

Of course, the greatest danger that Baldwin sees in going "home" again is the loss of one's manhood—the threat of rape, of castration, symbolic and real. He is obsessed with the image of the Black man hanging from a tree on a dark Southern road, blood gushing from his mutilated sex organ. As a matter of fact, in his view, "the past of a Negro is blood dripping down through leaves, gouged-out eyeballs, the sex torn from its sockets and severed with a knife."[34] Obviously this vision is no mere figment of Baldwin's imagination, but rather a vision motivated by the many actual instances of castration that frequently accompanied lynchings in the South. In this act, as Frantz Fanon has noted, "The penis, the symbol of manhood, is annihilated, which is to say that it is denied";[35] or as Baldwin states it simply, "a man without balls is not a man."[36] Thus, ironically, in Baldwin, the Black man who goes South, in finding his identity, risks his manhood, which is so much a part of that identity.

Commenting on the desire of a white guard to use him sexually, Caleb Proudhammer tells his brother that this was the most threatening danger which he faced in the South—the threat to his manhood; the threat of rape.[37] And the reason that Richard Henry cannot survive in the South, of course, is his insistence on being a man. His father says after his death, "I tried to help my son become a man. But manhood is a dangerous pursuit here."[38] That Lyle's killing of Richard is an effort to emasculate him is suggested when after Lyle's first shot Richard cries, "Why have you spent so much time trying to kill me? Why are you always trying to cut off *my* cock?"[39]

Baldwin faced the same threat of emasculation during his first trip South in 1957. Though he has written of that trip many times since then, it is not until the 1972 publication of *No Name in the Street* that he has discussed this particular incident, perhaps proving the truth of his assertion twelve years earlier that "All art is a kind of confession. . . . All artists, if they are to survive, are forced, at last, to tell the whole story, to vomit the anguish up."[40] A part of the anguish that perhaps completes the story of why he can't go home again is the "unbelievable shock" he experienced when he found himself in a situation where one of the most important and most powerful white men in a Southern state which he was visiting was, Baldwin writes, "groping for my cock."[41] Realizing the power of this man who could with a phone call prevent or provoke a lynching, Baldwin continues, "Therefore, one had to be friendly; but the price for this was your cock."[42] The inescapable implications of this, Baldwin concludes, is that the slave knows he is a slave "because his manhood has been, or can be, or will be taken from him."[43]

Thus, ironically, having found after much agonizing searching, his home, in the South, and, of course, in a larger sense, in America, Baldwin realizes that he cannot go home again. The very place that discovers for him his identity, his manhood, also threatens to rob him of it and denies him the peace and rest for which he seeks and which he had expected to find at home. He laments:

> [How] bitterly weary I was of wandering, how I hoped to find a resting place, reconciliation, in the land where I was born. But everything that might have charmed me merely reminded me of how many were excluded, how many were suffering and groaning and dying, not far from a paradise which was itself but another circle of hell. Everything that charmed me reminded me of someplace else. Someplace where I could walk and talk, someplace where I was freer than I was at home, someplace where I could live without the stifling mask—made me homesick for a liberty I had never tasted here, and without which I could never live or work. In America, I was free only in battle, never free to rest—and he who finds no way to rest cannot long survive the battle.[44]

Notes

1. Erik Erikson, *Identity: Youth and Crisis* (New York: W. W. Norton and Company, 1968), p. 310.

2. James Baldwin, *Notes of a Native Son* (Boston: The Beacon Press, 1955), p. 27.

3. Margaret Mead and James Baldwin, *A Rap on Race* (Philadelphia: J. B. Lippincott Company, 1971), p. 188.

4. James Baldwin, *Going to Meet the Man* (New York: The Dial Press, 1965), p. 140.

5. John A. Williams, *This Is My Country Too* (New York: The New American Library, 1965), p. 169.

6. Chester Himes, "Dilemma of the Negro Novelist in the United States," *Beyond the Angry Black*, ed. John A. Williams (New York: Cooper Square Publishers, 1969(, p. 55.

7. Langston Hughes, *The Big Sea* (New York: Alfred A. Knopf, 1940), p. 325.

8. Saunders Redding, "Reflections on Richard Wright: A Symposium on an Exiled Native Son," *Anger and Beyond: The Negro Writer in the United States*, ed. Herbert Hill (New York: Harper and Row, 1966), p. 204.

9. Mead and Baldwin, *A Rap on Race*, p. 81.

10. James Baldwin, *Notes of a Native Son*, p. 122.

11. James Baldwin, "Notes," *The Amen Corner* (New York: Dial Press, 1968), p. xiii.

12. W. E. B. Du Bois, *Dark Princess: A Romance* (New York: Harcourt, Brace and Company, 1928), pp. 8-9.

13. Baldwin, "Notes," *The Amen Corner*, xiii.

14. James Baldwin, *No Name in the Street* (New York: The Dial Press, 1972), p. 71.

15. James Baldwin, *Tell Me How Long the Train's Been Gone* (New York: The Dial Press, 1968), p. 330.

16. Baldwin, "Encounter on the Seine," *Notes of a Native Son*, p. 121.

17. Baldwin, *No Name in the Street*, p. 51.

18. Philip Sterling, ed., *Laughing on the Outside: The Intelligent White Reader's Guide to Negro Tales and Humor* (New York: Grosset and Dunlap, 1965), p. 206.

19. Baldwin, *No Name in the Street,* p. 55.

20. *Ibid.,* p. 72.

21. *Ibid.,* p. 58.

22. Baldwin, "Stranger in the Village," *Notes of a Native Son,* pp. 169–170.

23. Mead and Baldwin, *A Rap on Race,* p. 256.

24. James Baldwin, *The Fire Next Time* (New York: The Dial Press, 1963), pp. 112–113.

25. Baldwin, *No Name in the Street,* pp. 51–52.

26. *Ibid.,* p. 66.

27. *Ibid.,* p. 68.

28. Baldwin, "Notes of a Native Son," *Notes of a Native Son,* p. 86.

29. Baldwin, *No Name in the Street,* p. 70.

30. *Ibid.,* p. 74.

31. *Ibid.,* p. 57.

32. Baldwin, *Tell Me How Long the Train's Been Gone,* p. 209.

33. James Baldwin, *Blues for Mister Charlie* (New York: The Dial Press, 1964), p. 111.

34. James Baldwin, "Alas, Poor Richard," *Nobody Knows My Name* (New York: The Dial Press, 1916), p. 213.

35. Frantz Fanon, *Black Skin, White Masks,* trans. Charles Lam Markmann (New York: Grove Press, Inc., 1967), p. 162.

36. Baldwin, *No Name in the Street,* p. 64.

37. Baldwin, *Tell Me How Long the Train's Been Gone,* pp. 233–234.

38. Baldwin, *Blues for Mister Charlie,* p. 103.

39. *Ibid.,* p. 120.

40. Baldwin, "The Northern Protestant," *Nobody Knows My Name,* p. 179.

41. Baldwin, *No Name in the Street,* p. 61.

42. *Ibid.,* p. 62.

43. *Ibid.*

44. *Ibid.,* p. 126.

The Embattled Craftsman: An Essay on James Baldwin

Houston A. Baker, Jr.°

> We are like the sensitive spring
> walking valleys like a slim young girl
> full breasted and precious limbed

°Reprinted from *Journal of African-Afro-American Affairs* 1, no. 1 (1977):28–51, by permission of the author and the journal.

and carrying on our lips the kiss of the world.
Only the naked arm of Time
can measure the ground we know
and thresh the air we breathe.
Neither earth nor star nor water's host
can sever us from our life to be
for we are beyond your reach O mighty winnowing flail!
infinite and free!

Margaret Walker

I

During the past two decades, James Baldwin has received more attention from literary and social critics than any other black American author. His writings have been enthusiastically applauded by statesmen, activists, high school students, and scholars alike. These responses to the Harlem sage are not surprising if one considers him an implacable agent of reform ceaselessly hammering at the American consciousness. Moreover, it once seemed he was like the streetcorner evangelist, appearing everywhere, weaving a sinuous rhetoric that urged us to repent because it was later than we thought. But reactions today are less enthusiastic, and one explanation is the writer's discovery of an unequivocal relationship with his culture. On one hand, there are two few critics versed in Black American culture to testify to his present stance. On the other, there are many who vaguely (and with some terror, one imagines) realize what his progression implies. The result has been an increased effort to view Baldwin in the light cast by his earlier works.[1] It is as though one of our more prolific modern writers never moved beyond a fall to the threshing floor. An examination of his novels and of selected essays, however, reveals a quest that has brought him firmly to his feet and left him speaking in an "engaged" Black voice. His journey has been circular, beginning and ending with the Black urban masses, but his perceptions of Black Americans and of the artist's relationship to them as seen in *Go Tell It On the Mountain* (1952) and *If Beale Street Could Talk* (1974) are markedly different. Rather than (in the words of Twain to Howells) an old derelict on unfamiliar seas, James Baldwin today seems representative of timeless impulses in Black American culture.

II

Born in 1924, James Arthur Baldwin did not become part of a family until Emma Berdis Jones married David Baldwin in 1927. The boy could then number bastardy *and* oppression as his ironical legacy. "Ironical" because the format of some of the most accomplished Black American writing includes a nameless narrator who confronts a bleak

situation. The recurrent themes in Baldwin's canon are both autobiographical and traditional: a quest for identity and a drive to be
free. And as a promising writer must, he made creative capital of his
early experiences.

"One Sunday Morning" (1937),[2] a sketch published in a junior
high school newspaper, depicts a tramp whose desire to become an
actor has been thwarted by his parents. The tramp is now a broken
man. The young boy to whom he tells his story rewards him with a
quarter. The youngster is presumably better prepared for his own
creative calling, having given up worldly goods and learned a tale of
stifling convention. The artist, the creator, the spokesman as a victim
of oppression forced to draw from his own life the meaning of
existence—this is a stock figure for Baldwin. One might call it the
embattled craftsman.

It would be simplistic to say a writer never escapes his primary
experiences, e.g., Richard Wright remained a "Mississippi pickanniny"
all his life. It seems correct, however, to assert that authors often
shape some fundamental experience into a pattern that continually
lends weight to their work. If this is the case, one is justified in
noting the juvenilia mentioned above. The persecuted artist who sees
his own youthful struggles as symbolic is surely in accord with a
literary tradition whose most patent mode is autobiographical. Baldwin's traditionality, in short, is reflected by the fact that Frederick
Douglass's *Narrative,* Langston Hughes's *The Big Sea,* Richard Wright's
Black Boy, Ralph Ellison's *Invisible Man,* and Malcolm X's *The Autobiography of Malcolm X* could all be subtitled: "How I became the
narrator presently addressing you," or "A message to America from
a spokesman who may save your life." Baldwin is at his most assured
as a Black autobiographer appalled by his countrymen's myopia.
Whatever he writes is fiercely social because he assumes that not a
categorical "Negro," but a very particular Negro named James Baldwin is America's metaphor.[3]

The first long work in his canon is *Go Tell It On the Mountain.*[4]
The book opens on its protagonist's fourteenth birthday, and before
it concludes, John Grimes has: explored the "broadway" of whiteness
and damnation, wrestled the handsome, young ideal of the Temple
of the Fire Baptized, fallen on the threshing floor of the Lord, assumed
(problematically, to be sure) the cultural burden of the saints, and
"come through" blessed by Elisha's holy kiss. From the description,
one could infer a "big book." Actually the novel is quite succinct.
Its landscape is almost totally interior, and action is confined to twenty-
four hours. The work, in fact, is a compressed treasure, one of the
few unflawed gems in Baldwin's corpus. The setting, which is indis-
putably Harlemesque in outlook, tone, and detail, helps account for
this. The author is on home ground, presenting himself, so to speak,

in his own backyard. Ten, agonizing years went into the work's composition, and its title seems to celebrate both the protagonist's movement toward acceptance and hope and the author's triumphant hallelujah of creative fulfillment.

John Grimes's opposition is his father. Baldwin's was the oppressive memory of his own father. John is baffled by elders who have made their way from "improbable fields down South" to the narrow enclave he calls home. Their pictures on the mantle are beside the statue of a coiled serpent ready to strike. They are, thus, associated with that traditional knowledge that will be John's when he sees into their lives. The boy has already looked upon his father's nakedness and heard Gabriel's lust in the still hours of the night. But there is more to come.

The history begins with slavery, and its details include: family disruption, engaged animosity, rape, barrenness, lynchings, religious hypocrisy, and murder. And there is no transformation in the promised land of the North; here, there is only frustration, continuing hypocrisy, malignancy, and acrimony. John Grimes's burden is this frightening, Black humanity for which Baldwin insists we never have to battle but only to accept.[5] Since John only vaguely apprehends his past and present while on the threshing floor, his acceptance must be termed provisional. Still, he realizes he has been born into a new life where the struggle with his father will take on new dimensions. At the conclusion, he says "I'm ready. I'm coming, I'm on my way" and returns to his grimey, claustrophobic apartment alone. Elisha, his momentary companion, has walked into the sunrise.

Having endorsed a religion that is "more than a notion," John has also ensured the victor's role in the novel for a Black cultural tradition. That tradition, when the book closes, has received a sensibility which may eventually become sufficiently profound and tough to make it articulate. The quest was set in "Many Thousands Gone": ". . . the fact is not that the Negro has no tradition but that there has as yet arrived no sensibility sufficiently profound and tough to make this tradition articulate."[6]

With the completion of *Go Tell It On the Mountain,* Baldwin was in the position of the man who creates the features of his face and thereby forges the collective conscience of his race. He was free. Autobiographical recall led to the recovery of a self he deemed essential. This identity might be called, as I have stated earlier, that of the embattled craftsman. And it is this moving, brooding, somber figure who serves as the narrator of the next work, *Notes of a Native Son,*[7] a collection of essays published in 1955. The title essay is the longest in the volume. Its setting (not unexpectedly) is Harlem. The life detailed by the essay is much like John Grimes's, but there is a temporal and spatial expansion that carries readers to the narrator's "red summer" in New Jersey. It is the muggy time of the father's death and of the 1935 Harlem riot. Significantly, the action of *Go Tell It On the Mountain* is set in 1935. The essay, then, constitutes part of that "fifth act" at which Michel Fabre has so astutely hinted.[8] Here we have John Grimes with a resonant voice and a philosophy that advocates, if not love, at least, not-hate. The narrator realizes that hatred has eaten inward to his father's soul and consumed the man in madness. He himself has almost been lynched for his behavior in the discriminatory glitter of a Newark restaurant. We now know the father's fall, but we do not know his wrestlings. There is implicit exoneration here if one considers the narrator's own perplexity before whose empty bottles of life waiting to be filled. He does not have a clear recourse from the violence that hatred and frustration produce. But he must continue to search because there is new life coming into the world. A baby is born as the father lies dying.

Whatever answers the narrator offers are likely to be on the grand scale because he has travelled and achieved the distance he seems to feel is required to set his personal experiences in perspective. Essays such as "A Question of Identity" and "Stranger in the Village" sketch the Black man's relationship to America and condemn the moral innocence of whites who seek to escape the import of this relationship. We are alone with our unique past on this solid mass of ground called America. There is no hiding place, and if Blacks and whites do not face this truth, the day will come when no one has shelter from a cosmic wrath. The organization of *Notes of a Native Son* reveals Baldwin's progression. The first section contains a statement of his aesthetics: what one must be concerned with as an artist. Section two is set in Harlem. And part three details the writer abroad, having attained the requisite position for his critique. But the achieved exile did not turn out as the craftsman had hoped it would. The introduction to *Nobody Knows My Name* sums it up rather nicely: "These years [in Paris] seemed, on the whole, rather sad and aimless to me. . . . In America, the color of my skin had stood between myself and me; in Europe, that barrier was down."[9]

But the introduction continues in the following manner: "Nothing is more desirable than to be released from an affliction, but nothing is more frightening than to be divested of a crutch. It turned out that the question of who I was was not solved because I had removed myself from the social forces which menanced me—anyway, these forces had become interior, and I had dragged them across the ocean with me. The question of who I was had at last become a personal question, and the answer was to be found in me" (p. 11).

In *Nobody Knows My Name*, the quarrels with Wright and Gide continue. The concern with the role of the Black artist is expanded in "Princess and Powers," and cinema criticism appears again in "The

Northern Protestant." To go on listing, however, is to risk the charge that like the small boy in a toy shop one has felt compelled to touch everything. If we bypass the treatment of white vis-à-vis Black writers, there is left the title essay, which deals with the South. It is notable that an author whose protagonist in his first novel has, at least, a mystical glimpse of the "Ole Country" misses so completely the deeper layers of his ancestral soil.[10] In "Nobody Knows My Name," the narrator is all statistics, generalizations, and romantic set pieces. He is the observer who, after telling us what the return to his father's land is supposed to mean, proceeds as a journalist to record the prosaic (or fantasized) reality he perceives. Baldwin, in short, does not give life to those awesome and "improbable fields" down south. While he is again "sitting in the house" called America, his grasp of a landscape uniquely his own remains tenuous. This results, possibly, from his having "everything on his mind."[11] The essays collected in *Nobody Knows My Name* are disparate, and only an elaborate structure could reconcile so many unsettling doubts and desperate longings.

Determined to be an honest writer, realizing the question of color obscures the question of self, and bent on expending every ounce of stamina to "look on himself and the world as they are,"[12] Baldwin finished *Another Country* (1962). According to some, this novel reveals the "public vision" of its writer.[13] Their argument runs as follows: Baldwin's work in the civil rights movement spurred him to new heights of activism and resulted in creative efforts that manifest a sense of the "outside" world. In the context of the present discussion, however, *Another Country* seems a logical outgrowth of earlier writings. The embattled craftsman is always at the center of concentric circles: his family, the larger Black society, and the white world. And *Another Country* actually starts exactly where *Go Tell It On the Mountain* does—in Harlem. Rufus, a portrait of the Black artist as refugee, was born and raised in an uptown apartment. Downtown, he is merely an untidy young boy. He is a musician, though, and physically alluring enough to attract a poor, white, southern female to the bandstand. "Do you love me?" the refrain of a saxophonist, becomes Rufus and Leona's "let's try to love one another." But the burden of their respective personalities proves too formidable, and they end by destroying each other. The rage of the Black artist is futile unless he is strong enough to cease battling for his humanity by those "brutal criteria" bequeathed by Leona's forefathers. And the white female is driven mad as an ironic victim before a past she does not understand. The Black man leaps screaming off a bridge cursing God. The white woman proceeds to an asylum.

The supporting cast's reaction to Rufus's fate comprises the bulk of *Another Country*. Each character feels he or she has failed the dead musician. And through Ida they try to understand what has

happened to the Black artist and what is presently happening to
them. It is as though Baldwin, has, at this point in his career, rejected
one possible development of John Grimes. The Black boy from Harlem
can not survive as a raging, screaming, sexually-aggressive Black
creator pleading for the white world's acceptance. Such a course
merely carries one to the dead end of self-destruction encountered
by Baldwin's father. The substitute for this version of the artist is
Eric Jones. The tramp actor of "One Sunday Morning" appears as
the free and sensitive soul, a self-exiled actor who has decided to
return to his native land. He is the recipient of guiltless homosexual
love. White and successful, the embattled craftsman has returned
from Europe to tell us all. He will tell us all—and show us too.

Like a multifaceted cross, Eric spreads his grace in many directions. He is center stage, and his loving firmness brings both Vivaldo
and Cass to the light. He has had to fight his own, pitched battles
in a world that has denied him, but past confrontations with his father
and with his own Joeys (the name of David's young paramour in
Giovanni's Room) have now been set in order. He is ready, at any
moment, for a command American performance.

Meanwhile, another artist is finding her tortuous way to stardom.
Ida is turning Black tradition—the blues—to profit. In a capitalistic
society where doors were closed to Black creativity, she is certain
to encounter difficulties. And the Black artist as prostitute is an
important figure in this novel filled to the brim with artistic spirits.
If Rufus could not obtain satisfaction from a southern, white woman,
Ida can certainly achieve her ends with a white producer and with
Rufus's failed savior, Vivaldo. One is led gently to view Ida's sordid
ascent as positive. She moves domestically-nude about the kitchen at
the conclusion of the novel, explaining her degradation to the dis-
tressed artist Vivaldo. The clouds have passed away when she and
Vivaldo come through. Another way of viewing this scene is as an
ironic comment on what being an American creator involves. Prostitution seems required for Blacks (the giving of a *very* sexual love
to those almost helplessly incapable of grasping anything else, e.g.,
Baldwin's own altruism with graphic orgasms). Black flagellation seems
the key for whites. Without the stern instruction (added to the dark
eros) of the Black artist, white artists are doomed to stalled vision,
incomplete works of art. To be simplistic, the view set forth is that
the Black artist has to move far beyond the strictly aesthetic demands
of his field if he wishes to achieve success in a racist society. Further,
there seems an insistence that the white American artist is forever
lost unless he encounters head on the implications of his society's
racism and expiates his own guilt through a masochistic confrontation
with the Black other. This is not a pleasant reflection. But it does

seem to mirror one of Baldwin's conceptualizations of his own experiences.

It hardly seems overstatement to say *Another Country* is *not* a prolegomenon for a homosexual revolution. And when one turns to *The Fire Next Time,*[14] one can see how the novel fits into a total corpus. The voice in the 1963 volume of essays is that from *Notes of a Native Son,* but the vision is *Another Country's.* The boy from Harlem starts again at square one, but this time his autobiographical recall is from a position of eminence. Turning formerly veiled eyes upon the territory surrounding him, he is merciless in his rejections. The church which John enters in *Go Tell It On the Mountain* is scathingly exposed as part of the American power game. The Muslims are scrutinized but eventually put aside because the narrator is a writer and likes "doing things alone" (p. 97). Whites are unsparingly castigated for their fear of "sensuality," which is a rejoicing in life. Hope resides in "love": a commitment to self-knowledge and a refusal to foster the blindness which plunges the world into terror and loneliness. When love moves to the fore, power games will end, and the world will be safe from the fires of judgment.

I have, of course, emphasized the long essay, "Down at the Cross." "My Dungeon Shook," the first essay in *The Fire Next Time,* is less a prelude or introductory essay than an act of good faith on the part of the narrator. It sets the process championed in the final essay in motion, cautioning a nephew not to take false steps already explored by the author. "Down at the Cross" constitutes the careful—the very careful and brilliant—second view of experiences seen elsewhere. It bestows an order on the self's movement through time and space that was unavailable before *Another Country.* Only the few are "conscious" and can contribute to the world's salvation because precisely this handful has made the arduous journey toward self-identity. The work seems Baldwin's most accomplished essay and marks the real end of his first youth. The Black writer has reached the end of his initial quest in a narrowing rite of passage.

III

One of the curious, but predictable, impulses in American literary criticism is its tendency to ignore, shamelessly exploit, or say the same things about an author who is no longer young or who has reached a certain eminence. Middle age is a national trauma, and it seems unforgivable in the lives of our artists. The only interesting problems appear to be those of beautiful, bitter, and exacting youth. Hence, one does not find the great, startled eyes of James Baldwin on the covers of well-known periodicals today, nor does one discover his by-line inside.

That stock figure in the canon has felt the weight of this. A famous artist, one who has conquered the city, he is just as embattled as in his youth. Though they are more numerous, his domiciles are still a trouble to his spirit. The explanation resides in the betrayal of good faith represented by "trials, assassinations, funerals, and despair."[15] And it is complicated by the fact that: "In this place, and more particularly, in this time, generations appear to flower, flourish, and wither with the speed of light" (p. 178). To the foregoing he adds: "I don't think that this is merely the inevitable reflection of middle age: I suspect that there really has been some radical alteration in the structure, the nature, of time" (p. 178). Without being reductive, one might say success found the craftsman on the far side of the watershed marked by the death of Martin Luther King. His achieved city is smitten by plague, and he: "could scarcely be deluded by Americans anymore, one scarcely dared expect anything from the great, vast blank generality; and yet one was compelled to demand of Americans—and for their sakes, after all—a generosity, a clarity, and a nobility which they did not dream of demanding of themselves" (p. 10).

In *Tell Me How Long the Train's Been Gone*,[16] the middle aged Leo Proudhammer's heart has literally stopped beating. Having arrived at the crest created by his fame, he is brought low by the driving sacrifices and bewildering obstacles confronted during his climb. The road travelled is sketched for readers in the narrator's autobiographical reflections in the hospital. The actor of "One Sunday Morning" and *Another Country* is, thus, Black, celebrated, and convalescent. One suspects his illness is as much spiritual as physical, for the first section of *Tell Me How Long the Train's Been Gone* carries the self-deprecatory title, "The House Nigger." And the second part asks: "Is There Anybody There?" The favored servant of the big house is looking for connections. The glory train has already departed.

It began, of course, in a Harlem apartment where a Barbadian father and a New Orleans mother watched Leo and his brother Caleb go forth to meet a desperate world. Caleb bears the brunt of this world's cruelty: the violent streets, the false charge of theft, a prison farm, and a racist army. Having suffered unspeakable degradation and unanswerable treachery, he finds release in the Black church. He, in fact, represents Leo's alter ego, what John Grimes could have become without his compulsion to create.

Leo, the younger brother, does not have as far to run because a large part of the course has already been covered by Caleb. Nonetheless, his track is rocky. He will not prostitute himself to Saul, the director of the actors' workshop, nor will he embrace (without the sternest analysis) those "roles" whites demand of him. Rejection, denial of his talent, and a very tangible hunger are the results of this insubordination. His refusal to be locked into pathetic stereotypes is shared by Barbara King, wealthy heiress of a southern family. Defying her parents' expectations, she devotes her life to a search for self-knowledge and to a concomitant love for Leo Proudhammer. Barbara and Leo are the Greenwich Village generation of the fifties. They are the relatively conscious few among that group who have stood in the path of a fast-approaching holocaust. Others, like Jerry, have attempted the struggle and failed. To the question of the second section, therefore, Leo and Barbara can answer with each other's names. Unlike Rufus and Leona, they have been wise and committed enough to forge a union. But this is not enough. It is a dry salvation that does not result in a new life. And the offspring provides the title of the third section, "Black Christopher."

Christopher Hall is the Columbus of the post-civil-rights world. He represents the youth of a new generation: revolutionary, hopeful, aggressive. He loves space and, given a full set of options, would "tear this house down." Margaret Walker's lines, "Let a bloody peace be written. . . . Let a race of men rise and take control" capture the endorsement Leo and Barbara give their surprising progeny. A bond of commitment—a joining of North and South, Black and white—across the color line has lent a final hope to America. The assumptions behind this proposition are not without their weak points, however, since Leo remains unsure of what he must do for or with Christopher. And while he provides material comfort and a degree of understanding, it is impossible to assume he truly understands his young lover. The best Barbara can manage is incest.

Tell Me How Long the Train's Been Gone, then, remains strikingly open-ended. Black Christopher's Christian party is outnumbered, but with guns (and cameras) supplied by the interracial family, they will both seize and record (as revolutionary artists?) the time. Their articulate energy is as ill-defined as the flashing panorama seen at a San Francisco discotheque toward the end of the novel:

> On the wall were four screens, and, on these screens, ectoplasmic figures and faces restlessly writhed, moving in and out of each other, in a tremendous sexual rhythm which made me think of nameless creatures blindly coupling in all the slime of the world, and at the bottom of the sea, and in the air we breathed, and in one's very body. From time to time on this screen, one recognized a face. I saw Yul Brynner's face, for example, and, for a moment, I thought I saw my own. (p. 369)

This is veritably a whirring chaos, the primeval swamp from which a new world will, perhaps, emerge. One is not sure whether the recognizable figures are being consumed in fury or participating in the ritual. The presence of the immigrant actor may simply indicate

the theatricality of it all. But the young, Black street people dancing
a rite which the narrator is "witnessing, not sharing," a rite "older
than that, in forests irrecoverable," offer testimony to a surging force
making its way toward a world more attractive.

Speaking of Christopher, a prime generator of this force, Leo
remarks: "I heard his cry because it was my own. He did not know
this—did not know, that is, that his cry was my own—but he knew
that *his* cry had been heard." The novel's focus is, thus, the street.
How do the street people feel about Leo? Does he have a connection
with those "goggle-eyed," awkward, shy Black people who are fom-
enters of the coming judgment? If he has a role to play, *Tell Me
How Long the Train's Been Gone* seems to suggest the stage must
be shared with Barbara King. There is, one may feel, some confusion
about the direction of the embattled craftsman. The artist and the
revolutionary have formulated a truce that is both tentative and
uneasy. Moral suasion is useless before whites like the King family
(the bland, southern generation—or the innocently chirping television
group) and a simple speaking part on the nation's platforms will no
longer suffice.

The craftsman has gone full circle to return home. When John
Grimes leaves the temple on a Sunday morning, the "silent [Harlem]
avenue" stretching before him is vividly described as "like some gray
country of the dead." There is no life here, only the moving gutter
water filled with excrement, vomit, "dead sperm." The people are
sleeping, and when they awaken, it will be as John's tormentors. He
longs, therefore, to "stare past the bitter houses" and see into the
heart of things. The irony is that the monstrous heart turning an
"astounded universe" is revealed to the narrator of *No Name in the
Street* (1972)[17] as the inexorable Black heart. Its locus is the avenue
left behind for Paris and other points of the embattled craftsman's
journey.

If Leo Proudhammer answers Christopher's call with some uncertainty, James Baldwin not only hears a cry, but also seeks to
explain and extend it in *No Name in the Street*. He assumes a
colloquial voice, repeatedly asserts his alliance with "old street rats"
like Malcolm X, and unequivocally condemns the white West. He is
standing once more on home ground, speaking without fear or shame.
This is not to say his analysis is unduly chic. No effort that seeks to
explicate and compare contemporary Third-World revolutionary impulses and their implications for the West can be labelled merely
chic—or simplistic. What one has in the creator at his most forthright.

He begins with autobiographical recall. Five years old and in
Harlem, he finds his father smiling and his mother kind. The scenes
are almost painfully domestic compared to those participated in by
the Sisyphian toiler of *Go Tell It On the Mountain*. And if the father's

image quickly becomes one of a tyrant, there is left the fond memory of siblings banded together to protect the mother—and themselves. The brothers and sisters form an attractive unit, and the narrator insists it was (at least in part) a desire to be with them that brought him back from Paris. His sister Gloria, moreover, is a constant companion in the experiences recounted in *No Name in the Street*. The family is almost redeemed by the relationship of its young.

But the narrator's overriding concern is a larger family, one that includes the Western nations and their Third-World adversaries. What is forcefully portrayed is the death of the white, paternalistic elders—in France, Britain, and the North and South of the United States. Having always been worthy of the Biblical indictment, "Ye are liars and the truth's not in you," the wicked are now being chased out of the world. Blackness, defined as a "great spiritual condition," represents the energy standing in direct opposition to the mindless force declining empires exert to preserve their tabernacles. Those of the white West, however, have "neither . . . son nor nephew" remaining in their dwellings because their heirs have seen their wickedness and taken to the streets in search of salvation. They find Black people there, but no bonds. For the heirs are, and have always been, untrustworthy, unknowing. The refrain that stands so aptly in contrast to this delineation of whites is "O Pioneers." Crossing the barren stretches of the West's failing plains, young people like Dorothy Counts and a new pantheon of Black heroes like Ralph Shuttlesworth, Medger Evers, Malcolm X, Martin Luther King, Bobby Seale, and Huey Newton have given indisputable proof that "The white man's sun has set."

There is much more in the volume. But a treatment of the narrator's view of the South, his revised assessment of the value of Western history, and his detailed reflections on Black heroes he has known would consume a disproportionate amount of space. The most interesting point in light of the present analysis is the implied alteration in the role of the Black artist/autobiographer. If Baldwin has a public voice, it is to be found in *No Name in the Street*. Here, he speaks of and for the Black masses. He seems a rather more fluent avatar of David Walker: a man championing violent revolt.

And yet, there are strained hesitations, subtle retreats, and patent withdrawals from this role. Blacker-than-thou militants are scorned with a vengeance. Revolution and fanaticism are viewed as equally suicidal. The Beverly Hills Hotel and Watts are miles (and centuries) apart; the author remains in the hills. Malcolm X is a gentle, noble soul, a "genuine revolutionary." The craftsman remains opposed to Malcolm—until it is time to compose the story of a martyr. Eldridge Cleaver is a revolutionary, and the narrator sets himself as artist against Cleaver's calling.

The shift in point of view, which is actually a clearer perception of the bifurcated self, is forshadowed in *Tell Me How Long the Train's Been Gone. No Name in the Street* simply reinforces it. "Life's inexorable mathematics" have left the narrator's childhood friend in the streets. They have, in turn, elevated the craftsman to the heights, where his task remains that of a chronicler. He may *understand* the life of the avenue (lauding the Black Panthers and their programs), but he knows he can never again be an integral part of such a life. A younger, more fiery generation does not even know his name. And it is they who will give birth to a new world.

Both the revolutionary and the artist, however, are gifted with vision, and their roles may, in fact, be complementary. In *No Name in the Street* they are viewed as such because the narrator functions as a poet. He has his own personal experiences in mind, and Martin Luther King's assassination forces him to the depths of consciousness and provides a significant order. He juxtaposes and conflates events until they come together in an original and elucidating pattern. "Only poets," he says, "since they must excavate and recreate history, have ever learned anything from it." The Black poet, in this instance, is the Black autobiographer of *No Name in the Street.* He is a man of more lively sensibility, one who appears cut off from the dust and heat of battle. Finally, however, he is the man who illuminates for the revolutionary both the precedents and the total meaning of an all-encompassing conflict. The poet's apparent isolation is simply a socially-mandated withdrawal into a self tempered and instructed by experience. Not all of the narrator's dichotomizing, therefore, should be seen as the quarrelsome resistance of middle age to relinquish (in the words of Leo Proudhammer): ". . . all that I most treasured, wine, talk, laughter, love, the embrace of a friend, the light in the eyes of a lover, the touch of a lover, that smell, that contest, that beautiful torment, and the mighty joy of a good day's work . . ." Any component of this bourgeois list must be stolen by the revolutionary and the artist alike. Each must live each moment as though it were his last. The mortality of neither is more certain than the storm (Gwendolyn Brooks has called it a "whirlwind") "rising to engulf us all."

Having forged a new definition of his role, an explanation that makes more precise the traditional accomplishments of the Black autobiographer, the embattled craftsman is now prepared to render his penultimate vision. *If Beale Street Could Talk* (1974)[18] presents this in an interesting and persuasive narrative. The novel's characters and settings represent both general qualities and moral concepts. The tight Harlem apartment, the avenue, and the awesome inhabitants have been allegorized. The conclusion of *No Name in the Street* reads: "Now, it is the Virgin, the alabaster Mary, who must embrace the despised black mother whose children are also the issue of the Holy Ghost." *If Beale Street Could Talk* begins with the epigraph: "Mary / Mary / What you going to name / That pretty little baby?" The issue in question is the child of Clementine and Alonzo, two Harlem young people. Tish, who has recently discovered her pregnancy, is the narrator. Significantly, the book opens with Tish standing before a mirror. Unlike David in *Giovanni's Room,* she is forcefully aware of her situation, and she is accepting, loving, filled with life. The tale she rehearses is slight, but its deep structure is resonant.

Fonny has been compelled to leave home by a self-righteous mother and two scolding, mulatto sisters. Only his stepfather, Frank, has provided relief. He has taken an apartment in Greenwich Village where he works as a sculptor of wood. It is in Fonny's studio that Tish conceives. A white policeman (reminiscent of Lyle Britten in *Blues For Mister Charlie*) is determined to arrest the young artist and is passionate for his beautiful companion. The results are foreordained. At the opening of the novel Fonny is in jail charged with rape, and most of the book presents the other characters' efforts to gain his release. When his bail has almost been secured, the stepfather commits suicide. The novel ends with the crying of the newborn baby.

The most telling revision of earlier views in the canon is to be seen in the love and understanding provided by Tish's entire family and by Fonny's stepfather. The enclosed space of the apartment has become a source of fortitude and affection. The young lovers and their families, moreover, embody the complexities of the lives of the street people. There are shortcomings to spare, but beneath (or beyond) them is a genuine concern for one another. And here, finally, fathers are undeniably positive figures. It is the family (in Tish's case, an almost holy one whose spiritual head is Joseph) that nurtures the lives of the young couple. Fonny, the embattled craftsman as political prisoner, has always found refuge and solace with Tish's family. And the Rivers' reaction to the daughter's pregnancy is a committed effort to save the couple and their developing creation.

As the mother of the artist's child, Tish is a radically revised Barbara King. She is a forceful Black presence who breaks down— as she states it—"some heavy shit." Unlike the puzzled Leo Proudhammer awaiting his cue, her man is the powerful craftsman attempting to hew life from an intractable substance. The offspring is not yet formed. It is like the figures trapped in wood at Fonny's studio. The craftsman himself is represented by a carving similar to these. He gives Tish's mother a statue that portrays a man in great pain attempting to escape the wood that entraps him. Such Michel-angelesque sculptures carry the burden of the novel's meaning.

A renaissance is at hand, a Black rebirth fostered and overseen by the young. The street people have given rise to our salvation. The embattled craftsman is supported by the will of the family and the love of the Black madonna; both are dedicated to his freedom. A people "full of healing" will bring forth a messiah:

The baby asked,
Is there not one righteous among them?

An informed reader knows the answer. It is contained in the title and content of *No Name in the Street.*

IV

His penetration of the deeper levels of his people's history, his hard-won transcendence of social and psychological barriers that block his own and his group's identity, and his allegorization of experience provide release for the embattled craftsman. Beale Street becomes articulate, announcing the longed for second coming. The Black artist's quest for selfhood and a concomitant alliance with his culture culminates in a lyrical vision wrestled from the dense log of personal experience. Like an accomplished African artisan, he brings life from primeval matter.

The movement of the canon is torturous. Tentative conclusions, reversals, vague affirmations of even vaguer orthodoxies, and restless turnings of a spirit that refuses to be stilled provide a baffling combination. But recovery of the self's experience, which, by dint of history, is also a group's experience, is never easy. Ama Aidoo's statement in a review of *The Beautiful Ones Are Not Yet Born* seems, on first view, to sum up the argument: "So it should be easy . . . to see there have never been people to save anybody but themselves, never in the past, never now, and there will never be any saviors if each will not save himself. No saviors. Only the hungry and the fed."[19]

But further reflection shows that, for Baldwin, such intense individualism will not suffice. All of those who are Black and hungry shall become not only the fed, but also the ones who provide the substance of a new life. The embattled craftsman's part is fundamental in this transition. Though he is not in the streets violently confronting the wickedness that seeks to destroy us and may, in fact, be a prisoner for a time to both himself and society, he nonetheless aids our salvation.

What did we do to be so Black and so blue becomes: "What did I do to be so Black and so blue?" Innumerable slave narrators, Wright,

Ellison, and other Black authors have addressed this question and given cogent answers. For Baldwin, the causes are manifold, but his own most recent response is: "I'm (we're) blue / But I (we) ain't going to be blue always." And neither, one might add, is the world at large. For the Black writer and his people are, indeed, this land's salvation. They are beyond the West's "mighty winnowing flail." Having harrowed a frightening abyss, they stand "infinite and free."

Notes

1. Stanley Macebuh, *James Baldwin: A Critical Study* (New York: Third World Press, 1973), offers a telling example of such criticism.

2. Cited in Fern Marja Eckman, *The Furious Passage of James Baldwin* (New York: Popular Library, 1966), pp. 47–50.

3. Richard Wright, "The Literature of the Negro in the United States," in *White Man, Listen!* (Garden City: Doubleday and Co., 1957), p. 71.

4. New York: Alfred A. Knopf, 1953.

5. James Baldwin, "Many Thousands Gone," in *Notes of a Native Son* (Boston: Beacon Press, 1955), p. 42.

6. *Ibid.*, p. 36.

7. *op. cit.*

8. Michel Fabre, "Fathers and Sons in James Baldwin's *Go Tell It On the Mountain*," in Keneth Kinnamon, ed., *James Baldwin* (Englewood Cliffs: Prentice-Hall, 1974), p. 124.

9. New York: Dell Publishing Co., 1968, p. 11.

10. Daryl C. Dance, "You Can't Go Home Again: James Baldwin and the South," *CLA Journal*, XVIII (1974), 81–90. Professor Dance has treated in some detail Baldwin's inability to catch the deeper resonances of the Black, Southern experience.

11. ". . . With Everything on My Mind" is the heading of the second section of *Nobody Knows My Name.*

12. *Nobody Knows My Name*, "Introduction," p. 12.

13. Macebuh, *James Baldwin*, p. 100.

14. New York: Dell Publishing Co., 1964.

15. *No Name in the Street* (New York: Dial Press, 1972), p. 196. The quotations that follow are taken from the same work.

16. New York: Dial Press, 1967.

17. *op. cit.*

18. New York: New American Library, 1975.

19. In G. D. Gillam, ed., *African Writers on African Writing* (Evanston: Northwestern University Press, 1973).

The Economic Evolution of
James Baldwin
Craig Werner°

A comprehensive secularization has been taking place in James Baldwin's writing.[1] In the economic dimension of his work, as in the political and racial dimensions, Baldwin has been de-emphasizing purely spiritual approaches to problems and adopting a perspective stressing social action in the face of an oppressive environment.

A number of factors have contributed to an atmosphere of confusion in the critical reaction to Baldwin's writing. Determining Baldwin's precise position at any time is no simple task, and as a result of the highly charged topical nature of his basic concerns, a great deal of analysis suffers from the intrusion of the critic's personal political prejudices. Occasionally critics have commented directly on the economic elements of Baldwin's work. A quick survey reveals a bewildering variety of positions.

At one extreme, Eldridge Cleaver claims that Baldwin's work is "void of a political economic, or even social reference."[2] While Cleaver expresses a minority view, undertones of the criticism are included in Philip Bonosky's accusation that Baldwin tacitly accepts the American dream.[3] Irving Howe, adopting a more balanced tone, echoes a part of Bonosky's attack, writing, "Buried deep within this seemingly iconoclastic writer is a very conventional sensibility, perfectly attuned to the daydream of success."[4]

Robert Brustein, conversely, has accused Baldwin of being a wild-eyed propagandist. To Brustein, Baldwin embodies the "bad" elements of protest literature, of "everything he once professed to deplore."[5] Robert Bone, slightly altering the same theme, interprets Baldwin's increasing involvement with social issues as an admission of his failure to grow as an artist.

Less frequently, Baldwin has drawn praise for his social and economic positions. Calvin Hernton praises Baldwin as a spokesman "not just for the middle class but for the masses of people."[6] But even those sympathetic to his basic position tend to fault Baldwin's treatment of economic issues. Stephen Spender notes that, in passages, *The Fire Next Time* "reads like a Marxist writing in 1860 about the German or British working class" but is disappointed that Baldwin refuses to recognize that "The American Negro is in effect a world proletarian."[7]

°Reprinted from *CLA Journal* 33 (1979):12–31, by permission of the author and the journal.

Most of the attitudes expressed by the critics have at least a limited validity but almost all suffer from an inability to deal adequately with the changing nature of Baldwin's perceptions. Writing on the political (but using terms which apply directly to the economic) dimension of Baldwin's thought, Donald Gibson divides Baldwin's career into three stages:[8] an early "apolitical" stage, a transitional "concerned" stage, and a recent "militant" stage.[9] One of the chief indicators of this evolution has been Baldwin's growing willingness to recognize and deal directly with economic issues. His public positions on economics, those articulated in his essays, reviews and speeches, clearly delineate the three-stage pattern.

While the early Baldwin recognizes the presence of economic forces and often analyzes them cogently, he denies them a prominent role in the final solutions to central problems. This de-emphasis of economics relates to his own youthful association with, and break from, the socialist-Communist movement. He left the movement partially because of his growing awareness of the abuses of Stalinism and partially because of a feeling that the Communists were cynically exploiting blacks for political ends.[10] But, more significantly, he realizes that the unique pressures of the American situation result in a disruption of the Communists' theoretical equation between the aims of blacks and those of the working class. Criticizing Earl Conrad's *Jim Crow America,* Baldwin writes: "He reduces the problem, therefore, to an essentially economic one, the solution to which will be found in a coalition of black and white in the ranks of American labor. But this attractive hypothesis demands of labor an organization, awareness, and power it does not have; it assumes a homogeneity in this most diverse of nations; and it discounts the profound ambition of the laborer to enter the middle class."[11]

Despite the explicit dissociation from primarily economic philosophies, Baldwin was not writing from an economic void. Even in the early stage, he recognizes several crucial economic issues which he emphasizes in his later work. He sees a complex apparatus working for the economic exploitation of the ghetto through high rents, low quality, and general lack of safeguards against abuse. "The Harlem Ghetto" and "Fifth Avenue Uptown" extensively catalog the economic injustices which have a debilitating effect on the life of the individual ghetto resident.[12] The essay "Notes of a Native Son" discusses not only the plight of Baldwin's father, but that of the average ghetto breadwinner whose home life is ruined by the humiliation and unanswerable demands built into the system.[13] Baldwin stresses that some level of economic security is necessary before the individual can improve the spiritual quality of his life.[14]

Even while attacking America's institutional structure, however,

Baldwin argues that economic injustice is primarily a symptom of a deeper spiritual poverty, because "what produces it, after all, is something we don't want to look at, and that is the person."[15] This typifies Baldwin's stance prior to the later 1950s. He clearly recognizes economic pressure as an aspect of the general problem but turns to the individual condition when seeking answers.

In retrospect the tone of Baldwin's middle stage appears quite cautious, but in the context of the early 1960s and Baldwin's own early development, it is distinctly radicalized. The new tone results largely from a deepening concern with the inexorable mechanism of the economic system. Baldwin evinces an increased sympathy with the ghetto dweller, ground into inarticulate despair by forces beyond his understanding, and reveals a developing sense of the central importance of economics in the oppression of blacks in the United States ". . . the black men were brought here as a source of cheap labor. They were indispensable to the economy . . . [Reconstruction] was a bargain between North and South to this effect: 'We've liberated them from the land and delivered them to the bosses.' When we left Mississippi to come North we did not come to freedom. We came to the bottom of the labor market and we are still there."[16]

Still reticent to adopt radical economic proposals, however, Baldwin rejects the Black Muslim concept of a separate black economy.[17] Part of this rejection is based on realistic doubts concerning the source of black capital and the ability of an autonomous economy to survive external pressure. Part, though, is temperamental, a reflection of Baldwin's spiritual approach to problem solving.

For even while demanding institutional change, Baldwin still perceives spiritual transformation as the final answer. He argues that the basic social framework must be altered if blacks are to reach "equality," but emphasizes his belief that institutions are invariably reflections of a nation's spiritual condition.[18] The spiritual, rather than the economic, condition still dominates Baldwin's attention, but in line with his changing perspective, he focuses on the spiritual condition of the nation rather than that of the individual.

The tone of Baldwin's "militant" stage is unambiguous. It is angry, impatient. Its emergence corresponds almost precisely with Baldwin's return to a socialist (though not a Communist) economic position. No longer reticent to deal with specific institutions, he now calls for a direct attack on America's powerful conglomerates. He dismisses labor unions as part of a larger oppressive framework.[19] For the first time, Baldwin directly rejects the capitalist system: "One has been avoiding the word capitalism and one has been avoiding talking about matters on that level. But there is a very serious flaw in the profit system which is implicit in the phrase itself . . . the

Western economy is doomed. Certainly part of the crisis of the Western economy is due to the fact that in a way every dime I earn, the system which earns it for me . . . is standing on the back of some black miner in South Africa, and he is going to stand up presently."[20]

Baldwin emphasizes the need for group solidarity and stresses the similarity between the oppression of the ghetto dwellers in America, the English working class, and the inhabitants of the third world.[21] In words directly related to Marxist idiom, Baldwin calls for redistribution of the "means of production" and predicts the downfall of the capitalist system in the face of a sort of historical imperative.[22]

As a result of these perceptions Baldwin finds himself back in a position similar to that of his early years. He has come nearly full circle and endorses a socialist perspective.[23] But even while stressing the need for "radical alteration in all of our social arrangements, social and economic arrangements," Baldwin admits "no one seems equipped at the moment to even envision them."[24] This, strangely enough, leads Baldwin back to the beginning of a second circle, to a reliance on the spiritual as the source of change. Even in the newly developed, explicitly economic context, Baldwin maintains his belief, though much less prominently than previously, that a basic opposition of spiritual values underlies the problem. Speaking of the black third-world power axis, he notes: "We represent a civilization. I don't mean, literally, the African civilization or the Indian civilization or whatever. I mean a sense of life, which is the only thing that civilizes anybody. And which for mercantile, commercial reasons, to put it a bit too simply, the rise of Europe attempted to destroy."[25]

Baldwin's most recent book, *The Devil Finds Work,* simultaneously attacks the system's social and spiritual weaknesses. Even while raging against the highly visible film industry which, for economic rewards, is willing to abandon all vestiges of artistic or moral integrity, Baldwin stresses that the relationship between institutional and individual evil is extremely close. The "devil"—Baldwin's metaphor for the degeneration of human values—Baldwin writes, "has no need of any dogma—though he can use them all—nor does he need any historical justification, history being so largely his invention."[26]

In the end, then, Baldwin's public position remains essentially poetic rather than political. To be sure, his poetry is now community poetry as opposed to individual poetry. But although he has after a long and sometimes tortured evolution, given full recognition to economic forces, he retains a longing for a world free from these forces, a world where "men and women will be different. They will have to make money obsolete. Life is worth more than that."[27]

Critical discussion of Baldwin's economic position has been limited almost entirely to his essays. Economics in the novels has sometimes been recognized in passing as one element of the characteristically oppressive environment, and, occasionally, discussions of politics or morality are rich in economic implications.[28] But there has been very little explicit analysis of the manner in which the novels reflect Baldwin's evolving public position and even less recognition of the importance of economic pressures in shaping his characters' actions.

Although Baldwin's first novel, *Go Tell It on the Mountain,* is almost completely devoid of explicit economic discussion, economic pressures play a vital part in shaping the characters. Baldwin's fictional treatment of the pressures parallels his treatment of similar issues in his early essays—considering both individual and racial effects.

On the individual level, Baldwin presents the elusive but immediate effect of the oppressive environment on the main characters, John and his father Gabriel. John's aspirations are molded by his economic surroundings. Living in a deprived situation of claustrophobic poverty, he dreams a traditional dream of a world "where he would eat good food, and wear fine clothes, and go to the movies as often as he wished."[29] But reality punctures his dream and he realizes that for him, the future is more likely to include a cramped Harlem apartment and a menial job.

Economics exerts a more severe, if less direct, influence on John through its effect on Gabriel, whose native cruelty and harshness are accentuated by the pressures of providing for his family. Elizabeth excuses Gabriel's harshness to their son Roy on the grounds that the father works hard in his attempt to feed the family, and even Roy tacitly grants the argument with his silence. Economic forces in his past also helped mold Gabriel's character. His early idealism proves insufficient when confronted with the cynical economically motivated preachers at the revival meeting, and the demands for money which result from Deborah's pregnancy force him first to steal and then to go out on the road to preach for money. These experiences engender the hypocritical cynicism which sets the tone for Gabriel's life and leads to the angry bitterness which he projects onto John.

Baldwin devotes Part II of *Go Tell It on the Mountain* to the backgrounds both of the individual characters and of the black race as a whole. A pervasive economic pattern quietly emerges aimed at limiting individual aspiration.

Beginning with slavery, represented by Florence's mother, economics (in this case the status of the black man as property or cheap labor) plays a crucial role in shaping the racial experience. The

Southern "free" experience suffers a distinct warping effect under economic pressure. Both the church corruption and the "immoral" success of Elizabeth's pimp father stem from an underlying lack of economic opportunity.

The dream of economic opportunity inspires the northward migration of both Florence and Elizabeth. Elizabeth's "pretext" for moving to New York is "to take advantage of the greater opportunities the North offered colored people; to study in a Northern school, and to find a better job than any she was likely to be offered in the South" (p. 161). But she rapidly feels the subsequent general disillusionment with the North: "There was not, after all, a great difference between the world of the North and that of the South which she had fled; there was only this difference; the North promised more. And this similarity: what it promised it did not give and what it gave, at length and grudgingly with one hand, it took back with the other" (p. 163).

This disillusionment paves the way for the most recent chapter of the racial story as the crushing pressures of the Northern ghettos, many of them economic, begin to replace the Southern lack of opportunity. Economics forms the basis for one of Florence's major complaints concerning Frank: "He had never made enough money to buy the home she wanted, or anything else she really wanted, and this had been part of the trouble between them" (p. 84). Economics is more devious, but just as debilitating, in its effect on Elizabeth and Richard, who are forced to delay their marriage because they lack economic security. Their inability to hire a competent lawyer ultimately contributes to the feeling of impotence before the system which results in Richard's suicide.

Although economics is present as an oppressive force at each step of the racial journey, the terms of Baldwin's solution in *Go Tell It on the Mountain* are religious rather than secular.[30] John's conversion agony includes a recognition of the oppressed situation of blacks with a faint economic undertone. However, the climax results in a turning away from, rather than a confrontation with, the external pressures, and John is "in battle no longer, this unfolding Lord's Day, with this avenue" (p. 216). After presenting a subtle picture of a variety of social problems, Baldwin chooses to resolve them primarily in spiritual terms. From an economic perspective, *Go Tell It on the Mountain* remains unresolved.

The action of *Giovanni's Room*, Baldwin's second novel, takes place within a narrow frame and lacks the immediate ramifications of each of his other works. But within the frame, economics helps direct the characters' actions. The economic backgrounds of the central characters, David and Giovanni, provide the source of the tensions which lead to a tragic outcome. David, his roots in a middle-class, cocktail-party home, rejects "the work, which fed me only in the most brutally literal sense"[31] but is unable to ever quite free himself from the bourgeois obsession with money. Giovanni, on the other hand, is ultimately imprisoned by the "laws of actual and emotional poverty" (p. 41) which dominate the immediate setting of *Giovanni's Room*.

External economic pressures direct the plot development from the outset. The lovers are brought together only after David has been evicted from his hotel for failing to pay his bills, has been refused financial aid by his father, and has turned to Jacques for support. Jacques and David then meet Giovanni at a homosexual bar where he is, "in effect, for sale" (p. 40). After economic pressures contribute to the meeting, they recede from prominence, allowing a pastoral interlude in the relationship. Giovanni is making plenty of money. David is able to relax. In effect, external pressures have taken the day off.[32]

Economic forces reassert themselves only after the bliss of the relationship has worn away. The loss of Giovanni's job at Guillaume's bar precipitates the lovers' estrangement. After David's departure, economic desperation accelerates Giovanni's final decline: first to Jacques, then to the level of the common street boys, and finally back to Guillaume and the robbery-murder. But although the world insists on the economic interpretation of Giovanni's crime (the robbery motive), David (probably presenting Baldwin's attitude) realizes the inadequacy of that limited point of view and points out that the cash register remained untouched.

In economic terms, the theme of *Giovanni's Room* centers on the characters' use of economic attitudes to evade underlying spiritual difficulties. The tendency exists in the rich—Jacques and Guillaume—who immerse themselves in their affluence to blot out their future inevitable despair; it exists among the petty shopkeepers who "must have come into the world hungry for banknotes" (p. 69); it exists in the street boys who "appraise" each new face "to within a decimal" (p. 72); and it exists in David, whose spiritual decline parallels Giovanni's physical decline and manifests itself in an increasing reliance on safe economic interpretations of events.

David first evades a spiritual issue when he explains his relationship with Giovanni to Hella in cold economic terms which, if not precisely inaccurate, are dishonest. David says, ". . . kids like Giovanni are in a difficult position. This isn't, you know, the land of opportunity—there's no provision for them. Giovanni's poor, I mean he comes from poor folks, and there isn't much he can do. And for what he can do, there's terrific competition. And, at that, very little money, not enough for them to be able to think of building any kind of future" (p. 178). When David accuses Giovanni of seeking to dominate their relationship, he reveals the extent to which the economic obsession, rooted in his middle-class background, as poisoned his mind. His hysterical claim that "You [Giovanni] want to go out and be the big laborer and bring home the money, and you want me to stay here and wash the dishes" (p. 188) is extremely distorted.

This type of economic perception cannot cope with the experiences of *Giovanni's Room,* and David is forced by his realization of the source of Giovanni's decline to abandon his attempt to lose himself in a safe, economically comfortable life with Hella. So, as in *Go Tell It on the Mountain,* Baldwin asks not for a confrontation with the oppressive institutional environment, but for an alteration in the individual's basic spiritual attitude.

Another Country, Baldwin's third and most controversial novel, represents a turning point in his perception of economic forces. Whereas previously economics was merely one of several strands in the "social fabric" it now stands out (along with race) as the most prominent aspect of the oppressive environment. For Rufus Scott, "the weight of this city was murderous" with its controlling principle "the money they made on black flesh, the money the whole world made."[33] The cynical attitude underlying the economic system emerges in the words of Steve Ellis, the television producer: "I'm just realistic. . . . I figure that everybody's out for himself, to make a buck, whether he says so or not. And there's nothing wrong with that. I just wish more people would admit it, that's all. Most of the people who think they disapprove of me don't disapprove of me at all. They just wish that they were me" (p. 222). The novel bears witness to Ellis' accuracy, for the central metaphor of *Another Country* is prostitution—selling one's integrity for an economic reward. While most of the main characters prostitute themselves in some way, Baldwin's judgments on them vary with his perception of the pressures which force the prostitution.[34]

Richard Silenski, who writes a successful commercial novel out of spiritual despair, has entirely abandoned his integrity in exchange for economic rewards. The Silenskis personify the emptiness of the American dream, and there is a hard grain of truth underlying Richard's bitterly sardonic remark that "the rest of us, trying to love a woman and raise a family and make some loot—we're whores" (p. 208).

Rufus and his sister Ida are driven by far more crushing forces, and, to a limited degree, their prostitution is an affirmative action—a statement of defiance rather than of surrender. The manner in which economic forces operate on Rufus is complex. His despair stems partially from his inability to support Leona financially and leads to heavy drinking, which in turn leads at least indirectly to the loss of her job, which in turn worsens the basic economic problem faced by the couple. Of course this is only part of the massive alliance of forces, spiritual and social, which results in Rufus' suicide. Ida accepts Ellis' offer in a desperate attempt to escape a similar fate. She tells Richard's wife Cass: "You've never decided that the whole world was just one big whorehouse and so the only way for you to make it was to decide to be the biggest, coolest, hardest whore around, and make the whole world pay you back that way" (p. 293). Even the characters who are not prostituting themselves directly show a susceptibility to its appeal. For example, Vivaldo (who, significantly, frequents the Harlem prostitutes and therefore helps perpetuate the system) admits to himself that he finds Ellis' success highly appealing.

Another Country includes, for the early Baldwin, a typical movement toward a personal, rather than a social, solution. Cass explicitly rejects social perspectives and Ida returns to Vivaldo rather than continuing her commercial-sexual association with Ellis. Ellis clearly presents an unacceptable alternative. But Baldwin leaves untouched the specifics of *how* to escape the pressures which drive the characters to prostitution.

The chief example of a personal solution in *Another Country* is the homosexual relationship of Eric and Yves, which parallels that between David and Giovanni in *Giovanni's Room* and is susceptible to similar criticism as propaganda. As in the earlier novel, the economic pressures of hunger and poverty play a role in bringing the pair together, but vanish completely to allow a pastoral interlude in a "rented garden" (p. 158). In this garden, Baldwin presents the ideal adjustment of personal stances toward economics. Eric has been able to reject the middle-class dream of his past and break away from the white South with its dream of guaranteed security, and Yves has been able to rise above the pressures of the streets, saying, "I have not to be a whore just because I come from whores" (p. 177). It seems, however, to be mainly luck which allows the lovers the luxury of their economics-free existence. They love away from, not in the shadow of, economic oppression.

Baldwin provides an implicit criticism of his own vision in the juxtaposition of Yves and Leroy. Spiritually there is little difference in the textures of their characters, but Leroy, as a black American, cannot escape into the economic vacuum of a "rented garden." Recognizing the unavoidable barrier of their disparate economic positions, he tells Eric: "I can't be thinking about leaving. I got my Ma and all them kids to worry about" (p. 173).

Baldwin's plea (communicated through Vivaldo and Ida, as well as Eric and Yves) seems to be for a spiritual dissociation from the oppressive system. While recognizing the ability of the system to crush the individual (and expressing the situation very well), he remains primarily committed to individual change, a concept which the terms of his own vision cast into grave doubt.

When Leo Proudhammer, narrator and central figure of Baldwin's fourth novel, *Tell Me How Long the Train's Been Gone,* denies a reporter's assertion that "there are much more important things than just paying the rent,"[35] he quietly reveals Baldwin's developing attitude. Economic pressures, an angry tone, and willingness to directly attack oppressive institutions characterize the first novel of Baldwin's most recent period.

Baldwin emphasizes the squalor and poverty of both the Harlem and the Village settings, which create and aggravate numerous strains in the relationships between Leo and his family and friends. He extends the economic focus to the mercenary, cruel townspeople of the workshop setting and the workshop itself, which subtly perpetuates traditional economic cliches. Leo, limited to manual work with props, finds himself trapped in a subservient role wherever he turns.

In addition Baldwin stresses the self-perpetuating nature of the system. The disbelief which answers Leo's early ambition to become an actor and the bitterness with which Caleb surveys his future following his release from jail are aspects of the same built-in limitation.[36] Barbara King's attack on her brother Ken's defense of the economic system contrasts stark reality with glittering theory: "None of those boys who work for you are going to make their own way, you've seen to that— you've helped to see to that—they can't even join a union" (p. 357).

The anger which dominates *Tell Me How Long the Train's Been Gone* is accompanied by Baldwin's growing tendency to identify characters in terms of their social class rather than their individual peculiarities.[37] Leo identifies himself in terms of his class background rather than his individual success. At a New York rally, Leo stresses his solidarity with the crowd of the "poor and defenseless" (p. 83). Similarly, he perceives his success in Konstantine's play as a class, rather than an individual, triumph. Christopher's condemnation of Ken *points up* the specifically economic issues underlying the class structure: "You had a good thing going for you. You'd already killed off most of the Indians and you'd robbed them of their land and now you had all these blacks working for you for nothing and you don't want no black cat from Walla Walla being able to talk to no black cat from Boola Boola. If they could have talked to each other, they might have figured out a way of chopping off *your* heads and getting rid of *you.* . . . So you gave us Jesus. And told us it was the *Lord's* will that we should be toting the barges and lifting the bales while you sat on your big, fat, white behinds and got rich" (p. 355).

The class theory leads Baldwin to endorse the goal of solidarity among the oppressed. Typically, Baldwin sees a spiritual basis for this solidarity, based on a balance between practical survival and spiritual dignity resulting from dissociation from the system's values. Leo's mother, who resists the pressures of the ghetto stores which both exploited and insulted her, provides the first glimpse of the desired attitude. The West Indian restaurant owner for whom Leo worked also serves as a model; she sends most of her money back to Trinidad, never seeks praise, and had a "black dignity, hard to assail" (p. 283). Baldwin indicates the possibilities of interracial solidarity through his pictures of Barbara and Konstantine, who maintain their ideals even when threatened with economic reprisals.[38]

Leo, who in the final stages of the novel seems to be serving as a mouthpiece for Baldwin, militantly rejects the basic system, indicating a new willingness to speak in institutional rather than individual terms: ". . . it is always possible that if one man can be saved, a multitude can be saved. But in fact, it seemed to me that Christopher's options and possibilities could change only when the actual framework changed" (p. 255). Leo predicts an inevitable upheaval, seemingly on the basis of a kind of historical-economic imperative: "This groaning board was a heavy weight on the backs of many millions, whose groaning was not heard. Beneath this table, deep in the bowels of the earth, as far away as China, as close as the streets outside, an energy moved and gathered, and it would, one day, overturn this table just as surely as the earth turned and the sun rose and set" (p. 366).

Baldwin's one concrete tactical suggestion, which he develops at greater length in *If Beale Street Could Talk,* is that the oppressed *use* the system whenever possible, play on its built-in weaknesses. Leo plays on the white policemen's fears of losing their pensions, their essentially economic fears, when he is arrested. Madeleine backs him up, saying, "I don't always like being an heiress, but that doesn't mean I'm not prepared to use it" (p. 205). The final "guns" solution, however, seems hasty and is not developed in any depth. Although Baldwin has demonstrated an awareness of the necessity for social action, he remains uncertain over the precise form such action is to take and, like Leo, he seems to be "waiting for my cue" (p. 370).

Baldwin's more recent novel, *If Beale Street Could Talk,* is a book about the dispossessed for whom economic injustice is of primary importance. Tish, the narrator, implies Baldwin's basic economic position with a metaphor which recurs at points of extreme tension: "The poor are always crossing the Sahara. And the lawyers and bondsmen and all that crowd circle around the poor, exactly like vultures. Of course, they're not any richer than the poor, really, that's why they've turned into vultures."[39] Her lover, Fonny, points to the self-perpetuating nature of the system in his condemnation of the ghetto vocational school, which is "really teaching the kids to be slaves" (p. 39). Baldwin frequently issues reminders that the basic situation is NOT improving. Riding the subway, Tish reflects: "I looked around the subway car. It was a little like the drawings I had seen of slave ships. Of course, they hadn't had newspapers on the slave ships, hadn't needed them yet; but, as concerned space (and also, perhaps, as concerned intention) the principle was exactly the same" (pp. 123–124).

While Baldwin had previously recognized the basic nature of the economic system, *If Beale Street Could Talk* represents a major advance in his analysis of the relationship between the system and the individual. Baldwin recognizes that a large degree of direct involvement with the system is inescapable. Officer Bell may be spiritually beneath notice, but he has the power to put Fonny in jail on the flimsiest of evidence. And once Fonny has been jailed, the other characters must deal directly with the economic system, which not only has the resources to hide witnesses, but demands a great deal of money for support of the "special investigations" which provide the only hope for Fonny's ultimate release.

Once again, Baldwin establishes a spiritual economy which is created by very nearly inverting the material economic scale. Baldwin believes that the dispossessed must thoroughly and unambiguously reject the system which is oppressing them, and he approves solely of those characters who have dissociated themselves from the system's economic perception of value. Fonny and Tish refuse to allow economic considerations to crush their love. Tish's family (and Fonny's father) refuse to allow their "dreams of security" to control their actions. The "good" landlord and the Spanish restaurant owners refuse to accept money which they know is needed elsewhere. A Dickensian generosity underlies the actions of the characters who provide the spiritual center of gravity for *If Beale Street Could Talk*.

While Baldwin maintains his desire for an island removed from economic forces, his vision has become far less romantic. Fonny does not ignore the difficulties of rejecting the system, but accepts them as inevitable and refuses to buckle. He says: "So, all I'm trying to tell you, Tish, is I ain't offering you much. I ain't got no money and I work at odd jobs—just for bread, because I ain't about to go for none of their jive-ass okey-doke" (p. 90). This spiritual dissociation from the system provides the characters with a frame of mind which allows them to use the system against itself. Tish's father expresses the practical base of the philosophy of dissociation: "If we start worrying about money now, man, we going to be fucked and we going to lose our children. That white man, baby . . . he *want* you to be worried about money. That's his whole game. . . . I ain't worried about they money—they ain't got no right to it anyhow, they stole it from us—they ain't never met nobody they didn't lie to and steal from. Well, *I* can steal, too. *And* rob. How you think I raised my daughters?" (p. 135). This philosophy leads to a practical economic "attack" (actually a defense for Fonny) on the system. Tish describes the tactics: "Joseph is working overtime, and so is Frank. Ernestine has to spend less time with her children because she has taken a job as part-time secretary to a very rich and eccentric young actress whose connections she intends to intimidate and use. Joseph is coldly, systematically, stealing from the docks, and Frank is stealing from the garment center and they sell the hot goods" (p. 139).

But beyond the immediate actions necessitated by Fonny's arrest, Baldwin introduces an incomplete, but gradually focusing, vision of the future. He stresses solidarity with the dispossessed of the third world, for which the Puerto Rican "favella" is a stark emblem. On returning from Puerto Rico, Sharon comments: "I don't speak no Spanish and they don't speak no English. But we on the same garbage dump. For the same reason" (p. 199). Baldwin rests his fervent hopes on the future generation and pledges himself to creating a maximum degree of freedom in which it can develop its possibilities. Once again Sharon expresses Baldwin's defiant attitude: "We ain't going to let nobody put chains on that baby. That's all" (p. 200). But Frank's suicide, resulting at least partially from the economic forces represented by the loss of his job, serves as a grim reminder of the tenacity of the problem. Baldwin is no longer willing to dismiss it from his final vision. Nonetheless, the vision remains grimly optimistic. The successfully freed (although not completely free) Fonny and the messianic-apocalyptic baby combine at the end of *If Beale Street Could Talk* in a poetic statement of what, for the present, is both Baldwin's spiritual message and his secular warning: "Fonny is working on the wood, on the stone, whistling, smiling. And, from far away, but coming nearer, the baby cries and cries and cries and cries and cries and cries and cries and cries and cries, cries like it means to wake the dead" (p. 213).

This picture of Fonny as artisan fills a gap in Baldwin's economic vision. To oversimplify only slightly, economic systems must answer three basic questions: (1) What will be produced? (2) Whom will it be produced for? (3) How will it be produced? Prior to *If Beale Street Could Talk,* Baldwin had concentrated on the first two questions. His answers, in basic terms, were: (1) necessary (rather than luxury-consumerist) products, such as improved housing and medicine, and (2) for the laboring class equally with the managing—or capitalist—class. Fonny's obsession with, and pride in, his craft implies Baldwin's answer to the third question: an individual, or atomistic, system as opposed to a corporate, or mass production, system. So far Baldwin has avoided dealing with the difficulties raised by this approach, difficulties such as drastically decreased production in some areas. At any rate, *If Beale Street Could Talk* is clearly not intended as an economic manifesto and provides a rough sketch of Baldwin's thought, which is sufficient in its fictional context.

Baldwin's novels, then, present a constantly refined critique of the American economic system and suggest a general direction for future action. They are ever more willing to deal directly with the institutional basis of the problems. They maintain, however, a strong spiritual undercurrent which helps raise their social message above propaganda to the level of poetry. A comprehensive secularization has been taking place in James Baldwin's writing. It is not yet, and probably will never be, complete.

Notes

1. This article was written before Baldwin's last published novel [ed. note].

2. Eldridge Cleaver, "Notes on a Native Son," in Keneth Kinnamon, ed., *James Baldwin: A Collection of Critical Essays, Twentieth Century Views* (Englewood Cliffs, N.J.: Prentice-Hall, 1974), p. 75.

3. Bonosky's article, "The Negro Writer and Commitment," *Mainstream,* February 1962, pp. 16–22, charges that Baldwin's approach is "empty of all history and ideology, all meaningful struggle, especially class struggle . . . Mr. Baldwin's answer to oppression is the organization man and wall to wall suburbs." However, Bonosky abuses the text so badly (he frequently fails to register obvious irony on Baldwin's part) that his position deserves only passing consideration.

4. Irving Howe, "James Baldwin: At East in Apocalypse," in Kinnamon, p. 103.

5. Robert Brustein, "Everybody's Protest Play," *New Republic,* 16 May, 1964, p. 34.

6. Calvin Hernton, "A Fiery Baptism," in Kinnamon, p. 114.

7. Stephen Spender, "James Baldwin: Voice of a Revolution," *Partisan Review,* 30 (1963), 258.

8. Donald Gibson, "Ralph Ellison and James Baldwin," in *The Politics of 20th Century Novelists,* ed. George Paprichas (New York: Hawthorne, 1971), pp. 307–320. Although with any living author it is impossible to confidently identify stages of development, we can nonetheless trace a distinct change in Baldwin's attitudes. For the purposes of this essay, we shall consider Baldwin's early stage as extending through *Nobody Knows My Name,* most of which was written significantly earlier than its publication in 1961. The controversy over Richard Wright and the corollary rejection of "protest" literature provide the key to this period which, Gibson claims, "omits political, economic and social concerns" entirely. The middle period, which is much harder to define and will probably eventually be seen as a stage of one of the other periods, centers on *The Fire Next Time,* published in 1963. Gibson says that Baldwin at this stage is "more socially conscious" but maintains a "moral rather than a political stance." The recent, militant period had clearly begun by 1968, but some intimations are discernible as early as the production of *Blues for Mr. Charlie* in 1964. Gibson, who concentrates his discussion of the militant period on *Tell Me How Long The Train's Been Gone,* sees it as "sympathetic to the political perspective."

9. In "James Baldwin's Message for White America," *Quarterly Journal of Speech,* 58 (1973), 142–151, Gregory Howe and W. Scott Nobles argue that "in spite of this

increasing militancy in Baldwin's rhetoric, the structure of his message has not been significantly altered." Their observation that Baldwin's "solution to the race problem is primarily an individual redemption rather than a strategy for governmental action" is generally accurate. But, as I shall demonstrate, Baldwin's perception of the relationship between the individual and the social group has changed.

10. Baldwin's personal disillusionment with the Communist movement parallels the general disillusionment in the black community associated with the "sell-out" of World War II. Only recently has Baldwin freely discussed the meaning and motivation of his early political experience. Prior to 1970 only a passing reference to "my brief days as a socialist" in *Notes of a Native Son* (New York: Bantam Books, 1955), p. 58, alluded to his youthful leftist leanings. More recently, however, *No Name in the Street* (New York: Dell Publishing Co., 1972), pp. 29–35, has provided a detailed account of his early political involvement.

11. Baldwin, "Too Late Too Late," *Commentary*, 7 (1949), 96. This uncollected review of several books on the black economic condition provides an indispensable glimpse into Baldwin's early attitudes.

12. Baldwin, "The Harlem Ghetto," in *Notes*, pp. 47–60. "Fifth Avenue Uptown," in *Nobody Knows My Name* (New York: Dell Publishing Co.,, 1961), pp. 53–64. The contrast of the ghetto with the relative affluence of surrounding areas recurs frequently in Baldwin's work as a major source of emotional impact.

13. Baldwin, "Notes of a Native Son," in *Notes*, pp. 71–97.

14. Baldwin recognizes, but at this stage does not heavily emphasize, the role of economics in dispossessing the black man of his cultural heritage. The American black's search for historical identity, Baldwin observes, is "abruptly arrested by the signature on the bill of sale" (*Notes*, p. 144).

15. Baldwin, *Nobody*, p. 126.

16. Baldwin, "A Talk to Teachers," *Saturday Review*, 46 (21 December 1963), 43.

17. Baldwin, *The Fire Next Time* (New York: Dell Publishing Co., 1963), pp. 108–111.

18. *Ibid.*, 115–120.

19. "How Can We Get the Blacks to Cool It?" *Esquire*, July 1968. This interview serves as a good basic introduction to the tone of Baldwin's most recent period. Baldwin's personal reaction can be seen as a mirror of the black community's growing militancy, which, in general, characterized the late 60s. A great deal of Baldwin's anger at the economic system relates directly to the labor unions. He says, "They don't want the unions broke [racially] because they're afraid of the Negro as a source of competition."

20. Baldwin and Margaret Mead, *A Rap on Race* (New York: Dell Publishing Co., 1961), p. 173.

21. Although Baldwin speaks primarily of the condition of blacks, he willingly admits that oppressed whites suffer from many of the same pressures and shows a somewhat tempered scorn for the black middle class.

22. Baldwin, *Rap*, p. 144. In "An Open Letter to My Sister, Miss Angela Davis," *New York Review of Books*, 7 January 1971, pp. 15–16, Baldwin claims "the system is doomed because the world can no longer afford it."

23. Baldwin, *Nobody*, p. 174.

24. Baldwin, *Rap*, pp. 69–70.

25. Baldwin and Nikki Giovanni, *A Dialogue* (Philadelphia: J. B. Lippincott Co., 1973), p. 71.

26. Baldwin, *The Devil Finds Work* (New York: The Dial Press, 1976), p. 121.

27. "An Interview with James Baldwin," *Black Scholar,* January 1974, p. 36. Baldwin's vision of a world without attitudes shaped by money (directly or indirectly) resembles Charles Dickens' vision of generosity. Baldwin has said that Dickens provided much of his favorite childhood reading.

28. See especially Charles Newman, "The Lesson of the Master: Henry James and James Baldwin," in Kinnamon. Newman comments, "Baldwin's characters are similarly unaffected by conventional economic problems. . . . the economics of both situations are only manifestations of more significant and complex problems" (p. 60).

29. Baldwin, *Go Tell It on the Mountain* (New York: Dell Publishing Co., 1953), p. 19.

30. While the tone of the ending of *Go Tell It on the Mountain* presents a major critical problem, it seems acceptable for the purposes of this discussion to assume that Baldwin wishes to indicate a provisional, though by no means blithe, approval of John's action.

31. Baldwin, *Giovanni's Room* (New York: Dell Publishing Co., 1956), p. 31. Baldwin's portrait of David's father can be seen as a criticism in miniature of the American dream.

32. The portrait of David and Giovanni introduces the "homosexual paradise" in Baldwin's writing. Homosexual relationships typically are accompanied by a freedom from extreme economic pressures. While there may be valid artistic reasons for de-emphasizing economic issues when focusing narrowly on love relationships, Baldwin seems to imply a cause-and-effect relationship between homosexuality and economic freedom which may be seen as propagandistic.

33. Baldwin, *Another Country* (New York: Dell Publishing Co., 1962), p. 10.

34. The racial element seems quite prominent in determining Baldwin's sympathies. The black host of the party in Chapter I provides the basic reason when he defends his opportunism as a form of repaying the economic system in kind.

35. Baldwin, *Tell Me How Long the Train's Been Gone* (New York: Dell Publishing Co., 1968), p. 248.

36. The secularization of Baldwin's attitude since his early period is indicated by the comparison of the harsh judgment which now attends Caleb's conversion with the relatively sympathetic view of John's conversion in *Go Tell It on the Mountain.*

37. Baldwin's willingness to generalize indicates the shift in his perspective on social issues. It also presents him with the technical problem of "mouthpiece" characters who are able to present Baldwin's positions and still retain fictional autonomy. The problem is less prominent in *Tell Me How Long the Train's Been Gone,* where Leo Proudhammer is a male character of approximately Baldwin's age. With Tish in *If Beale Street Could Talk,* a female of a younger generation, the discrepancy between Baldwin's thoughts and Tish's believable fictional character becomes noticeable. When Tish explains the relationship between the black woman and the black man in almost precisely the same terms Baldwin uses in his conversation with Nikki Giovanni, the problem becomes a glaring one.

38. Konstantine's play, significantly, is based on the similarities between the plight of black Americans and that of Welsh miners. The identification follows an essentially economic-class line.

39. Baldwin, *If Beale Street Could Talk* (New York: The Dial Press), p. 7.

The Divided Mind
of James Baldwin

C. W. E. Bigsby°

Lionel Trilling once observed that there are certain individuals who contain the "yes" and "no" of their culture, whose personal ambivalences become paradigmatic. This would seem to be an apt description of a man whose first novel was published twenty-five years ago, a man whose career has described a neat and telling parabola and whose contradictions go to the heart of an issue which dominated the political and cultural life of mid-century America: James Baldwin. And it is perhaps not inappropriate to seize the occasion of this anniversary and of the publication of his new novel, *Just Above My Head,* to attempt a summation of a writer, once an articulate spokesman for black revolt, now living an expatriate existence in southern France.

To date, Baldwin has written six novels: *Go Tell it on the Mountain* (1954), *Giovanni's Room* (1956), *Another Country* (1962), *Tell Me How Long the Train's Been Gone* (1968), *If Beale Street Could Talk* (1974), *Just Above My Head* (1979); four books of essays: *The Fire Next Time* (1963), *Nobody Knows My Name* (1964), *Notes of a Native Son* (1964), *No Name in the Street* (1972); two plays: *Blues for Mr. Charlie* (1964), *Amen Corner* (1968); and one book of short stories: *Going to Meet the Man* (1965). Born in Harlem in 1924, he left in 1948 for France, driven out by despair of the racial situation. He returned in 1957 and in the heady days of the Civil Rights movement found himself a principal spokesman—his polemical essay, *The Fire Next Time,* appearing at a crucial moment in black/white relations. Outflanked by the events of the late sixties, he retreated again to Europe. His more recent novels have failed to spark the popular or critical interest of his earlier work.

What follows is not offered as a detailed critical analysis of his literary work but as an account of a career and a mind instructively divided, a sensibility drawn in opposing directions.

James Baldwin spent the first part of his career compensating for his deprivation and the second part compensating for his success. He sought invisibility in racial terms by going to Paris, and ended up by becoming the most visible black writer of his generation. His career was in part generated by the rise of the Civil Rights movement, as white America looked for an explanation for the crisis which had

°Reprinted from *Journal of American Studies* 14, no. 2 (1980): 325–42, by permission of the publisher, Cambridge University Press.

apparently arrived so suddenly; and it was eventually threatened by that movement, which in time produced demands for racial and aesthetic orthodoxy which potentially left him stranded in his equivocal role as mediator and prophet, when the dominant model for black art became fierce commitment and cultural separatism. Having fled a role as writer and individual which was determined by the colour of his skin, he discovered that that colour was in fact to be the key to his art. Wishing to dispense early with the obligation to act as spokesman, he came to recognize a responsibility to articulate, if not the demands, then the feelings of those whose own frustrations and courage were otherwise expressed in mute suffering or simple action. What Baldwin has become he once travelled four thousand miles not to be.

Both the act of refusal and the ultimate acceptance are characteristic gestures of a writer who has always been drawn in two apparently mutually incompatible directions. It was not simply that his early faith in the moral responsibility of the individual and the possibility of social change was destroyed, though he has said as much: "There was a time in my life not so very long ago that I believed, hoped . . . that this country could become what it has always presented as what it wanted to become. But I'm sorry, no matter how this may sound: when Martin was murdered for me that hope ended."[1] It is that from the very beginning the optative mood had been in battle with a sullen determinism, the present tense constantly invaded by the past. Catonian warnings in his work have alternated with expressions of sensual salvation. His has indeed always been a schizophrenic style, as he has in turn presented himself as suffering black and alienated American, social outcast and native son. It is a rhetorical style which at its best captured the cadences of hope and rebellion which characterized the early days of the civil rights movement, and which at its worst degenerated into unashamed posturing of a kind which failed to inspect with genuine moral honesty the realities which he had once exposed with such authority.

For Baldwin, the self is sometimes a series of improvizational gestures and sometimes a moral constant which has only to be exposed to become operative. And there is at the heart of his work, beneath the level of contingent event and social determinant, an unexamined confidence in the possibility of action and the recovery of ethical purpose. Constraints are arbitrary and irrational; hatred and rage the product of a history which is real but susceptible of transcendence. Through assailed from within and without by a corrosive mythology, the individual consciousness contains resources entirely adequate to the task of distilling meaning from social chaos, while the alliance of consciousness provides the principal means of resisting an isolation which is part social and part metaphysical.

At the heart of his work is a Christian belief that grace is a gift of suffering and that love has the power to annihilate the primal space between the self and its perception of itself, between the individual and the group. Racial and national categories, though real and though reflecting a symbolic heritage, exist to be transcended, for he is convinced that society clings so desperately to rigid definitions—sexual and social—more from a need to project a sense of order than from a belief that such distinctions contain any real clue to the nature of human possibilities. The Negro, in fact, is in large part a fiction, a convenient hierarchical invention. As an emblem of unrepressed needs and of uninhibited sexuality, he becomes a convenient image of the dark, spontaneous and anarchic dimension of human life. His social subordination thus stands as a symbol of society's control over its own anarchic impulses. As a consequence he is offered a role whose significance is not limited to its social utility. Thus, when he resists that caricature the consequent appeals by the dominant society to "law and order" have metaphysical as well as pragmatic implications.

In Baldwin's work the self resists the peripheral role which seems its social fate, and the primary agent in this resistance is the imagination. It is an imagination with the necessary power to project alternative worlds, to conceive of a society which can escape its own myths and consciously break its own taboos. The communicative act involved in art (virtually all of his protagonists are artists of one kind or another, including musicians, actors and novelists) becomes in itself a paradigm of a desired social interaction, while the individual's imposition of order, implied by the creative act, becomes a model for a coherence which is generated by the sensibility and not imposed by social fiat. And this presumption of an imaginative control of the world necessarily implies a rejection of that religion which historically has proved a secondary means of social control. Rejection of God is a natural extension of rebellion against the power of the state.

There is a demonstrable logic of revolt. The creation of an autonomous self relies first on a rejection of the authority of the father (his personal revolt against his father recurs in his work) and then that of white society and of God. The self emerges, in a familiar liberal way, by a slow rejection of elements extraneous to that self. Such a process frequently involves pain and Baldwin remains enough of a puritan to believe that this is a key to truth. But salvation, paradoxically, lies in a leap from belief into scepticism. Baldwin eplaces the authority of social and metaphysical dictat with an authority of the sensibility. Faith gives way to a secular belief in the authenticating power of the self.

Baldwin's characters are highly self-conscious, reflecting not only upon their social situation but on the nature of their consciousness itself. The question of identity is constantly presented to them. Indeed, it is often a clue to literal survival, so that it becomes in itself a literary event. And the particular problem which confronts them is that the usual stratagems of definition now fail. History, memory and belief are at odds with the drive for self-creation and the need for personal alliances which can deny the reality of boundaries. Thus his characters tend to adopt an ambiguous stance with regard to time, appropriating to themselves the right to define process and resist versions of historical progress which threaten to subordinate them to an alien logic.

His use of the internal monologue itself implies the existence of a resistant self which is apart from and not contained by the externalities which otherwise seem to define the limits of action and character. This is the functioning imagination, the artist within, which creates even as it analyses. His are not novels which are primarily concerned with social change in the sense of a re-allocation of power; what matters to him is the altered consciousness of the individual. He is interested in process, in the interplay between the experiential and the given. The stream of consciousness becomes an image for the flow of experience and responses which provide the basis for a definition of the self. And, indeed, in a sense, one can find in William James's discussion of the stream of consciousness a justification for Baldwin's attempt to have his cake and eat it; his feeling that the self is both its own creation and an existent fact which has merely to be exposed to another level of consciousness. In *The Principles of Psychology* William James says that, "if the stream as a whole is identified with the self far more than any outward thing, *a certain portion of the stream abstracted from the rest* is so identified in an altogether peculiar degree, and is felt by all men as a sort of innermost centre within the circle, of sanctuary within the citadel constituted by the subjective life as a whole."[2] For Baldwin this is less a spiritual essence than a sense of moral certainty, an intimate reality available to the individual who learns the necessity to engage experience with a sensibility undistorted by social presumptions.

The problem which Baldwin fails to engage is precisely how that integrity of the self can be projected into a social scale; why the withdrawal into love should be seen as an adequate model for social action since it is frequently born out of a denial of that social action. This is something which he largely leaves to his essays. Baldwin can dramatize the moment and even the process which results in that moment; but he is, for the most part, unable to sustain that moment to the point at which it becomes an enabling strategy. The impersonal power which limits individuality seems too immune to such epiphanies to grant anything but momentary release from its definitional authority.

For Norman Mailer, the world can be made over by the personality, which can counterpose its own energies to that of society and which can release a neutralizing flood of language which, in effect, reduces the physical world to the status of backdrop: the subject of the drama is the self, the social world existing only in so far as the individual is prepared to grant it a role. Personal history becomes as authentic as public history. But for Baldwin history cannot be shrugged off with such a casual gesture. His lack of social freedom, as a Negro, contrasts markedly with that of a man who can seriously run for the office of Mayor of New York, and who apparently has a kind of romantic faith in the fact that social forms are plastic enough to be moulded by the sheer power of the will. As Baldwin has never tired of telling people, the black American knows otherwise. He is all too aware of the injunctions, written and unwritten, which spell out the limits of his freedom; to cross those boundaries is to risk a reaction which is real in the sense of Dr. Johnson's definition of the term. Yet in fact he himself was tempted by solutions every bit as romantic as those advanced by Mailer, and his commitment to invoking the sinister lessons of history is always balanced by a contrary faith in a grace which can dissolve such determinism.

In his attack on Baldwin, in *Advertisements for Myself,* Mailer accused him of not being able to say "Fuck you" to the reader. It was an even more naïve remark than it seemed in that it failed to recognize that sense of oppression from which Mailer was immune but which had led Baldwin to be a writer; it also failed to recognize that all of his work was in effect an attempt to discover a basis on which such a contemptuous dismissal of society could be affectuated, while longing, as LeRoi Jones and Eldridge Cleaver cruelly pointed out, for precisely that gesture of inclusion which would obviate such a response.

For Baldwin, will, crucially allied with imagination and a sensitivity to the pressure of other selves, becomes a force with the power, if not to overcome social realities, then to forge other alliances than those sanctioned by history and power. But this is not quite the confident self of the transcendentalists. In each of his books self-analysis is not only provoked by pain; it is the source of pain. Society's power is scarcely diminished. The most that the individual can hope for is to win a small psychic territory within which the harsh pragmatics of the public world no longer operate. Nor is love quite the panacea which it appears, for it, too, is infected by materialism, by the urge to power and by the demands of history and myth. And though, as suggested above, Baldwin is never clear as to whether identity is laboriously constructed out of the interplay of sensibility and event, or whether it is a resilient moral principle concealed beneath social habiliments, in neither sense is he confident of its ability to command public acquiescence. (And this, of course, is the source of the pressure which led him to social protest outside of his novels. As a public spokesman he sought to provoke changes which would allow greater space for the self which, as a novelist, he felt was the real agent of transformation.)

Like Emerson and Thoreau he felt the need to resist those conventions and beliefs which passed for an adequate description of the real, in favour of a spiritual self-reliance, limited only by its obligations to remake the public world, whose deceptions and inadequacies were rejected not in the name of privatism but of truth. But Baldwin inhabits a more sceptical world and his racial identity is forced to concede more power to social fictions than was that of the New England moralist.

In a sense, of course, America has always prided itself on its improvizational qualities, and in his essays Baldwin has repeatedly insisted on the parallel between the Negro in search of selfhood and the American intent of distilling a national identity. And he was clearly right in insisting on his American-ness. It is stamped on his imaginative enterprise. But the fluidities of the American system have historically not extended to the Negro. On this the country had been absolute. Where everything else has changed, to Baldwin this at least has remained a constant. And in this respect the experience of black and white is dissimilar. Certainly the irony of Baldwin claiming an American heritage in his early books of essays at the moment when facilities in southern towns, which he himself was not to visit until his early thirties, were still segregated, was not lost on his critics. Yet Baldwin's view was that though American identity and history had indeed been built on a denial of human complexity and freedom, this was a denial of an essential American idealism to which he wished to lay claim. His resistance to protest fiction (see "Everybody's Protest Novel") and, implicitly, to the naturalistic novel, lay precisely in the fact that it denied access to this idealism, that it made the self into a simple product of biological and environmental determinism. It denied the possibility of escape. And that, arguably, is at the heart of Baldwin's work: the need to forge a truce with determinism and with punishing social constraints, a truce which can sustain the individual even, perhaps, in face of the knowledge of its inevitable collapse. The escape to Europe is simply an attempt to create geographically that space for manoeuvre which in America has to be won through an exertion of imagination or will.

But the ironies emanating from his American identity were not simply those contained in the obvious dissonance between American idealism and reality. As he himself fully realized, his very articulateness is itself fraught with ambiguities which seem to nail him permanently to a paradoxical view of self and cultural identity. Indeed, Baldwin has always been aware of the special problem of language for the black writer. "It is quite possible to say that the price a Negro pays for becoming articulate is to find himself, at length, with nothing to be articulate about."[3] The word becomes a barrier, indeed a protection, between the self and experience. The reduction of social events to language becomes in itself a form of excape. Initially, experience intervenes between the self and the articulation of that experience, but in turn language intervenes between the self and the experience. He is crushed from two directions.

"The root function of language," Baldwin suggests, "is to control the universe by describing it."[4] But the black finds that access to language is not access to power, to control over his environment or himself. Language becomes disfunctional. Historically, of course, it betrayed him more fully into the power of those who sought to control him by offering means to facilitate that control. And once a possession of that language he becomes, perforce, heir to those very cultural presumptions to which he is formally denied free access. In turn he is then blessed or fated with a fluency which draws him steadily away from his own past. He is thus left with a cultural inheritance characterized by ambiguity, self-doubt, and linguistic paradox. And Baldwin's work carries his mark. The personal pronoun, as he applies it, in *Nobody Knows My Name* and *Notes of a Native Son,* means sometimes Negro and sometimes American, a pronominal uncertainty which goes to the heart of that concern with identity which characterizes so many of his essays and so much of his work. And when he assumes an identification with his American self against his racial identity the effect is more ambivalent. For the cultural nationalists of the sixties his assertion that "Our dehumanization of the Negro . . . is indivisible from our dehumanization of ourselves: the loss of our identity is the price we pay for our annulment of his,"[5] is an expression of a desire for cultural assimilation which goes beyond a rhetorical device.

His rhetorical style, particularly that of the latter part of his career, is, in fact a product of the battle to enforce his authority over language, to make it accommodate itself to an experience which it had been designed to justify and impose. As he put it, "you've simply got to force the language to pay attention to you in order to exist in it."[6] The central problem, as he explained to Margaret Mead in 1970, was "how are we ever going to achieve some kind of language which will make my experience articulate to you and yours to me? Because you and I have been involved for all our lives . . . in some effort of translation."[7]

Protest was implied in Baldwin's stance as an essayist. He was indeed a mediator, explaining the Negro to America by translating his experience into American terms, by establishing his own struggle for identity as of a kind with that of the American, anxious to distil meaning from history and experience. Like Ralph Ellison, he is essentially calling for the restoration of American idealism, and sees the route to that as lying through the individual: "An honest examination of the national life proves how far we are from the standard of human freedom with which we began. The recovery of this standard demands of everyone who loves this country a hard look at himself, for the greatest achievements must begin somewhere, and they always begin with the person."[8]

His trip to Paris in 1948 was an American search for personal and national identity in an Old World which could render up an image of the New partly from its own desire to translate promise and threat into concrete form, and partly from its own ability to conceive of an American luminous with a meaning derived from those very contradictions which the American writer frequently found so disabling. In part, of course, it was the old game of discovering the limits of the self by abstracting it from the viscous world of its daily setting; it was an attempt to see what could survive such spiritual surgery—an act of definition by elimination, an attempt to find which conflicts were internal and definitional and which part of a dialectic between the unexamined self and the social projections of that self. For a black American it afforded the only opportunity to venture outside of the myth which defined him, and, in a curious way, protected him, in so far as it offered a self-image requiring only acceptance. Here, as Baldwin knew, he would be judged for himself, or at least in the context of other compulsions than the familiar ones. Yet it was as an American that he found himself responding, as an American that Europeans perceived him. And what he learned was the impossibility of distinguishing a clear line between the self and the culture in which that self develops. Once in Europe he felt as "American as any Texas G.I.," freed from the necessary reflexes which had once concealed his own identity from others and hence, eventually, from himself.

It was a move which sprang from the conviction that neither an unquestioned community of suffering, nor an assumed American homogeneity, offered a real clue to personal meaning. Baldwin wanted to find out "in what way the *specialness* of [his] experience could be made to connect [him] with other people instead of dividing [him] from them."[9] And that specialness could only be abstracted by removing himself from a culture whose definitions of him sprang from compulsions shaped partly by history and partly by the pressure of a perverted puritanism and a hermeneutic of suffering and guilt.

"Everybody's Protest Novel" was not so much a necessary assault on a major icon of black literature as it was an expression of his desire to resist the role which he could feel being pressed upon him. To be a Negro writer was to be reduced to a socio-literary category. His subject was not just himself, in the sense that it always is for the writer, it was *himself as Negro.* And his assault on the protest novel was an attempt to create sufficient space for himself to operate, outside of the terms which it seemed his fate to embrace. As he said in the introduction to his early book of essays, *Notes of a Native Son,* "I have not written about being a Negro at such length because I expect that to be my only subject, but only because it was the gate I had to unlock before I could hope to write about anything else."[10] At the beginning of his career, already writing his first novel, he felt the need to establish his own right to be seen outside the terms which seemed to mark the limits prescribed for the black novelist, by white society on the one hand, and by the moral demands of black suffering on the other.

He reacted against the Bigger Thomas of Richard Wright's *Native Son,* he admitted, partly because he seemed to him to represent a possibility which had to be rejected if he was to escape a self-destructive rage. In an early story, called "Previous Condition," published in 1948, he displaces this violence into the imagination of his protagonist: "I wanted to kill her, I watched her stupid, wrinkled frightened white face and I wanted to take a club, a hatchet, and bring it down with all my weight, splitting her skull down the middle where she parted her iron-grey hair."[11] But Baldwin is less interested in the literal discharge of hatred than in its power to distort the psyche, to warp personal and private history. It was precisely to escape such a distortion that he fled to Europe, a process which he describes in "This Morning, This Evening, So Soon," published in *Going to Meet the Man,* which remains one of his best stories and one which is crucial to an understanding of his position.

It concerns a black American actor/singer who lives in France with a Swedish woman, Harriet, and their son, and is in part an explanation of the sense of release which expatriation granted to him. For though he concedes a determining power to race, religion and nationality, the story is offered as evidence of the fact that such determinants are deadly if they are not transcended: "everyone's life begins on a level where races, armies, and churches stop."[12] And the gift of ex-patriation is precisely such a transcendence, for it enables individuals to confront themselves and others outside of the constraining power of myth.

Black men and white women free themselves of a public rage

and coercive power which, in America, would have become private compulsions. They are also free of a language which might otherwise throw its own reductive net around them. As the protagonist's sister observes, "Language is experience and language is power."[13] The failure of black Americans, as she sees it, is that they employ a language of power which must be ironic since it is detached from their experience. And yet this, of course, is Baldwin's language too and the story can be seen as a confessional work of some honesty. For the protagonist recognizes that his success has in part been generated by a refusal to be identified too closely with the misery of his people, by associating himself, on the contrary, with those responsible for their suffering. It has also been dependent on his refusal to grant any ambiguity to French social attitudes. France had removed the cataract from his eyes, with respect to America, at the cost of a moral myopia with regard to French attitudes.

A brief return to America reminds him that there his life is a concession offered to him by whites. But a conversation with his French director also reminds him that suffering is not a black prerogative. For he had lost a wife and son in the war and knows the weight of history as well as the black American. The real American sin is presented as an innocence of history, a failure to perceive that the past demands a price from the present. And this is a message which Baldwin himself felt increasingly obliged to underline as his career developed.

For Baldwin, Europe's function was precisely to release him from an identity which was no more than a projection of his racial inheritance. It was not, as LeRoi Jones was later to imply, that he wishes to deny his colour but rather that he recognized the danger implicit in allowing public symbols of oppression or resistance to stand as adequate expressions of the self. As he said in his introduction to *Nobody Knows My Name,*

> In America, the colour of my skin had stood between myself and me; in Europe, that barrier was down. Nothing is more desirable than to be released from an affliction, but nothing is more frightening than to be divested of a crutch. It turned out that the question of who I was was not solved because I had removed myself from the social forces which menaced me—anyway, those forces had become interior, and I had dragged them across the ocean with me. The question of who I was had at last become a personal question, and the answer was to be found in me.[14]

For it was Baldwin's assumption that the question of colour, crucially important on a moral level, concealed a more fundamental problem, the problem of self. And it is in that sense that he felt most American.

But he negotiates a privileged position for himself by claiming

an American identity (while naturally disavowing the guilt for a
prejudice which he did not originate and for a history which he
played no part in determining), and simultaneously embracing a Negro
identity (while declining the cultural temporizing and disabling pa-
thology which he otherwise identifies as the natural inheritance of
the black American). Both American and Negro search endlessly for
identity. Only Baldwin, in the eye of the storm, realizes that it resides
in stillness, in an acceptance, not of injustice nor of public roles, but
of the authenticity of the self. His failure lies in his inability to reveal
the authenticating process at work. Sexuality is clearly a part of it;
in some way, supposedly, it tells the truth that the intellect denies.
It offers a vital clue, he feels, both to the American need to dramatize
innocence and to the real roots of prejudice. In his essay "Nobody
Knows My Name," he coyly hints that desegregation battles have to
do with "political power and . . . with sex."[15] Now, on an obvious
level, he is clearly right. It was certainly never an argument about
educational theories. But the link between that observation and the
obsessive question of identity is not so clear. Meanwhile his own
sexual ambiguity was itself a confusing factor, acceptance for him
meaning the difficult task of accepting the real nature of his bisexuality,
abandoning illusion for reality.

On the face of it the American problem with regard to sex was
somewhat different. It was that sexuality had so often been presented
as an absolute, as a metaphor for evil or anarchy, or, alternatively,
utopian bliss, that it could not be so easily integrated into a realistic
model of society. Its metaphoric weight was simply too great. But
for Baldwin acceptance implied precisely that elevation of sex into
metaphor, so that in virtually all of his work it stands either as an
image of exploitation and abuse, or of an innocence with the power
to transform social reality: sex as weapon, sex as redemption. In other
words he is never more American than in his symbolic perception
of sexuality, and what he presents as a kind of emotional realism is
in fact a familiar form of sentimentality. It can be found just as easily
in Hemingway, in Tennessee Williams, and in Normal Mailer and is
no more sophisticated here, except that Mailer, whom Baldwin actually
attacked for his sentimentality, purports to see sex as a dialectical
term. Baldwin, in struggling to escape the sexual myths which sur-
round the Negro in America, has simply succumbed to others.

He suggests that Wright placed violence where sex should have
been, because he was unable to analyse the real nature of the rage
which he perceived; but Baldwin himself endows sex with a brutal
physicality which is in effect a simple transposition of social violence.
Having claimed in his essays that it is principal, in his novels he
presents it as agent, while the ambiguities of sexual contact, in part
an expression of self, in part a surrender of self, in part aggression,

in part submission, become an enactment of the ambivalence implied in the self's confrontation with society and the tensions of racial relationships. For if in suppressing the Negro, white Americans were in fact "burying . . . the unspeakably dark, guilty, erotic past which the Protestant fathers made him bury,"[16] then the release of that erotic self should serve to heal the wound opened up by that denial of the whole man. And Baldwin was by no means alone in this assumption. What he adds in the presumption that the existence of the Negro has facilitated his disruption of identity, that he has collaborated in a myth of black sexual potency. The risk is that in releasing this sexuality in his own work he is in danger of endorsing the metaphoric presumptions of those Protestant fathers or, as bad, generating a false image of reconciliation.

In a graceless essay called "Alas, Poor Richard," following Richard Wright's death, he asserted that "the war in the breast between blackness and whiteness which caused Richard such pain, need not be a war. It is a war which just as it denies both the heights and the depths of our natures, takes, and has taken visibly and invisibly, as many white lives as black ones." For him, Wright was "among the most illustrious victims of this war."[17] Borrowing one of Wright's favourite phrases, he had, he suggested, wandered in a no man's land between black and white. The act of reconciliation simply lay beyond Wright's imagination. But what, then, does Baldwin offer? Only, it appears, the fact that whiteness has lost its power and that blackness will soon do so. Thus the crucial act of reconciliation will take place in the moral sensibility of the Negro. But to be made flesh, however, it must assume a reality beyond that privileged environment. And the only way in which he can dramatize it is in the literal embrace of black and white, a coition which, like that implied, but mercifully not enacted, at the end of Hawthorne's *The House of the Seven Gables,* will produce a moral synthesis. The trouble is that, for Baldwin, history cannot be so easily propitiated by simple images of sexual union.

For Baldwin, society is bound together by fear of our unknown selves. In other words, he offers us a neat reversal of the Lockean model. Men form society not to protect their freedom but to evade it. The notion is a Freudian one, so it is perhaps not surprising that the force he invokes to neutralize this process in his work is sexuality. This becomes the key to a real sense of community. The sentimentality of such a conviction is clear and may account for the real evasions which are to be found at the heart of so much of his own work. For social evil is thus seen as deriving from a desire for order and a fear of "our unknown selves . . . which can save us—'from the evil that is in the world.' "[18] Indeed by this logic the victim creates himself by accepting the need for social structure and granting it his acquiescence, when all the time "our humanity is our burden, our life; we need not battle for it; we need only to do what is infinitely more difficult—that is, accept it."[19]

In the case of his attack on *Native Son,* he is offering a severe misreading, for far from being trapped within sociological generalizations, far from reducing complexity to simplicity and failing to engage the dangerous but liberating freedom of the individual, the genuinely subversive quality of that novel lies not in its attack on American society but in its conviction that individual action and the individual mind are not socially determined or socially bound. It is true that Wright's novel was a curiously schizophrenic work, with the individualistic drive of the narrative operating against an adjectival insistence on constriction and the deterministic weight implied by its sectional headings: Fear, Flight, Fate. It is equally true that, if events constitute successive stages in the liberation of the sensibility, they are also, by inverse law, stages in the diminishing world of social possibilities. But Baldwin was saddled with the same paradox. He wishes to presume both that the self is real and pre-social, and that it cannot exist apart from its determinants. The result is a curious and distinctive tension between what he sees as an American sensibility and a free-ranging existential self—yet another example of his manichean imagination which sees himself as the product of the Old World and the New, black and white, vengeance and love, male and female, probing intellect and liberating imagination. It is a dialectical process of which the self is the putative synthesis. And, to Baldwin, this is an American process.

To Baldwin, the objective of the novelist is to serve truth, which he defines as "a devotion to the human being, his freedom and fulfilment." To see the individual as only an image of a race is to exchange reality for symbol, a life for a cause. And this was the real target of "Everybody's Protest Novel"—the retreat into metaphor. And just as Moby Dick was not to be understood either as type or as emblem, so the individual's reality lies outside his availability as public symbol. Baldwin could already feel the pressure of the public role he was inevitably offered and which he felt the need to resist. "What is today offered as his [the black writer's] Responsibility," he said, "is, when he believes it, his corruption and our loss."[20] Curiously, *Native Son's* vulnerability to Baldwin's criticism lay less in the element of protest, which is the source of its central ambiguity, than in the vague mythologizing of the social impulse which Bigger Thomas feels. The edge of his newly-discovered identity blurs at the very moment of its coalescence. Baldwin suggests that American uncertainty about identity, and American disregard for the identity of others, derive from a contempt for history and historical process. Doubtful of historical logic, the American has tended to distrust time and to value experience—to assume that identity therefore is the product of events outside of time. A name is no more than the emblem of a man until it is claimed in action. The result is a social formlessness which masquerades as freedom but actually smacks of anarchy. And this breeds a Hemingwayesque pragmatic morality which is as likely to validate racism as anything else. It is, he suggests, an American confusion to think that it is possible to consider the person apart from all the forces which have produced him, since American history turns on the abstraction of the individual from his social and cultural setting. And yet this is precisely Baldwin's assumption, since, as we have seen above, when it serves his purpose he too posits the existence of a primary self outside of and unaffected by history. This, indeed, is a clue to a basic contradiction in his position which enables him both to use the moral self to indict the social world and the social world to explain the collapse of self.

The recurring pain to which Baldwin avers in the alienation from self and from the cultural experience of the Negro, an alienation which is not neutralized by expatriation, as this intensifies the guilt and adds a further level of ambiguity since now he must battle for possession of an American identity which if the source of his pain, is also the key to its transcendence. As he puts it in a 1950 essay, "Encounter on the Seine," "To accept the reality of his being an American becomes a matter involving his integrity and his greatest hopes, for only by accepting this reality can he hope to make articulate to himself or to others the uniqueness of his experience, and to set free the spirit so long anonymous and caged."[21] More than this, like Wright, he felt that the black experience not merely offered a clue to American moral ambiguity but that it functioned as metaphor, that "in white Americans he finds reflected—repeated, as it were, in a higher key—his tensions, his terrors, his tenderness" and that "in this need to establish himself in relation to his past he is most American, that this depthless alienation from oneself and one's people is, in sum, the American experience."[22]

Having previously argued, in his essay on the protest novel, against metaphoric reductivism, he now strains, as expatriate, to transform his own experience into an emblem of dispossession in precisely the same way that Wright had done in a series of works starting with Native Son and running through "The Man Who Lived Underground" and The Outsider. Where he does try to establish a distinction it is that between the social and the metaphysical image, yet this is a distinction which he finds it difficult to sustain. It now turns out that his real rejection of Wright's novel lies in what he takes to be the inaccuracy of its portrait, in its faulty sociology, a conviction that the problem is being engaged too soon, at a level which denies not so much the complexity of the Negro, as that of an essential human nature. For he feels that "the battle is elsewhere. It proceeds far from us in the heat and horror and pain of life itself where all men are betrayed by greed and guilt and blood lust and where no man's hands are clean."[23] It remains unexamined since, as Camus realized, the logic of this position is that if all men are guilty then all men are innocent. If the sociological approach implies the possibility of facile solutions then assertions of an immutable human nature, generating social action, leave one with the sentimentalities of evil and innocence, with desperate images such as that which concludes but scarcely resolves Steinbeck's *The Grapes of Wrath*, in which social realities are invited to defer before the reassertion of human goodness. For this was a paradox he was not ready to engage, indeed has never engaged, since he has continued to dramatize human action as a battle between good and evil, a battle which he believes to characterize American political and cultural presumptions. Out of the sociological frying pan and into the metaphysical fire. Knowing that "anyone who insists on remaining in a state of innocence long after that innocence is dead, turns himself into a monster,"[24] his puritan mentality continued to play with manichean ideas.

The essence of his contradictions was exposed very effectively in a conversation between Baldwin and Margaret Mead which took place in 1970—a discussion in which the anthropologist acts as a useful restraining influence on the writer's sentimentalities and on his increasingly casual use of language. Baldwin was intent on establishing an historical guilt, incurred by the act of enslavement, but inherited by white Americans of the present. In this respect, he admitted himself to be something of an Old Testament prophet. But he also wished to offer the possibility of absolution, and the resultant contradiction between an ineradicable guilt and a necessary grace, which has characterized so much of his work, was carefully exposed by Margaret Mead. Speaking of the process of enslavement of blacks, he describes it as "the crime which is spoken of in the Bible, the sin against the Holy Ghost which cannot be forgiven."[25] The exchange which followed reveals his tendency to let language and imagery outstrip his convictions:

MEAD: Then we've nowhere to go.

BALDWIN: No, we have atonement.

MEAD: Not for the sin against the Holy Ghost.

BALDWIN: No?

MEAD: I mean, after all, you were once a theologian. . . . And the point about the sin against the Holy Ghost is that—

BALDWIN: Is that it cannot be forgiven.

MEAD: So if you state a crime as impossible of forgiveness you've doomed everyone.

BALDWIN: No. I don't think I was as merciless as the Old Testament prophets. But I do agree with Malcolm X, that sin demands atonement.

MEAD: Whose sin? I mean, you're making racial guilt—

BALDWIN: No.

MEAD: Yes. You are.

BALDWIN: I'm not talking about race. I'm talking about the fact.

MEAD: But you are. . . . You're taking an Old Testament position, that the sins of the fathers are visited on their children.

BALDWIN: They are.

MEAD: The consequences are visited on the children.

BALDWIN: It's the same thing, isn't it?

MEAD: No, it's not the same thing at all. Because it's one thing to say, All right, I'm suffering for what my fathers did—

BALDWIN: I don't mean that, I don't mean that! I don't mean that at all! I mean something else! I mean something which I may not be able to get to . . .

MEAD: . . . but when you talk about atonement you're talking about people who weren't *born* when this was committed.

BALDWIN: No. I mean the recognition of where one finds oneself in time or history or now. . . . After all, I'm not guiltless, either. I sold my brothers or my sisters—

MEAD: When did you?

BALDWIN: Oh, a thousand years ago, it doesn't make any difference.

MEAD: It *does* make a difference. I think if one takes that position it's absolutely hopeless. I will *not* accept any guilt for what anybody else did. I will accept guilt for what I did myself.[26]

Jean-Paul Sartre makes a similar point in *Anti-Semite and Jew* when he observes that "if one is going to reproach little children for the sins of their grandfathers, one must first of all have a very primitive conception of what constitutes responsibility."[27]

What Baldwin's comments to Margaret Mead demonstrate is a desire, evident throughout his published works, to present history as present reality, to establish a social responsibility which, because he chooses to dramatize it in terms of sin and guilt, he is unable to establish as an active principle. The Old Testament prophet denies the efficacy of New Testament grace. The writer who wishes to establish a racial indictment is thus inhibited from dramatizing the need for racial reconciliation which is a conviction which he holds with equal force. His desire to establish his belief that individuals are responsible moral creatures is simultaneously undermined by his conviction that their crime is ineradicable and human beings ineluctably wicked. The problem does not reside in language alone, but in his own terrible ambivalences which lead him to accuse and defend, condemn and rescue with equal conviction. The deficiency is an intellectual one.

Even now, in one mood, he sees a solution in some kind of symbolic union of black and white for which he can find no historic justification and for which he can establish no social mechanism. When asked, some twenty-five years after his first essay, how he meant to go about securing his solution to the problem, his reply was simply "I don't know yet." And then, slipping into the opposite mood, which has always been the other side to this sentimental vision, he offered the only solution which he could see: "Blow it up."[28]

Notes

1. James Baldwin and Margaret Mead, *A Rap on Race* (London: 1972), pp. 245–46.

2. Quoted in Frederick Hoffman, *The Mortal No* (Princeton: 1964), p. 332.

3. James Baldwin, *Notes of a Native Son* (London: 1965), p. 3.

4. Ibid., p. 141.

5. Ibid., p. 19.

6. Baldwin and Mead, *A Rap on Race*, p. 58.

7. Ibid., p. 180.

8. James Baldwin, *Nobody Knows My Name* (London: 1965), p. 98.

9. Ibid., p. 17.

10. Baldwin, *Notes of a Native Son*, p. 5.

11. James Baldwin, *Going to Meet the Man* (New York: 1966), p. 76.

12. Ibid., p. 127.

13. Ibid., p. 129.

14. Baldwin, *Nobody Knows My Name*, p. 11.

15. Ibid., p. 87.

16. Ibid., p. 169.

17. Ibid.

18. Baldwin, *Notes of a Native Son*, p. 15.

19. Ibid., p. 17.

20. Ibid., p. 11.

21. Ibid., p. 102.

22. Ibid., p. 104.

23. Ibid., p. 35.

24. Ibid., p. 148.

25. James Baldwin and Margaret Mead, *A Rap on Race* (London: 1972), p. 186.

26. Ibid., pp. 186–87.

27. Jean-Paul Sartre, *Anti-Semite and Jew,* trans. G. J. Becker (New York: 1965), p. 16.

28. Baldwin and Mead, *A Rap on Race,* p. 250.

James Baldwin's Blues

Marlene Mosher°

For James Baldwin, the black American blues may have seemed a natural vehicle in which to express his ideas. For incidents in his own life bore many similarities to the *content* of many blues lyrics: early abandonment by the "man" in his life (his father—in fact, Baldwin was an "illegitimate" child); continued questing for love— the love of his mother (and, later, of his stepfather and his eight half-brothers and half-sisters); extreme poverty; frequent hunger; and incessant subjection to white American racism. Baldwin's own nature, too, seems like that of a blues: he honestly looks at the horribleness of a situation, but he does *not* give up. Accordingly, the "message" of Baldwin's various works is, foremost, how blacks can survive in a racist America. Like Baldwin's fiction, essays, and plays, "the blues . . . recognize that there is something wrong with this world, something absurd about the way that white people treat black people." Like Baldwin, "the blues singer articulates his mood, and thus provides a degree of transcendence over the troubles of this world." Traditionally, "singing the blues" has promoted black survival: "When the blues caught the absurdity of black existence in white America and vividly and artistically expressed it in word and suitable music, it afforded black people a certain distance from their immediate trouble and allowed them to see and feel it artistically, thereby offering them a certain liberating catharsis. That black people could transcend trouble without ignoring it means that they were not destroyed by it."[1]

This theme of surviving despite tremendous odds is persistent in Baldwin's writings. It permeates his fiction from one of his earliest mature short stories ("Sonny's Blues," written in 1948; first published in 1957) to his recent novel *If Beale Street Could Talk* (1974). It is

°Reprinted from *CLA Journal* 26 (1982):112–24, by permission of the author and the journal.

underscored in his personal essays and in his two major dramas, *Blues for Mister Charlie* (1964) and *The Amen Corner* (begun, 1952; first performed, 1965).

As Baldwin made clear in *The Fire Next Time,* there are many ways of dealing with life's disappointments,[2] and these various ways are examined throughout Baldwin's fiction, dating from the early short story "Sonny's Blues."[3] Some of those ways are usually seen by Baldwin as being either cowardly or dishonest: relying on drugs in order to "block out life" (as Sonny's friend does, in "Sonny's Blues"), accepting the role selected for you by "the Man" (as Sonny's elder brother does), fleeing into the armed services (as both Sonny and his brother do), relying on God (as some of the former street people in "Sonny's Blues" do). Creating (and communicating through) art—especially a blues song—is, however, seen in most of Baldwin's works as being both courageous and helpful to others. Like Albert Murray, Baldwin seems to consider that "the whole point of the blues idiom lyric is to state the facts of life. . . . It would have the people for whom it is composed and performed confront, acknowledge, and proceed in spite of, and even in terms of, the ugliness and meanness inherent in the human condition. It is thus a device for making the best of a bad situation."[4] This explains why Sonny, despite several fitful starts, finally succeeds in playing "Sonny's Blues" only at the very end of the story. To communicate through the blues, one must be honest and one must also have suffered deeply. These characteristics are finally perceived by Sonny's elder brother to be also present in the whistling of his Harlem pupil. This student, who has surely repeatedly found his head "bumped abruptly against the low ceiling of [his] actual possibilities," has become "filled with rage": "[He] was whistling a tune, at once very complicated and very simple; it seemed to be pouring out of him as though he were a bird, and it sounded very cool and moving through all that harsh, bright air, only just holding its own through all those other sounds."[8] This whistled tune functions—for the boy's fellow students—just as "Sonny's Blues" does for his audience: it helps them, for a moment, to be free of their bonds.

Only those who *have* suffered (and have overcome their torment) can understand the message of the blues. Hence, the whistling student and the whores and streetman of "Sonny's Blues" effectively communicate to other sufferers through their music; likewise, many of Sonny's listeners understand and are strengthened by Sonny's blues. These people have all "been 'down the line,' . . . [so they] know what this music is about."[6] Though Sonny's particular sufferings are his own, deep suffering is common to all his hearers; even Sonny's elder brother—whose tiny daughter, Grace, dies of polio during the course of the story (p. 337)—is at last attuned to the common suffering expressed by Sonny's blues. Yet, the blues here move far *beyond* being a mere "lament" (for Sonny has—at least temporarily—overcome his tormentors); Sonny's brother acknowledges: "[I]t [the song] was no longer a lament. I seemed to hear with what burning he had made it his, with what burning we had yet to make it ours, how we could cease lamenting. Freedom lurked around us and I understood, at last, that he could help us to be free if we would listen, that he would never be free until we did" (p. 346). The elder brother's statement effectively echoes Creole's earlier assessment of the blues: "There isn't any other tale to tell, it's the only light we've got in all this darkness."[7] The blues provides, then—both for singer and for hearers—at least a temporary flight above the morass of one's daily condition.

In *The Amen Corner*[8] gospel hymns serve as precursors of the blues as a tool for black survival; here, as "in the [earlier] black spirituals, the image of heaven served functionally to liberate the black mind. . . . Blacks were able, through song, to transcend the enslavement of the present and to live as if the future had already come."[9] Hence, Sister Margaret Alexander and the poor members of her small storefront church are continually emphasizing that though "I walk the lonesome road / . . . I'm in His care, / . . . No evil thoughts can harm me / 'Cause I'm so glad I'm in His care" (p. 528). This faith in "the image of heaven" can, however, also enable one to gloss over the negative aspects of ones own life; it is sometimes an "escapist route" that permits one to avoid facing the truth. Baldwin himself came to consider his own early career as a minister (from ages fourteen to eighteen) to have been somewhat escapist (like the preaching career of Sister Margaret), to have been a mere survival "gimmick." Hence, in *The Fire Next Time* he noted the reaction to the daily horrors of life in Harlem: "Many of my friends fled into the service. . . . Others fled to other states and cities. . . . Some went on wine or whiskey or the needle. . . . And others, like me, fled into the church" (pp. 32–33). Similarly, it is only after Sister Margaret gives up the "escapist" hymns and beliefs of her storefront church, after she openly confronts both the disappointments in her own life and her own failures as a wife and mother, that she is "fit" to sing the blues. She now openly admits her need for the love of her husband, Luke, and she seems determined, at play's end, to *try* to rise above her disappointments in this life and to *try* to accept both the death of her husband and the departure "into the world" of her over-protected son, David (p. 586).

It is surely significant that, though basically as "gospel" play, *The Amen Corner* is dedicated to the musicians Nina (Simone), Ray (Charles), Miles (Davis), "Bird" (Charlie Parker), and Billie (Holiday) (p. 519); for Baldwin himself came to consider "freedom" to be characteristic of only "some gospel songs [while] . . . in all jazz, and especially in the blues, there is something tart and ironic, authoritative and double-edged" which helps oppressed blacks to survive.[10] The "theme song" that underlies *The Amen Corner* is, significantly, "The Blues Is Man,"[11] and Sister Margaret matures, during the play, from being over-dependent on "God" and gospel hymns to relying on herself and other blacks (particularly her "experienced" sister, Odessa) and the blues for survival. She is finally able to admit, "I tried to put my treasure in heaven where couldn't nothing get at it and take it away from me and leave me alone. I asked the Lord to hold my hand:" (p. 582). She has learned, too late, the truth that, dying, Luke shared with his and Margaret's eighteen-year-old son, David: "Son— don't try to get away from the things that hurt you. The things that hurt you—sometimes that's all you get. You got to learn to live with those things—and—use them" (p. 554). Only very near the end of *The Amen Corner* does a recording of Luke's music ring through the rooms of Sister Margaret's apartment, effectively "drowning out" the gospel hymns being sung by the assembled congregation. The effect of this music is to show that *all* the regular inhabitants of that household (Odessa, David, and Sister Margaret) are now willing to face life's miseries honestly.

The painful lesson learned by Sister Margaret and David is similar to that learned by the most important characters in Baldwin's more convoluted play, *Blues for Mister Charlie*:[12] Meridian and Richard Henry, Parnell James, and Juanita. Young Richard—who has earlier rejected the sermonizing, spiritual-singing and insistence on non-violence of his father, Meridian—has been living in New York City, where he had gone expecting to find a kind of "freedom" that he had been denied down South. Having quickly learned that the North was really not much different, racially, from the South, Richard was driven to seek refuge in both whoring and drugs, before, finally, he was able to become a successful musician. After having "done time" for selling heroin, Richard returned to the South, to regroup before attempting to resume his career as a musician. Richard, like the main characters in "Sonny's Blues" and *The Amen Corner,* has matured because of his experiences: in a discussion with his grandmother, Mrs. Wilhelmina Henry, Richard reveals that he considers himself wiser— and also stronger—than his father, Meridian. Though his father has repeatedly visited New York, "Daddy don't know nothing about New York. . . . He never saw New York. Finally, I realized he wasn't never going to see it—you know, there's a whole lot of things Daddy's never seen? I've seen more than he has" (p. 254). Because he is honest with himself, Richard has greater understanding of the world than his father does, but he also has a strong determination to live *in* the world. Unlike his father, he will *not* retreat—neither from life

nor from love. He is determined to "walk" in the world—a man—
with Juanita, his woman, alongside him.

Because of Richard's strong convictions—which are shared (though
to a lesser degree) by the young black protesters in the play—Richard
is seen as a threat to Southern "rednecks" like Lyle Britten. Hence,
Britten *kills* Richard soon after the latter's return to the South. Though
Richard is, in fact, dead throughout Baldwin's play (and is seen only
in a series of flashbacks), Richard's strong music is heard intermit-
tently. Both Richard's music and his example serve to force the other
significant characters in the play to appraise honestly black—and
white—life in the American South. Juanita learns, from Richard, the
importance of honesty, courage, and love—as do many of the other
blacks in the play, as well as Parnell, the "white liberal." For the
first time in his life Parnell acknowledges the undercurrent of "rage—
maybe hatred" in his black townspeople's words and songs. "You've
heard it before," says a now more honest Meridian; "You just never
recognized it before. You've heard it in all those blues . . . you
claim to love so much" (p. 266).

Just as Sonny's blues served both to enlighten and to strengthen
his audience, so Richard's music functions with his hearers. It helps
to pull the black community together. Even white Parnell—who, like
Sister Margaret, has dared to finally be honest with himself—is
somewhat strengthened in the end. Rejecting his own former two-
facedness, Parnell embraces Richard's honesty. Significantly, he moves
out, in the final scene, not exactly *with* Juanita, Meridian, and other
black protesters, but at least "walk[ing alongside them] in the same
direction" (p. 313). Though the other whites from Plaguetown have
seen both Richard's example and his music only as causes to lament
their forcibly changing lifestyles, Parnell—like all the blacks in the
final scene—gains strength and a sense of wholeness from his brief
encounter with Richard and his music.

Again, in *Another Country*[18] Baldwin presents a character much
like Sonny, Luke Alexander, and Richard Henry: here Rufus's music
and his example become the forces that help sustain his younger
sister, Ida, and his white friends (and lovers), Vivaldo Moore and Eric
Jones. Like Baldwin's earlier hero-musicians, Rufus suffered very much
before he was able to become a successful musician. A resident of
New York City, he had almost been "crushed" by his life in the city
before discovering the power of jazzs and the blues to help him,
psychologically, "hold back" the time of his destruction (pp. 4–5).
For a brief interlude Rufus, like Sonny and Richard Henry, was
able—through his music—to help both himself and his listeners deal
with the daily horrors of life in New York City—which horrors were,
for him, caused primarily by "all those white sons of bitches out
there" (p. 67).

Unfortunately for Rufus, he shared the ambiguous love-hatred for whites that is very common among Baldwin's black characters. By having allied himself with Leona, a poor-white Southerner who was "lost" in New York, Rufus in effect severed his umbilical cord to black music. Significantly, the very *first* night that Rufus spent with Leona occurred after "he had played the last set of his last gig" (p. 9). After his fateful alliance with Leona, Rufus is never again able to sustain himself through his music. This fatal discordance is hinted at early in the novel as Rufus "remembering Leona, . . . began to walk, very slowly now, away from the music" (p. 6). Though he can still "hear, in . . . [a Bessie Smith] blues, something which spoke to his troubled mind," he can only "wonder how others have moved beyond the emptiness and horror which faced him now (p. 49); he can no longer move beyond his own troubles. Lacking the sustaining force of his music, Rufus moves inexorably (in Book One) to his suicidal plunge from the George Washington Bridge. Not only is Rufus unable to save himself, but he also destroys Leona—who was, haltingly, hoping to gain strength from her alliance with Rufus (p. 12); after Rufus's fierce treatment of her, Leona also "retreats" from life's horrors—into permanent insanity (p. 71).

Despite her own death, Rufus (who was bisexual) continues to provide his sister, Ida, and his closest (white) male friends and lovers, Vivaldo Moore and Eric Jones, with strength. Despite their whitness, both Vivaldo and Eric have finally been able to "love" and "understand" Rufus (as Ida does); these three have "all been up the same streets" and they all, finally, are inspired by Rufus to resist the easy urge "to lie" (p. 52)—both to themselves and to each other. All three become, in effect, "blues people," as they "confront, acknowledge, and proceed in spite of, and even in terms of, the ugliness and meanness inherent in the human condition."[14]

Throughout *Another Country* Baldwin refers to blues and jazz greats: W. C. Handy (epigraph, Book One), Fats Waller (p. 8), Charlie Parker (p. 14), Bessie Smith (pp. 49–54; 82–83; 232–38), Billie Holiday (pp. 158 and 398), and the book is also replete with references to minor (unnamed) musicians. Moreover, Baldwin reiterates the idea that these musicians have enormous social value: "[S]ecrets, the secrets of everyone, were only expressed when the person laboriously dragged them into the light of the world . . . and made them a part of the world's experience. Without this effort, the secret place was merely a dungeon in which the person perished" (p. 112). Significantly, at Rufus's burial ceremony, three young blacks from Rufus's neighborhood—all of whom also knew Rufus well—perform what might be deemed "Rufus's blues": [A]ccompanied by "a guitar" and "a fiddle," a young girl sings the "tense . . . bitter and . . . swift" song of Rufus's transient "victory" over life's horrors (pp. 122–23). And these blues linger in Vivaldo's consciousness, long after that time, to strengthen him (p. 126).

It becomes clear in Books Two and Three of the novel that only those persons who dared both to love Rufus and to be honest with themselves can hope to survive in Baldwin's fictional world. When Ida sings a blues "for my brother" (pp. 255 ff.), "something appeared in her face which had not been there before, a kind of passionate, triumphant rage and agony" (p. 256). In this scene she manifests a strength that supports her in the final scene as she confesses her infidelity with Ellis to Vivaldo. Yes, unlike the hearers of Sonny's blues, Ida's audience is unwilling to face the common thread of her suffering, to move to the higher plauteau she has reached.

The main themes explored in Book One in connection with Rufus—black-white relations (exploitation, vengeance, and love) and sexuality (heterosexuality, homosexuality, and bisexuality)—come up again and again throughout *Another Country*. As in a blues song, they are given as many variations as there are characters being treated; for Baldwin sees no "correct" black-white relationship and no "right" form of sexuality: he sees only variations. Only when one is *honest* about the particulars of his own experience can he become stronger *because* of those experiences; likewise, only when one recognizes the commonality of human suffering can one profit from the particular sorrows of others: hence, Vivaldo grows as a result of "Rufus's funeral blues," but Ida's (more cowardly) audience fails to benefit from her own "blues."

The principal final confrontations—Eric's honest self-confrontation regarding his sexuality, Vivaldo and Ida's truthfulness with each other—seem to have resulted, in part, from each character's knowledge of, and love for, Rufus. By drawing on what he learned from Rufus's particular life-experiences, each is finally able to become more honest, to go on from where he is, refusing easy capitulation to his past behavior. *Another Country* shares, then, the sense of (at least temporary) "victory" that is common to most blues.

Baldwin's most successful melding of the blues and the novel forms is surely his recent novel *If Beale Street Could Talk*.[15] Taking as his title a line from an old W. C. Handy blues,[15] Baldwin seeks to recreate—in a New York City setting—the early part of this century. Though Beale Street actually offered few opportunities for success to blacks (and has been memorialized in one well-known black poem as a street that offered blacks no more than "a grave yard / At one end, / A river, / At the other"),[17] it grew to fame as the "birthplace" of the black American blues. It is both the stultifying effect of white American racism and the value of the blues (and, by extension, of other forms of creative expression) as a tool of survival that Baldwin is attempting to depict in his modern, novelistic version

of the "Beale Street Blues." And, once again, Baldwin presents a
variety of responses by nonwhites caught in this racist situation. As
in all of Baldwin's works, the weak and the cowards are ultimately
destroyed by the racist system, while those who can overstep their
bonds—especially through creativity—are able to survive.

The strongest male character in this novel is Alonzo ("Fonny")
Hunt, who, like Richard Henry, early rejected the "submissive" nature
of his father (Frank) and insisted on being treated like a man, whoever
was confronting him. His refusal to have Tish (*his* girl) "attacked"
by a "young, greasy Italian punk" (pp. 167 ff.) brought him into
direct confrontation with entrenched white American racism—in the
person of Officer Bell (a "psychological brother" to Richard Henry's
murderer, Lyle Britten). Throughout the novel, Bell and other white
racists pursue Fonny, his family, and his friends—hoping to keep all
of them "in their place." That Fonny is aware of his situation and
that he refuses to buckle under to whites' expectations are clear in
his social actions as well as in the sculpture he creates in his small
Bank Street apartment. For Fonny is a sculptor, not another of
Baldwin's musicians. His very first sculpture is made of "black wood,"
"a naked man with one hand at his forehead. . . . One foot seems
planted, unable to move, and the whole motion of the figure is
torment" (p. 43). Regarding the survival value of this statue (and of
Fonny's sculpting), Tish says: "Fonny had found something that he
could do, that he wanted to do, and this saved him from the death
that was waiting to overtake the children of our age" (p. 44). Moreover, not only did Fonny save himself: Tish says that, as she "clung
to Fonny, perhaps Fonny saved *me*" (p. 45). Fonny as "creator/
savior" seems, then, closely akin to Baldwin's earlier musicians.

Though Fonny's particular mode of expressing himself is sculpting, the importance of the blues as a tool of survival is made clear
throughout *If Beale Street Could Talk*—particularly in relation to
Tish, Baldwin's black heroine. A traditional function of "singing the
blues" is clearly to help both singer and hearers "achieve enough
understanding and strength to deal with [and to overcome] the past
and present hurt,"[18] and the parallel function of creating and surviving
is clarified by Baldwin through his portrait of Tish. After Tish's family
have learned that she is expecting Fonny's baby and that Fonny's
family probably won't help financially to get a lawyer who can free
Fonny from the Tombs (where he has been incarcerated for a crime—
rape—that he did not commit) in time for him to be the baby's
"legal" father at the time of its birth, they gather together, turn "the
lights very low," and listen "to the music" (p. 50): "It was as though
we were a picture, trapped in time: this had been happening for
hundreds of years, people sitting in a room, waiting for dinner, and
listening to the blues. And it was though, out of these elements, . . .

out of this rage and a steady, somehow triumphant sorrow, my baby was slowly being formed" (p. 51). For Tish, the creative impulse results, at novel's end, in the birth-cries of her (and Fonny's) baby.

As was true in Baldwin's own childhood neighborhood, white American racism effectively "controls" many nonwhites in the fictional New York City of his many characters. Fonny's father is finally driven to suicide, while his mother has long ago retreated to the church. His sisters, by "trying to be white," have become almost nonbeings. Fonny's closest male friend, Daniel Carty, has resorted to drugs and, finally, has been completely unmanned as a result of his barbarous mistreatment while in jail (pp. 125–27).

When Tish's mother, Sharon Rivers, travels to Puerto Rico in search of Fonny's supposed rape victim, Mrs. Victoria Rogers (who is herself "retreating"—into madness), she finds the disease of white American racism *there*, too. Sharon first listens to a young singing group sing "I Can't Get No Satisfaction" (p. 187), then visits the dwelling of Victoria Rogers— who lives, along with countless other poor Puerto Ricans, atop a crowded, steaming *favella* (garbage dump), where they are methodically being victimized by whites. In this inferno, Sharon is assailed on all sides by radios blaring the blues:

> There must be two thousand transistor radios playing all around them, and all of them are playing B. B. King. Actually, Sharon cannot tell what the radios are playing, but she recognizes the beat: it has never sounded louder, more insistent, more plaintive. It has never before sounded so determined and dangerous. This beat is echoed in the many human voices, and corroborated by the sea—which shines and shines beyond the garbage heap of the *favella*. (p. 205)

Looking back on this experience, Sharon declares: "We [blacks and Puerto Ricans] on the same garbage dump. For the same reason" (p. 226). Baldwin's message is again clear: in such a racist setting, the blues make survival possible.

Throughout Baldwin's works, blacks in the United States are presented as being victimized by most whites. The means of surviving in such a setting is, Baldwin suggests, to be both honest (especially with oneself) and creative. The majority of those who do survive draw both understanding and strength from the black American blues. Even Fonny, though a sculptor, shares a common "theme song" with Tish. Reminiscing of Billie Holiday, the two temporarily overcome their main obstacles (poverty and racism) by hugging each other, laughing, and singing, "All my life is just despair / but I don't care" (p. 128). Baldwin himself, though writing in nonsong form, usually writes "blues." Like his hero-musicians, Baldwin draws his strength from honestly confronting—and overcoming—his would-be restrainers. As he told Fern Marja Eckman in her biography, *The Furious*

Passage of James Baldwin, his early "plays and poetry and short stories" constituted "an act of love. . . . It seemed a way to save myself and a way to save my family. It came out of despair. And it seemed the only way to another world."[19]

Notes

1. James H. Cone, *The Spirituals and the Blues: An Interpretation* (New York: The Seabury Press, 1972), p. 125.

2. James Baldwin, *The Fire Next Time* (New York: Dell Publishing Co., 1962).

3. James Baldwin, "Sonny's Blues" in *Dark Symphony: Negro Literature in America,* ed. James A. Emanuel and Theodore L. Gross (New York: The Free Press, 1968), pp. 319–47.

4. Albert Murray, *The Hero and the Blues,* The Paul Anthony Brick Lectures, Ninth Series (Columbia, Mo.: Univ. of Missouri Press, 1973), p. 36.

5. "Sonny's Blues," p. 320.

6. *The Fire Next Time,* p. 61.

7. "Sonny's Blues," p. 346.

8. James Baldwin, *The Amen Corner,* in *Black Theater: A 20th Century Collection of the Work of Its Best Playwrights,* ed. Lindsay Patterson (New York: New American Library, 1971), pp. 519–88.

9. Cone, *The Spirituals and the Blues,* p. 95.

10. *The Fire Next Time,* p. 60.

11. See *The Amen Corner,* pp. 527–28.

12. James Baldwin, *Blues for Mister Charlie,* in *Contemporary Black Drama,* ed. Clinton F. Oliver and Stephanie Sills (New York: Charles Scribner's Sons, 1971), pp. 233–313.

13. James Baldwin, *Another Country* (New York: The Dial Press, 1962).

14. Murray, *The Hero and the Blues,* p. 36.

15. James Baldwin, *If Beale Street Could Talk* (New York: New American Library, 1974).

16. W. C. Handy, "Beale Street Blues," in *Blues: An Anthology,* ed. W. C. Handy, 3rd ed. (New York: Macmillan, 1972), pp. 116–19.

17. Waring Cuney, "Beale Street," in *Calvalcade: Negro American Writing from 1760 to the Present,* ed. Arthur P. Davis and Saunders Redding (Boston: Houghton Mifflin Co., 1971), pp. 375–76.

18. Sherley Anne Williams, "The Black Musician: The Black Hero as Light Bearer," in *Give Birth to Brightness: A Thematic Study in Neo-Black Literature* (New York: The Dial Press, 1972), p. 146.

19. Fern Marja Eckman, *The Furious Passage of James Baldwin* (New York: M. Evans and Co., Inc., 1966), p. 46.

James Baldwin's Vision of Otherness and Community

Emmanuel S. Nelson[*]

James Baldwin, in his dialogue with Nikki Giovanni, states that "people invent categories in order to feel safe. White people invented black people to give white people identity. . . . Straight cats invented faggots so they can sleep with them without becoming faggots themselves."[1]

This apparently flippant but disarmingly candid assertion contains one of the central aspects of Baldwin's vision of otherness and community.[2] To Baldwin, personal as well as collective failures stem from the inability of individuals to confront the "darker" side of their human nature. Out of this failure comes the mechanism of scapegoating: racial and sexual minorities become visible symbols of the "darker" side—the buried repressions, disturbing anxieties, and hidden pathlogies—of the members of the Establishment majority. This failure to face, deal with, and accept the darker impulses of one's own soul—so dramatically portrayed in the play *Blues for Mister Charlie,* in which we witness whitetown and whitechorus standing in angry opposition to blacktown and blackchorus, thus presenting a sad picture of a divided humanity and divided self—has two immediate implications. First, such a denial of an aspect of one's human nature amounts to a denial of a part of one's own humanity, and it robs that individual of any genuine sense of identity; second, it incapacitates that individual from fruitful and fulfilling interpersonal and communal experience. Hence Baldwin's vision of otherness and community is closely related to and dependent on his vision of self.[3]

Search for self-identity, therefore, is one of the central themes of Baldwin's fiction as well as nonfiction. Almost all of his protagonists—from John in *Go Tell It on the Mountain* to Arthur in *Just Above My Head*— are involved in an agonizing quest for self. And reaching a genuine sense of self and forging an identity depend largely on self-knowledge and self-awareness which, according to Baldwin, come only through suffering. In other words, suffering, if endured creatively, leads to self-knowledge, which, in return, can offer the possibility of achieving a genuine sense of self. Hence, suffering has humanizing power and redemptive potential. If many of the Black characters in Baldwin's fiction are presented as morally superior to most of the white characters—an aspect of his works that

[*]Reprinted from *MELUS* 10, no. 2 (1983):27–31, by permission of the author and the journal.

has annoyed many critics like Robert Bone and Stephen Spender—
it is *not* because those characters are Black, but because their blackness inflicts additional suffering on them, suffering that can be uplifting
and humanizing. And if homosexual characters, like Eric in *Another
Country,* play a redemptive role—again an element of Baldwin's
moral universe that has elicited negative reactions from Robert Bone,
Denis Donoghue, Eldridge Cleaver, and many others—it is *not* because
those characters are homosexual, but because their homosexuality
intensifies their suffering, suffering that has redemptive possibilities.
Hence, blackness and homosexuality in Baldwin's fiction assume met-
aphorical functions: they are both sources of agony as well as means
of redemption; they bring suffering, but, if dealt with courageously,
they can lead to self-knowledge, self-acceptance, and the forging of
a genuine self-identity.

But self-discovery is never an entirely private battle: it can be
achieved only in spiritual communion with others. Again, the bridge
of suffering can enable one to define oneself through a committed,
compassionate, and reciprocal understanding of the other. This concept is movingly developed in one of Baldwin's finest short stories,
"Sonny's Blues," in which the older brother understands himself
through a recognition of Sonny's—his younger brother's—anguish.
By understanding Sonny's pain and accepting his humanity, his brother
understands and accepts himself. This idea of conquering the void of
otherness through recognition and acceptance of another's humanity
is examined on a broader scale in the novel *Just Above My Head.*
The narrator, Hall, attempts to understand himself through gaining
an understanding of his brother's anguished life. He gains that knowledge largely because he examines his brother's life with compassion
and loving commitment. David in *Giovanni's Room,* on the other
hand, fails to achieve a valid sense of self or span the chasm of
otherness mostly because of two major flaws: first, he fails to forge
his human identity through an acceptance of his sexuality and the
suffering it entails; second, he lacks the capacity for communication
with the commitment to another individual, which, according to
Baldwin, is the core element of genuine love. David's failure to face
himself and the existential void within him inevitably leads to moral
and spiritual blindness: he uses Hella and Sue to "confirm" his
heterosexuality; he is revolted by the Parisian homosexual underworld,
but fails to discern the pain behind promiscuity;[4] and his unwillingness
to commit himself to Giovanni, largely a result of the young American's
reluctance to confront and come to terms with his own sexual self,
drives the Italian into tragic circumstances. Similarly, Rufus in *Another
Country* fails to accept his blackness with dignity and deal with his
bisexuality creatively; hence, he fails to accept Leona's whiteness and

her womanhood. Their relationship, therefore, terminates in disaster. Ida and Vivaldo, on the contrary, achieve at the end at least a semblance of stability in their relationship; that stability, though precarious, is reached only after their bitter but open and honest confrontation with themselves and with each other.

Self-discovery in Baldwin's fiction, however, is not always a result of private anguish and loving commitment to another individual; it is also dependent on identification of the individual self with group experience and tradition. Tradition, or heritage, is what one carries from his cultural past involuntarily; it is indispensable to achieve self-discovery, for "to see oneself as part of an historical process, as entrusted by the past with a legacy for the future,"[5] is to have identity. Hence community plays a central role in Baldwin's novels. Often his characters' quests for identity reveal their need for communal identification. He implies that for an individual to accept himself and develop a healthy ability to commune with another, he must come to terms with his racial past. For example, the backdrop for John's desperate quest for identity in *Go Tell It on the Mountain* is his ancestral past: the lives of Elizabeth, Gabriel, and Florence collectively constitute a microscopic but complex picture of the Black experience. And Baldwin suggests that his adolescent protagonist, to forge his identity, must examine, understand, and accept his collective racial past. John has to come to terms with the pain and humiliation that are part of his heritage, but he must also recognize his people's monumental dignity and their triumphant capacity for survival.

A similar concept of the relationship between self and community emerges in *Blues for Mister Charlie,* a play that chronicles its protagonist's developing sense of self. In the beginning Richard perceives the humiliations of his racial past as signs of weakness and tries to define himself in opposition to that collective experience.[6] But as the play moves along, he becomes increasingly sensitive to the beauty and strength that have come out of the appalling suffering of his people. It is in his gradual identification with the collective, communal Black experience from which he had originally alienated himself that he finds his self and strength. Likewise, in the short story "Sonny's Blues," Sonny and his brother find themselves and each other through the medium of the blues—a musical form that has evolved out of the African's nightmarish experience in America. In their moment of reciprocal recognition, they realize that family ties and skin color alone are not what they have in common; they recognize that they share an entire racial experience.

This idea of finding selfhood and strength through community is more elaborately developed in Baldwin's poignant novel *If Beale*

Street Could Talk. Here the family—symbolic of community—emerges as a source of enduring strength to the individual. The Rivers family, which consists of Tish, Ernestine, Joe, and Sharon, is nurturing and protective. It is united in love and commitment; therefore, it is able to offer stiff collective resistance to external oppression. The various members of the Rivers family as well as Fonny Hunt emerge as proudly individualistic characters, but they are eager to unite communally to launch a ceaseless battle for justice. Baldwin's implication is clear: one ought to establish one's individual identity and find one's center within oneself, not in opposition to but in harmony with one's communal identity. From such self-definition comes strength for the individual as well as the community. In other words, the individual, while strengthening the community, draws strength from it in return.

The significance of community in an individual's quest for selfhood is further stressed in *Tell Me How Long the Train's Been Gone.* Leo, the novel's central character, is a phenomenally successful Black actor. His very success, however, isolates him substantially from his roots; his frustrating heterosexual involvement with Barbara King, a white actress, further undermines his precarious contact with his community. But Leo achieves a greater sense of self through his homosexual commitment to Black Christopher. That achievement not only signifies the aging actor's honest acceptance of his sexuality and his willingness to commit himself to and commune with another individual, but, above all, signals his return to his racial roots. Through his commitment to Christopher, he identifies with the young militant's revolutionary political and racial ideology, his proud assertion of blackness. Their relationship eventually fails, largely because of the substantial difference in their age and a weakening of their commitment to each other. In spite of their failure, however, Leo finds in his involvement with Christopher the central justification for his life. Since he is much older than the young revolutionary, he develops an almost paternal concern for the latter and, in turn, for the ideals of racial and social justice that Christopher has passionately committed himself to. Thus Leo's quest for identity and meaning ultimately involves a return to identification with and commitment to his community, his group tradition. Such an idea, however, is not a call for racial provincialism. On the contrary, since Baldwin intends the Afro-American experience as a metaphor for human experience in general, he implies that one can bridge the void of otherness and achieve a genuine sense of self only through one's identification with the humanity within all men and women. And in a real sense, all of his works constitute a magnificent assertion of the oneness of the human spirit that unites the family of mankind.

Thus, Baldwin suggests that one can achieve a genuine and liberating sense of self only through complete acceptance of one's self, through loving commitment to another, and through identification with one's community. His works collectively present his vision of the vital relationships between the self, the other, and the community. That vision, no doubt, has been substantially shaped by his private anguish as a mistreated stepson, Black, and homosexual—as a member of the outcast America. His vision is a product of his own struggle to define the chaos of his experience to achieve an orderly sense of self. In the depths of his despair he has forged his own identity, and through his works he has helped us shape our own.

Notes

1. James Baldwin and Nikki Giovanni, *A Dialogue* (Philadelphia: Lippincott, 1975), pp. 88–89.

2. I wish to thank Professors Claude Summers (University of Michigan), Dorothy Lee (University of Michigan), Ronald Bieganowski (University of Wisconsin), and John Shawcross (University of Kentucky) for their insights on this topic. They were my fellow-panelists in a workshop on Baldwin's fiction at the 1981 MLA Convention in New York City, where this paper was first presented.

3. Ronald Bieganowski, "James Baldwin's Vision of Otherness in 'Sonny's Blues' and *Giovanni's Room*," MLA Convention, New York City, 28 December 1981.

4. Stephen Adams, *The Homosexual as Hero in Contemporary Fiction* (New York: Barnes & Noble, 1980), p. 41.

5. Eliot Schere, "*Another Country* and Sense of Self," *Black Academy Review*, 2 (Spring-Summer, 1971), 93.

6. Shirley Ann Williams, "The Black Musician: The Black Hero as Light Bearer," in *Give Birth to Brightness* (New York: Dial, 1972), p. 166.

Fathers, Gods, and Religion: Perceptions of Christianity and Ethnic Faith in James Baldwin   Sondra A. O'Neale°

In a 1965 television interview for the BBC, British author Colin MacInnes said to James Baldwin: "You spoke just now of the soul, the soul of the black man, the soul of the white man. I never have been able to make out, Jimmy, whether you are or are not a religious writer. Does the concept of God mean something to you? Are you a believer in any sense, or not?" As he has done so often when

°This essay was written for this volume and appears here for the first time by permission of the author.

people have tried to pin him down to traditional modes of religious persuasion, Baldwin answered MacInnes in ambiguities based on his own redefinitions of "the church as church," salvation as that which "we must do to save each other," and love as that which is not passive but "something active, more like a fire, like the wind."[1] Perhaps not realizing that Baldwin's "fire-wind-energy" simile alludes to Acts 2, where it is recorded that the Holy Spirit came down "like a violent, rushing wind and tongues as of fire rested on seventy fearful disciples,"[2] MacInnes did not steer Baldwin toward acknowledging the debt that his literature owes to a deep intellectual contemplation of black America's centuries-old struggle to formulate a Christian faith that would assuage and reconstitute the evil-oriented identity that white Christian culture had imposed upon them (i.e., interpretations of the Cain and Ham curses and interpolations of the significance of skin color, predestination, heathenism, sin, and hell).[3] Nor did MacInnes acknowledge that Baldwin's relationship to what the critic called "religion"—presumably the traditional European-centered view that is the basis of American Protestantism: belief in a God whose holiness is imbued in puritanical white; a written word that calls for redemptive purging of nonpure, vis-à-vis nonwhite, phenomena from His world; and an orthodox, spiritless, liturgical form keeping strict legalistic step with a deterministic force that assures white believers of spiritual, political, and economic superiority—is, like that of all black American writers since 1760, an inherently different idea of religion. On the surface one cannot ascertain whether or not Baldwin is a "religious writer" because his works do not reflect the traditional treatment of Christianity in black American literature. Instead, Baldwin examines the enigmas of human affections absent in Christian professors; the failure of the Christian God to thwart the persistent onslaught of His African children; and the insistence of those children to forge a "normal" dependent interaction with that God. These witnesses are empirical evidences of God in Baldwin's world, and he exploits them to excess so that he can mold a composite God, discover His personality, and fathom His intentions toward black people.

Although scholarship has touched upon the recurrent father-son motif in Baldwin's works,[4] there has been little discussion of those images for an understanding of his (and black America's) search for God and for an iconography that is not totally and suicidally antipathetic to the dominant culture. Baldwin often codifies his variable perceptions of a puritanical, unloving God as a woman-mother (e.g., Margaret Alexander in *Amen Corner*); however, his use of female characters and feminine symbolism to conceptualize these possibilities is a study in itself. This essay explores the multifarious complexities of Baldwin's concepts of fatherhood and how they impinge on his search—for a sympathetic Father/God—an odyssey that he deliberately identifies as the collective historic experience of the race and its artists.

Indeed, a close critical and theological exegesis—that includes traditional religious consciousness in the canon of black American literature—of Baldwin's writings reveals these themes and gives credence to what is already suspected: that more than the heritage of any other black American writer, Baldwin's works illustrate the schizophrenia of the black American experience with Christianity. Much of the symbolism, language, archetypal rhythm, and thematic call for justice in his essays are so steeped in Christian ethics that his readers may become deafened to the tragicomic Christian pathos that is agonizing at the heart of the Baldwin message. Agonizing because, in ways similar to those of the transformed biblical disciples, the experiential anointing and ethereal vision that fourteen-year-old Baldwin received on the threshing floor of a Harlem storefront church in 1938 is at constant warfare with the unremitting oppression he receives from the world. When he sought relief in art, the divisiveness of this apparently irreconcilable dichotomy dominated his world view, his theology, and his writing. By that time, however, Baldwin also knew that by wrestling with that dichotomous angel in the public arena of his own written word, he was unveiling the agony of simultaneous disappointment and hope in the psyche of the race. That agony is evident in the earliest offerings to the canon of black American literature. Even in the mid-eighteenth century, Africans enslaved in America, while sincerely acknowledging their own conversions to Christianity, nonetheless deplored the white man's use of the same Bible both to convert and to enslave them. They also haltingly revealed their various inabilities to reach satisfactory faith-embracing conclusions (or at least to express them in a manner palatable to doubting black readers) on such doctrines as color symbolism; predeterminism; the infinite, omnipotent sovereign will of God; the Old Testament curses placed on Cain and Ham, presumably in perpetuity; and the New Testament reenslavement of Philemon.[5] For instance, in his poem "A Dialogue Between the Kind Master and the Dutiful Servant" eighteenth-century New York slave, poet, and essayist Jupiter Hammon, the first black to publish in America, craftily tells his religious master that he cannot follow him for life's guide and example because the master himself is not a true Christian; yet he is reduced to telling his slave audience in a sermon, "As Black and despised as we are," that nevertheless, God, "Our Father," will save "us" (i.e., from hell and slavery—concepts merged as one in the literature up to the 1870s) if "we" obediently trust in Christ. Hammon promised that this same God will also eventually judge (i.e., in eternity) the white man for his unjust behavior.[6] But Hammon's faith was firm. His admissions were not to engender doubt but to establish belief.

Phillis Wheatley continued the tensions of faith in, among other salient poems, her famed poetic lines, "Remember, *Christians, Negroes,* black as *Cain,* / May be refin'd, and join th' angelic train."[7] Other black poets, essayists, and narrative authors of the period, such as Briton Hammon, Olandah Equiano, Benjamin Banneker, John Marrant, and George Moses Horton—all slaves—expressed themselves in similar fashion.[8] In the nineteenth century, freed or escaped slaves, such as David Walker, J. W. C. Pennington, James Whitfield, Nat Turner (who led a slave revolt based on his faith in the righteous judgment of the Old Testament God), Sojourner Truth, William and Ellen Craft, Frances E. W. Harper, and, most prominently, Frederick Douglass, expressed complete faith in the reality of the conversion experience, in the inerrant totality of Scripture, and in the absolute love and fatherhood of their God.[9] While their stance as freed men and women was more militant than that of enslaved writers of the earlier period, their militancy involved a clear distinction between Christianity as they knew it and Christianity as it was practiced in the white world. Their faith in God, as reflected in the literature, was unswerving, and their relationship with Him could not be violated by injurious whites.[10] In the epilogue of his shorter *Autobiography,* Douglass clearly distinguishes between black Christian faith and white Christian practice:

> What I have said respecting and against religion, I mean strictly to apply to the *slaveholding religion* of this land, and with no possible reference to Christianity proper; for, between the Christianity of this land, and the Christianity of Christ, I recognize the widest possible difference—so wide, that to receive the one as good, pure, and holy, is of necessity to reject the other as bad, corrupt, and wicked. To be the friend of the one, is of necessity to be the enemy of the other. I love the pure, peaceable, and impartial Christianity of Christ: I therefore hate the corrupt, slaveholding, women-whipping, cradle-plundering, partial and hypocritical Christianity of this land. Indeed, I can see no reason, but the most deceitful one, for calling the religion of this land Christianity.[11]

In the secularized Harlem Renaissance of the 1930s, God is either absent from artistic expression or mentioned (i.e., as the saving grace and artistic folk source of the black church) with reverence. Doubt or rejection is for an unredeemed, oppressive society. Representative works include James Weldon Johnson's *God's Trombones,* Zora Neale Hurston's *Their Eyes Were Watching God,* Langston Hughes's "Cross," "Bound No'th Blue," and "Brass Spittoons," and the third section of Jean Toomer's *Cane,* with the wise, though blind, preacher, Father John.[12] Perhaps the most cogent example of the black American

writer's slight but expanding distancing from traditional racial concepts of God in that period occurs in a poem, "Yet Do I Marvel,"
by Baldwin's high school teacher Countee Cullen (Baldwin attended
DeWitt Clinton High School in the Bronx from 1938 to 1942, during
which time Cullen was employed as a teacher and supervisor of the
school magazine, the *Magpie*, of which Baldwin was editor and to
which he contributed):[13]

> I doubt not God is good, well-meaning, kind,
> And did he stoop to quibble could tell why
> . . . .
> Inscrutable His ways are, and immune
> . . . .
> What awful brain compels His awful hand,
> Yet do I marvel at this curious thing:
> To make a poet black, and bid him sing![14]

These were Baldwin's black literary progenitors, in whose works
he was well read. In their volume entitled *Dialogue*, he tells Nikki
Giovanni:

> Now I can see what I owe to Richard [Wright] and what I owe to
> Chester [Haines], what I owe to Langston Hughes and what I owe
> to W. E. B. DuBois and what I owe to Frederick Douglass. But I
> could not see that when I was twenty. I don't think anybody can
> see that at twenty. But you see they were, on one level, simply
> more exalted victims. . . . And it takes a long time before you
> accept what has been given to you from your past. What we call
> black literature is really summed up for me by the whole career,
> let's say, of Bessie Smith, Ray Charles, Aretha Franklin, because
> that's how it's been handed down, since we couldn't read or write,
> as far as they knew. And it was at one time a crime to be able to
> read if you were black. It was punishable by law. We had to smuggle
> information, and we did it through our music and we did it in the
> church. You were talking before about the church you went to visit.
> I thought about the Apollo Theater. The last time I saw Aretha,
> what did she do at the Apollo Theater but turn it into a gospel
> church service—! And that's true religion. A black writer comes out
> of that; I don't mean he has to be *limited* to that. But he comes
> out of that because the standards which come from Greece and
> Rome, from the Judeo-Christian ethic, are very dubious when you
> try to apply them to your own life.[15]

Baldwin's position in *The Fire Next Time* is in the tradition of
black Christian protest:

> Negroes in this country—and Negroes do not, strictly or legally
> speaking, exist in any other—are taught really to despise themselves
> from the moment their eyes open on the world. This world is white
> and they are black. White people hold the power, which means that

they are superior to blacks (intrinsically, that is: God decreed it so), and the world has innumerable ways of making this difference known and felt and feared.[16]

He joins the black church in search of at least spiritual kinship: "My friend was about to introduce me when she looked at me and smiled and said, 'Whose little boy are you?' Now this, unbelievably, was precisely the phrase used by pimps and racketeers on the Avenue when they suggested, both humorously and intensely, that I 'hang out' with them. Perhaps part of the terror they had caused me to feel came from the fact that I unquestionably wanted to be *somebody's* little boy."[17] But then he posits that the deity's historic treatment through His white representatives renders Him a nihilistic, loveless icon that cannot or will not proffer comfort at black men's altars. His rhetoric is strikingly atypical of ethnic conversion experience:

> All I really remember is the pain, the unspeakable pain; it was as though I were yelling up to Heaven and Heaven would not hear me. And if Heaven would not hear me, if love could not descend from Heaven—to wash me, to make me clean— then utter disaster was my portion. Yes, it does indeed mean something—something unspeakable—to be born, in a white country, an Anglo-Teutonic, antisexual country, black. You very soon, without knowing it, give up all hope of communion.[18]

Instead of finding cardinal faith on the threshing floor, he concludes that God is indeed white and that the black man cannot obtain redemption in the universe:

> The universe, which is not merely the stars and the moon and the planets, flowers, grass, and trees, but *other people,* has evolved no terms for your existence, has made no room for you, and if love will not swing wide the gates, no other power will or can. And if one despairs—as who has not?—of human love, God's love alone is left. But God—and I felt this even then, so long ago, on that tremendous floor, unwillingly—is white. And if His love was so great, and if He loved all His children, why were we, the blacks, cast down so far? Why? In spite of all I said thereafter, I found no answer on the floor—not *that* answer, anyway—and I was on the floor all night.[19]

As his writing develops, he not only continues the thematic ambiguity between possibilities of individual faith in and societal practice of Christianity as a religious system, he goes beyond the point of doubt about white practice to question the validity of life-alternating salvation in the black church, and he imperiously accuses God of being at best a weak, powerless, detached, "watch-maker" creator and at worst a white-skinned being who truly does (as slave masters and Puritans declared) hate and predetermine His nonwhite creation for servitude. No black American writer before Baldwin had quite the literary nerve (i.e., to risk separating himself from the mainstream of Christian black America) or the agnostic impertinence (i.e., his frequent self-recriminations for slipping toward blasphemy)[20] to question openly the justice, judgment, and sincerity of God.

Yet Baldwin claims to have had a traumatic Christian conversion. He was an ardent licensed preacher of the Gospel for three years, during which time he absorbed all facets of Christian doctrine, denominational practice, and, most importantly, biblical image, symbol, narrative, and meaning. His biblical allusions and references to the black nation's spiritual consciousness are innumerable. Today he claims membership in one of the largest Baptist churches in Washington, D.C.[21] He reveres as much today the Christian commitment of Martin Luther King and Medgar Evers as he did when he joined hands with them in the civil rights movement.[22] The unfailing optimism, seen in the entirety of his works, that only love within and between the races will ultimately save America and its black citizens is rooted in the philosophy of Christian faith.[23]

In spite of the above claims, an objective look at the constantly apposed treatment of his own experience and of the collective black Christian experience, leads to the suspicion that Baldwin really does not believe in the possibility of a spiritual epiphany to lift the black man above the environment of his anguish. At least he seems to accept the prevailing social theories that treat Christianity as simply a force to keep black people insensitive to the need for more immediate freedom. Both aspects can be seen in John Grimes's conversion, in *Go Tell It on the Mountain* under the jealous eye of his cruel, oppressive stepfather, an un-Christian minister; in the tawdry, fractious, loveless relationships in the midst of "devout" religious fervor in *Amen Corner*—wretched "saved saints" who will not stoop to save the dying father, Luke Alexander; likewise in the spineless father, Rev. Henry, in *Blues for Mr. Charlie,* whose prayers and example of Christian meekness are powerless against the congregation of white "Christian" lynchers, who kill his son in the name of God; and in that very precise essay "Many Thousands Gone," he sardonically says that even the white man knows his "Negroes" got "real" religion. The smug white persona expresses what the mainstream really feels about the "Negro":

> In the case of the Negro his shameful history was carried, quite literally, on his brow. Shameful; for he was heathen as well as black and would never have discovered the healing blood of Christ had not we braved the jungles to bring him these glad tidings. As he accepted the alabaster Christ and the bloody cross—in the bearing of which he would find his redemption, as, indeed, to our outraged

astonishment, he sometimes did—he must, accept that image we
then gave him of himself. . . .[24]

The persona concludes that his simple dilemma must be borne in
mind if one wishes to comprehend Negro psychology.

Today, thirty-eight years after the appearance of Baldwin's first
successful, quasi-religious novel, *Go Tell It on the Mountain,* critics
are displeased with his continuing reliance upon religious themes.
They want him to leave the arena of the black church and the black
family portrayed again in his latest work, *Just Above My Head,* and
"write about something more in keeping with the contemporary
problems of Black America."[25] Such advice misses Baldwin's point
altogether, for he believes that understanding the black man's dilemma
with Christianity is axiomatic to dealing with these contemporary
problems—a position that on many levels is no different from the
beloved Dr. King's admonishments or those of Malcolm X, who,
because of the untenable hypocrisy of practiced Christianity, disa-
vowed his father's Baptist faith; or of the contemporary black writers
of the seventies and eighties who for the most part have rejected
Christianity as a basis for moral standard and have turned to Islam
and other African religions.[26] Baldwin says in "Everybody's Protest
Novel": "The African, exile, pagan, fell on his knees before that God
in Whom he must now believe; Who had made him, but not in His
image. This tableau, this impossibility, is the heritage of the Negro
in America: *Wash me,* cried the slave to his Maker, and I shall be
whiter, whiter than snow! For black is the color of evil; only the
robes of the saved are white. . . . This reality, in the same nightmare
notion, he both flees and rushes to embrace."[27]

Although Martin insisted that the black man was made in God's
image and Malcolm and Elijah Muhammed held that there definitely
must be two gods—one white and one black, with the white one
and his white offspring being indisputable devils—Baldwin concluded
that at the core of the question was an unsolved mystery with an
illusive, incomprehensible God, sometimes white, sometimes black,
with variant earthly fathers as representatives of the origins of man's
being and causality. Perhaps one reason that they could be so absolute
and he could not was that they had at least the psychological security
of knowing a true father in the flesh while he did not. Surely, the
Reverend David Baldwin was not his real father. Not only had his
mother finally confessed that James was born out of wedlock, the
boy spoken of in *Go Tell It on the Mountain, The Fire Next Time,*
and *Nobody Knows My Name* intuitively knew that this mean, in-
secure, spiteful man could not be his father. In his constant daily
behavior, the elder Baldwin made it clear that James was not among
his chosen sons.

Within the cosmology of biblical narrative is of course the Cain story in which God and his image, Adam, denied Cain the honor of an elder son because he had murdered his younger brother Abel. They gave the inheritance of the lineage to a third son, Seth, and banished Cain from the familial community to wander as a vagabond on the earth. To support slavery, white theologians said that the mark God put upon Cain to establish his identity on the earth was black skin.[28] A thorough student of ancient lore, Baldwin was aware that the rejection he suffered from Mr. Baldwin made him quite analogous to Cain. As mimicked in the interpersonal relations in *Go Tell It on the Mountain*, David Baldwin, the younger son, was the reverend's beloved namesake. Thus, the harsh father—most succinctly because of his ministerial profession—becomes a symbol of the Calvinistic God, who had likewise cursed the African to a base position of sonship.

The young Baldwin yearned to know his "real" father. Why had he deserted him, denied him name and legitimization? Was it a matter of an unworthy son or of an irresponsible father? In either case, again as with Mr. Baldwin, the alienation becomes a representative allegory for the absence of an adequate protective father in the black man's life. The sociological implications, both in black American experience and in Baldwin's works, are obvious. The awesome limitations of a racist society will not allow any of his male characters to be economically or socially functioning fathers, or serve as role models for young men to follow. Both in life and as a personal source for his young black male characters, the steps of initiation thus presume that other "fathers" in the community are available as viable substitutes. In both his life and his work, Baldwin turns first to the church and then—discarding all but its spiritually artistic forms (i.e., its music as the cradling forerunner of jazz and the blues as contrasted in "Sonny's Blues")—to the world of art and literature.

Thus, Baldwin's chaotic, essentially orphaned childhood, his conversion, and the symbolic relationship with his "earthly" fathers are merely his metaphors for the religiously inconclusive psyches of the race. The black man's relationships with the Father-God of Christianity early became a central Baldwin thesis. For him, there is no other moral standard by which whites can be judged and through which, in vindicating black peoples, the Christian God can absolve himself as the moral center of the universe. In a commentary of the black preacher's socialization of the Gospel, Baldwin makes the assumption that the confessed spiritual piety has always been an ambiguous veneer veiling demands for social justice:

> The word "belief" has nearly no meaning anymore, in the recognized
> languages, and ineptly approaches the reality to which I am referring:
> for there can be no doubt that it is a reality. The blacks had first

been claimed by the Christian church, and then excluded from the company of white Christians—from the fellowship of Christians: which taught us all that we needed to know about white Christians. The blacks did not so much use Christian symbols as recognize them—recognize them for what they were before the Christians came along—and, thus, reinvested these symbols with their original energy. The proof of this, simply, is the continued existence and authority of the blacks: it is through the creation of the black church that an unwritten, dispersed, and violated inheritance has been handed down. The word "revelation" has very little meaning in the recognized languages: yet, it is the only word for the moment I am attempting to approach.[29]

An innate perfectionist, the younger Baldwin found these absolutes quite compatible with the orderings of causal existence offered by the church. After his "conversion" experience, the directions for life were quite easy: "An eye for an eye and a tooth for a tooth." "Do unto others as you would have them do unto you." God, on behalf of the suffering saints, would quickly punish the wicked. Although such simplistic answers presented ideal solutions, Baldwin soon learned that they were not easily transferrable into his expanding world. He notes in *The Fire Next Time* that all authority appeared to come from God to subversive white representatives, without whose permission the Harlemites indeed did not seem to be able to "live, move, or have their being."[30]

Even more perplexing, it became equally evident during Baldwin's three years in the ministry that although God did not seem to be doing His part, perhaps God's moral standard was operating in justifiable judgment against black Christians. They themselves were not fulfilling the laws necessary to receive the savior's blessings. Baldwin confesses in *The Fire Next Time:*

> There was no love in the church. It was a mask for hatred and self-despair. When we were told to love everybody, I had thought that that meant *everybody*. But no. It applied only to those who believed as we did, and it did not apply to white people at all. But what was the point, the purpose of *my* salvation if it did not permit me to behave with love toward others, no matter how they behaved toward me?[31]

Therefore, all external truths that were supposed to complement the new Christian's internal ecstatic experience—the Christian church and the Christian community—were in complete contradiction to it. White Christians, to the shouting black pentecostal church, were devils to be exorcised, not brethren to be loved. Yet the blacks themselves were either humble inheritors of some future earth or heaven; or pitiful imitators of the hypocritical whites whom they despised. Herein were the seeds planted for his agonizing message.

For the next forty years, Baldwin examined these polarities in his fiction, drama, and prose. He looked into, if not resolved, the mystery that the "Church Fathers" had left untouched, and he wrote to influence a national reconciliation between the hope of Christian love that he may have tasted as a young man and the intolerable realities of hate in professing disciples. The ensuing philosophy of his dilemma is best stated in his denial of faith in the "Down at the Cross" essay, in which he states that the black man's experiential condition rendered it impossible for him (Baldwin in particular and the race in general) to find salvation in the black church.

Because Baldwin knew such a theorem was heretical to the Christian doctrine he was supposed to preach, he searched for a medium other than the pulpit in order to work out and affirm both a proper communal response for those who had valid spiritual experience and a proper holocaust judgment for those who profess salvation without manifesting universal love. This reordering becomes the philosophical foundation on which he creates. In all of his works, he emphasizes these extremes in a multileveled metaphor that has the ultimate vortex of estrangement from the father.

Baldwin's call for the reunion of fathers and sons is a modern continuation of the cosmic replay, both in the Bible and in America's religious culture, of the Trinity. The father—"white," light, pure, righteous judge of the universe—had to forsake, to "blacken" with the stain of sin, to sacrifice his only son. It was a necessary sacrifice. Mankind, black or white, could not be saved without it. But the gift of universal, unpredestined salvation for which Christ died on the cross has, in succeeding generations, been stolen by evil forces and persons who want to gain wealth and power. In much popular antebellum American literature, most sympathetically in *Uncle Tom's Cabin,* in steps the black man, chosen from eternity as the type of Christ. Through loving self-sacrifice, in obedience to his heavenly father's will, the black sacrificial son must redeem that gift for his own generation and for the salvation of the nation. He must in love lay down his freedom, his dignity, his life for his "lost" white brother. It is also so much of an archetypal pattern in American literature and theology, a pattern that Baldwin hates. But as much as he despised it in Stowe's novel, which he read over and over as a boy, it is nonetheless one of the solutions that he sets forth to reconcile America. This is why he could not espouse the Moslem faith of Elijah Mohammed—it was a doctrine of hate. As deeply as he understands the racial foundations of American power, Baldwin has never been able to hate the white man.

Herein lie additional levels of depth in the "father" symbolism. Baldwin advocates a reunion between white fathers and black sons— an action that is not only incredibly idealistic and in most cases impossible, but one that blacks as well as whites probably find repulsive. Historically in the literary canon, awareness of the specific identity of white parentage only intensifies the bitterness of black disinheritedness and heightens the sense of schizophrenia.[32] Additionally, with this thesis, Baldwin transgressed a movement in black aesthetics that demanded that black writers turn away from the tragic mulatto theme that had dominated white authorial portrayal of blacks as well as the post–Civil War birth of black American literature. In the historicity of these issues, Baldwin was well versed. Nevertheless, he insisted, especially in his early works, that for total self-discovery and purgation, blacks, indeed, all Americans, must face the horror of "The Great White Father."

Continuing aspects of the mulatto theme, he says in *The Fire Next Time* that the American Negro must accept the history of his white parentage, that he is neither totally African, nor Moslem, but "a unique creation; he has no counterpart anywhere, and no predecessors. . . . I am called Baldwin . . . because I was kidnapped by a white Christian named Baldwin, who forced me to kneel at the foot of the cross. I am, then, both visibly and legally the descendant of slaves in a white, Protestant country, . . . this is what it means to be an American Negro."[33] There is also the poignant prayer by Meridian Henry, in *Blues for Mr. Charlie,* lamenting the murder of his only son at the hands of a white pseudo-Christian terrorist: "But can I ask the children forever to sustain the cruelty inflicted on them by those who have been their masters, and who are now, in very truth . . . their parents? What hope is there for a people who deny their deeds and disown their kinsmen and who do so in the name of purity and love, in the name of Jesus Christ?"[34] That parentage is both physical and spiritual. Baldwin wants the white religious zealot who placed the African on the auction block to be held accountable for his failure to demonstrate the Christian protectorate that he promised in Christ. Further, he wants the white biological forefather, through the repentance of his heirs, to face the retribution of damnation for the heinous crime of denying, enslaving, and murdering his own sons.

Another point that violates the black aesthetic endeavors to reverse the images of Africans in American culture is set forth in Baldwin's generic identification of the black self as "Devil":

> In our church, the Devil had many faces, all of them one's own. He was not always evil, rarely was he frightening—he was, more often, subtle, charming, cunning, and warm. So, one learned, for example, never to take the easy way out: whatever looked easy was almost certainly a trap. In short, the Devil was that mirror which could never be smashed. One had to look into the mirror every day— *good morning, blues / Blues, how do you do? / Well, I'm doing all*

right Good morning / How are you:—check it all out, and take it all in, and travel. The pleading of the blood was not, for us, a way of exorcising a Satan whom we knew could never sleep; it was to engage Satan in a battle which we knew could never end.[36]

If, as he repeated to Margaret Mead in *A Rap on Race,* the "good" Christian God is white and is vengeful toward black persons, is he saying later in *The Devil Finds Work* (as indicated in the title and the theme of the book) that blacks indeed represent God's opposite? Or is he merely speaking of that tiger to be tamed within the universal self that transcends race and color?

Aspects of the metaphor that most fill Baldwin's cup of anguish are the angry, self-depreciating relationships between black fathers and sons as a necessary insulation against the white world. He suspected that it was shame at having created a black son to perpetuate the myth that caused his natural father to disown him. Likewise, the ambivalent love-hate memories of his religiously violent stepfather were a vehicle for apprehending a causal iconography symbolic of the black man's relationship with God and society. Ultimately, one who is brought up to expect that any tender mercy can turn to cruelty cannot be disillusioned. In *The Devil Finds Work,* he acknowledges the effectiveness of the elder Baldwin's negativistic training and patriarchy:

> The pride and sorrow and beauty of my father's face: for that man I called my father really *was* my father in every sense except the biological, or literal one. He formed me, and he raised me, and he did not let me starve: and he gave me something, however harshly, and however little I wanted it, which prepared me for an impending horror which he could not prevent. This is not a Western idea, but fathers and sons arrive at that relationship only by claiming that relationship: that is, by paying for it. If the relationship of father to son could really be reduced to biology, the whole earth would blaze with the glory of fathers and sons.[36]

This image culminates in a father's acrimonious disapproving of Anglicized theories of black manhood. But, ultimately, Baldwin's texts and personal direction indicate that neither his religious stepfather nor other ministers in the church provided significant answers for an initiate whose questions were more than superficial. In *Notes of a Native Son,* he reminisces about the variety of the old man's life:

> "But as for me and my house," my father had said, "we will serve the Lord." I wondered, as we drove him to his resting place, what this line had meant for him. I had heard him preach it many times. I had preached it once myself, proudly giving it an interpretation different from my father's. Now the whole thing came back to me, as though my father and I were on our way to Sunday school and

I were memorizing the golden text. . . . I suspected in these familiar lines a meaning which had never been there for me before. All of my father's texts and songs, which I had decided were meaningless, were arranged before me at his death like empty bottles, waiting to hold the meaning which life would give them for me. This was his legacy: nothing is ever escaped.[37]

In his move from biological, familial, and church fathers, Baldwin—and, consequently, those among his black male characters who achieve reconciliation—eventually finds ostensibly compatible generative role models among the black artists and intellectuals who fostered his artistic development. His subsequent art became a journal of his search in self and society for evidence of God and His love. In that other world of the unseen black spirit—literature, art, jazz, black language, and blues—he finds authority figures who can guide him and other thoughtful young men unable to adjust to the holocaustic horror into which they had been born: "the American despair, the search, in our country for authority. . . . The streets of my native city were filled with youngsters searching desperately for the limits which would tell them who they were, and create for them a challenge to which they could rise."[38]

As seen earlier in a discussion of the strand of biblical symbolism in the works of black American writers since the eighteenth century, the racial literary heritage gave Baldwin at least a transitional basis on which to move from religious "principling" into modern secularized art and philosophy. Although he mastered the latter, he never fully renounced the former, which for his purposes was the more functional form. But he realizes that he is attempting to "marry" incompatible elements in agnostic art and traditional black Christian faith. His conflicting emotions when in late adolescence he moved away from the church and his ministerial calling are explored not only in *The Fire Next Time* and *Notes of a Native Son*, but are perhaps most eloquently expressed in both Sonny's ("Sonny's Blues") and David's *(Amen Corner)* experiences when they suffer parental rejection because they must steal away to discover nonecclesiatical epiphanies in the ethereal grasp of black music.

Biographically, Baldwin's earliest artistic mentor was not really Countee Cullen but the prolific (and, even now, barely recognized) genius, visual artist Beauford DeLaney. He was the first adult to assure Baldwin that the world of art and thought did not freakishly separate him from acceptable ethnic experience. When Baldwin visited Beauford's studio and lamented his abject poverty, the restricting duty to support eight younger brothers and sisters, and his inherent failure to maintain employment at any of the menial tasks he continually tried to swallow, he found in Beauford an understanding, compassionate friend. Beauford finally told Baldwin, who had lost his umpteenth dishwasher's job, "Perhaps you simply don't belong there," and encouraged him to pursue his writing instead.[39] When the often sick and ultimately imcompetent ministerial stepfather died, it was DeLaney—not black churchmen—to whom James Baldwin turned. The elder artist provided a haven for the young man, now freshly terrified at the prospect of total responsibility for the family. Beauford appealed to the neighborhood for donations to supplement his own generous cash gift, which was needed for the funeral because the impoverished family lacked the money to bury the father. Baldwin's brother David; his associate, dancer and choreographer Bernard Haskell; and distinguished black American literary critic Dr. Richard Long (who himself was strongly influenced by DeLaney and who first began his lifelong friendship with Baldwin through DeLaney) all agree with Baldwin's claim that DeLaney was the true father of Baldwin's art. In later years, Baldwin, after an intermittent but compatible association with DeLaney, was able to repay the artist's gracious gesture when he, Long, and Haskell not only buried DeLaney, who died in neglect and obscurity in Paris, but withstood the attempts of an avaricious French government to confiscate his paintings.[40] Later Baldwin and Long coedited *Beauford DeLaney Retrospective Exhibition: Harlem Studio Museum* as a final tribute to a talented "father" who had encouraged them to let nothing inhibit their creative dreams.

Apart from Beauford's support, Baldwin was primarily on his own; though his quixotic initiative was also influenced by the world of black music, which beckoned him from Harlem's streets, as well as the consummate neighborhood and the downtown Forty-Second Street New York libraries (with their titular attempts at integration). In one interview, his brother David painfully recalls the benignly discourteous treatment that Baldwin received from Richard Wright and other members of the post-Renaissance New York circle. Later, the venerable Sterling Brown was one of the few prominent black writer/scholars who had published during the Harlem Renaissance to support Baldwin or his works when *Amen Corner* opened at Howard University in 1956. Brown single-handedly withstood the irate reaction of conservative black scholars who were deeply disturbed at Baldwin's portrayal of black life and language and at his irreverence for the black church.[41] Although Wright interceded to get the budding writer an early fellowship to work on *In My Father's House* (the first title of the novel that later became *Go Tell It on the Mountain*), the true character of their relationship and of Wright's refusal to sponsor or associate with the younger writer is barely seen in "Alas, Poor Richard" or "Everybody's Protest Novel."

Like many black writers and artists who failed to find a congenial environment for their work in America, Baldwin set sail for France in 1948. He found some respite with white expatriots, but Beauford and Hoyt Fuller—the founder of *Negro Digest* and *Black World,* which were the major sources for publication of black writers in the fifties and sixties, and *First World* in the seventies—were mainstays of solace and encouragement. After hearing about his work, Hoyt wrote to Baldwin from Chicago to encourage him and to invite submissions. Through their correspondence and later acquaintance, Baldwin grew to respect Fuller as one of the few men who understood what he was trying to do.

Any conceptualization of Baldwin's quest for fathers must, of necessity, include a discussion of his own influence as an innovator in the mainstream of black American literature. Historically, Baldwin should be seen as the last black American writer to exploit as a major theme the black man's relationship with Christianity. Conversely, he may be considered the first black American writer to distance himself from the lone enduring black institution, the black church, not by its notable absence (as with Wright, Ellison,[42] and other blacks writing in the first half of this century; for example, Ann Petry, Nella Larsen, Sterling Brown, Chester Himes, Paule Marshall, Robert Hayden, and William Demby), but by his overtly persistent portrayal of its lack of authentic Christian commitment. In this and his subsequent treatment of homosexuality as an acceptable form of human love (in *Giovanni's Room* and, most recently, in *Just Above My Head*)—a position he knew was not compatible with orthodox Christian behavior and thus utterly shocking even to black sophisticates—Baldwin opened the floodgate for contemporary anti-Christian, nonbiblically based black American literature. In most of his works, he only questions divine existence while still courting its allegiance, but his boldness invited younger writers to complete the schism between black art and black faith.

The schism between white-practiced Christianity and black American art was always axiomatically present. For two hundred years, black writers examined the Bible and indicted white society for the incorrigible refusal to love oppressed people (as the Bible commands); however, they agreed with the black preacher that faith in the true God and in His deliverance of them was the only accessible power upon which an enslaved or oppressed people could rely. In their works, the black church itself and faith as exercised in the hearts of black believers were sacrosanct.

Ironically, Baldwin intended his literature to influence national and personal reunification. He hoped that white fathers would repent and acknowledge their sons: that black fathers would be men of strength and love while throwing off the shackles of Tomism and that God the Father, indicated in even those oft-repeated prayerful exclamations, "God knows," would reveal the black man as an equally chosen son. The Trinity would then be restored. The thrust of his message is that the validity of Christianity can best be measured by how it has affected the colored peoples of the world. That effect "seems" instead to resolve solely in oppression. I say "seems" because Baldwin still attempts to separate the visible history of black America's experience with Christianity from the spiritual, visionary experience that both he and the race may have internalized. The reality of that unseen spiritual truth, codified in his novels by the suffering blues and tarrying spiritual motifs, enables him to keep advocating that the demonstrable love of Christ will bring to earth that paradise revealed on the threshing floor and fulfill that prophecy in Amos 9:7, "Are ye not as children of the Ethiopians unto me, O children of Israel?" Then Baldwin can have peace with the heritage of his forefathers. Then and only then will his quest end and he can unhesitantly acknowledge oneness with the Christian God, his father. Until that essence of true Christianity is revealed, Baldwin's dissociation from variant fathers tempts him to withhold absolute commitment. The totality of his theme is a cosmologically oxymoronic statement in both language and philosophy that sensible faith in an unseen God cannot transcend experience in self, race, or society. Faith, even in one's own soul, is difficult to capture in artistic medium. In an uncontrived moment, Baldwin jocularly confessed to Nikki Giovanni, "Well, it depends on what you mean by God. . . . I've claimed Him as my father and I'll give Him a great time until it's over because God is our responsibility."[43] Although that is not belief, it at least indicates that his search for God, his primal father, is not abandoned.

Notes

1. "Race, Hate, Sex, and Colour: A Conversation," By James Baldwin with James Mossman and Colin MacInnes, *Encounter* 25 (1965):55–60.

2. Acts 2:1–5. The allusion has more a pentecostal than fundamentalist flavor, as this, the more emotional mold, is essentially Baldwin's church background.

3. Most basic texts on American slavery deal with theological supports manipulated to support that institution. Studies going into the greatest detail are Winthrop D. Jordan, *The White Man's Burden: Historical Origins of Racism in the United States* (New York: Oxford University Press, 1974), and *White Over Black: American Attitudes Toward the Negro, 1550–1812* (Chapel Hill: University of North Carolina Press, 1968); and Roger Bastide, "Color, Racism, and Christianity," in *Color and Race,* ed. John Hope Franklin (Boston: Houghton Mifflin, 1968).

4. See Michel Fabre, "Fathers and Sons in James Baldwin's *Go Tell It on the Mountain,*" in *James Baldwin: A Collection of Critical Essays,* ed. Keneth Kinnamon (Englewood Cliffs, N.J.: Prentice-Hall, 1974); see also Therman B. O'Daniel, "James Baldwin: An Interpretive Study," *College Language Association* 7 (1963):37–47.

5. See the entries of ex-slaves in Roger Burns, *Am I Not a Man and a Brother: The Anti-Slavery Crusade of Revolutionary America, 1688–1788* (New York: Chelsea House, 1977); and Dorothy Porter, *Early Negro Writing, 1760–1837* (Boston: Beacon, 1971). The story of Philemon is in the New Testament epistle bearing his name.

6. Jupiter Hammon, "A Dialogue Entitled the Kind Master and a Dutiful Servant," in *America's First Negro Poet: The Complete Works of Jupiter Hammon of Long Island*, ed. Stanley Austin Ransome, Jr. (Port Washington, N.Y.: Kennikat, 1970).

7. Phillis Wheatley, "On Being Brought from Africa to America," in *The Poems of Phillis Wheatley*, ed. Julian D. Mason (Chapel Hill: University of North Carolina Press, 1966), 7.

8. Briton Hammon, *A Narrative of the Uncommon Sufferings and Surprising Deliverance of Briton Hammon, a Negro Man* (Boston, 1760); John Marrant, *A Narrative of the Lord's Wonderful Dealings with John Marrant, a Black, 1785*, in *Narratives of North American Indian Captivities*, vol. 17 (New York: Garland, 1978). See *Black Writers of America* for other authors cited.

9. The most inclusive anthology is Richard Barksdale and Keneth Kinnamon, *Black Writers of America* (New York: Macmillan, 1972). Hammon's poem is in *America's First Negro Poet*, ed. Ransome. The Crafts' narrative is William Craft and Ellen Craft, *Running a Thousand Miles for Freedom or The Escape of William and Ellen Craft from Slavery*, collected in *Great Slave Narratives*, ed. Arna Bontemps (Boston: Beacon, 1969). Sojourner Truth's most famous speech is in the Burns Collection.

10. See Benjamin E. Mays, *The Negro's God as Reflected in His Literature* (New York: Russell & Russell, 1938).

11. Frederick Douglass, *Narrative of the Life of Frederick Douglass: An American Slave* (Boston: Anti-Slavery Office, 1845; reprint ed., Garden City, New York: Anchor/ Doubleday, 1973).

12. James Weldon Johnson, *God's Trombones: Seven Negro Sermons in Verse* (New York: Viking, 1927); Zora Neale Hurston, *Their Eyes Were Watching God* (Urbana: University of Illinois Press, 1978). Hughes's poems are in Barksdale and Kinnamon. Jean Toomer, *Cane* (New York: Liveright, 1975).

13. See Carolyn Wedin Sylvander, *James Baldwin* (New York: Ungar, 1980), 1–7. See also chapter 1 of Fern Marja Eckman, *The Furious Passage of James Baldwin* (New York: M. Evans; distributed by J. B. Lippincott, Philadelphia, 1966).

14. Countee Cullen, "Yet Do I Marvel," in *Black Writers of America*, 531.

15. James Baldwin and Nikki Giovanni, *A Dialogue* (New York: Lippincott, 1973), 36–38.

16. James Baldwin, *The Fire Next Time* (New York: Dell, 1962), 39–40.

17. Ibid., 43.

18. Ibid., 45.

19. Ibid., 46.

20. See Baldwin and Giovanni, *Dialogue*, 36–38. See also "Down at the Cross," in *The Fire Next Time.*

21. Interview (April 1981) with James Baldwin and Dr. Eleanor Traylor of Washington, D.C., one of the organizers of an appreciation day for James Baldwin's mother in 1979 at the Baptist church that Baldwin subsequently joined.

22. Baldwin is currently working on a studied biography of the lives of Martin Luther King, Malcolm X, and Medgar Evers. His esteem for Martin is mentioned often in his works. See, for example, *Dialogue*, 25.

23. Baldwin admitted at various times that Christianity, not the church but the religion itself, was one basis of his own moral philosophy. See Margaret Mead and James Baldwin, *A Rap on Race* (New York: Lippincott, 1979), 85–89.

24. James Baldwin, "Many Thousands Gone," in *Notes of a Native Son* (Boston: Beacon, 1955), 29–30.

25. Critical reception of *Just Above My Head* has been mixed. These remarks

were included in a BBC broadcast on National Public Radio in 1982. See also *Booklist*, 1 October 1979, 216; *New York Times Book Review*, 23 September 1979, 3; *Times Literary Supplement*, 21 December 1979, 150.

26. Dr. Martin Luther King, "Letter from a Birmingham Jail," in *Why We Can't Wait* (New York: New American Library, 1963), 76–95.

27. Baldwin, "Everybody's Protest Novel," *Notes*, 21.

28. Genesis, 4.

29. James Baldwin, *The Devil Finds Work* (New York: Dial, 1976), 114.

30. Baldwin, *Fire*, 40.

31. Ibid., 57–58.

32. The tragic mulatto theme and its attendant schizophrenic psychosis are treated variously and continually in black American fiction, beginning with such early novels as William Wells Brown's *Clotel; or The President's Daughter* (London: Partridge & Oakley, 1853) and Francis E. W. Harper's *Iola Leroy; or Shadows Uplifted* (Philadelphia: Garringgues Brothers, 1892). See Robert Cone's *Negro Novel in America*, rev. ed. (New Haven: Yale University Press, 1965), for a discussion of the theme.

33. Baldwin, *Fire*, 114.

34. James Baldwin, *Blues for Mr. Charlie* (New York: Dial, 1964), 77.

35. Baldwin, *Devil*, 116.

36. Baldwin, *Devil*, 30.

37. Baldwin, *Notes*, 112–13.

38. James Baldwin, "The Northern Protestant," in *Nobody Knows My Name* (New York: Dell, 1954), 180.

39. I am preparing a biography of James Baldwin. Much of the material in this section of the essay was obtained from conversations and interviews with Mr. Baldwin, his family, and associates. I am indebted to the Emory University Grants and Research Committee for a fellowship for support in obtaining these interviews and documentation in the course of this research.

40. Interviews with James Baldwin, Bernard Haskell, David Baldwin, and Richard Long, April 1980 and August 1980.

41. Interview, James Baldwin, June 1981.

42. Richard Wright's bitter exposure to Christian dogma was through his overbearing grandmother's relationship with the Seventh-Day Adventist Church, a denomination that had no historical axis in black American historical traditions. Thus, other than his hatred of her religious hypocrisy in *Black Boy*, his scenes are not religious and certainly did not reflect a church experience of his own. In *Invisible Man*, religion is confined to the rhetoric of the college campus and other political forums. Other than metaphors of groupism that also allude to the Communist party, Ellison avoids condemnation of the black church.

43. Baldwin and Giovanni, *Dialogue*, 38.

Essays on Fiction

Temple of the Fire Baptized   Richard K. Barksdale°

James Baldwin has written a very fine first novel [*Go Tell It on the Mountain*]. It is a story by a Negro, about Negroes, set in a predominantly Negro environment; and yet it is not essentially a "Negro" novel. Herein lies Mr. Baldwin's signal achievement. The plot, related in a series of superbly articulated flashbacks, is not grounded on race relations nor the sociology of the Negro. The author is not intent on analyzing the social dilemma of certain specific Negro characters, but he is intent on analyzing the spiritual dilemma of certain people who happen, in this instance, to be Negroes.

The principal characters in the novel are the Grimeses—Gabriel, the preacher father; Elizabeth, his careworn, sorrow-ridden wife; John, her bastard son; and Florence, Gabriel's unbendingly dignified sister. The plot is concerned with the effects of a highly surcharged emotional religion on the dreams, aspirations, values, and experiences of these characters. And this religion which fills the book and activates the plot is just as important as any character in the book. It is a quintessential, fire-and-brimstone Protestantism—ascetic, sin-laden, emotionally and musically rich, and colorfully anthropomorphic. It is the religion of the unlettered masses in several sections of Protestant America—the religion of the impoverished rural South, and the religion of the slum-ridden urban North. Mr. Baldwin so describes the reactions of his characters to this religion that no one character's reaction ever becomes a socially conditioned reaction to a socially conditioned "Negro" religion. The conflicts which sear the soul of each character are conflicts which are concerned with ethical values and patterns of conduct, and these are preeminently the concern of religion, whatever the color of a man's skin. Mr. Baldwin never forgets this fact, and this is the great merit of his work. His is essentially a religious novel. Hence, there is no mockery in his description of the

°Reprinted from *Phylon* 14 (1953):326–27, by permission of the author and the journal.

almost Dionysian revelry of the "Saints" of the "Temple of the Fire Baptized"—no mockery of their songs and of their wordless religious ecstasy in their storefront church, no mockery of their emotional gyrations before the altar of deliverance. Mr. Baldwin's message to sophisticated, skeptical, utilitarian America is that such a religion is part of the American scene and that it merits quiet acceptance, not patronizing tolerance.

Inevitably, in a religious novel, the character becomes more important than either plot or setting. This is true of Go Tell It on the Mountain. Although the reader knows that the action takes place either in Harlem or in the deep South, the setting is never particularized to any great extent. The author quite justifiably concentrates on character analysis—through introspective flashbacks, through passages of sharply authentic dialogue, and through his own objective comments.

The crowning point of the novel undoubtedly is John Grimes' mystical experience on his fourteenth birthday. This incident occurs after the reader has been given a full account of the life and experiences of the other three principal characters—Gabriel and Elizabeth Grimes, and John's Aunt Florence. Their past lives, seen in retrospect, have been filled with sin, cruelty, deceit, and hypocrisy; but John's mystical experience, described in a powerfully poetic prose, furnishes a beautiful climax to the action of the novel. When John Grimes sees the Lord and envisions the marraige of light and darkness, the misery and folly of his elders are forgotten. The storm of their lives is over, and the reader sees the blue sky of the young man's mystical affirmation.

James Baldwin, I repeat, has written a very fine first novel.

A Homosexual Dilemma   Leslie A. Fiedler*

For what seems a long time but surely can be no more than a few years, I have been watching James Baldwin's work—not merely reading it, but watching it, warily, hopefully—a little incredulously. I have had the sense that here for once was a young Negro writer, capable of outgrowing at the same moment both qualifications and becoming simply a writer. Giovanni's Room, whatever its limitations, is a step in this direction—that is to say, a step beyond the Negro

*Reprinted from the New Leader 39 (1956):16–17, by permission of the author and the journal.

writer's usual obsession with his situation as a Negro in a white culture, an obsession which keeps him forever writing a first book.

I do not mean to imply that the writer who is also a Negro can afford to ignore the deepest passions and conditions of his growing up, and Baldwin has, indeed, treated those passions and conditions in his earlier novel, *Go Tell It on the Mountain*. But he must, I am convinced, *break through*, find ways of registering his identity and outsidedness through other symbols than the accidental, autobiographical one of skin color. Our very concern with Negro-white relations has tended to make a cliché of every aspect of them, and the writer who accepts them as *the* subject lays up for himself a life of exasperation and frustration. It is not easy to make poetry of sociological banalities, especially if one approaches them already committed to righteousness and self-pity.

There is not only no Negro problem in Baldwin's new book; there are not even any Negroes—and this, I must confess, makes me a little uneasy. His protagonist, David, is a shade *too* pale-face, almost ladies-magazine-Saxon, gleaming blond and "rather like an arrow"; but this is not what troubles me finally. It is rather the fact that he encounters no black faces in his movements through Paris and the south of France, that not even the supernumeraries are colored; so that one begins to suspect at last that there must *really* be Negroes present, censored, camouflaged or encoded. It is a little like the feeling of Trilling's *Middle of the Journey,* in which no Jew is permitted to enter a world of intellectual Communists and fellow-travelers. In the mature novel toward which Baldwin is progressing, surely Negro characters will be present, at the periphery or in the center, as the exigencies and probabilities of the story demand—a full world fully rendered.

Giovanni's Room does not create such a full world in any sense. It is a tightly focused book, a novella rather than a novel—dense at its best moments, thin at its worst, but always spare. There are only three characters who count: David himself, the American girl Hella, and the Italian homosexual Giovanni. David, who has never faced up to anything himself, is driven to make a choice between marriage to Hella and a life with Giovanni in the miserable room on the outskirts of Paris that serves as a symbol of the shoddiness, the isolation, the appallingly naked intimacy of such an affair. Not even choosing in full awareness, but drifting and fleeing, he abandons Giovanni, who in his desolation and poverty is led to commit a murder and is finally guillotined. But David cannot, in the end, marry Hella at all, her very touch having become repulsive to him; and he is left to a life of degradation and self-reproach, punctuated by furtive affairs with sailors.

It is all very moral and melodramatic, almost a little morality play in modern dress, in which the characters tend to become allegorical and life is portrayed as exacting consequences more bloody and final than its usual fumblings attain. There is something quite old-fashioned about the basic fable; indeed, David's despair after his unalterable rejection of Giovanni recalls phrases from books long confined to the ten-cent tables of second-hand book stores. "All my vivid realization of how utterly base I myself had been, and of your unspeakable agony, caused by me, your despair, your humiliation, all my remorse . . . my sense of what I had wantonly flung away, and lost beyond all recovery . . . in a word, all my love—love that had lain as I supposed dead, now suddenly had come to, never to let me rest any more. . . ." The feeling is the feeling of Baldwin's book, but the words are those of a character in a novel published in 1887 and called *The Yoke of the Thorah.*

Indeed, there is a clue here. The earlier protagonist, a Jew, has reached his final pitch of despair by refusing to marry the Gentile girl with whom he was truly in love, by failing to cast off the "yoke of the Torah." But he might well have been (and *was* in the novel of a few decades later) a white boy giving up his Negro mistress, a social climber rejecting the poor (and pregnant) girl for an heiress; it is a basic American plot—a staple of popular fiction wherever it dares approach the problematical. But it is the gimmick of Baldwin's book to have made the poor but worthy girl a poor but worthy fairy, and thus to have dissolved the sentimental assurance of the older versions into a quite contemporary sort of ambiguity. A writer need be only a little enlightened to recommend (heartily and tearfully) breaking through economic or religious or social conventions to marry the girl one loves. But what if the girl is a *boy?* The moral concern remains, but where is the assured moral answer?

"You are the one who keeps talking about *what* I want," Giovanni insists at one point to David. "But I have only been talking about *who* I want." In terms of Baldwin's novel, this conflict between the "what" and "who" approach to love comes to stand for a deep conflict of the American and European conscience. It is David, the American, who feels driven to ask not "Can I love Giovanni?" but "Can I love a *man?*," just as his ancestors, of whom, despite his expatriation, he is so proud ("My ancestors conquered a continent, pushing across death-laden plains . . ."), might have asked: Can I love a Jew, a Negro, a dissolute woman, one older than myself? We are back now to *The Ambassadors,* to Henry James and the clash between the recent American notion that experience is itself a good and love the great experience, and the more ancient American conviction that there are clean and unclean loves and that only what is clean is good.

It is the most amusing of Baldwin's wry ironies to portray the last stand of Puritanism as a defense of heterosexuality. But if David is our latest Last Puritan, he is by that very token the most uncertain of them all. He knows he cannot endure the stench of Giovanni's room, of Europe; but no more can he return to the well-washed Hella, to a clean America. And what of Hella, what of women in a world where men are as lost as David? "David," she cries, "please, let me be a woman. . . . It's *all* I want. . . ." But what *he* wants he does not know, and it requires his confidence in his own maleness to define her. "But if women are supposed to be led by men and there aren't any men to lead them, what happens then?"

I do not finally believe in Baldwin's sense of "the lack of sexual authority" in our world; but I believe he believes in it and feel the consequences of such a belief as he renders them in this book. Beneath the melodramatic statement, he is attempting a tragic theme: the loss of the last American innocence, the last moral certainty—that the mirror does not lie, that little boys are boys, little girls girls. Once more, Hella is his mouthpiece: "Americans should never come to Europe. . . . It means they never can be happy again. What's the good of an American who isn't happy? Happiness was all we had." But Hella sees only part way; if beyond happiness there is despair, beyond morality bewilderment, past despair and bewilderment there is God. Baldwin is finally a religious writer, though his religion is desperate and tentative in the expected modern manner. The last word, after all, is with David, who has betrayed everything, in his appeal to the "heavy grace of God," and in his cry to his deepest self, "I must believe, I must believe. . . ."

Outcasts in a Caldron of Hate   Granville Hicks°

James Baldwin's *Another Country* is a novel about love and hate, and more about hate than love. In its totality and with all due allowance for occasional weaknesses in the writing, it is one of the most powerful novels of our time. The complexities of love have seldom been explored more subtly or at greater depth, and perhaps the power of hate has never been communicated with a more terrifying force.

The novel begins with Rufus Scott, a Negro, once a drummer in a jazz band, now penniless and desperate. We go back to Rufus's

°Reprinted from *Saturday Review* 45 (1962):21, by permission of the author and the journal.

meeting with a poor white girl from Georgia named Leona, and we follow their relationship as, torn between love and hate, Rufus tortures and degrades Leona until she loses her mind. He is driven to destroy both her and himself, and Baldwin traces the process with relentless fury.

This episode takes less than a hundred pages, but then we are introduced to a variation of its theme. After Rufus's death, Vivaldo Moore, his best friend, falls in love with Rufus's sister Ida. She is as full of hatred of white people as Rufus, and his fate has intensified her bitterness. Her relationship with Vivaldo is not so violent as Rufus's with Leona, but it is ambivalent in the same way, and if the outcome, so far as the novel goes, is not so calamitous, we have no great cause for hope.

These are not the only varieties of love we encounter. Cass and Richard Silenski, older friends of both Rufus and Vivaldo, are at the outset a happily married couple, but Richard achieves success with a second-rate novel, and the disillusioned Cass turns away from him. And there is Eric, an actor who has been living in France. We see him first with Yves, a French boy of the streets to whom he is strongly attached. Later, after his return to New York, while waiting for Yves to join him, he becomes involved in strange ways with Cass and Vivaldo.

Baldwin does not underestimate the power of love, mysterious as its operations seem to be; but it is the power of hate that one really feels as one reads the novel. In certain of the essays in *Nobody Knows My Name* (*SR*, July 1, 1961) Baldwin has said directly enough that Negroes hate white people, and, if anybody needs to ask, he has explained why. It is, however, one thing to say that hatred exists and another to make it palpable, as he so magnificently does in the opening section about Rufus and again in the final account of Ida's confrontation of Vivaldo. Perhaps all Negroes do not feel as Rufus and Ida and Baldwin himself do, but if they don't, he convinces us, they ought to.

His hatred is not limited to the resentment that Negroes so legitimately feel towards the white people who have abused and exploited and scorned and despised them through the centuries. He has painted a Dantesque picture of New York—the heat, the stench, the gross inhumanity. And, rightly or wrongly, he sees New York as the symbol of contemporary American civilization. It is significant that most of his characters are outcasts—Rufus and Ida because they are Negroes, Eric because he is a homosexual, Cass out of disdain for her husband's false values, and Vivaldo because he cannot conceive of self-fulfilment except by way of alienation. The only characters who are willing to exist within the framework of contemporary society are contemptible—Richard Silenski, who welcomes a cheap success, and a cynical and empty impresario named Ellis. American writers, Baldwin argued in an article he wrote for the New York *Times Book Review* last winter, must accept the fact that the United States is becoming a second-rate power. This may be true; but now I can see that, true or not, it is what Baldwin wants to believe.

As I pointed out in my review of *Letting Go* (*SR,* June 16, 1962), Philip Roth also takes a dark view of present-day American civilization; but his discontent seems, in comparison with Baldwin's, no more than a kind of fractiousness, the peevish complaint of a spoiled child. American life in Baldwin's account is a terrifying barbarism. The very violence of the language he uses is itself an expression of horror; all the words have appeared in print before, but they have never been employed so ruthlessly to express disgust and to inspire disgust. The book itself is and is meant to be an act of violence.

The novel opens with a scene of such intensity that there seems to be nowhere for Baldwin to go, but in fact he matches it again and again. From his very first book, *Go Tell It on the Mountain,* it has been clear that he has a fine gift of language, but he has never before come anywhere near the sustained power of *Another Country.* There are lapses, to be sure. He describes, for instance, a party given by Cass and Richard Silenski, and the description is almost completely commonplace. Sometimes, when the heat is off, he slips into banality: " 'Ah!'—she shrugged merrily, and took a deep drag on her cigarette—'I wasn't consulted.' " Again: "Her face, then, made one think of a mischievous street boy. And at the same time there gleamed in her eyes a marvelously feminine mockery." But when two persons confront one another, whatever their sexes, whatever their color, Baldwin finds the words that will make us feel what they are feeling.

It has to be said, of course, that Baldwin's experience of America is limited, and limited in drastic and terrible ways. He does not know the America I know any better than, if as well as, I know his America. But every writer's experience is limited in one way or another, and the question is simply what he is able to make of it. What Baldwin has to say about contemporary civilization seems to me only partly true, but in so far as it is true at all, it is of the utmost importance. He compels one to participate in a kind of life that is horrible and that is important because it is horrible.

The novel is an explosion, but that does not mean that it is uncontrolled or artless. Baldwin seems to move haphazardly from character to character, but in fact the novel is shaped with rigorous care. Rufus, though he dies on page 88, dominates the whole book. Eric's entry on the scene comes relatively late, but it has been carefully prepared for. The lives of the various characters are closely related, and it is Baldwin's art that makes the relationships seem so natural and uncontrived. He is not only a powerful writer; he has become a skilled craftsman. I hope that, in the controversy the book is bound to arouse, his great gifts as a novelist will not be overlooked.

Blues for Mister Baldwin   Joseph Featherstone°

The blues are an attempt to retain the memory of pain, to transcend catastrophe, not by taking thought—for that often only adds to the pain—but by an attitude, a nearly comic, nearly tragic lyricism. The best stories in James Baldwin's new collection are blues, fragments of his vast and cureless sorrow. One, "The Outing," is a beautifully disciplined piece of writing. It is hard to know which to admire more, the ironic precision of the characters or the despairing eloquence with which Baldwin spells out a vision of their fate. In subject and time, "The Outing" is an early effort. The Hudson River excursion of a Harlem church evokes the world of Baldwin's first and best novel, *Go Tell It On the Mountain* (1952). Here again he describes the tension in the Negro community between the saved and the wavering young, whose burning time is upon them. The hearts of the saints are easy; they know, in their cosmic smugness, the peace that passes understanding. But for the unsaved, growing into consciousness of evil on the Harlem streets and within themselves, there is no peace. The prose is bleak; there is an ugly spareness to the church life. There is none of the rhetorical grandeur that lifted up the experience of the store front churches in *Go Tell It On the Mountain,* none of the Pentecostal ecstasies of God's hand striking the redeemed down onto the dust of the floor, the world rocking on its foundations. Here the lives of the saints are empty too, and the poetry is mostly pathos: the iron of the trap, the defenselessness of the young flesh caught in it.

"Come Out the Wilderness" and "Sonny's Blues" were both written in the late fifties. The first again renders Baldwin's ghastly vision of the moral chaos of New York, this time through the eyes of a Negro girl who has escaped North into the dreary landscape of fulfillment. She is sharply seen, a study in pity and rage. She loves a white artist who is sure to leave her; and in one scene, where she lunches with a young Negro executive, Baldwin marvelously creates her scorn and self-hatred, her brave, hopeless love for the white artist, her panic as she realizes the unlikelihood of love flowering in

°Reprinted from the *New Republic* 153 (1965):34–36, by permission of the author and the journal.

this wilderness. "Sonny's Blues" is poised on the edge of certain of the unsolved problems of Baldwin's grand failure, *Another Country* (1962). In its own right, though, "Sonny's Blues" is close to a success, the most completely imagined story of the collection, next to "The Outing." It is written with detachment; sweet objectivity rare for Baldwin who in much of his recent writing has been unable to distinguish between himself and his characters. The story relates the attempt of a Negro schoolteacher, very square, to understand his brother Sonny, a jazz musician and on-and-off dope addict. Variations on its theme have filled all of Baldwin's works: it concerns what Robert Bone has described as the priestly function of the sufferer in Baldwin's fiction. He who manages to endure suffering is set free; more important, he can set others free through his sacramental ministrations. Sonny's jazz solo flows from his cracked heart and his sickness. As he plays, the broken pieces of his life fuse for once into a whole which his brother hears and comprehends. It is an extraordinary story, but its testimony is not, in the end, altogether persuasive. There is, first of all, the problem of language, which constantly dogs Baldwin: for all his eloquence, he has a hard time sticking to any one tone. Here the brother's sober, square speech is set against Sonny's hip idioms, which in their inarticulate way are meant to point to deeper levels of experience. Yet at the final, the deepest level of experience, the transforming power of the jazz solo is described in unexpectedly religious terms: "And he was giving it back, as everything must be given back, so that, passing through death, it can live forever." The terms seem wrong; clearly this is not the voice of Sonny or his brother, it is the intrusive voice of Baldwin the boy preacher who has turned his back on the store front tabernacles but cannot forget the sound of angel's wings beating around his head.

Despite Baldwin's scornful rejection of the "God-shops," life is constantly weighed in the balance against an unearthly time when he rode the whirlwind of absolute love. The lives of the characters in these stories seem to posess an extra dimension of emptiness, because he sees them against the possibility of a very different kind of life: a life of ceremonies and mysteries touching the absolute. He is searching for another city and another country. Like the great moralizing novelists, he is a preacher; he writes to bear witness. It would be ridiculous, as well as rude, to tell him he should take another tack. My complaint is simply that the total hunger aching inside him has has driven him on to invest certain aspects of secular life—notably sex—with a blasphemous grace, and, alas, the grace is artistically unconvincing. The beauty of the language in *Go Tell It On the Mountain* brought the hero's experience of salvation to life; and, faithful to the spirit of the blues, Baldwin left much of the book's anguish unresolved. But in recent works he has made larger and larger claims for his various instruments of salvation, while the instruments themselves have become less and less convincing. When, in *Another Country,* Baldwin gives us the word about the redeeming majesty of the orgasm—multiracial, heterosexual, or homosexual— you sense a lack of artistic control, to say nothing of a loss of common sense.

The stories in this collection thus leave us with the problematic Baldwin of *Another Country,* with his rich promise, his prophet's ambition, his magnificent sense of urban desolation, his lapses of tone, and the spurious religiosity of his sex. There are no resolutions here, no new departures. The four first-rate stories—"The Outing," "Sonny's Blues," "Come Out the Wilderness," and "Previous Condition"—were all written before 1958. The title story seems to be a recent effort; it is reminiscent of, though not quite as terrible as, Baldwin's misguided play, *Blues for Mister Charlie* (1964). Here again, he attempts the compassionate feat of entering into the mind of a Southern racist, in this case a deputy sheriff dealing with civil rights demonstrations. Despite its gruesome stylized lynching scene, "Going to Meet the Man" has the same trivial effect as *Blues for Mister Charlie:* it appears that what all this racial fuss stems from is the white man's inability to get it up. After so much suffering and anguish, so many thousands gone, the indictment of the South that emerges is that it's square.

In *Notes of a Native Son* (1955) and *Nobody Knows Ny Name* (1961) Baldwin argued that part of the race problem was white America's refusal to confront reality, especially the reality of pain, tragedy, violence, sex, and death. This inability to understand forbidden impulses and secret terrors made it hard for the American to know himself; and from a crazy structure of inhibitions and lies followed the fantasies and projections which were the white picture of the Negro. It was a complex and profound argument, full of anger and understanding. Reading "Going to Meet the Man," you dimly recognize the outlines of the argument, reduced to inanely simple terms. It is almost like reading the Book of Job in the form of a comic.

James Baldwin is at his best as himself. His finest work is self-revelatory: the fictional selves who walk the troubled regions of his mind, or the dramatic self created in essays like *The Fire Next Time* (1963). This is a source of both weakness and strength. The weakness centers around his difficulty seeing his characters plainly through the distorted lenses of his self-pity and self-love. The strength lies in his ability to endow his experience, his feelings, with universal significance. This one figure, surrounded by darkness, is lit with a light of unbelievable intensity. Thus when Baldwin speaks of beauty, a particular undertone of yearning reminds you of the ugly child who put pennies over his eyes to make them go back. Nor are his encounters with the Negro churches or the Black Muslims simply reported; they are aspects of his lost self, the child who wondered in Harlem whose little boy he was. And the race troubles of America are the intersection of James Baldwin and history. Look what you have done to me, says the prophet whose country has endangered his salvation; look at my wounds. What is heard is something more, and something less, than the voice of the Negro. It is the voice of James Baldwin, crying to you from his private wilderness.

His Cardboard Lovers

Mario Puzo°

Tragedy calls out for a great artist, revolution for a true prophet. Six years ago James Baldwin predicted the black revolution that is now changing our society. His new novel, *Tell Me How Long the Train's Been Gone* is his attempt to re-create, as an artist this time, the tragic condition of the Negro in America. He has not been successful; this is a simpleminded, one-dimensional novel with mostly cardboard characters, a polemical rather than narrative tone, weak invention, and poor selection of incident. Individual scenes have people talking too much for what the author has to say and crucial events are "told" by one character to another rather than created. The construction of the novel is theatrical, tidily nailed into a predictable form.

It becomes clearer with each book he publishes that Baldwin's reputation is justified by his essays rather than his fiction. It may be that he is not a true or "born" novelist. But it must be said that his essays are as well written as any in our language; in them his thought and its utterance are nothing less than majestical. He has, also, the virtues of passion, serious intelligence and compassionate understanding of his fellow man. Yet it would seem that such gifts, enough for critics and moralists and other saintly figures, are not enough to insure the writing of good fiction. Novelists are born sinners and their salvation does not come so easily, and certainly the last role the artist should play is that of the prosecutor, the creator of a propaganda novel. A propaganda novel may be socially valuable *(Grapes of Wrath, Gentlemen's Agreement),* but it is not art.

Tell Me How Long the Train's Been Gone is written in the first-

° Reprinted from the *New York Times Book Review*, 23 June 1968, 5, 34, by permission of the author and the journal.

person singular, the "I" person, perhaps the most misused, most misunderstood technique today, from its irrelevance in Mailer's *The Deer Park* to its crippling effect on Styron's thought and style in *The Confessions of Nat Turner*. It doesn't do Baldwin any good here because the "I" person should never be used in a novel of social protest, which this is. Why? Because it doesn't work.

To be specific, the "I" person should be used in either of two ways (geniuses are excused): either to narrow the focus, to let the main character telling the story filter everything through his own particular vision of the world and of himself; and to get away with it he has to be someone with a special vision—nutty or eccentric, not balanced. (Donleavy's *The Ginger Man* is a good example.) Or the "I" person should be a minor character telling us about a main character who is basically unexplainable and perhaps would be unbelievable if presented in the third person *(The Great Gatsby)*. The best use of the "I" person is in Célines' *Death on the Installment Plan*, where you get the wild "I" person observing a great romantic character in the balloonist-inventor-charlatan, Courtial des Pereires. Both are nutty and both are a treat.

What the "I" person cannot be is a bore, or a moralist in a straight-out polemical way. In Baldwin's book the "I" person hero is both. His name is Leo Proudhammer; he has risen from the slums of Harlem to become the most famous Negro actor in America and the opening chapter has him suffering a massive heart attack on stage. We get flashbacks covering his life while he is being given emergency first aid and then while he is recovering in the hospital. The flashbacks are done in thin theatrical fashion rather than novelistic technique, and this doesn't help.

The flashbacks showing Leo Proudhammer as a child growing up in Harlem are the most successful sections of the book. His alienated, bitterly religious father (who appears often with slight variations in Baldwin's fiction) and Leo's brother Caleb are the only characters who come alive. Leo loves Caleb, and when the white society humiliates Caleb, arrests and beats him before the younger brother's eyes, Leo is traumatized. When Caleb is released from prison and runs away to California, Leo feels deserted and the effect on him is disastrous. He succumbs to all the seductions of the ghetto streets and finally becomes the kept boy of a pimp-gangster. Fascinating material but Baldwin just tells us what happened to Leo in a few lines; he doesn't show us, doesn't create it. And this is exactly where the use of the "I" person technique could have been effective.

Still, the relationship between the two brothers is always moving and sometimes heartbreaking. The family life is honestly portrayed. Here in the streets of Harlem, in the dark bedrooms, the dangerous hallways, the chanting churches, Baldwin is at his best. Leo as a child is an interesting and alive character. Unfortunately, the novel next moves into the phony milieu of the theatrical world, and we get Leo as an important actor who muses that the kiss he plants on a nurse's forehead will probably keep her from washing. The theater as background for a serious novel so earnest in tone is simply not right. Not here anyway.

Leo is 19 years old when he escapes Harlem and moves to Greenwich Village, sharing living space with a young, white, unmarried couple. Barbara is a pretty girl, Kentucky bred; Jerry is an amiable fellow of Italian parentage. By this time Leo is bisexual, but his relationship with the young couple is completely innocent. All three of them are concerned only with becoming actors and they finagle their way into the strawhat dramatic workshop of a famous theater guru, whose characterization is done with deadly wit.

Inevitably, Barbara and Leo become lovers. Jerry is terribly hurt but understands. Barbara and Leo have their troubles with the natives of the strawhat village, and finally this and other pressures make them split up. They remain close friends as they climb the ladder of success. In fact, Barbara is on stage with Leo when he suffers his heart attack 20 years later, and she helps nurse him back to health.

Leo finally finds happiness with a young Black militant named Christopher. Barbara seduces Christopher because she wants to recapture the young Leo (I think), Leo forgives them both (Christopher has an equally classy excuse), and everybody remains friends and lovers. Christopher takes Leo to some black-power meetings and Leo agrees that the blacks must get guns. Finally Leo, completely recovered from his heart attack, is again in the wings waiting for his cue, ready for work he loves. Ready for life!

If this makes the book sound like a soap opera, that's exactly right. White Barbara, white as snow, is right out of a slick magazine, flat as cardboard. At the end of the book Barbara tells Leo she has always loved him and will always continue to love him. Her lines are extravagant, theatrical; she will always come to him when he calls. Barbara gives this speech at the age of 39; she is rich, she is famous, she has been presented as a reasonably intelligent woman. She has known Leo for 20 years. And yet we are asked to believe that the only man in the whole world she can love forever is a Negro homosexual actor. This is a romantic condescension equal to anything in *Gone With the Wind,* in that Baldwin does not recognize a parallel revolution, the feminine against the masculine world. In the conception of Barbara's character, in the undying-devotion speech, Baldwin glorifies a sexual Uncle Tom.

Baldwin's greatest weakness as a novelist is his selection of creation of incident. Time and again his conclusions are not justified by narrative action. Too many of his characters are mere cardboard. There are scenes that are simply echoes of the literature of the thirties, and they were cornball even then.

It is possible that Baldwin believes this is not tactically the time for art, that polemical fiction can help the Negro cause more, that art is too strong, to gamy a dish for a prophet to offer now. And so he gives us propagandistic fiction, a readable book with a positive social value. If this is what he wants, he has been successful. But perhaps it is now time for Baldwin to forget the black revolution and start worrying about himself as an artist, who is the ultimate revolutionary.

A Quite Moving and Very
Traditional Celebration of Love   Joyce Carol Oates°

Though our turbulent era has certainly dismayed and overwhelmed many writers, forcing upon some the role of propagandist or, paradoxically, the role of the indifferent esthete, it is really the best possible time for most writers—the sheer variety of stances, the multiplicity of "styles" available to the serious writer, is amazing. Those who are bewildered by so many ostensibly warring points of view and who wish, naively, for a single code by which literature can be judged, must be reminded of the fact that whenever any reigning theory of esthetics subdues the others (as in the Augustan period), literature simply becomes less and less interesting to write.

James Baldwin's career has not been an even one, and his life as a writer cannot have been, so far, very placid. He has been both praised and, in recent years, denounced for the wrong reasons. The black writer, if he is not being patronized simply for being black, is in danger of being attacked for not being black enough. Or he is forced to represent a mass of people, his unique vision assumed to be symbolic of a collective vision. In some circles he cannot lose— his work will be praised without being read, which must be the worst possible fate for a serious writer. And, of course, there are circles, perhaps those nearest home, in which he cannot ever win—for there will be people who resent the mere fact of his speaking for them, whether he intends to speak for them or not.

°Reprinted from the *New York Times Book Review*, 26 May 1974, 1–2, by permission of the author and the journal.

If Beale Street Could Talk is Baldwin's 13th book and it might have been written, if not revised for publication, in the 1950's. Its suffering, bewildered people, trapped in what is referred to as the "garbage dump" of New York City—blacks constantly at the mercy of whites—have not even the psychological benefit of the Black Power and other radical movements to sustain them. Though their story should seem dated, it does not. And the peculiar fact of their being so politically helpless seems to have strengthened, in Baldwin's imagination at least, the deep, powerful bonds of emotion between them. *If Beale Street Could Talk* is a quite moving and very traditional celebration of love. It affirms not only love between a man and a woman, but love of a type that is dealt with only rarely in contemporary fiction—that between members of a family, which may involve extremes of sacrifice.

A sparse, slender narrative, told first-person by a 19-year-old black girl named Tish, *If Beale Street Could Talk* manages to be many things at the same time. It is economically, almost poetically constructed, and may certainly be read as a kind of allegory, which refuses conventional outbursts of violence, preferring to stress the provisional, tentative nature of our lives. A 22-year-old black man, a sculptor, is arrested and booked for a crime—rape of a Puerto Rican woman—which he did not commit. The only black man in a police line-up, he is "identified" by the distraught, confused woman, whose testimony is partly shaped by a white policeman. Fonny, the sculptor, is innocent, yet it is up to the accused and his family to prove "and to pay for proving" this simple fact.

His fiancée, Tish, is pregnant; the fact of her pregnancy is, at times, all that keeps them from utter despair. The baby—the prospect of a new life—is connected with blacks' "determination to be free." At the novel's end, Fonny is out on bail, his trial postponed indefinitely, neither free nor imprisoned but at least returned to the world of the living. As a parable stressing the irresolute nature of our destinies, white as well as black, the novel is quietly powerful, never straining or exaggerating for effect.

Baldwin certainly risked a great deal by putting his complex narrative, which involves a number of important characters, into the mouth of a young girl. Yet Tish's voice comes to seem absolutely natural and we learn to know her from the inside out. Even her flights of poetic fancy—involving rather subtle speculations upon the nature of male-female relationships, or black-white relationships, as well as her articulation of what it feels like to be pregnant—are convincing. Also convincing is Baldwin's insistence upon the primacy of emotions like love, hate, or terror: it is not sentimentality, but basic psychology, to acknowledge the fact that one person will die, and another survive simply because one has not the guarantee of a fundamental human bond, like love, while the other has. Fonny is saved from the psychic destruction experienced by other imprisoned blacks, because of Tish, his unborn baby and the desperate, heroic struggle of his family and Tish's to get him free. Even so, his father cannot endure the strain. Caught stealing on his job, he commits suicide almost at the very time his son is released on bail.

The novel progresses swiftly and suspensefully, but its dynamic movement is interior. Baldwin constantly understates the horror of his characters' situation in order to present them as human beings whom disaster has struck, rather than as blacks who have, typically, been victimized by whites and are therefore likely subjects for a novel. The work contains many sympathetic portraits of white people, especially Fonny's harassed white lawyer, whose position is hardly better than the blacks he defends. And, in a masterly stroke, Tish's mother travels to Puerto Rico in an attempt to reason with the woman who has accused her prospective son-in-law of rape, only to realize, there, a poverty and helplessness more extreme than that endured by the blacks of New York City. While Tish is able to give birth to her baby, despite the misery of her situation, the assaulted woman suffers a miscarriage and is taken away, evidently insane. Nearly everyone has been manipulated. The white policeman, Bell, seems a little crazy, driven by his own racism rather than his reason. He is a villain, of course (he has even shot and killed a 12-year-old black boy, some time earlier), but his villainy is made possible by a system of oppression closely tied up with the mind-boggling stupidities of the law.

For Baldwin, the injustice of Fonny's situation is self-evident, and by no means unique. "Whoever discovered America *deserved* to be dragged home, in chains, to die," Tish's mother declares near the conclusion of the novel. Fonny's friend, Daniel, has also been falsely arrested and falsely convicted of a crime, years before, and his spirit broken by the humiliation of jail and the fact—which Baldwin stresses, and which cannot be stressed too emphatically—that the most devastating weapon of the oppressor is that of psychological terror. Physical punishment, even death, may at times be preferable to an existence in which men are denied their manhood and any genuine prospects of controlling their own lives. Fonny's love for Tish can be undermined by the fact that, as a black man, he cannot always protect her from the random insults of whites.

Yet the novel is ultimately optimistic. It stresses the communal bond between members of an oppressed minority, especially between members of a family, which would probably not be experienced in happier times. As society disintegrates in a collective sense, smaller human units will become more and more important. Those who are without them, like Fonny's friend Daniel, will probably not survive.

Certainly they will not reproduce themselves. Fonny's real crime is "having his center inside him," but this is, ultimately, the means by which he survives. Others are less fortunate.

If Beale Street Could Talk is a moving, painful story. It is so vividly human and so obviously based upon reality, that it strikes us as timeless—an art that has not the slightest need of esthetic tricks, and even less need of fashionable apocalytic excesses.

Blues for Mr. Baldwin   Darryl Pinckney°

James Baldwin, born in Harlem in 1924, became a boy preacher when he was fourteen. He left the church when he was seventeen and transformed himself into a writer of extraordinary rhetorical refinement, but there remained in his style, in his baroque sense of grievance, the atmosphere of the pulpit. In works like *The Fire Next Time* (1963), an exalted rhetoric rushes out, as in a sermon, to meet the bitterness of American life.

In 1948, when Baldwin was twenty-four, he was seized by what appears to have been a claustrophobia of the spirit and went to France, from which he has never really returned. Exile freed him to contemplate his homeland. *Notes of a Native Son* (1955), a collection of essays striking in their subtlety of language, shows a mind deeply knowledgeable about the psychological costs of racism and skeptical toward the ideological complacencies and inherited ideas that define so much of the analysis of the racial conflict on both sides.

Moralistic fervor, a high literary seriousness, the authority of the survivor, of the witness—these qualities made Baldwin unique. In his best work, he is drawn to the ways in which life can go wildly wrong, to examinations of the damage done the individual by society. Another bloodied stone is always waiting to be turned over. A sense of mission has guided Baldwin's development as a writer. He was truly born with his subject matter, and yet for a long time his work showed a feeling of distrust for the promises of "pure" literature, a sense of its impotence, both personally and as a political weapon. In his youth Baldwin wanted to be identified not as a black but as a writer. It is a conflict he has never resolved.

Just Above My Head is a long and ambitious novel in which we

°Reprinted with permission from the *New York Review of Books,* 6 December 1979, 32–33. ©1979, Nyrev, Inc.

find again many of Baldwin's obsessions. He returns to the Harlem and the church of his first novel, *Go Tell It on the Mountain* (1953); to the homosexuality of *Giovanni's Room* (1955) and *Another Country* (1962); and to the social and political outrage that has inspired all his work. Whether the visions of the past are still vivid is another question.

Hall Montana, the narrator of *Just Above My Head,* tells the story of his dead brother Arthur, a celebrated gospel singer, and in so doing Hall hopes to make sense of his own life, shatter his grief. Arthur was called "the Soul Emperor," and Hall was his manager. When the novel opens, Arthur has been dead two years, of a heart attack in the basement men's room of a London pub. Hall is tolerant, loving, grateful for children and wife, filled with memory and family feeling, and also schooled in the hardships of being black. His voice, however, is not very fluent and this makes for something of a strain in such a long work. The burden of editorial omniscience, including what his brother felt while having sex, forces Hall's imagination to do more work than it can bear.

Hall is the witness to Arthur's life, and Baldwin, we feel, has compelled him to testify. The story takes the form of a saga, bringing in three decades of history and shared experiences. Not only does Hall remember the sufferings of his family and friends, but his memories continually shift to embrace a sweep of black life: family relations, work, the importance of music, the influence of religious feeling, the intensity of the Freedom Movement. This is a story of costly, wearying struggle, mainly concentrating on Hall, his brother Arthur, and their lifelong friend, Julia Miller.

Julia has been a child evangelist, willful and arrogant, spoiled by possessive parents, but she has lost her faith after the death of her mother and fallen into a violent, incestuous relationship with her dandyish, weak father. The Montana family helps her to escape to New Orleans. Later, back in New York, she becomes Hall's mistress. She abandons him and goes to Africa, where, in search of liberating experience, she takes a lover. Her younger brother Jimmy, open and innocent, becomes Arthur's accompanist and devoted lover. Even when they are flung apart, these four people appear as members of a troubled, tightly knit family, each preoccupied with the feelings of the others. Hall's tone is so intense and so sprawling, that everyone who has entered his or Arthur's life, however briefly, is touched by it.

Most of the action takes place off stage. Intimates and strangers race in and out of the book. Arthur is always on tour—with his quartet as a young man in the South; or as an increasingly famous solo performer in Canada and Europe. The young Hall is drafted, and sent to Korea. Julia is swept off to Abidjan. The novel is composed mostly of earnest conversations about unfulfilled longings and absent friends—testimony given at bars, meals with the family, and other social events.

> She was talking to me about something which was happening to *us*.
> This was the strangest and most grueling sign of respect anyone had given me, in all my life.
> "And so, I had to think about it. *I* knew what was holding me here."
> She reached out and put one hand in mine, for a moment.
> "I would have liked to be able to have said—to myself—that it was you. But I would have been lying—to myself, and to you, and I love you too much for that."
> She dropped my hand, and nibbled at her rice. The restaurant was full, but not yet inundated, we had, for a moment, a haven.

A "haven," one might say, from the agitated movements, the abrupt arrivals and departures that are intended to satisfy the need to have something happen in this novel. Here, as throughout Baldwin's other work, flight is at the center of the psychological drama. The characters believe in the possibilities of another evening, a different place, a new face. The world is revealed to them at night, in the hours of nakedness, drinking, and truth-telling.

Although Hall tells many detailed anecdotes of the adolescent years of Julia and the two brothers, particularly Arthur, as they move into maturity his narration becomes more urgent and elliptical, as if he were uneasily aware that the story he wished to tell is too large. Crucial moments that would help us understand what he and his brother were going through are only hinted at. For instance, Hall mentions that there were troubles near the end of Arthur's life, that he is said to have suffered from dissipation and cruelties and weariness. But Hall never returns to any of this, so we learn an important part of Arthur's fate only through rumor.

Arthur himself never emerges from the shadows of his brother's descriptions, but it is clear that he is very different from the subversive heroes of Baldwin's earlier novels. He is homosexual, but seen sentimentally, continually as a member of a family, the doting younger brother, the loving son. He is meant to be a kind of artist hero, hardworking, dedicated, tragically undone by the rages of their lives. He unfortunately lacks the willfulness and chaotic interest of other artists in Baldwin's fiction—the jazz musician Rufus Scott in *Another Country,* the actor Leo Proudhammer in *Tell Me How Long the Train's Been Gone* (1968). For Baldwin, the time for a daring portrayal of the homosexual as outcast appears to have passed. He seems now to be trying to make a sentimental truce between the outcast and the family, meaning the black community. Arthur goes to bed with many young lovers and longs to be "married" to them. In fact, he gets married as a boy, when he is fourteen, to Crunch, eighteen, a member of the gospel quartet in which Arthur gets his first professional experience in the Harlem churches and on the road in the South. Crunch is a repentant lady killer.

In *Nobody Knows My Name* (1961), Baldwin wrote, "In most of the novels written by Negroes until today . . . there is a great space where sex ought to be; and what usually fills this space is violence." He himself confronted the subjects of interracial sex and homosexual encounters in *Another Country.* Sexual honesty contained healing possibilities for the disturbed psyche. "He held Eric very tightly and covered Eric's body with his own, as though he were shielding him from the falling heavens." However, in this new work, Arthur sees his homosexuality as a liability, a potential source of rejection. "But nothing less than confession is demanded of him. He dreams of Jimmy, and comes, almost, to prefer the dream because dreams appear to be harmless; dreams don't hurt. Dreams don't love, either, which is how we drown. Arthur had to pull himself to a place where he could say to Paul, his father, and to Hall, his brother, and to all the world, and to *his* Maker, *Take me as I am!*"

For Baldwin, it once seemed possible that spiritual bondage could be overcome by belief in a transcendent passion. Freedom from sexual and racial bigotry was the only redemptive possibility for the individual confined and menaced by society. In Baldwin's fiction homosexuality is symbolic of a liberated condition; but in *Just Above My Head* this theme is dropped—rejected, one might say—by having the homosexual characters imitate heterosexual behavior. By the time Arthur dies, he and Jimmy have been married fourteen years, complete with in-laws.

The anxious tone of this novel is a long way from the romantic melancholy of *Giovanni's Room,* a book neglected not only because of its homosexual protagonists but also because in it Baldwin was writing exclusively about white characters, though he was hardly the first black writer to do so.

> Until I die there will be moments, moments seeming to rise up out of the ground like Macbeth's witches, when his face will come before me, that face in all its changes, when the exact timbre of his voice and tricks of his speech will nearly burst my ears, when his smell will overpower my nostrils. Sometimes in the days which are coming—God grant me the grace to live them—in the glare of the grey morning, sourmouthed, eyelids raw and red, hair tangled and damp from my stormy sleep, facing, over coffee and cigarette smoke, last night's impenetrable, meaningless boy who will shortly rise and vanish like the smoke, I will see Giovanni again, as he was that night, so vivid, so winning, all of the light of that gloomy tunnel trapped around his head.

Abandoning his idealism about love, Baldwin now writes sentimentally not only about Arthur but about the entire Montana family. The parents are wise, forgiving, and everyone is uniformly resilient and "caring." If Baldwin means to honor the family as one of the reasons why blacks have, if nothing else, survived, his way of doing so is hardly convincing. Giving to the family generous amounts of noble qualities results in a neat symmetry: *us* versus *them.* The hagiographic approach helps to account for the flatness and didacticism of this work, as it did of Baldwin's last novel, *If Beale Street Could Talk* (1974), a book that was also dogmatic in its insistence on families and marriage as joyous alliances against an oppressively conceived "them." From Baldwin's other writings, one knows he has had a far more complicated idea of the family.

Increasing disillusionment over the years may have led Baldwin to search for something like a "people's book." But there is a repetitious and inert quality to *Just Above My Head.* Attempting to be earthy, to render a vernacular, black speech, Baldwin loses something when he declines to use the subtle language of his essays. In many ways the bombast in Hall's narration creates not a closeness to the material but a peculiar distance from it. In using a kind of ordinary language, hoping for what Richard Wright once called "the folk utterance," Baldwin has denied himself the natural lyrical mode of expression for which he has such a high gift.

Eldridge Cleaver's irresponsible attack in *Soul On Ice* may help to explain the turn in Baldwin's work. Cleaver claimed that Baldwin's work revealed a hatred of blacks, of himself, and a sycophantic love for whites, manifested in a racial death wish. Baldwin, according to Cleaver, attacked Wright's *Native Son* and dismissed Norman Mailer's *The White Negro* because he despised and feared masculinity. Cleaver also described the black homosexual as counterrevolutionary, castrated by the white man. His assault was doubtless prompted not only by the propaganda of Black Manhood but also by his own anti-intellectualism. The intimidation of Baldwin was extreme; along with many other black writers he faced the threat of being branded as a collaborator. Even as late as 1972, Baldwin could only answer by saying that he thought Cleaver merely felt impelled to issue a warning because he saw Baldwin as "dangerously odd, . . . of too much use to the Establishment to be trusted by blacks."

The fury of the Black Power movement seemed to demand of Baldwin a new set of definitions with which to express his loathing of America's racial troubles. In the long essay *No Name in the Streets* (1971), he charged Western societies with the "lie of their pretended humanism"; he once described how the "irresponsibility and cowardice" of the intellectual community during the McCarthy era first alerted him to the hypocrisy of rational liberalism. The political events of the Sixties—upheavals, assassinations, and secret police persecutions—fully confirmed his suspicions. Baldwin had made a choice, one he hoped to realize in his writing.

As Harold Cruse pointed out, however, Baldwin was not much interested in identifying social and economic causes. He always conceived of racial and political injustice as deriving from sin and requiring salvation, an argument rooted in his Christian training. His many exhortations to collective conscience went unheard. The nation did not atone for the sin of slavery and still moves away, indifferent, unchastised. Baldwin's exasperation with this "emotional poverty" has brought him to repudiate most of the claims of Western culture— "I don't believe in the wagons that bring bread to humanity"—and to seek a refuge, however delusory, in black solidarity.

It would appear from this book that he is weary of battling alone and wishes for a wider, more popular acceptance, a coming home to the "folk." There is a sad irony here. When Baldwin was young, in Paris, he quarreled with his "spiritual father," Richard Wright, over Baldwin's attack on the genre of protest novels. Wright felt betrayed and Baldwin defended himself by saying that all literature may be protest but not all protest was literature. Later, when recalling Wright's isolation from other blacks in Paris, his aloneness, his alienation, Baldwin wrote: "I could not help feeling: *Be Careful. Time is passing for you, too, and this may be happening to you one day.*" Baldwin now writes as if he is haunted by this prophecy. *Just Above My Head,* with its forced polemical tone, represents a conversion of sorts, a conversion to simplicities that so fine a mind as Baldwin's cannot embrace without grave loss.

Religious Symbolism and Psychic Reality in Baldwin's *Go Tell It on the Mountain*   Shirley S. Allen°

James Baldwin's first novel, *Go Tell It on the Mountain,* deserves a higher place in critical esteem than it has generally been accorded.

°Reprinted from *CLA Journal* 19 (1975):173–99, by permission of the author and the journal.

Although critics have recognized its widespread appeal, often asserting that it is Baldwin's best work, and although teachers of literature have incorporated it into the standard curriculum, they assume that the work is primarily important as an interpretation of "the black experience," comparing it with *Invisible Man, Native Son,* and Baldwin's own essays.[1] Certainly, *Go Tell It on the Mountain* is an authentic and convincing presentation of a wide range of that experience from the days of slavery in the South to the Harlem of Baldwin's youth, and obviously Baldwin weaves the black-versus-white theme into the central conflict as inextricably as it is woven into the daily consciousness of the characters; but the major conflict of this novel, unlike *Invisible Man* and *Native Son,* is not black against white, but the more universal problem of a youth achieving maturity, with literary parallels in *David Copperfield, Great Expectations, The Brothers Karamazov,* and Hawthorne's "My Kinsman, Major Molineux." Its excellence as a "Negro novel" has obscured its relevance to other human concerns, particularly the process described by the psychiatrist Rollo May in *Man's Search for Himself* (which appeared in the same year as Baldwin's novel) as "cutting the psychological umbilical cord."[2] The central action of the novel is John's initiation into manhood—a ritual symbolization of the psychological step from dependence to a sense of self; but most critics describe the conversion as the acceptance of his blackness.[3]

A contributing factor to the misinterpretation of the novel is Baldwin's extensive use of Biblical allusion and Christian ritual for symbolic expression of the psychic realities he wishes the reader to experience. Although critics have commented on the religious setting, they have generally missed its symbolic importance. Colin MacInnes, for example, remarks that the story is "saturated with religious feeling" like *The Scarlet Letter* and *Pilgrim's Progress,* but discusses the religion's effects—"usually repellent"—on the lives of the characters rather than its symbolic use.[4] John R. May finds evidence of an apocalyptic theme and D. E. Foster of the theme of the Fall, but in both cases the tendency to look for themes typical of black writers obscures insight into the pervasive religious symbolism peculiar to this novel,[5] just as for other critics the symbolism is obscured by their effort to describe the novel as a typical illustration of the Adamic myth in American literature.[6] Howard M. Harper speaks of the specific use of Biblical symbolism when he points out the identification of the hero with John the Baptist, but he fails to see the relevance of "The Seventh Day"—the title of Part One—perhaps because he is unaware that in Biblical terms Saturday, not Sunday, is the seventh day.[7] Because the symbolism is essential to understanding *Go Tell It on the Mountain,* critics, missing the clues, have found fault with

Baldwin's art. So, Marcus Klein writes, "In fact, the dark that John goes through is not so substantial as the scheme of the novel hopes for. Much of it is just Biblical reference. John doesn't really know the lives of his aunt, his stepfather, and his mother. Only the reader does. And that is a technical fault.[8] Perhaps a better understanding of the symbolism will lead to critical re-evaluation, since Baldwin's most serious "technical fault" may be his assumption that most readers are as familiar with the Bible as the members of his childhood Harlem community were.

I

From the very beginning of the novel Baldwin clearly indicates the central importance of the religious symbolism. The title, taken from a Negro spiritual, suggests not only the basic Christian setting of the action, but also the kind of symbolism we are to expect. In different versions of the folk hymn the command, "Go tell it," refers to the good news (gospel) that "Jesus Christ is born" or to the message of Moses to the Pharaoh, "Let my people go." The ambiguity of the allusion in the title is intentional and also suggests the unity of Old Testament and New Testament faith that is characteristic of the Christian belief described in the novel—the teachings of a sect formed from Baptist practices and Calvinist doctrines, grounded in frequent reading of the King James translation of the Bible, and influenced by the needs, hopes, and artistic expression of Negro slaves. A poignant example of the perfect blending in Baldwin's novel of the Old Covenant with the New occurs in the old black woman's prayer for her daughter Florence as the family huddle in their dark cabin listening for the hoofbeats of white riders intent on rape and arson: "Lord, sprinkle the doorpost of this house with the blood of the Lamb to keep all the wicked men away."[9] The doctrine of the Paschal Lamb is intuitively grasped by a people who identify themselves with the children of Israel in Egypt and the suffering Christians in the early Roman empire.

This same coupling of Exodus with the Book of Revelation occurs in the song "Go Tell It on the Mountain" when the speaker asks, "Who's that yonder dressed in white?" and is answered, "Must be the children of the Israelities." The question is an echo of the question put to John of Patmos in Revelation 13:14. "Who are these robed in white?" and therefore suggests the identification of the children of Israel with the "saved" in John's apocalyptic vision. The cry, "Go tell it!" thus becomes the cry of all the faithful from the beginning of history to the judgment day; and the phrase "on the mountain" further links Moses' Mount Sinai and John's Mount Zion with one of the best passages in scripture: the second Isaiah's exhortation to the

Jewish exiles, "O Zion, that bringest good tidings, get thee up into the high mountain; O Jerusalem, that bringest good tidings, lift up thy voice with strength."

By this multiplicity of Biblical allusion, the cry "Go tell it on the mountain" is much more than the announcement of good news: it is a shout of faith in ultimate victory while the struggle and suffering are still going on. Jesus is born, but he has still to face the cross. The Israelities still have to survive the wilderness and conquer the promised land, the freed captives have to cross the desert and rebuild Jerusalem, and the seventh seal has yet to be opened before God will "wipe away all tears from their eyes." Because of all the allusions, all of which Baldwin reiterates in the course of the novel, the title becomes symbolic of the specific human situation when a costly break with the past has been made and a new road, beset with dangers but promising salvation, has been undertaken. This is clearly the situation of the protagonist at the end of the novel.

Immediately after the title Baldwin has placed a quotation from the same chapter of Isaiah alluded to in the title: "They that wait upon the Lord shall renew their strength; they shall mount up with wings like eagles; they shall run and not be weary, they shall walk and not faint." This epigraph reinforces the symbolism of the title by making specific its allusion to the situation in Isaiah 40 where the prophet is promising the Lord's help to the released captives in their effort to cross the desert and shout from the mountain top the good news to the cities of Judah. Their release is thus symbolically identified with the main action of the novel, John's release from childish dependence on his parents; and therefore, the prophet's promise of the Lord's protection applies also to John in his hazardous journey through the wilderness of life. On the last page of the novel as John stands on the threshold of his family's house, shaken by the emotional trauma of his release and trembling with fear that he may fail in his new role of adult, Elisha says to him, "Run on, little brother. . . . Don't you get weary."[10] Those who find the novel's ending ambiguous fail to catch in Elisha's words the echo of Isaiah's promise, "They shall run and not be weary," as well as the shout of faith in ultimate victory which is implied symbolically by the title.

Baldwin's use of Biblical allusion in the title and the first epigraph to give symbolic meaning to John's conversion and to interpret the event is typical of his use of symbolism throughout the novel. Each of the three parts has a title and two epigraphs referring to the Bible or Christian hymns, and each of the prayers in Part Two begins with a quotation from a hymn. Two of Gabriel's sermons, based on Biblical texts, are paraphrased at some length. The thoughts and spoken words of almost all the characters are larded with passages from the King James version, and the major characters are identified with their favorite texts of scripture. The doctrines, ritual, songs, and visual symbols of the Baptist church are equally pervasive in the words and events of the novel. But all this religious apparatus, like the central scene of the tarry service itself, is used not simply as psychological and social milieu for the action, but also to give symbolic expression and archetypal meaning to the characters and events. Biblical allusion in *Go Tell It on the Mountain* serves some of the same purposes as the Homeric myth in *Ulysses* and the Olympic paraphernalia in *The Centaur,* but Baldwin's use of the religious apparatus is more like that of Dostoyevsky in The *Brothers Karamazov* than that of Joyce and Updike in one important respect: the symbolism arises naturally out of the setting. This very integration of symbolic apparatus and milieu is perhaps the reason critics have missed the symbolism—a case of not seeing the forest for the trees.

In Part One, Baldwin uses Biblical allusion to set the major conflict in much larger dimensions than the specific situation of the fourteen-year-old John Grimes confronting his stepfather in problems of family relationships, Christian belief, and racial attitudes. The title of this part, "The Seventh Day," gives a more universal significance with its double allusion to the creation myth in Genesis and the holiness of the Sabbath in Mosaic law. John's fourteenth birthday is like the seventh day of creation in that it marks the end of the creative process for him—the moment at which a completed, whole individual emerges from the process that begins in his mother's womb and continues through the nurtured years until the psychological umbilical cord is cut. His birthday falls on Saturday, the Biblical Sabbath, a day set apart for making one's account with God. The relevance of this symbolism to the psychic realities of John's situation is made immediately clear as the reader is plunged into John's thoughts upon awakening. He is obsessed with fear of his father's domination, troubled by awareness of his sexual maturity, reluctant to leave his mother's protection, and feeling pressure from all sides urging him to take his stand among the adults of the church community in which he lives. The two epigraphs following the title of this part further establish the nature of the conflict in symbolic terms. The quotation from Revelation invites "whoever will" to "take the water of life freely," while the quotation from the church song expresses John's fear of accepting the invitation: "I looked down the line, / And I wondered."

The effect of this religious symbolism is to keep the reader aware of the universal elements in John's struggle so that its significance will not be lost amid the specific details and particular persons complicating his conflict. The symbolism prevents us, for example, from mistaking John's peculiar problem as a black taking his place in a society dominated by whites for the more basic problem, common to all humanity, of a child taking his place in adult society. The symbolism also keeps us from being sidetracked by the specific personality of Gabriel or the fact that he is not John's real father, since he is named for the angel of the Annunciation and therefore symbolically is the agency of fatherhood. We are to see John in the larger view as a human child struggling against dependency and finding a sense of his own selfhood through the initiation rite practiced in his community, even though Baldwin has fully realized that struggle in the specific circumstances of Harlem, the fully rounded human characters of the Grimes family, and the particular heritage of American Negro religion.

II

Even the aspects of John's struggle that are peculiar to his situation—racial persecution, his father's preference of his younger brother, and the ritual practices of the Baptist sect—are carefully linked to archetypal patterns by means of Biblical allusion and religious symbolism.

The racial situation is lifted to a more universal plane by equation of the Negroes' sufferings in America with those of the children of Israel in Egypt and the early Christians in the Roman Empire. This symbolic identification is not only implied by many allusions throughout the novel, but also specifically stated in Florence's account of the days of slavery (p. 76).

Moreover, John himself is identified with the saint John who was on Patmos in the time of Roman persecution. Although the names Gabriel and Elizabeth and the allusion in the novel's title to the herald of the advent of the Messiah suggest symbolic linking of John Grimes with John the Baptist, Baldwin has more clearly identified him with the John of Revelation. For example, when John setting off to celebrate his birthday emerges from Harlem into midtown Manhattan, he runs up a hill of Central Park "like a madman" and looks down with a feeling of exultation on the "shining city which his ancestors had seen with longing from far away" (p. 35). The parallel with John of Patmos glimpsing the New Jerusalem could hardly be missed—"And he carried me away in the spirit to a great and high mountain, and showed me that great city"—but Baldwin makes identification sure by using a turn of speech characteristic of the Book of Revelation in the King James translation, the repetition of the name "John" after the personal pronoun. "Then I John saw the holy city" is deliberately mimicked in Baldwin's "Then he, John, felt like a giant." Furthermore, at the climax of the novel when John Grimes is in the throes of his mystical experience, he gains strength to struggle toward the light by remembering words from the Negro spiritual about John of Patmos:

I, John, saw the future, way up in the middle of the air . . .
I, John, saw a number, way in the middle of the air. (p. 229)

I, John, saw a city, way in the middle of the air,
Waiting, waiting, waiting up there. (p. 232)

Through such symbolic identification Baldwin lifts his hero's problem of being a victim of persecution out of his particular racial situation in twentieth-century United States and places it in a larger historical and religious context.

He gives a still more universal significance to the black-versus-white problem by another device of religious symbolism. During the first major episode of the novel, Harlem and, by implication, the black race are linked with dust and dirt. First he describes the kitchen that is constantly scrubbed but which "no labor can ever make . . . clean;" then he gives John's inner cry against his father, "He who is filthy, let him be filthy still"; and immediately afterward he describes John's Saturday morning task of dusting and sweeping the front room (pp. 21, 22, 27). When we remember that the family name is Grimes, we accept this symbolic identification of John's environment and heritage with dust. But the dust itself is described in highly connotative words that link it symbolically with sin. The dirt "triumphs" beneath the sink; it lives behind the stove 'in delirious communion with the corrupted wall;" and it is piled on the rug by "demons" (pp. 21, 27). John's cry against his father echoes John of Patmos, speaking of sinners not to be saved on the judgment day. Before the tarry service can begin, the church must be dusted, swept, and mopped; but even so when John is lying on the floor before the altar, there is dust in his nostrils, and he must be lifted out of the dust to be saved. So, symbolically, as John's salvation will come only by rising above the innate or inherited sinfulness of man, so his achievement of maturity or self-identity will come only by rising above the innate and inherited conditions of race, locality, and family. The linking of Harlem with dust and of dust with sin makes clear that John is struggling against forces more universal than white persecution of blacks in America.

Similarly, Baldwin takes pains to set John's relationship to Gabriel against archetypal patterns in order to emphasize the universal aspects of their conflict. Critics who have accused Baldwin of sentimentality and lack of artistic distance for making Gabriel John's stepfather, like those who find it a technical fault that the true relationship is never revealed to John, have overlooked the symbolism.[11] With consummate artistry Baldwin has reversed the usual situation of an adolescent searching for his own identity: whereas it is fairly common for a fourteen-year-old to wish that his parents were not his real parents—a psychological result of the incompatibility he feels between himself and them, John never suspects that his father is not his real father. John finds the strength (or is given the grace) to stand up to his father without having a basis for questioning Gabriel's right to authority over him, and therefore Baldwin is not guilty of providing an easy way out for his hero. At the same time the reader, knowing Gabriel's history, sees John's conviction that his father doesn't love him as something more than a projection of adolescent insecurity. This ironic inversion suggests that the psychic reality of an Oedipal situation may reflect external reality.

Baldwin, by means of Biblical allusion, substitutes Hebrew archetypes for the Freudian Greek myth in interpreting the father-son confrontation. Gabriel sees the situation in terms of Abraham and Ishmael when he thinks, "Only the son of the bondwoman stood where the rightful heir should stand" (p. 128). He has already used as a text for one of his sermons Paul's translation of the story (in Galations 4:21–31) into an analogy to explain the difference between those bound by the law and the "children of promise" (p. 117). To Gabriel, John is Ishmael, "born after the flesh," and so must be exiled in order to protect the inheritance for Roy, the true son of the promise, Isaac.[12]

But Baldwin does not allow us to accept Gabriel's view of the father-son conflict. In this case as in several others, he shows us by use of the very religious faith Gabriel professes that Gabriel has misconceived his own relationship to scriptural paradigms. John is not Ishmael, but Jacob, who supplanted his brother Esau as the accepted heir against the wishes of his father and with his mother's encouragement. The symbolic identification is prepared for in the early episodes of the novel, where John is encouraged by his mother and Roy is clearly regarded by his father as his true heir; and it is made explicit before the end of Part One in the wrestling scene before the beginning of the tarry service. Before Jacob could claim the birthright, won on the human level by "buying" it from Esau and by tricking his father into giving it, he had to wrestle with an angel of the Lord. So John on the night of his initiation into the community of saints wrestles with a strong and holy young man who represents the Lord. Baldwin describes John's wrestling with Elisha in language that identifies it as more than a playful encounter and makes it a serious test of John's strength. John sees his victory as a manifestation of his power and is "filled with a wild delight" (p. 58). Baldwin has already prepared the reader for Elisha's role as John's guardian angel by giving some history of their friendship and emphasizing Elisha's holiness, but more explicitly he identifies Elisha after the wrestling match as a "young man in the Lord; who, a priest after the order of Melchizedek, had been given power over death and Hell"—recalling the words and Messianic connotations of Psalm 110. Throughout John's ordeal on the threshing floor Elisha continues his symbolic role as the angel of the Lord: his interposed body prevents Gabriel from striking his stepson (p. 171); his voice guides John through the dark; and his parting kiss is called "the seal ineffaceable forever" like the seal of God on the foreheads of the saved in the Book of Revelation (p. 253). Like Jacob, John wrestles with an angel of the Lord to win his place as the recipient of his father's reluctant blessing and as the heir to leadership of the chosen people in spite of his brother's birth-based claim. Like Jacob, who received the new name Israel, John wins his Christian (baptismal) name: " 'He come through,' cried Elisha, 'didn't he, Deacon Grimes? The Lord done laid him out, and turned him around and wrote his *new* name down in glory' " (pp. 252–253). Baldwin's italics, besides emphasizing the identification with Jacob and the relation to Christian doctrine, remind us that John's real name is not Grimes, although he may never know it. By use of the Jacob archetype, Baldwin suggests that as the spirit has triumphed over the flesh in John's conversion, so in psychic terms his consciousness of self has overcome adverse family circumstances.

Similarly, the sectarian ritual of the Temple of the Fire Baptized becomes symbolic of a more universal human experience through association with Biblical patterns. The ritual colors of the store-front church are given their full Biblical significance by careful use of suggestive language in the first part of the novel. The red altar cloth is called "scarlet," and the golden cross glows "like smothered fire." The saints are dressed in white "from crown to toe," and their white caps seem "to glow in the charged air like crowns." Such metaphors and connotative words give the colors the symbolic meaning they have for Isaiah—"Though your sins be as scarlet, they shall be as white as snow"—and for John of Patmos in his vision of the golden Jerusalem.

Then in Part Two these same colors are carefully associated with particular psychological perceptions in the lives of John's family, especially of Gabriel. His potential for fatherhood is described as "white seed." His passion for Esther is identified with scarlet: "She was associated in his mind with flame; with fiery leaves in the autumn, and the fiery sun going down in the evening over the farthest hill, and with the eternal fires of Hell" (p. 130). In his dream of God's promise to him on the top of the mountain, Gabriel sees himself as "all golden" among the elect in their white robes (p. 126). And when he learns that Esther is carrying his baby, a high window of the house turns turns to "spun gold" (p. 146).

In Part Three the colors are used to express both John's religious experience and his psychic perceptions about his parents. He sees the cross on the altar as a "golden barrier" keeping his father, mother, aunt, and friend from coming down to help him (p. 221). Thus it becomes a symbol for both the religious salvation and the adulthood that separate them from him while suggesting the isolation felt both by a soul in the presence of God and by a youth who must throw off childish dependence. John then thinks of the "mountaintop, where he longed to be, where the sun would cover him like a cloth of gold (p. 223). This deliberate echo of Gabriel's dream symbolizes John's need to take his rightful place as an adult by receiving the covenant traditionally handed down by father to eldest son, at the same time suggesting that this is God's promised salvation. That he sees "his mother dressed in scarlet and his father dressed in white" indicates his psychological perception of the relationship between his parents (p. 227). And finally, his salvation is achieved when he grasps the Christian doctrine that God accepts and dwells with *sinful* man—an understanding that comes to him through the symbolic colors of the ritual of the Lord's Supper:

> Now this service was in a great, high room, a room made golden by the light of the sun; and the room was filled with a multitude of people, all in long, white robes, the women with covered heads. They sat at a long, bare, wooden table. They broke at this table flat, unsalted bread, which was the body of the Lord, and drank from a heavy silver cup the scarlet wine of His blood. Then he saw that they were barefoot, and that their feet were stained with this same blood. (p. 231)

That the blood of salvation is scarlet, the color of sin, reveals to John the possibility of his own eligibility; and then he sees the Lord, and the darkness is filled with light: "The light and the darkness had kissed each other, and were married now, forever, in the life and vision of John's soul" (p. 232).

On the religious level, the colors express his conversion—his understanding and acceptance of the central Christian belief. On the psychological level, the colors express his growth into maturity through the perceptions that his sexual impulses are common to humanity (even his parents), that both black and white men share the heritage of sin in the "army of darkness," and that the golden cloak of manhood belongs to him in spite of his father's opinion.

Besides color, another type of imagery relates John's experience in the tarry service to more catholic Christian ritual and through it to universal human experience. Because John has reached the age at which he is expected to make his commitment to the church, to be "saved," in the presence of the community, this ritual performance is the equivalent of confirmation, bar mitzvah, and the initiation rites of many other religious communities. In Christian doctrine, however, the true initiation rite is baptism, and therefore the practice of confirmation, becoming a member of the congregation, or "making your witness"—made necessary by the long-established practice of infant baptism—is considered a completion of the baptismal rite. Baldwin gives John's experience its basic Christian significance by describing it in terms of the imagery of birth and thus emphasizing the traditional concept of baptism as regeneration accomplished after symbolic death by drowning. From the moment John begins to face his decision, his descent into darkness is described as drowning: "Their faces, and their attitudes, and their many voices rising as one voice made John think of the deepest valley, the longest night, of Peter and Paul in the dungeon cell, one praying while the other sang; or of endless, depthless swelling water, and no dry land in sight, the true believer clinging to a spar" (p. 88). His mind is "awash with visions;" he is "at the mercy of this sea;" and he goes down "to the bottom of the sea" (pp. 89, 166, 221). This sea is described in imagery and connotative words that link it both with the amniotic fluid surrounding a foetus and with the depths of the subconscious:

> There was an awful silence at the bottom of John's mind, a dreadful weight, a dreadful speculation. And not even a speculation, but a deep, deep turning, as of something huge, black, shapeless, for ages dead on the ocean floor, that now felt its rest disturbed by a faint, far wind, which bid it: "Arise." And this weight began to move at the bottom of John's mind, in a silence like the silence of the void before creation. (p. 89)

As the tarry service goes on, Baldwin makes the birth metaphor an explicit analogy for Christian conversion:

> With this cry, and the echoing cries, the tarry service moved from its first stage of steady murmuring, broken by moans and now and again an isolated cry, into that stage of tears and groaning, of calling aloud and singing, which was like the labor of a woman about to be delivered of her child. On this threshing-floor the child was the soul that struggled to the light, and it was the church that was in labor, that did not cease to push and pull. . . . For the rebirth of the soul was perpetual. (p. 127)

And at the same time John's experience as the child about to be born, facing "this staring, waiting mouth," is explicitly connected with his confrontation of knowledge about his parents that is buried in his subconscious—thoughts he has never before confronted "in such a narrow place" (p. 164). As he admits to himself his hatred of his father, he realizes that "in the darkness of his heart" is "something he must find"; and the process of probing his subconscious is again described in sea imagery: "His mind was like the sea itself: troubled, and too deep for the bravest man's descent, throwing up now and again, for the naked eye to wonder at, treasure and debris long forgotten on the bottom" (p. 166). That this process of fighting through the darkness of the mind is necessary to achieve both the religious salvation and psychological maturity is suggested by the linking of both in the birth imagery of Elizabeth's prayer:

> She thought of that far-off day when John had come into the world— that moment, the beginning of her life and death. . . . How long she had bled, and sweated, and cried, no language on earth could tell—how long she had crawled through darkness she would never, never know. There, her beginning, and she fought through darkness still; toward that moment when she would make her peace with God, when she would hear Him speak . . . as, in that other darkness, after eternity, she heard John cry. As now, in the sudden silence, she heard him cry: not the cry of the child, newborn, before the common light of earth; but the cry of the man-child, bestial, before the light that comes down from Heaven. (p. 216)

In the third part John's mental and physical anguish on the threshing floor is described in birth imagery. The rhythmic chanting of the saints and the beating of their feet are like throbbing blood vessels and muscular contractions; sudden silences are like the intermission of labor, which he knows will resume; and the voice that calls, "Go through," is the final push through the narrow passage. His painful struggle to face subconscious knowledge matches this physical pattern of crescendo and intermission as each new climax of insight is followed by utter exhaustion and fear. And at the end of his ordeal John is told to rise up and "talk about the Lord's deliverance" (p. 234). His heart is "newborn and fragile," and he speaks "in the new voice God had given him." This figurative language enables us to see John's conversion as a second birth both in the Christian sense of regeneration and in the psychological sense of stepping from childhood into maturity, becoming fully separated from the parental womb and speaking in a manly voice instead of a childish treble. Although the second birth is only symbolically accomplished in a particular event and we are aware that John's new state is not the end of the struggle—the "terrors of the night" are not finished— we are given assurance of his victory in both the religious and psychological spheres by the reiteration in the speeches of Praying Mother Washington and Brother Elisha of Isaiah's promise: "They shall run and not be weary."

III

The main action of *Go Tell It on the Mountain* is thus clarified and linked with universal human experience through the use of religious symbolism; but even more remarkable, perhaps, is Baldwin's use of Biblical allusion to explain the psychic realities of three other characters: Florence, Gabriel, and Elizabeth—the older generation from which John must differentiate himself to find his own identity. Some critics have objected to the extensive use of flashbacks in this novel and to the tenuousness of their connection with the main action.[13] Many of these objections can be removed, I believe, by a better understanding of the religious symbolism that links the events recounted in "The Prayers of the Saints" with the psychological perceptions John attains on the threshing floor. The use of colors discussed above is only one of several devices that integrate the facts of his parents' lives, which he does not know, with his new awareness of the true relationships, which he grasps psychologically during his ritual initiation into manhood.

In the basic structure of the novel the prayers of the saints are linked with the threshing floor in that all four characters are kneeling before the same altar in hopes of obtaining the same boon—salvation. Florence, Gabriel, and Elizabeth, who have all participated in the family crisis brought on by Roy's injury, are seeking divine help in a desperate situation just as John is. For them, to be sure, this occasion is not the ritual conversion nor initiation into adulthood; but just as the rebirth of the soul is perpetual, according to the doctrine of the Grimeses' church, so the struggle to attain maturity is continual, according to psychological theory.[14] The rules for successful prayer, which are given at the beginning of Florence's prayer, apply to all four supplicants: "Her mother had taught her that the way to pray was to forget everything and everyone but Jesus; to pour out of the heart, like water from a bucket, all evil thoughts, all thoughts of self, all malice for one's enemies; to come boldly, and yet more humbly than a little child, before the Giver of all good things. . . . And God did not hear the prayers of the fearful, for the hearts of the fearful held no belief" (pp. 72–73). The successive attempts by Florence, Gabriel, and Elizabeth to win salvation by qualifying under these rules prepare us for John's encounter and increase the tension as each one fails to meet the test. Florence cannot empty her heart of malice, against "niggers," against men, and especially against her brother Gabriel; so she falls back with the hand of death on her shoulder. Gabriel cannot come humbly, but only with proud confidence in his own righteousness; so he remains in fiery darkness. Elizabeth cannot come boldly, but only in fear of her own unworthiness; so she ends in weeping and struggling through darkness still.

On the psychological plane the situation is analogous. The rules for successful prayer are easily translated into criteria for maturity, so that as each character re-thinks the events of his life, we see how each failed to find his own identity in growing from dependency to self-reliance. Florence, filled with the sense of unworthiness that is typical of children who are deprived of parental love, reacted with fierce determination to prove her own worth by leaving home, going north, and finding a husband who would amount to something. Her fear of her mother, hatred of her family and race, and her proud facade (compare the account of her marriage she gives Elizabeth with the facts as she privately remembers them) are evidence of the rebellion that masks continuing dependency. Gabriel, spoiled and dominated by a mother who was as strong as a man, shows the characteristics of the typical Oedipal victim: his guilt feelings drove him to harlots, who were safely unlike his mother, and prevented him from loving Deborah, whom he married as a surrogate mother. In his conversion, which is carefully described as an antithesis to John's, he could not go through the darkness alone, but only with the aid of his mother's spiritual presence and her voice singing (p. 108). His career as a preacher was devoted to her: "If only, he felt, his mother could be there to see—her Gabriel mounted so high!" (p. 120). That he had to marry Deborah in order to achieve a sense of reality is evidence that he never achieved selfhood (p.110). Elizabeth, neglected by her mother and separated from the father she adored, is unable to emerge from childish dependency on men. She fell into Richard's arms—"waiting for her since the day she had been taken from her father's arms"—when he called her "little girl" (pp. 181, 185). She was afraid to tell him of her pregnancy, and after his death she was unable to make her way alone. She married Gabriel without loving him, as an escape from the struggle, "like a hiding-place hewn in the side of the mountain" (p. 213).

The prayers of the saints, then, function as prototypes for John's ordeal on the threshing floor, setting both the religious and psychological conditions for salvation. When John's turn comes, the reader is fully aware of the dangers and the seriousness of the test. The basic structure of the novel thus emphasizes the central importance of John's experience and suggests a parallel between him and the archetypal hero of myth who must face a crucial test of strength or grace or wit—the riddle of the Sphinx or the sword in the stone—which other men fail. Indeed, John's progress through his fourteenth birthday resembles at many points the pattern of the mythic hero-adventure which Joseph Campbell sees in the myths of all cultures: his acceptance of the call, his trials during initiation "in a dream landscape of curiously fluid, ambiguous forms," his attainment of the ultimate boon through supernatural help covertly given by an agent whom he met at the entrance of the region, and his return to the world in a new state of freedom.[15]

Structurally the prayers of the saints are linked to "The Threshing

Floor" by another device, which also increases the tension felt by the reader. In the course of each prayer there is a return to the scene before the altar so that we are reminded of John's progress while we are still involved with the older generation. The very facts of his parents' lives, juxtaposed to his present crisis, increase our fears that John will fail as they do to reach the top of the mountain, since we see that their attitudes toward him resemble those of the previous generation toward them and therefore are likely to produce the same result: fear, guilt, and hatred that prevent the child from attaining psychological independence. We wonder if it is an endless chain of psychological cause and effect—the sins of the fathers visited upon the children for endless generations, and with John we ask, "Could a curse come down so many ages?" (p. 224).

John's negative answer to this question, which is his salvation, evolves from his new perception of his parents as separate from himself with their own sins and psychological problems. This perception, at once allowing him to empty his heart of evil thoughts, malice, and fear and giving him a sense of his own identity, come to him (mystically) and to the reader (explicitly) through symbolism based on Biblical allusion. Like the mythical hero undergoing the trials of his initiation, John's experience resembles the dreams and hallucinations of a patient in psychoanalysis, which Campbell describes as a "journey of darkness, horror, disgust, and phantasmagoric fears."[16] But the dream landscape of John's mind is inhabited by religious symbols of the Hebrew-Christian tradition, so the reader does not have to be a psychoanalyst to interpret them. Although the symbolism is complex, Baldwin carefully alerts the reader by pinpointing the Biblical sources early in the novel and by repeating his texts in different situations so that they run through the three parts as themes that link characters and events. Much of the poetic intensity and psychological subtlety of Part Three derives from the use of these themes, with all their acquired symbolic meaning, to illuminate John's psychic experience on the threshing floor by relating it to the events of the morning and the past lives of his family.

As the first example of Baldwin's technique, let us look at his use of the last chapter of the Book of Revelation to give John insight into Gabriel's character. He first draws the reader's attention to this chapter by using a quotation from it as the epigraph of Part One. Almost immediately afterward he uses another passage from it for John's first expression of hatred toward his father: "He which is filthy, let him be filthy still." (p. 22). With remarkable economy Baldwin uses this allusion for several purposes. It at once connects the dirt of Harlem with John's family heritage and with sin. Since the passage is a pronouncement of damnation at the last judgment on those who are currently sinful, it is in John's mouth a child's curse of his father.

Psychologically it expresses the childish trick of turning against a parent the very punishment the parent normally uses against the child, since Gabriel is always warning his children of their imminent damnation with such texts as "Set thine house in order." But there is also a latent irony in this inversion which becomes explicit when Gabriel repeats the quotation in his guilty despair after the affair with Esther (p. 154). The reader, as Marcus Klein points out, wants John to know Gabriel's guilt, forgetting or not believing the promise John's mother gave him that morning: "The Lord'll reveal to you in His own good time everything he wants you to know" (p. 34). At the moment John needs to know the truth about Gabriel a wind blows over him reminding him of another verse of the same chapter: "Whosoever loveth and maketh a lie" (p. 222). The wind, whether of the Holy Spirit or psychic inspiration, imparts the necessary insight into Gabriel's hypocrisy and enmity by recalling to his memory a Biblical text juxtaposed to one he has recently applied to his father.

A more complex example of Baldwin's technique is his use of Gabriel's favorite text, "Set thine house in order." The earliest mention of the text is ironic in its contrast between Gabriel's assumption that his own house, by which he means the state of his soul, is in order and the reader's knowledge of the serious disorder of his household (p. 34). Another irony is suggested when the text is used for the second time, at the beginning of Florence's prayer: "For the message had come to Florence that had come to Hezekiah: *Set thine house in order, for thou shalt die and not live*"(p. 73). The repetition of Gabriel's favorite text in a situation that gives it the most literal meaning, the imminence of physical death, implies that Gabriel is unaware of his own death sentence, which (as suggested by Baldwin's autobiographical essay, "Notes of a Native Son") may already have been pronounced. This repetition, enforced by the explicitness of the allusion, should send any reader not as well versed in scripture as Baldwin's characters to the story of King Hezekiah's illness, which is twice recounted in the Old Testament—once in the Book of Isaiah, frequently quoted in this novel.

King Hezekiah is alluded to four times in Gabriel's prayer when he speaks of asking for and receiving a sign from God (pp. 129, 156, 157, 170). The sign is again stressed at the climax of Elizabeth's prayer when she accepts Gabriel's interpretation of her and her baby as the sign for which he, like Hezekiah, has asked the Lord (p. 214). And at the end of the novel Gabriel counters Florence's threat of revelation by insisting on the significance of his "sign" (p. 245). But the reader, remembering Hezekiah's sign, the turning of the sun ten degrees backwards, understands that Gabriel has mistaken the sign God gave him. The true sign (also suggested by the gold imagery, which is linked with salvation and the assumption of manhood in this novel) occurs when he is given the opportunity to take Esther and their unborn child as his own: "He moved toward the house, which now—high, gleaming roof, and spun-gold window—seemed to watch him and to listen; the very sun above his head and the earth beneath his feet had ceased their turning; the water, like a million warning voices, lapped in the buckets he carried on each side; and his mother, beneath the startled earth on which he moved, lifted up, endlessly, her eyes" (p. 146). Here again Old Testament and Christian symbolism—Hezekiah's sun and the golden cross (crown, Jerusalem)—are combined to express the psychic reality, Gabriel's chance for maturity, which he cannot accept because of his infantile dependence on his mother. From this point on Gabriel's confidence in his sign is ironic, and the reader understands that the Lord has not forgiven him.

Gabriel's favorite text is used, finally, to convey to John during his ordeal the full force of his father's hatred. In his psychic confrontation with his father the dreadful menace of the statement, "For thou shalt die and not live," forces John to examine the sin that his father is going "to beat out of him," and he suddenly grasps the basically sexual nature of the conflict between father and son—a necessary step in his salvation (p. 222). For the reader the quotation is again ironic because we already know what John intuitively grasps, that Gabriel's "house"—in this context, his sexual sins stemming from Oedipal fixation—is far more disordered than John's.

Baldwin's most important use of Biblical symbolism to express the psychic realities of the older generation and to interpret John's sudden comprehension of them centers in the theme of God's covenant with Abraham. The theme is suggested in the first pages of the novel by parallels between Gabriel and the patriarch who holds the covenant on behalf of the whole tribe and passes this power to his son with his blessing. Gabriel has spiritual as well as temporal authority, so John must kneel to his father before he can kneel to the Lord (p. 20). It is "his father's church" as well as "his father's house," and John's rebellion against him includes rebellion against the whole race: "He would not be like his father, or his father's fathers" (p. 18). Later his father's fathers, the Negro slaves, are identified with Abraham's tribe in Egypt. In John's dreams of escaping his father, he sees himself as "the Lord's anointed," an epithet Florence uses of Gabriel in expressing her reluctance to bow before Gabriel's God (pp. 35, 72).

In Gabriel's prayer the theme becomes more explicit. Before his conversion he wants to become "the Lord's anointed," and his fear of dying in a state of sin is expressed in terms of God's covenant with Abraham—the promise of an heir "out of thine own bowels" and "seed" that shall outnumber the stars—given in Genesis 15.

Gabriel feared that "where he had been would be silence only, rock, stubble, and no seed; for him, forever, and for his, no hope of glory. Thus when he came to the harlot, he came to her in rage, and he left her in vain sorrow—feeling himself to have been, once more, most foully robbed, having spent his holy seed in a forbidden darkness where it could only die" (p. 105). His first important sermon is concerned with sexual sin and paternity, based on a text from St. Paul: "and if ye be Christ's, then ye are Abraham's seed, and heirs according to the promise" (pp. 116–117). He marries Deborah to "continue the line of the faithful, a royal line" after waking up one night to find himself "covered with his own white seed" and then dreaming that God called him to the top of a mountain, showed him the elect, and promised (in the word of the Lord to Abraham), "So shall thy seed be" (pp. 124–126). His reaction to Esther's pregnancy is horror that "the seed of the prophet would be nourished" in the womb of a harlot (p. 146). His sons are named (ironically by Esther and in most religious earnestness by Gabriel) Royal and Roy to preserve their symbolic identification with the kings of Israel from Saul, who was anointed by the Lord, to Jesus, whose title is Christ or Messiah, "the anointed One."

For Gabriel salvation is connected with lawful paternity. When Roy calls him a bastard, he considers it a curse (p. 128). His hatred of John is doubly inspired by this religious conviction: first, because the "son of the bondwoman" might stand in the place of the "rightful heir," and second, because Elizabeth, mother of the prophet, might have contaminated Roy by not thoroughly repenting the conception of John. The Covenant theme expresses both Gabriel's psychological motivation—his thirst for power and his feeling of sexual guilt—and its result—his behavior toward Deborah, Esther, Elizabeth, Roy, and John. Through this symbolic identification with Abraham we understand Gabriel.

But Baldwin, using the same symbolism, takes us a step farther and leads us to forgive him, for this novel is more like *Great Expectations* than *David Copperfield* in that the child-parent conflict is set in a larger social context. If Gabriel is Abraham, his people are the children of Israel in the wilderness. As he makes a preaching tour in penitence for his treatment of Esther, he sees how white oppression has driven the blacks away from the Lord into the wilderness of lechery, gambling, drinking, and jazz:

> There seemed . . . no woman . . . who had not seen her father, her brother, her lover, or her son cut down without mercy; who had not seen her sister become part of the white man's great whorehouse; . . . no man whose manhood had not been, at the root, sickened, whose loins had not been dishonored, whose seed had not been scattered into oblivion, into living shame and rage, and into

endless battle. Yes, their parts were all cut off, they were dishonored, their very names were nothing more than dust blown disdainfully across the field of time—to fall where, to blossom where, bringing forth what fruit hereafter, where?—their very names were not their own. Behind them was the darkness, nothing but the darkness, and all around them destruction, and before them nothing but the fire— a bastard people, far from God, singing and crying in the wilderness! (pp. 155–156)

Gabriel's mother had seen her older children sold out of her house and one taken into her master's house where she could not go. Deborah had suffered rape and mutilation which Florence barely escaped. Elizabeth's mother and father were both "part of the white man's great whorehouse," and her Richard was "cut down" by the white man. Like the Israelites in the wilderness their only salvation must be strict obedience to the Lord's commandments in an effort to fulfill the covenant that promised them their own land and a name of their own.

Understanding this, who could not forgive Gabriel's mother her fierce determination to establish Gabriel in the covenant, even at the cost of her daughter's happiness; or Elizabeth's parents their neglect born of despair; or Gabriel his decision that he "would not go back into Egypt for friend, or lover, or bastard son" (p. 156)? The question that remains is whether the curse must be passed down. Is there no way to prevent Gabriel's understandable concern to establish his royal line and Elizabeth's understandable refusal to climb to the top of the mountain from warping a new generation? John's ordeal on the threshing floor is the crucial test, and the reader approaches it with the feeling that only a miracle can save him.

The miracle, whether it comes from the Holy Spirit visiting the two or three gathered in his name or from the evocation of subconscious knowledge by the group therapy of the tarry service, happens through the agency of Biblical passages. First John sees the relation of racial persecution to sexually based father-son hatred through the story of Noah and his son Ham. His father's accusing stare of hatred makes John feel naked and reminds him of the only serious sin he is conscious of—masturbating in the bathroom (p. 223). (Here the critics go wildly astray, both those who assume that his masturbation is an indication of homosexual tendencies induced by Oedipal love and those who assume that his labeling of the act as sin indicates religious neurosis.)[17] By association of ideas he remembers that he, like Ham, has seen his father naked. Religious symbolism interprets the experience: the bathtub is dirty, suggesting sin, and his father's penis reminds him of the serpent and the rod, both symbols of Moses, the lawgiver. He recognizes the source of his hate and understands Noah's reason for cursing Ham: sexual rivalry between the father-king and the son-subject—the Biblical parallel to the Oedipus situation.

The curse on Ham—"A servant of servants shall he be unto his brethren"—suggests racial persecution since John is aware of modern use of the ancient Jewish excuse for enslavement of the Canaanites as justification for white enslavement of blacks. For a desperate moment he considers the possibility that the passage really means that "all niggers had been cursed," as he listens to the mocking voice of the unbelief within him, which has been urging him to get up off the floor and walk out of the church. But the anger expressed in his father's approaching footsteps resounding "like God's tread in the garden of Eden, searching the covered Adam and Eve" gives him the insight that this curse is common to all men—all the sons of Adam, not just the sons of Ham—and that it is "renewed from moment to moment, from father to son"—not by God's fiat.

After a short rest another labor pain begins, signaled by a crescendo of sound that John identifies as the rage and weeping he had heard around him all his life. It is the sound "of boundless melancholy, of the bitterest patience, and the longest night; of the deepest water, the strongest chains, the most cruel lash; of humility most wretched, the dungeon most absolute, of love's bed defiled, and birth dishonored, and most bloody, unspeakable, sudden death" (p. 228). To leave childhood is to join the ranks of unprotected adults who suffer all the ills that flesh is heir to, and in John's case, adults who suffer the additional ills of being despised, rejected, and spat upon by other men, the "armies of darkness." There will be no one in those armies to take care of him, to heal him and lift him up. He is terrified and dreads leaving the womb.

Just as in the first crisis Biblical passages gave him the insights needed to see his fear and hatred of his father as a universal problem, so again they lessen the terrors of adulthood by calling up the testimony of the ages. Looking on the armies he asks, "Who are these? Who are they?" and so becomes John of Patmos looking at the persecuted who will be saved (p. 229). He thinks of their sufferings in the words of Paul: "Thrice was I beaten with rods, once I was stoned, thrice I suffered shipwreck. . . ." These quotations forge the link in his chain of understanding so that he sees the love of God specifically offered to the persecuted, whether they are victimized by Egypt, Babylon, Jerusalem, Rome, or New York. Their robes "stained with unholy blood" and their feet "bloodstained forever" relate them to the sacrificial Lamb of God. John then sees that all men are both persecutors and victims, trampling over each other in the struggle of life: "the strong struck down the weak, the ragged spat on the naked, the naked cursed the blind, the blind crawled over the lame" (p. 232).[18] In accepting manhood he is accepting the human condition, which is redeemed by the love of God.

The love of God becomes, in the end, the cloak of manhood, which is golden like the cross. After seeing the light, John stands up as an adult. He is no longer dependent on his mother, who he senses is claimed by the dead even though he knows nothing of Richard. And he is able to stand up to Gabriel, sensing that he is the "enemy . . . that wants to cut down my soul," although he suspects nothing about his true paternity. God by baptism has given John a new name, independent of the name Gabriel had fought so hard to keep from him in defending his own earthly kingdom of "royal" lineage. John has gone a step beyond Gabriel's lament for American Negroes, that "their very names were nothing more than dust blown disdainfully across the field of time;" he sees that all earthly names are "Grimes"— dust and sin—that all men are subject to the curse renewed from moment to moment from father to son. In becoming a man he has rejected not only childish dependency on his mother and fear of his father, but also racial bondage. When the light and the darkness kissed each other, he became no longer a child of the bondwoman but an heir according to the promise—not Ishmael but Isaac, not bound by the racial law of circumcision or Noah's curse on Ham, but redeemed from Adam's sin and justified by faith. Through religious symbolism Baldwin suggests that the conversion which frees John from sin is also his psychological initiation into maturity, which frees him from the umbilical cord, and racial hatred. "He was free . . . he had only to stand fast in his liberty. He was in battle no longer, this unfolding Lord's day, with this avenue, these houses, the sleeping, staring, shouting people, but had entered into battle with Jacob's angel" (p. 247).

Notes

1. See, e.g., Theodore L. Gross, *The Heroic Ideal in American Literature* (New York: Free Press, 1971), p. 167; Howard M. Harper, *Desperate Faith* (Chapel Hill: University of North Carolina Press, 1967), p. 144; Marcus Klein, *After Alienation, American Novels in Mid-Century* (Cleveland: World Press, 1965), p. 163; Therman B. O'Daniel, "James Baldwin: An Interpretive Study," *CLA Journal*, 7 (September, 1963), 38; and Nathan A. Scott, "Judgment Marked by a Cellar: The American Negro Writer and the Dialectic of Despair," in *The Shapeless God*, ed. Harry J. Mooney and Thomas F. Staley (Pittsburgh: University of Pittsburgh Press, 1968), pp. 159–164.

2. (New York: Norton, 1953), particularly in Part Two, "Rediscovering Self-hood."

3. See, e.g., Robert A. Bone, *The Negro Novel in America*, rev. ed. (New Haven: Yale University Press, 1965), pp. 217–225; D. E. Foster " 'Cause My House Fell Down'; the Theme of the Fall in Baldwin's Novels," *Critique: Studies in Modern Fiction*, 13 (1971), No. 2, 54–55; Albert Gérard (tr. McDowell), "The Sons of Ham,"

Studies in the Novel, 3 (Summer, 1971), 156; and Scott, "Judgment Marked by a Cellar," p. 161.

4. "Dark Angel: The Writings of James Baldwin," *Encounter,* 21 (August, 1963), rpt. in *Five Black Writers,* ed. Donald B. Gibson (New York: New York University Press, 1970), pp. 122–123. The same point of view is found in Edward Margolies, *Native Sons* (Philadelphia: Lippincott, 1968), pp. 109–114. A notable exception is Michel Fabre in "Pères et fils dans *Go Tell It on the Mountain* de James Baldwin," *Etudes Anglaises,* 23 (January–March, 1970), 47–61, where he not only points out some of the symbolism discussed in this article, but also suggests that the total structure of the novel resembles a Christian triptych. Another European critic, Albert Gérard (in "The Sons of Ham," pp. 149–151) sees the religious experience as central to the conflict and recognizes the universiality of the human moral problem on "a plane where racial conflicts have no part," but he is not concerned with symbolism.

5. "Images of Apocalypse in the Black Novel," *Renascence,* 23 (1970), 31–45, and " 'Cause My House Fell Down,' " p. 54.

6. See, e.g., David W. Noble, *The Eternal Adam and the New World Garden* (New York: Braziller, 1968), pp. 210–212, and Scott, "Judgment Marked by a Cellar," p. 163.

7. *Desperate Faith,* pp. 142, 144.

8. *After Alienation,* p. 181. From one of the first reviews, where J. H. Raleigh in the *Nation,* 176 (1953), 488, comments that "the final impact of the novel is somewhat muffled" to Michel Fabre's article in *Etudes Anglaises,* 1970, most critics have found the denouement unclear because (as I argue) they dismiss the symbolism as "just Biblical reference."

9. *Go Tell It on the Mountain* (New York: Dial, 1963, c. 1953), p. 74. Further references to the novel, which are given in the text, follow the pagination of this edition, different from the first edition.

10. Immediately after John's conversion Praying Mother Washington also echoes the passage from Isaiah used as epigraph: "Run on, honey, and don't get weary!" (p. 235).

11. See, e.g., Klein, p. 184, and Wallace Graves, "The Question of Moral Energy in James Baldwin's *Go Tell It on the Mountain," CLA Journal,* 7 (March, 1964), 219–221.

12. Acceptance of Gabriel's view, coupled with the tendency to see racial conflict as the basis of the action, has led some critics into unusual explanations of the father-son conflict. See Bone, "The Novels of James Baldwin," *Tri-Quarterly,* No. 2 (Winter, 1965), 8, and Foster, pp. 52–53.

13. See Paul Pickrel, "Outstanding Novels," rev. of *Go Tell It on the Mountain, Yale Review,* 42, (Summer, 1953), x, and the quotation from Klein at the end of my introduction.

14. Rollo May points out that the potentiality to become aware of selfhood is what is meant by the Biblical assertion that man is created in the image of God, and he adds: "Almost every adult is, in greater or lesser degree, still struggling on the long journey to achieve selfhood on the basis of the patterns which were set in his early experiences in the family." *Man's Search for Himself,* pp. 86–87.

15. *The Hero with a Thousand Faces* (Cleveland: World Press, 1956, c. 1949), p. 97. Campbell also connects this pattern with the psychic patterns of growth from dependency to adulthood.

16. *Ibid.,* p. 121. Baldwin describes a similar situation in his most recent novel, *If Beale Street Could Talk* (New York: Dial, 1974), pp. 105–106, speaking of Daniel, "who cannot abandon his mother, yet longs to be free to confront his life; is terrified

at the same time of what that life may bring, is terrified of freedom; and is struggling in a trap."

17. See, e.g., Klein, pp. 182–184; Harper, p. 145; and Scott, p. 160.

18. This perception is given artistic realization in *If Beale Street Could Talk*, where Daniel, Victoria, and Pietro are victims who become persecutors, and even the white lawyer is shown to be a victim.

Go Tell It on the Mountain: Religion as the Indirect Method of Indictment
Fred L. Standley[*]

Go Tell It on the Mountain (1953), James Baldwin's first novel, focuses upon the religious conversion of John Grimes, the protagonist, on his fourteenth birthday in Harlem's storefront Temple of the Fire Baptised.[1] The fictional parallels with Baldwin's own youth indicate clearly the autobiographical religious elements in the novel, for example, his conversion in Mother Horn's Pentecostal Faith Church; the three-year stint as a teenage preacher in the hymn-singing, gospel-shouting, hand-clapping, Bible-chanting Fireside Pentecostal Assembly; the ambivalent filial relation with David Baldwin, the stern stepfather, who was also a deacon and a pentecostal preacher; and an acute sense of need for escape from the horrors of ghetto experience—whether by jail, drugs, alcohol, or religion.

Typically, the numerous critics and commentators on Baldwin have consistently pointed to the primacy of the religious dimension of the novel in such descriptions as these: (1) "a story of religious experience among Harlem Negroes,"[2] (2) "a lyrical, poignant novel dealing with his early religious experiences in Harlem,"[3] (3) "an astutely integrated vision in which the fear of God and the despair of love are the fundamental forces."[4]

Indeed, upon initial examination *Go Tell It on the Mountain* appears to be permeated by a religious perspective manifesting readily discernible features drawn from the Judeo-Christian tradition: scriptural references, allusions and names, ecclesiastical practices, ritualist actions, and doctrinal concepts. For example, scriptural references, quotations, and allusions serve as the basic structuring devices for the novel. The title of the work is derived from a combination of the Christmas plantation song, "Go Tell It on the Mountain," and

[*]This essay was written for this volume and appears here for the first time by permission of the author.

scriptural passages from the Old Testament books of Exodus (19:12) and Isaiah (2:03, 40:09, etc.); while the novel's epigraph is derived from Isaiah (40:31). Likewise, each of the three sections of the novel, both in subtitle and epigraph, is drawn from biblical sources: part 1, "The Seventh Day," Genesis 2:02, Hebrews 4:04, etc.; epigraph—Revelation 22:17; part 2, "The Prayers of the Saints," Revelation 8:04; epigraph—Revelation 6:10; part 3, "The Threshing Floor," Genesis 50:10, Luke 3:17, etc.; epigraph—Isaiah 6:05.

A brief plot summary may be useful to substantiate the thesis. Part 1, "The Seventh Day," introduces the Grimes family living in Harlem, 1935. The young John Grimes feels constricted and frustrated by the repressive, hate-suffused, hell's-fire sermons of his stepfather, Gabriel, who is the spiritual leader of the Temple of the Fire Baptised. John struggles with guilt about sex, ambivalent emotions toward his parents, and latent hatred of whites.

Part 2, "The Prayers of the Saints," is complex and artistic and uses flashbacks of the Grimes' family background centering upon three prayers: one by Aunt Forence, sister of Gabriel; another by Gabriel; and the third by Elizabeth, John's mother. Florence's prayer reminisces about (1) the times of their mother and their expectations of black family life being dominated by the male; (2) her fleeing from the South about 1900 after having been asked by a white employer to become his "concubine"; (3) her relation with a former husband, Frank, whose caramel skin color eventually led to the termination of the marriage because of her disdain for his "common nigger" friends and her ironic, continued use of "them old skin-whiteners" while he stubbornly remarked "that black's a mighty pretty color." Florence's prayer ends "with terror and rage" as she asks God why "he preferred her mother and her brother, the old, black woman, and the low, black man, while she, who had sought only to walk upright, was come to die, alone and in poverty, in a dirty, furnished room?" (78).

Gabriel's prayer section recapitulates twenty years of his life; his earlier marriage to Deborah, "a holy fool;" the affair with Esther and the birth and death of their son, Royal; his own distaste for the "big, comfortable, ordained" evangelists at the Twenty-Four Elders Revival Meeting; his internal struggle between pietism and lust; and his ambivalence toward Elizabeth's bastard son, John.

Elizabeth's prayer recounts what various experiences of love have meant to her: the "furious affectation of maternal concern" toward her; the enforced "separation of herself from her father" by her aunt; life in New York with her first lover, Richard, and his ultimate suicide after being humiliated by the police; and her marriage to Gabriel after the illegitimate birth of John. Elizabeth "hated it all—the white city, the white world"—and she finds relief in the thought that "only

God could establish order in this chaos; to Him the soul must turn to be delivered" (151).

Part 3, "The Threshing Floor," emphasizes John Grimes's conversion experience on the floor before the altar surrounded by Mother Washington, Brother Elisha, and other "saints," while his mind is racked and tortured by the pangs of guilt, fear, and hatred. Finally, "in the silence something died in John, and something came alive," and at dawn he emerges from the Temple, smiling and confident about the future.

In spite of these obvious scriptural references, allusions, and names, and the seeming preoccupation with ecclesiastical and doctrinal matters, Go Tell It on the Mountain is not primarily a religious novel. It is instead a work embodying a major cultural concept of which religion is only one important dimension. A point of entree for interpreting the significance of the novel in this manner can be found in the essay "Culture: Negro, Black and Nigger," written a decade ago by anthropologist Johnetta Cole. This essay is an exploratory analysis of "the existence of a black subculture" which uniquely combines three components that authenticate the reality and viability of this subculture in predominantly white America: (1) those features drawn from white America, (2) those shared with all oppressed people, and (3) those particular to blacks.[5]

Within the latter group—that is, features peculiar to blacks—are elements that help to distinguish the essence of blackness, for example, soul, or style, or a combination. However, the most interesting feature of Cole's essay is the analysis of the four basic life-styles that comprise "nigger culture," namely, the street, down home, militant, and upward bound. Upward bound referred to the life-style of the "black bourgeoisie" and centered in better neighborhoods and integrated churches and clubs, in short, the black middle class. Militant described the political world and life-style of cultural and revolutionary nationalists, especially on college campuses and in high school black student unions and their ostensible concern with relief from oppression.

The street life-style, that is, the urban world of American blacks, highly stylized in behavior, appears initially to be dominant in Go Tell It on the Mountain. The locale for the novel is the urban North, a type of setting that the author later refers to as "another country" in a novel by the same name. The frequent descriptions and depictions of the city in Go Tell It express the gutter and grime, the impersonality and anonymity, the confinement and isolation of the sprawling and teeming metropolis with its "roar of the damned," a place "where no one cared, where people might live in the same building for years and never speak to one another" (141). While it may be true, as Addison Gayle suggests,[6] that "no writer knows the ghetto or its people better than Baldwin," and that the frequent descriptions in *Go Tell It* reinforce the urban scene as the "gray country of the dead" (186), it is really the "down-home" life-style that dominates and recurs consistently throughout this first novel.

Down home is, according to Cole, "a common expression among black Americans, indicating one's point of origin, down south, or the simple, decent way of life"; as a life-style it is "the traditional way of black folks . . . basically rural and southern" and centering in "the kitchens of black homes, in the church halls for suppers, and in the fraternal orders."[7] Within this broader cultural context *Go Tell It on the Mountain* embodies the experiences of the *down-home* life-style. The narrative lines of Gabriel, Florence, and Elizabeth involve reminiscences of their belongings to those transitional generations of the great migration earlier in this century when southern blacks left the rural areas of their origin for the northern cities, carrying their cultural heritage (including religion) with them. This *down-home* life-style pervades the novel and possesses inherent ironic implications for interpreting the central meaning of the book. Textual evidence abounds in testimony to this point. For example, on one occasion Frank asks: "What's them niggers doing down home? It ain't no bad news, is it?" (77). Similarly, Florence says in a conversation: "Them niggers down home, they think New York ain't nothing but one long, Sunday drunk . . ." (159). And Gabriel declares: "Don't know . . . tell me folks do things up North they wouldn't think about doing down home" (159). There are numerous other references to *down home*.

The interpretive point of entree for the novel, then, is a cultural concept rather than a religious concept, though assuredly religion is an aspect of it. Within that context this is not a novel about religion per se; rather it is a sociopolitical novel that subtly but savagely indicts a white controlled society that has radically delimited the lives and hopes of blacks by the pernicious doctrine and damnable practice of black inferiority. This in turn has led to fear, isolation, alienation, hatred, despair, and destruction. The novel is replete with passages of suffused hatred for and desired revenge upon the white world; for example, after Gabriel learns that a black soldier has been viciously beaten to death by a group of white men, "he dreamed of a white man's forehead against his shoe; again and again, until the head wobbled on the broken neck and his foot encountered nothing but the rushing blood" (123). Or, following the jailing of her lover, Richard, for a crime of which he is innocent, Florence "hated it all— the white city, the white world. She could not, that day, think of one decent white person in the whole world" (150). Thus, for those whose skin color offers no hope better than "the back door, and the dark stairs, and the kitchen or basement" (33), the alternatives seem limited to escapism by drugs, drink, and sex, or escape through the church; either of these forms is regarded equally as merely an anodyne in the novel. At the conclusion John Grimes has yet to learn the awful realities of the experiences recited in the lives of Florence, Gabriel, and Elizabeth; the options that open to him on "the threshing floor" in front of the altar are to leave the comminity of the faithful and thus court disaster, or to remain among the group and reduce his range of possibilities by embracing a hopeless otherworldliness divorced from reality. Thus, the novel indicts not only the white society's racism but also the black society's reliance upon a religious mode of behavior that is illusory and irrelevant to the brutalizing and dehumanizing experiences of daily living.

The primary literary technique for expressing the dual points of sociopolitical condemnation is irony. This is a novel of stasis rather than change; in spite of the fact that there seems to be a great deal of action, that action occurs during one day in March 1935, which is John's fourteenth birthday, though we also glimpse a previous time through the three sets of reminiscence already mentioned. Despite his religious conversion, nothing has changed for John Grimes at the end; in fact, the narrator says that in the throes of John's conversion experience, "in his moment of seizure an ironic voice insisted . . . that he rise from that filthy floor if he did not want to become like all the other niggers." Thus, John Grimes's joyful weeping remembrance of the scriptural passage "whom the Son sets free is free indeed" is an illusion. Nothing has changed in his environment or with his stepfather or in his conception of God; though John declares boldly "I'm ready. I'm coming. I'm on my way," the reader recognizes the irony inherent to the anticipation and has to counter: "Ready for whom? Coming where? On the way to what?"

Another indication of the technique of irony in the novel consists in the ethical norm as manifested in the community of saints in the Temple of the Fire Baptised, especially in their effort to be in the world but not of the world. Though the conventions of behavior are ostensibly established and enforced by the community of saints, each of the three principal saints—Florence, Gabriel, and Elizabeth—has his or her own secret code of predominant behavior at variance with and contradictory to the communal norm. Elizabeth's favorite scriptural passage is "All things work together for good for them that love the Lord" (Rom. 8:28), but loving the Lord has had no impact or made no change in the pain, suffering, or victimization of herself or her family in the past or present. Gabriel's favorite text is "set this house in order" (2 Kings 20:1), yet all of the households connected with him have been in perpetual disorder, and his fanatical belief structure has been a persistent rationalization for evading the responsibility that establishes order; the words of Gabriel, whose name literally means "God's messenger," are revealed to be words of deceit, despair, and destruction. In the case of Florence the words of the hymn serving as epigraph to her prayer section becomes the ironic indicator: "Light and life to all He brings, / Risen with healing in His wings." However, we discover that there has been neither light nor life nor healing in any of her experiences—the skin whiteners have not worked; and though a believer she ends the prayer section with a vision of the hands of death caressing her shoulders and a voice saying: "death's got a warrant out for you."

Go Tell It on the Mountain, then, is a novel embodying a cultural concept broader than merely a religious interpretation and indicting both blacks and whites for the nature of their society and their ways of dealing with it. By doing so the novel is also a prefiguration of themes and motifs that Baldwin was to pursue in subsequent fiction, drama, and essays. By revealing the intensity of passion, the ambiguity of motivation, the complexity of conflicting emotions, the inner struggles over love, joy, and pain, Baldwin derides and derogates those who would oversimplify the need for an authentic and effective mode of response to the white society's dominance over the black society's existence; and he reveals that refuge in an otherworldly orientation rationalized by a conception of God, whether held by blacks or whites, is an illusion and, therefore, damnation, not salvation. In this first novel, then, the author fictionalized an extension of two nonfictional theses that have since dominated his work as a man of letters: first, that "people who shut their eyes to reality simply invite their own destruction"; and, second, that "if the concept of God has any validity or use, it can only be to make us larger, freer, and more loving. If God cannot do this, then it is time we got rid of Him."[8] Thus, James Baldwin in Go Tell It on the Mountain borrowed the aesthetic principle of "indirect communication" advocated earlier by writer and philosopher Soren Kierkegaard. Just as Kierkegaard perceived that his first task was "to deceive people, in a true sense, into entering the sphere of religious obligation which they have done away with, but I am without authority,"[9] so was Baldwin as novelist cognizant of the fact that Go Tell It on the Mountain (1953) was being presented to the public in an era saturated not by "religious obligation" but rather by the religious "cult of serenity"—the era of Rabbi Joshua Liebmann's Peace of Mind (1946), Bishop Fulton J. Sheen's Peace of Soul (1949), Dr. Norman Vincent Peale's The Power of Positive Thinking (1952), and the Reverend Billy Graham's Peace With God (1953).[10]

Notes

1. *Go Tell It on the Montain* (New York: Signet-NAL, 1953); hereafter cited in the text.

2. "Reviews of Forthcoming Books," *Booklist,* 15 March 1953, 229.

3. James A. Emanuel and Theodore L. Gross, eds., *Dark Symphony: Negro Literature in America* (New York: Free Press, 1968), 297.

4. Stanley Macebuh, *James Baldwin: A Critical Study* (New York: Third World Press, 1973), 53.

5. Johnetta Cole, "Culture: Negro, Black and Nigger," in *New Black Voices,* ed. Abraham Chapman (New York: New American Library, 1972), 491–98.

6. Addison Gayle, Jr., "Cultural Nationalism: The Black Novelist in America," *Black Roots Bulletin* 1 (1971):7.

7. Cole, "Culture," 493.

8. James Baldwin, *The Fire Next Time* (New York: Dell, 1964), 67, 111.

9. Alexander Dreu, ed., *The Journals of Soren Kierkegaard* (New York: Oxford University Press, 1951), 348.

10. Ronald E. Osborn, *The Spirit of American Christianity* (New York: Harper, 1958), 210–11.

Baldwin's *Going to Meet the Man:* Racial Brutality and Sexual Gratification
Roger Whitlow°

The relationship between race and sexuality has long been described in the literature of Americans, both black and white, and was, in fact, the subject of the first work of fiction written by a black author, William Wells Brown's novel *Clotel: Or The President's Daughter* (1853). Interracial love and sexual attraction are treated in other important works of black fiction, such as Charles W. Chestnutt's *The House Behind the Cedars* (1900), James Weldon Johnson's *The Autobiography of an Ex-Colored Man* (1912), Jean Toomer's *Cane* (1923), Richard Wright's *Native Son* (1940), and Sarah E. Wright's *This Child's Gonna Live* (1969).

With the development of the psychologically self-concious age of post–World War II America came of course more penetrating approaches to the subject of race and sexuality—new and intense efforts not simply to *describe* the socio-historical facts of sexual

°Reprinted from *American Imago* 34, no. 4 (1977):351–56, by permission of the author and the journal.

attraction between members of different races, notably between blacks and whites, but to *explain* and *interpret* the actual working out of the manifestations of this attraction, through fantasies, dreams, and other vicarious as well as actual sexual experiences. Especially helpful have been such studies as Calvin Hernton's *Sex and Racism in America* (1965), Laurence Baughman's *Southern Rape Complex* (1966), William Grier and Price Cobb's *Black Rage* (1968), Eldridge Cleaver's *Soul on Ice* (1969), and Beth Day's *Sexual Life Between Blacks and Whites* (1972).

Perhaps the finest interpretaion of one facet of this relationship, the sexual stimulation and subsequent gratification which can be achieved through racial brutality is, however, found in James Baldwin's short story "Going to Meet the Man." Baldwin immediately establishes the problem to be resolved—white male impotence—as the story opens:

"What's the matter?" she asked.
"I don't know," he said, trying to laugh, "I guess I'm tired."
 "You've been working too hard," she said. "I keep telling you."
 "Well, goddammit, woman," he said, "it's not my fault!" He tried again; he wretchedly failed again. Then he just lay there, silent, angry, helpless. Excitement filled him just like a toothache, but it refused to enter his flesh. He stroked her breast. This was his wife. He could not ask her to do just a little thing for him, just to help him out, just for a little while, the way he could ask a nigger girl to do it. He lay there, and he sighed. The image of a black girl caused a distant excitement in him, like a far-away light; but, again, the excitement was more like pain; instead of forcing him to act, it made action impossible.[1]

Jesse, a white southern deputy sheriff, cannot perform sexually when confronted with only the "frail sanctuary" of his white wife to satisfy the sexual raging that he feels but cannot convert to physical action ("He moaned. He wanted to let whatever was in him out; but it wouldn't come out"). While he does not know what is tormenting him, he does sense the circuitous psychological route which he must take to produce the firmness by which, even through his wife, he can have at least temporary relief. And so he begins mentally tracing for his sleeping wife the events of the day: "There was this nigger today." And he tells of the black civil-rights activist who, though arrested and beaten, refused to tell his followers to stop singing:

He was lying on the ground jerking and moaning, they had threw him in a cell by himself, and blood was coming out his ears from where Big Jim C. and his boys had whipped him. Wouldn't you think they'd learn? I put the prod to him and he jerked some more and he kind of screamed—but didn't have much voice left. "You make them stop that singing," I said to him, "you hear me? You make them stop that singing." He acted like he didn't hear me and I put it to him again, under his arms, and he just rolled around on the floor and blood started coming from his mouth. He'd pissed his pants already." He paused. His mouth felt dry and his throat was as rough as sandpaper; as he talked, he began to hurt all over with that peculiar excitement which refused to be released.[2]

Already Jesse begins to stir sexually; thoughts of the electric prod burning the flesh and of the intimate responses of the black body, the release of its blood and urine, move Jesse closer to his objective of sexual potency. His mind now moves back in time to provide the final stimulus, back to his first exposure to sexual mutilation, when he was eight years old, back to what was, in fact, the molding of his own sexual nature. He recalls the jalopy driving into the yard to bring the electrifying news, "They got him," and the hasty arrangements of his family to join the other townspeople at the "picnic." Upon their arrival, after the lighthearted and excited greeting of friends, Jesse is placed upon his father's shoulders:

Now he saw the fire—of twigs and boxes, piled high; flames made pale orange and yellow and thin as a veil under the steadier light of the sun; grey-blue smoke rolled upward and poured over their heads. Beyond the shifting curtain of fire and smoke, he made out first only a length of gleaming chain, attached to a great limb of the tree; then he saw that this chain bound two black hands together at the wrist, dirty yellow palm facing dirty yellow palm. The smoke poured up; the hands dropped out of sight; a cry went up from the crowd. Then the hands slowly came into view again, pulled upward by the chain. This time he saw the kinky, sweating, bloody head— he had never before seen a head with so much hair on it, hair so black, black and so tangled that it seemed like another jungle. . . . Sweat was pouring from the hair in its armpits, poured down his sides, over his chest, into his navel and his groin. He was lowered again; he was raised again. Now Jesse knew that he heard him scream. The head went back, the mouth wide open, blood bubbling from the mouth; the veins of the neck jumped out; Jesse clung to his father's neck in terror as the cry rolled over the crowd. The cry of all the people rose to answer the dying man's cry. He wanted death to come quickly. They wanted to make death wait: and it was they who held death, now, on a leash which they lengthened little by little.[3]

Jesse has unwittingly become a participant in a white southern folk ritual, a primitive sex rite in which the society experiences, through the mutilation of the "outcast" figure, a communal orgasm. Jesse responds, as do the others, to the "hanging, gleaming body, the most beautiful and terrible object he had ever seen till then." And he observes the complete participation and response of his mother, who is gripped by the intense anticipation which precedes sexual fulfillment: "Her eyes were very bright, her mouth was open: she was more beautiful than he had ever seen her, and more strange." And as the moment of the inevitable castration nears, Jesse senses also his father's response as he feels "his father's hands on his ankles slip and tighten."[4] Then the climax comes, an act so decisive, so breathtaking—while in fact, so hideous—that all of the preliminary sensations are reduced to near insignificance:

> The man with the knife took the nigger's privates in his hand, one hand, still smiling, as though he were weighing them. In the cradle of the one white hand, the nigger's privates seemed as remote as meat being weighed in the scales; but seemed heavier, too, much heavier, and Jesse felt his scrotum tighten; and huge, huge, much bigger than his father's flaccid, hairless, the largest thing he had ever seen till then, and the blackest. The white hand stretched them, cradled them, caressed them. Then the dying man's eyes looked straight into Jesse's eyes—it could not have been for as long as a second, but it seemed longer than a year. Then Jesse screamed, and the crowd screamed as the knife flashed, first up, then down, cutting the dreadful thing away, and the blood came roaring down. Then the crowd rushed forward tearing at the body with their hands, with knives, with rocks, with stones, howling and cursing. Jesse's head, of its own weight, fell downward toward his father's head.[5]

Jesse's first orgasm is over; he has now been initiated into the folkways of his culture; he has, with the aid of his family and in the company of his community, participated in the destruction/communion of that figure which his society has deemed an object of both announced fear and secret admiration; and he, with his community, has symbolically eaten (beaten, burned, cut) the flesh and drunk (brought pouring forth) the blood. Jesse's society, the rural South, has sexually/spiritually sated itself upon the new man of sorrows, the black man whose legendary sexual prowess is absorbed, through this mutilation ritual, by Jesse's white culture. The initiation that Jesse, as well as the other communicants, has experienced, however, insures that, whether a boy of eight or a man of forty-two, he cannot know complete sexual gratification which is not accompanied by either the fantasy or the reality of racial torture and mutilation. And as Jesse's thoughts return to the present, he finds that his manhood has returned:

> Something bubbled up in him; his nature again returned to him. He thought of the boy in the cell; he thought of the man in the fire; he thought of the knife and grabbed himself and stroked himself and a terrible sound, something between a high laugh and a howl, came out of him and dragged his sleeping wife up on one elbow. She stared at him in a moonlight which had now grown cold as ice. He thought of the morning and grabbed her, laughing and crying

and laughing, and he whispered, as he stroked her, as he took her, "Come on sugar, I'm going to do you like a nigger, just like a nigger, come on, sugar, and love me just like you'd love a nigger."[6]

So, as the story closes, Jesse, whose manhood is restored through the imaginary infusion of himself, through communion, of black flesh and blood, makes his own transformation complete. For the purpose of the sexual pleasure that he can achieve in no other way, he *becomes* black, and he demands that his wife respond to him as such—an ironic confession, made only in the heat of desperate passion, that Jesse, his wife, the white South, can never know physical and psychic fulfillment without openly acknowledging the void in the "frail sanctuary" of themselves that can be filled only through their psychological assimilation with blackness.

Notes

    1. James Baldwin, *Going to Meet the Man* (New York: Dell Publishing, 1969), p. 198.
    2. *Going to Meet the Man*, p. 201.
    3. *Going to Meet the Man*, pp. 214–215.
    4. *Going to Meet the Man*, p. 216.
    5. *Going to Meet the Man*, pp. 216–217.
    6. *Going to Meet the Man*, pp. 217–218.

Words and Music: Narrative Ambiguity in "Sonny's Blues"

Keith E. Byerman°

"Sonny's Blues" has generally been accorded status as the best of James Baldwin's short stories. It tells of the developing relationship between Sonny, a musician and drug addict, and the narrator, his brother, who feels a conflict between the security of his middle-class life and the emotional risks of brotherhood with Sonny. The critics, who differ on whether the story is primarily Sonny's or the narrator's, generally agree that it resolves its central conflict.[1] If, however, resolution is not assumed but taken as problematical, then new thematic and structural possibilities are revealed. The story becomes a study of the nature and relationship of art and language. The com-

°Reprinted from *Studies in Short Fiction* 19 (1982):367–72, by permission of the author and the journal.

mentary on the story has centered on the moral issue; the purpose of this essay is to focus on the underlying aesthetic question.

According to Jonathan Culler, resolution can be accomplished in a story when a message is received or a code deciphered.[2] In most cases the message is withheld in some manner—through deception, innocence, or ignorance—until a key moment in the narrative. In the case of "Sonny's Blues," however, the message is apparent from the beginning and is repeatedly made available to the narrator. The story, in part, is about his misreadings; more importantly, it is about his inability to read properly. The source of this inability is his reliance on a language that is at once rationalistic and metaphoric. His sentences are always complete and balanced, and his figurative language puts on display his literary intelligence. Even in the description of his own emotional states, the verbal pattern overshadows the experience. Whenever the message is delivered, he evades it through language; he creates and then reads substitute texts, such as the messenger, or distorts the sense of the message by changing it to fit his preconceived ideas.

The message is first presented in the simplest, most straightforward manner, as a newspaper story: "I read about it in the paper, in the subway, on my way to work. I read it, and I couldn't believe it, and I read it again. Then perhaps I just stared at it, at the newsprint spelling out his name, spelling out the story."[3] The information is clearly there, "spelled out," a text that cannot be ignored. But the narrator's immediate action is to refract his emotions through metaphor: "I stared at it in the swinging lights of the subway car, and in the faces and bodies of the people, and in my own face, trapped in the darkness which roared outside" (p. 86). This oblique allusion to the underground man is followed in the next paragraph by a reference to the ice at the center of his emotional Inferno. What is noteworthy is that these images call attention to themselves as images and not simply as natural expressions of emotional intensity. His response has built into it a strong sense of the need for proper verbal expression. This deflection from emotion to art is accompanied by repeated statements on the impossibility of believing the message.

The second scene dramatizes and verifies the information presented by the newspaper story. The narrator encounters an addict who had been a friend of Sonny's. In fact, "I saw this boy standing in the shadow of a doorway, looking just like Sonny" (p. 88). Again there is a darkness and an explicit identification with Sonny. Again there is distancing through figurative language: "But now, abruptly, I hated him. I couldn't stand the way he looked at me, partly like a dog, partly like a cunning child" (p. 88). Such language prepares us for, while guaranteeing, the failed communication of this episode. The narrator is offered knowledge, but he chooses to interpret the messenger rather than the message. He expresses a desire to know, and remorse when he does not listen, but he also repeats his unwillingness to understand.

A further complication occurs when, in the midst of this encounter, the narrator turns his attention from the addict to the music being played in a bar. The mark of his refusal to know is in his act of interpreting those associated with the music. "The juke box was blasting away with something black and bouncy and I half watched the barmaid as she danced her way from the juke box to her place behind the bar. And I watched her face as she laughingly responded to something someone said to her, still keeping time to the music. When she smiled one saw the little girl, one sensed the doomed, still-struggling woman beneath the face of the semi-whore" (p. 90). Rather than listen to the conversation he is directly involved in, the narrator observes one he cannot possibly hear. In the process, he can distance himself by labeling the woman he sees. He is thereby at once protected from and superior to the situation. The music, a motif repeated in subsequent scenes, here is part of what the narrator refuses to know; he substitutes his words for the non-verbal communication that music offers. In telling the incident, he suggests that he is listening to the music to avoid the addict-messenger; in fact, their messages are identical, and he avoids both by imposing his verbal pattern.

A similar evasion occurs in the next major scene, which is a flashback within a flashback. The narrator's mother, after hearing her son reassure her that nothing will happen to Sonny, tells him the story of his father and uncle, a story that parallels the one occurring in the present time of the narration. Her story, of the uncle's death and the father's inability to prevent it, is a parable of proper brotherly relationships. After telling the tale, she indicates its relevance: " 'I ain't telling you all this,' she said, 'to make you scared or bitter or to make you hate nobody. I'm telling you this because you got a brother. And the world ain't changed' " (p. 101). The narrator immediately offers his interpretation: " 'Don't you worry, I won't forget. I won't let nothing happen to Sonny' " (p. 101). His mother corrects his impression: " 'You may not be able to stop nothing from happening. But you got to let him know you's *there*' " (p. 101).

No ambiguity can be found here. The message is clearly delivered, in transparent, non-metaphoric language. What prevents it from being received can only be the substitutions in the pattern. The musically-talented uncle is Sonny's double and the helpless father is the narrator's. This parallel structure makes the point obvious to the reader, but the fact that it is *only* parallel justifies the continuation of the narrative. In his positivistic way, the narrator will not believe what does not occur to his immediate experience or what cannot be contained within his linguistic net. His mother's fatalistic message cannot be so contained. Thus, the story must continue until he has both evidence and the means of controlling it.

The final scene of the story, instead of validating the meaning, only deepens the ambiguity. The bar where Sonny plays and the people in it are presented as alien to the narrator's experience. The room is dark and narrow, suggestive not only of a birth passage, but also of the subway where the narrator first felt troubled by Sonny. The musicians tend to fit stereotypes of blacks: Creole, the band leader is "an enormous black man" and the drummer, "a coal-black, cheerful-looking man, built close to the ground . . . his teeth gleaming like a lighthouse and his laugh coming up out of him like the beginning of an earthquake" (p. 118). The language grows more serious when the music itself begins: "All I know about music is that not many people ever really hear it. And even when on the rare occasion when something opens within, and the music enters, what we mainly hear, of hear corroborated, are personal, private, vanishing evocations. But the man who created the music is hearing something else, is dealing with the roar rising from the void and imposing order on it as it hits the air. What is evoked in him, then, is of another order, more terrible because it has no words, and triumphant, too, for that same reason" (p. 119). Little preparation has been made for such a reaction to the music. The act of the musician seems a creative response to the impinging chaos described in the opening subway scene. But this perception springs full-bodied from the brow of a man who has repeatedly indicated his antagonism to such music. One resolution of this apparent contradiction might be found in his comment about the terrible wordlessness of what he is hearing. A man committed to language, he finds himself confronted with a form whose power seems precisely its ability to create order without language.

In this context, it is highly significant that he immediately undertakes to explain the music through the metaphor of conversation. "The dry, low, black man said something awful on the drums, Creole answered, and the drums talked back. Then the horn insisted, sweet and high, slightly detached perhaps, and Creole listened, commenting now and then, dry, and driving, beautiful and calm and old" (p. 121). If the terror of the music is its lack of words, then to explain it as language is to neutralize its power. By creating the metaphor, the narrator can control his experience and limit its effect. He can make the music fit the patterns that he chooses.

This is not readily apparent in what he calls the "tale" of Sonny's music. "For, while the tale of how we suffer, and how we are delighted, and how we may triumph is never new, it always must be heard. There isn't any other tale to tell, it's the only light we've got in all this darkness" (p. 121). While music is changed to language, with the attendant change in meaning, and while the obsession is still with bringing light and thus reason, the narrator is opening up the meaning with reference to "we" and to the emotional conditions of suffering and delight. His language seems less logical and self-consciously artistic than before.

The specifics of the tale strengthen its emotional impact. The music frees the narrator and perhaps Sonny: "Freedom lurked around us and I understood, at last, that he could help us to be free if we would listen, that he would never be free until we did" (p. 122). The narrator's freedom comes through his recapturing and acceptance of the past; the music conjures up his mother's face, his uncle's death, Grace's death accompanied by Isabel's tears "and I felt my own tears begin to rise" (p. 122). Yet for all the emotional content, the form remains very logically, artistically structured. Sentences are very carefully balanced and arranged, the emotion is carried on such verbs as "saw" and "felt," and finally "we," after a series of generalizations, quickly becomes "I" again. This scene only has to be compared to the prologue of *Invisible Man* to demonstrate the extent of control. Both scenes deal with the emotional impact of the blues, but whereas Ellison's is surrealistic and high paradoxical, with its narrator barely living through the history of the vision, Baldwin's narrator remains firmly planted in the bar and firmly in control of the emotion he describes.

The story's underlying ambiguity has its richest expression in the final metaphor, a cocktail that the narrator sends to Sonny. As a symbolic representation of the message of the narrative, the scotch and milk transformed into the cup of trembling suggests the relief from suffering that YHWH promised the children of Israel. Thus, Sonny's suffering will be made easier by the narrator's willingness to be involved in his life. But, as in earlier cases, this is not the only possible reading. First, the drink itself, scotch and milk, is an emblem of simultaneous destruction and nurture to the system; it cannot be reduced to one or the other. Sonny's acceptance of it indicates that his life will continue on the edge between the poison of his addiction and the nourishment of his music.

The narrator's reading of the drink as the cup of trembling offers a second ambiguity, which is not consistent with the first, for it implies clear alternatives. The cup of trembling was taken from Israel when YHWH chose to forgive the people for their transgressions. But it was YHWH who had given the cup of suffering to them in the first place.[4] Thus, it becomes important to the meaning of the story which verse is being alluded to in the metaphor. If the cup is given, then Sonny will continue to suffer and feel guilt; if the cup is taken away, then Sonny returns to a state of grace. There is no Biblical reference to the cup merely remaining.

The choice of image indicates the continuation of the narrator's practice of reading events through the vehicle of his own language. But the very limits of language itself raise problems as to the meaning of the narrative. The need to turn an act into a metaphor and thereby "enrich" the meaning depends upon limitation in the use of language. The words, though, carry traces of meaning not intended. The result, as in this case, can be that the meaning can carry with it its very opposite. In such a situation, intended meaning is lost in the very richness of meaning.

"Sonny's Blues," then, is a story of a narrator caught in the "prison-house of language."[5] Both in describing experiences and explaining them, he is locked into a linguistic pattern that restricts his understanding. With the presentation of such a character, Baldwin offers an insight into the limits of language and the narrative art. In the very act of telling his story, the narrator falsifies (as do all story-tellers) because he must use words to express what is beyond words. The irony is that much of Baldwin's own writing—essays, novels, stories—is premised on the transparency and sufficiency of language rather than on its duplicity.

Clearly a dialectic is at work. "Sonny's Blues" moves within the tension between its openly stated message of order and a community of understanding and its covert questioning, through form, allusion, and ambiguity, of the relationship between life and art. With the latter, the story suggests that literary art contributes to deceit and perhaps anarchy rather than understanding and order. What makes this tension dialectical is that the artifice of narration is necessary for the existence of the story and its overt message. The measure of Baldwin's success is his ability to keep this tension so well hidden, not his ability to resolve the conflict. What finally makes "Sonny's Blues" such a good story is its author's skill at concealing the fact that he must lie in order to tell the truth.

Notes

1. See Stanley Macebuh, *James Baldwin: A Critical Study* (New York: Third World Press, 1973); Sherley Anne Williams, *Give Birth to Brightness* (New York: Dial, 1972), pp. 145–166; Harry L. Jones, "Style, Form and Content in the Short Fiction of James Baldwin," in *James Baldwin: A Critical Evaluation*, ed. Therman O'Daniel (Washington, D.C.: Howard University Press, 1977), pp. 143–150; Suzy Bernstein Goldman, "James Baldwin's 'Sonny's Blues': A Message in Music," *Negro American Literature Forum*, 8 (1974), 231—233; John Reilly, " 'Sonny's Blues': James Baldwin's Image of Black Community," *Negro American Literature Forum*, 4 (1970), 56–60; and Donald C. Murray, "James Baldwin's 'Sonny's Blues': Complicated and Simple," *Studies in Short Fiction*, 14 (1977), 353–357.

2. *Structuralist Poetics: Structuralism, Linguistics, and the Study of Literature* (Ithaca: Cornell University Press, 1975), pp. 202–238.

3. "Sonny's Blues," in *Going to Meet the Man* (1965; rpt. New York: Dell, 1976), p. 86. All further references to this work appear in the text.

4. See Isaiah 51:17–23.

5. The phrase comes from Frederic Jameson, *The Prison-House of Language: A Critical Account of Structuralism and Russian Formalism* (Princeton: University Press, 1972).

The Eye as Weapon in *If Beale Street Could Talk*   Trudier Harris°

If the eye is indeed the light to the soul, then James Baldwin lays many of his characters bare in *If Beale Street Could Talk* (Signet, 1975). The people in the novel, by looking at each other—not with just casual glances, but with *intense* eye contact—reveal many of their subconscious thoughts and feelings. On a superficial level, they use eye contact to fight battles that might require guns, knives, and other more physical weapons if the characters were in a different societal context and, on a deeper level, they use the eye to commune in metaphysical terms. If "Beale Street" could talk, the talk would be of people, people in trouble, people who love, suffer, sacrifice, and hope. Baldwin's novel is about them, about their interaction by voice, body language, and eye contact. This is the method by which he conveys to readers his belief in black community and spirituality.

Eye contact is both real and symbolic confrontation, be it for purposes of communion, seduction, or conquest. One character is usually dominating the other; the use of eye contact can result in calming a disturbed person down, inspiring a depressed person, encouraging sexual submission, or creating feelings of terror in persons who lack authority and social status. At the heart of all these confrontations is the idea of transformation, of converting people to a different point of view, of change of mind or change of attitude.

The concept of change by intense reflection (mirror, eyes) is introduced by Tish, the nineteen-year-old narrator, in the very first sentence of the novel and provides undercurrents throughout. "I look at myself in the mirror," she says, trying to understand the changes and transformations that have been thrust upon her. She is seeking for something in her own eyes that will convey such knowledge to her, a search for understanding that many of the later confrontation

°Reprinted from *MELUS* 5, no. 3 (1978):54–66, by permission of the author and the journal.

scenes center upon. At the outset Tish tries to understand how she got from her christened name of Clementine to the nickname of Tish. It would make sense, she observes, if people called her Clem. Is the answer somewhere in that reflection of subtleties she conveys to other people and now tries to understand for herself? Why has she been transformed in such an interesting way? She wonders the same about Fonny, her twenty-two-year-old lover, whose name is Alonzo and whose nickname might logically have been Lonnie. Looking into the depths of people's souls, as Tish looks into the mirror, and trying to get them to change, or at least to change their minds, is what many of the characters do in their eye-to-eye confrontations.

People who use this weaponry of the eye are usually fighting for ones they love, for *If Beale Street Could Talk* is indeed a story of love. It is the story of one family's struggle to get the lover of its younger daughter out of jail. Such a brief synopsis of plot, however, is almost an insult to the intensity of the story, to its carefully structured scenes of present and flashback action and to its perceptive, creative narrator. By using Tish, the youngest member of the Rivers family, as his narrator, Baldwin adds a dimension to this novel that has not been present in his earlier works. This dimension, that of female storyteller (a youthful, unsophisticated one at that), adds a measure of credence to the narration. Tish's innocence, along with her natural abilities at perception, draw the reader into the story and encourage empathy with her. Tish relates the story of her family's efforts to get Fonny, her lover and the father of her unborn child, out of jail. He has been falsely accused of rape by a Puerto Rican woman, a Mrs. Rogers, who is obviously parroting testimony fed to her by officer Bell, a white cop who is out to get Fonny for having publicly degraded Bell's badge and reputation. Tish's family (Joseph the father, Sharon the mother, and Ernestine the sister) have in effect adopted Fonny and made his struggle theirs. Although Fonny's father, Frank Hunt, assists in the efforts to free his beloved son, Fonny's mother and two sisters will not step down from their "high yaller" superiority long enough to concern themselves with a nappy-headed, backwards, and wayward son and brother. These conflicts within and among the two warring families (reminiscent of the Romeo and Juliet story to which Tish makes allusion) provide one of the major arenas for the weaponry of the eye.

Powerful eye contact is used several times in inter- and intra-familial confrontation between and among the Rivers and the Hunts, as those who love them work to keep Tish sane and healthy during her pregnancy and to get Fonny out of jail. As a means of announcing Tish's pregnancy to the Hunts, Joseph calls a summit meeting at his home. The eight people who should care most about Fonny are thus put into confrontation with each other; three of them obviously do not care. Mrs. Hunt has used her religion as a convenient crutch for years and has left her son "in the hands of the Lord," believing his term in jail will make him "surrender his soul to Jesus—" (p.79). His two sisters have rejected Fonny because they consider him an unsalvageable street person and beneath them since they at least have gone to City College. The intrafamilial divisions of color and status cause the three Hunt women to respond negatively to the announcement of the pregnancy. Mrs. Hunt describes the act of conception as "lustful" and concludes that the "Holy Ghost will cause that child to shrivel" in Tish's womb. Frank, outraged by his wife's curse of his unborn grandchild, knocks her to the floor; he and Joseph then depart, leaving the six women to confront each other.

Accusations fly back and forth between the women, threats are made, tears shed. When one girl ventures to comment that she, her mother, and her sister shouldn't have come, Ernestine, Tish's sister, an extremely forceful character and one of Tish's strengths in these times of trouble, takes control: "Ernestine stared at Sheila until Sheila was forced to raise her eyes. Then, Ernestine laughed, and said, 'My. I must have a dirty mind, Sheila. I didn't know that you could even *say* that word' " (pp. 87–88). By the power of eye contact, Ernestine forces Sheila to silence, forces her to make the look that will provide for the climactic undercutting of Sheila's sexual activities. Power and control, which Ernestine has here, are what the people fighting for Fonny need. The power of her eye contact puts Ernestine in the dominant position. Such control could possibly elicit or force a change of mind on Sheila's part concerning her brother. Unfortunately, the Hunt women are lost in their arrogance and no changes are forthcoming.

Tish, however, makes one last attempt to convert Fonny's female relatives. As the Hunt women are about to leave the Rivers' household, Tish bars the door, stands in front of Mrs. Hunt, and looks her "in the eyes." "That child," Tish says, "is in my belly. Now, you raise your knee and kick it out—or with them high heel shoes. You don't want this child? Come on and kill it now. I dare you" (pp. 89–90). Tish, in the position of control, looks into Mrs. Hunt's soul and sees the blackhearted villain that the woman reveals, by her rejection of the unborn child, is living there. In this confrontation of love and hate, Tish seems to be asking a question that will recur repeatedly: can hatred be allowed to win? Can Mrs. Hunt really feel the way she says she does about her unborn grandchild? Has she rejected Fonny to the extent that she will not accept his child? Can hatred, when it confronts love, still continue as hatred, or will Mrs Hunt, seeing the desperation and love in Tish's eyes, change her mind? Will she be transformed? Again, the question is the same as the basis of all such confrontations: Will the light of the soul have effect when actions and words do not?

The power of the eye is no less strong when it is used in situations where one family member is trying to calm other family members. There is still an idea of change, of transformation—that the love conveyed by one person will be transmitted to the other and bring him from a state of despair or depression to one of calmness and encouragement. Ernestine does this for Tish, and Joseph, at another point, does it for Frank. After Mrs. Rogers has left New York to return to Puerto Rico (or been sent away by Bell) and the difficulty of getting Fonny out of jail intensifies, Ernestine and Tish have a meeting in a bar to decide what is to be done. Ernestine is calm; Tish is discouraged and "frightened." Tish observes: "[Ernestine] looked at me very steadily. It may seem a funny thing to say, but I found myself admiring her guts" (p. 146). Ernestine then outlines her plan for someone to pursue Mrs. Rogers to Puerto Rico in an effort to poke holes in the state's case; she convinces Tish that Sharon, their mother, is the logical choice. As Ernestine talks, Tish is calmed and finally encouraged by the determination she sees in Ernestine's eyes (pp. 148–49).

Ernestine's task of encouraging Tish goes smoother by far than does Joseph's encouragement of Frank. Working against Joseph is the fact that Frank is a weak man, unsupported by wife and daughters and, in his own mind, fighting a losing battle. In another bar setting, Joseph and Frank try to decide how to raise money for Fonny's defense. In the face of Frank's discouragement, Joseph "stares at Frank in silence, and forces Frank to raise his eyes" (p. 153). Then Joseph begins to talk about raising money. "Frank looks up at him and says nothing—merely questions him with his eyes" (p. 153). As Joseph explains that they have never had money and will rob and steal if necessary, Frank is slowly brought to agreement and, in response to Joseph's comment that they have work to do, says: "You right, old buddy. Let's make it" (p. 155). The determination that Frank has seen in Joseph's eyes has inspired him, and his questions, for the moment, have been answered.

In Frank, however, hope flickers briefly and falters. Mrs. Rogers has a breakdown in Puerto Rico and connot return to testify against Fonny. The prosecutor maintains that Fonny will stay in jail until she can, which, to Frank's mind, may mean never. Frank receives the dire information from Joseph while they are sitting in the Hunts' kitchen; Frank's daughters are in the living room, laughingly having a good time. Joseph and Frank "watch each other for a rather awful moment, aware of the girls' laughter in the kitchen. Frank wants to make the laughter stop, but he cannot take his eyes from Joseph's eyes" (p. 229). Joseph has a hard time drawing Frank from the depths of his defeat, a hole made deeper by the giggling proof of the daughters' lack of concern for their brother. Joseph watches Frank deteriorate into tears and although the change does come, it is not as lasting this time around. The determination in Joseph's eyes is not transmitted to Frank in as innervating a form as it was before; Frank fails to see hope because his energy to keep coming back after defeats is almost gone at this stage.

Working for change of attitude or mind with family members has one important advantage—it presumably takes place in a receptive environment. The greatest test of the power of the eye as a weapon comes when family members must confront hostile environments; for example, when Tish and Fonny first confront Bell, the white cop. Tish has been aware of the alienation of people on the street, of the alienation of forces outside, throughout the novel (pp. 67, 102, 179). The love she and Fonny have is beautiful, and, it often affects people they come into contact with in very positive ways, but this is not universally true. Their little island of love is a fragile thing in the hostile sea of Harlem and is therefore susceptible to its many ravages. However, in an environment where everyone has more than his share of trouble, Tish correctly observes that when you're in trouble, you're alone.

Bell, one of the hostile forces outside, is the cause of that trouble. He tries to arrest Fonny for assault and battery after Fonny attacks an Italian junkie who has accosted Tish. When Tish sees Bell approaching, she puts her body between Fonny and Bell in the role of protector: "I was sure that the cop intended to kill Fonny; but he could not kill Fonny if I could keep my body between Fonny and this cop; and with all my strength, with all my love, my prayers, and armed with the knowledge that Fonny was not, after all, going to knock *me* to the ground, I held the back of my head against Fonny's chest, held both his wrists between my two hands, and looked up into the face of this cop. I said, 'That man—there—attacked me. Right in this store. Right now. Everybody saw it' " (pp. 168–69). Her awareness of what white cops do to black men forces Tish to take control; she realizes she must emasculate Fonny in this instance in order to save him. The the control and power that is symbolically represented by Bell's uniform comes through in his eyes. Tish records:

> Then, he looked back at me. Then, he looked at Fonny. I could not see Fonny's face. But I could see the cop's face: and I knew that I must not move, nor, if I could possibly help it, allow Fonny to move.
>
> "And where were you," the cop elaborately asked Fonny, "while all this"—his eyes flicked over me in exactly the same way the boy's eyes had—"while all this was going on between junior, there, and"— his eyes took me in again—"and your girl?"

"He was around the corner," I said, "buying cigarettes." For I did not want Fonny to speak. I hoped that he would forgive me, later.

"Is that so, boy?"

I said. "He's not a boy. Officer."

Now, he looked at me, really looked at me for the first time, and, therefore, for the first time, he really looked at Fonny. (p. 169)

When the cop threatens to take Fonny to jail for assault and battery, the Italian lady who runs the store where Tish has been attacked testifies in their behalf and Bell has no case. He determines to "get" Fonny. His eyes convey that message. Tish observes: "Bell's eyes are blue and . . . what I can see of his hair is red. He looks again at me and then again at Fonny. He licks his lips again" (p. 171).

Bell's eyes not only convey power and control; they also convey the possibility of symbolic rape, and image that is developed explicitly in later passages. Traditionally in the love-making situation, the male is dominant, the female submissive. The male, in a sense, uses his sex organ as a "weapon" to force the female to submit. Therefore, to make love to someone can be viewed as causing that person to submit to the "weapon" of love. Similarly, to seduce someone can mean overpowering that person in love as well as taking away means of resistance. To seduce Fonny (here intensified to rape), Bell would symbolically take away anything Fonny could use to fight back. Bell would put Fonny, in other words, in the position of woman in the lovemaking analogy. Fonny is to be "mounted," controlled by Bell through the legalistic system. Reduced to a weaker, submissive "woman," Fonny would restore to Bell the sense of power the storekeeper has taken away. This is the message of rape his eyes convey.

Then, too, hasn't the image of eye contact always been one of seduction? Doesn't Ernestine "seduce" Tish in trying to change her mind? Isn't the calming effect Joseph has on Frank a kind of seduction, with its own transformation, its own relief? Seduction as power, only hinted at in the family relationships, becomes obvious with Bell.

On occasions after the scene described above, Bell conveys his threat of rape by staring Tish and Fonny into submissive roles—if they happen to be alone (together they can fight, which is significant to their development of Fonny's defense). Bell's suggestive physical unbaring of Fonny and Tish is reminiscent of a comment Daniel, Fonny's friend, makes earlier. "I don't believe there's a white man in the country, baby, who can even *get* his dick hard, without he hear some nigger moan" (p. 133). Daniel suggests that whites get sexual stimulation (power) from the violence they commit against blacks, an idea not new to Baldwin and one he treated in his 1965

short story, "Going to Meet the Man." Bell's eyes, then, convey
power to be used against blacks for their destruction, a destruction
that would enhance Bell's sense of (sexual) power. Consider Tish's
observations:

> But I was beginning to learn something about the blankness of
> those eyes. What I was learning was beginning to frighten me to
> death. If you look steadily into that unblinking blue, into that pinpoint
> at the center of the eye, you discover a bottomless cruelty, a vi-
> ciousness cold and icy. In that eye, you do not exist: if you are
> lucky. *If* that eye, from its height, has been forced to notice you,
> if you *do* exist in the unbelievably frozen winter which lives behind
> that eye, you are marked, marked, marked, like a man in a black
> overcoat, crawling, fleeing, across the snow. The eye resents your
> presence in the landscape, cluttering up the view. Presently, the
> black overcoat will be still, turning red with blood, and the snow
> will be red, and the eye resents this, too, blinks once, and causes
> more snow to fall, covering it all. Sometimes I was with Fonny when
> I crossed Bell's path, sometimes I was alone. When I was with Fonny,
> the eyes looked straight ahead, into a freezing sun. When I was
> alone, the eyes clawed me like a cat's claws, raked me like a rake.
> These eyes look only into the eyes of the conquered victim. They
> cannot look into any other eyes. When Fonny was alone, the same
> thing happened, Bell's eyes swept over Fonny's black body with the
> unanswerable cruelty of lust, as though he had lit the blowtorch and
> had it aimed at Fonny's sex. When their paths crossed, and I was
> there, Fonny looked straight at Bell, Bell looked straight ahead. *I'm
> going to fuck you, boy,* Bell's eyes said. *No, you won't* said Fonny's
> eyes. *I'm going to get my shit together and haul ass out of here.*
> (pp. 211–12)

Bell maintains his victory; Fonny maintains his resistance. And as long
as Fonny will not submit, Bell uses the system to "fuck" him.
     The climatic image of rape comes on another occasion when
Tish, coming home from shopping, confronts Bell alone:

> I looked into his eyes again. This may have been the first time
> I ever really looked into a white man's eyes. It stopped me, I stood
> still. It was not like looking into a man's eyes. It was like nothing
> I knew, and—therefore—it was very powerful. It was a seduction
> which contained the promise of rape. It was rape which promised
> to debasement and revenge: on both sides. I wanted to get close to
> him, to enter into him, to open up that face and change it and
> destroy it, descend into the slime with him. Then, we would both
> be free: I could almost hear the singing.
>   "Well," he said, in a very low voice, "you ain't got far to go.
> Sure wish I could carry it for you, though."
>   I can still see us on that hurrying, crowded, twilight avenue,
> me with my package and my handbag, staring at him, he staring at

me. I was suddenly his: a desolation entered me which I had never
felt before. I watched his eyes, his moist, boyish, despairing lips,
and felt his sex stiffening against me. (pp.213–14)

Bell forces Tish into the role of the victim. On this sexual battlefield,
Tish can only imagine herself using her "weapon" successfully against
Bell and thereby freeing herself. She will be transformed from a state
of victimization to a state of freedom. The singing she imagines hearing
as indicative of that freedom is an image she also uses to describe
her sexual conversion with Fonny (p. 98). She has sexual power even
if Bell can seduce her on the social level, sexual power that is very
positive and which, between Fonny and Tish, is very sacred, as will
be seen.

Bell cannot or will not see the love that Tish and Fonny have
for each other; his own self image negates any such consideration.
Bell represents one kind of hostile environment—totally unsympa-
thetic and unrelenting. Pietro, Mrs. Rogers' lover/protector, presents
another hostile force against which the weapon of the eye, as wielded
by Sharon, is severely tested. In order to protect Mrs. Rogers, Pietro,
for different reasons, but just as staunchly as Bell, cannot allow himself
to be affected by the power of the eye. He has seen the woman he
loves raped and degraded by Americans and has taken her home to
Puerto Rico to safety. Then Sharon comes to ask Pietro to influence
Mrs. Rogers to change her testimony. While Pietro sympathizes with
Sharon and recognizes her noble motives, he cannot subject Mrs.
Rogers to further abuse. Sharon then tries to change his mind by
forcing him to look into her soul. *"Look at me,"* she demands in
answer to Pietro's question "What makes you think he [Fonny] didn't
do it?" (p. 188). Can the young Puerto Rican not see that this
grandmotherly woman is telling the truth? If her actions are ineffec-
tual, can her eyes possibly lie? Can't he see the love, the concern,
the genuine sense of commitment to freeing Fonny and getting at
the truth of the identity of Mrs. Rogers' rapist?

Again Sharon commands "Look at me" and tries to convey to
Pietro the love she has for Tish and her genuine belief that she is
not marrying her daughter to a rapist. Pietro is not convinced. Going
one step further in trying to make Pietro spiritually identify with the
situation, Sharon asks: "Are you a rapist?" Perhaps the chord she
wants to strike in Pietro is almost reached: "The dark eyes, in the
stolid face, staring, now directly into my mother's eyes, make the
face electrical, light a fire in the darkness of a far-off hill: he has
heard the question" (p. 191). Perhaps he sees in his own self-
consciousness the innocent Fonny who is locked away in jail in New
York. But his first commitment is to Mrs. Rogers' peace of mind and
he refuses to upset her by implying she has identified the wrong

man as her rapist. Sharon's first mission has failed; the light has not been bright or strong enough: "He looks at her, now very hard and cold" (p. 191).

Sharon, however, is not one to give up. When she fails with Pietro, she tracks down Mrs. Rogers and confronts her. Sharon immediately notices in Mrs. Rogers' face that "there is terror . . . and a certain covered terrified sympathy" (p. 202). But looks are indeed sometimes deceiving, and the Puerto Rican woman fights back. "She looks at Sharon, with bitterness. Sharon straightens and they are, abruptly, looking each other in the eye—each held, now, by the other" (p. 203). Victoria Rogers is as abused by American society as Fonny is and she makes as much of an effort to convince Sharon as Sharon does to convince her. "There is a plea in the girl's eyes," a plea for Sharon's understanding of the plight the girl is in and definitely a plea for Sharon to go away. The girl is frightened and tearful and does not respond as Sharon wants her to even when she is confronted with a picture of Fonny. Sharon reaches out and pulls the girl toward her—the direct confrontation: "'You pay for the lies you tell.' She stares at the girl. The girl stares at her. 'You've put a man in jail, daughter, a man you've never seen. He's twenty-two years old, daughter, he wants to marry *my* daughter—and'—Victoria's eyes meet hers again—'he's black.' She lets the girl go, and turns back to the window. 'Like us'" (p. 208). Mrs. Rogers is affected by Sharon's pleas and "tears rise in" her "dark, defeated, eyes." However, she cannot relive the experience of the rape or re-evaluate her identification of the rapist. To do so, as Ernestine has predicted, means insanity. "If she changes her testimony, she'll go mad. Or become another woman. And you [Tish] know how often people go mad, and how rarely they change" (p. 147). Sharon, therefore, by the power of the eyes, brings Mrs. Rogers to the brink of truth, only to cause her to fall down the other side of the precipice, into insanity.

The power of eye contact might sometimes fail with family members, it might fail with Bell, Mrs. Rogers and Pietro, but to Fonny and Tish, it is everything they have. It is the *saving* power that sustains them as they talk to each other at the Tombs through telephones separated by a glass partition. They see in each other's eyes what they cannot give by touching; they commune, they comfort. They create, in effect, a religion of love, a religion that has as its essential qualities loyalty, affection, and comfort. When Tish visits Fonny, she sees a "quickening look" in his eyes, a look that conveys to her the hope for deliverance and the unwavering love they have for each other. "I love his eyes" (p. 4), Tish says, bringing immediate notice to the eyes and the communion between herself and Fonny. She also frequently wonders if the baby will have Fonny's eyes.

To understand the creation of a religion of love and the climactic encouraging, transforming lovemaking that Tish and Fonny engage in through the glass partition when he is in jail, it is necessary to consider the images that are used to describe their earlier lovemaking. Their love has taken on a sacred quality. In describing their sexual encounters, Tish says that Fonny "rode deeper and deeper not so much into me as into a kingdom which lay just behind his eyes" (p. 52). This kingdom of love (God) is given validity in other expressions as well. Tish describes herself and Fonny as being one (p. 62). Time and again her sentences are redolent with phrases from gospel songs. She describes the atmosphere around them being changed after their discovery of love (p. 63—as in the song of religious conversion—"I looked at my hands, my hands looked new. I looked at my feet, they did too"), the "sacramental air" and "vows" (p. 176) of their love, and the transforming power of sex—"Fonny caressed me and called my name and he fell asleep. I was very proud. I had crossed my river. Now, we were one" (p. 177). To cross a river (as in Jordan) is as much an image of religion as it is of sex ("to cross over into camp ground"). To cross over is also to be changed, to be transformed in some way. Fonny and Tish, then, are thus converted into an unbreakable union with each other—to love and to save (figuratively and literally) each other by loving (the conversion is also suggested in the name changing that Tish observes on the first page of the novel). They will give each other emotional and spiritual support during Fonny's incarceration (in spite of the stone walls) and those who love Fonny will save him by rescuing him from a destructive and dehumanizing prison environment by their love. Fonny and Tish will look to no other source, save a human one, for whatever they may need. This view of humanity as the ultimate source of sustenance continues in other images Tish uses; she and Fonny see God reflected in each other.

Images casually hinted at elsewhere are made explicit in Tish's description of the first time she and Fonny made love (pp. 93–99). Initially, Fonny tries to convey his love for Tish through eye contact: "It was like nothing was happening in the world but us. I was not afraid. It was deeper than fear. I could not take my eyes away from his. I could not move. If it was deeper than fear, it was not yet joy. It was wonder. . . . 'And you know,' he said, still not moving, holding me with those eyes, 'that I've always been yours, right?' " He explains how he values his sculpture, how he will probably respond to her when they are married, and then "he stopped and looked at me, very quiet, very hard: there was a hardness in him I had barely sensed before. Within this hardness moved his love, moved as a torrent or as a fire moves, above reason, beyond argument, not to be modified in any degree by anything life might do. I was his, and he was mine—" Then, the creation of the love of religion. Tish records of Fonny: "he called me by the thunder at my ear," which brings to mind immediately the lines of the spiritual, "Steal Away" ("My Lord, He calls me, He calls me by the thunder / The trumpet sounds within my soul / I ain't got long to stay here.") As her lord calls her, Tish is "being changed" (the conversion). Says Tish, "a *singing* began in me and his body became *sacred* (my emphasis). When the river has been crossed, and sperm and blood are mingled, "the effect was as of some strange anointing. Or, we might have just completed a tribal rite" (p. 101). Tish's state of virginity is a pure offering on the altar of her lord, a purity that enhances the sacredness of their religion.

This new religion gets an immediate test of faith. Fonny has kept Tish out all night and brings her home to confront Joseph with the fact that they want to get married. The message of love is conveyed more in looks than in words and Fonny convinces the skeptical Joseph. "Joseph looked at him" and "They stared at each other again." "Both men, again, then measured each other." "Joseph looked hard at Fonny—a long look, in which one watched skepticism surrender to a certain resigned tenderness, a self-recognition. He looked as though he wanted to knock Fonny down; he looked as though he wanted to take him in his arms" (pp. 106–107). The kingdom behind the eyes is at last triumphant here. And Joseph is not the only convert. The Italian storekeeper who defends Tish sees the love she and Fonny have for each other (p. 171); so too does the Jewish man who rents the loft to them (pp. 163ff), and the Spaniards whose restaurant they frequent (pp. 69ff, 173ff).

With the strength of the religion established, it is no wonder then that Fonny and Tish can make love through glass. If tears are like orgasms (pp. 45–46), is it impossible for eyes to seduce? Tish comes to the Tombs near the end of the novel to inform Fonny of the numerous setbacks in trying to free him. "His eyes are enormous, deep and dark. . . . And he asks me, staring at me with those charged, enormous eyes, 'You all right?' " (p. 234). Then later, in her last interview with Fonny: "He was so skinny; he was so bruised: I almost cried out. To whom, where? I saw this question in Fonny's enormous, slanted black eyes—eyes that burned, now, like the eyes of a prophet. . . . We sat, and we just looked at each other. We were making love to each other through all that glass and stone and steel" (pp. 236–37). If God is dead, or at least gone from New York, Tish and Fonny can only cry out to each other: she and their coming baby save him from bitterness in jail. He experiences a conversion; he knows his own power to endure and to provide for their future life together. In responding to those eyes of a prophet, she says, "Where you lead me . . . I'll follow" ("Where He leads me, I will follow / Where he leads me, I will follow / I'll go with Him, with Him, all the way"). The religion of love is complete; Tish and Fonny are bound to each other eternally. Although for novel ends with Fonny still in jail, and Tish in labor, the realistic struggle for salvation will continue and the metaphysical one will give it sustenance.

Baldwin has ultimately used the eye as the light to the soul to recapture the essence of Christianity and plant its tenets in a new and fertile ground. From distortions, perversions, and hatred, the qualities of the Christian experience have beem reshaped into the essence of love, a love epitomized in the sacrifice of Jesus and now redefined and reflected in Tish's sacrifices for Fonny. This redefinition of a subject, Christianity, that Baldwin has treated again and again, is what makes the novel worthy of special note in the corpus of his works. It would have been the height of blasphemy for John Grimes (*Go Tell It on the Mountain,* 1953) to see God reflected in another human being. He had to thrash on the cold, bare church floor in his search for God, alone with those invisible forces which could damn him as quickly as they could extend a saving grace to him. The saints, including his mother and father, could watch, but they could not help him. In 1975, with Tish and Fonny, organized religion is passé to Baldwin. Mrs. Hunt, the institutional religious person in *If Beale Street Could Talk,* is painted as a clown, an anachronism, a fraud in her weekly ventures to church. She "loves Jesus" but ignores the plight of her son; she "loves Jesus" and scorns the husband who provides the fancy hats and clothes for her to get to her Jesus every Sunday. Baldwin suggests that the church has so distorted her vision of reality that she is beyond saving. On the one occasion Fonny and Tish accompany her to church (pp. 21–32), Baldwin reminds us, through Tish, that the place was once a post office. Zealous members of the congregation are remembered later in very unreligious connections: one dies of an overdose, another drops out of church to have an illegitimate child. Tish observes that on that Sunday the piano player, an "evil looking brother . . . attacked the keyboard like he was beating the brains out of someone he remembered" (p. 31). Tish later compares that Sunday's experience of walking into church with walking into the Tombs where Fonny is being held.

The people in the novel who thrive, work, and care about each other have no official record of church attendance. The Rivers go on occasions, such as Easter, and Frank doesn't go at all. They do not agonize over these decisions in their consciences, as a Gabriel or an Elizabeth or a Florence would in *Go Tell It on the Mountain.* They are people who are secure in themselves and what they can do for each other. They recognize no power other than themselves. No miracle will get Fonny out of jail, but stealing to get money for the lawyer might do it.

Closely tied to this new religion of love, of human beings interacting positively with and for other human beings, is Baldwin's attention to the black family. *If Beale Street Could Talk* is the realization of the family relationship Baldwin has been struggling for years to portray. Family members give freely but expect nothing in return. The Rivers and Frank put no restrictions on their love; they will make any sacrifice for Fonny and for each other. They recognize no god, no morality save that which is necessitated by the dictates of love. They are not bound by the guilt of a Gabriel or by the expectation that the people they give their love to should in fact be more pious than they are, as Gabriel expects of John. They are not bound by the submission of an Elizabeth who is grateful to Gabriel for having given her illegitimate son a name. They are not haunted by the self-hatred of a Rufus (*Another Country*, 1962), a hatred which destroys those upon whom it is projected, and which makes any semblance of family relationship impossible. They are not confused by interracial emotional involvement, as are many of the characters in *Another Country* and *Going to Meet the Man* (1965).

In *If Beale Street Could Talk*, Baldwin has turned to look at what solid black family and love relationships can be when they are motivated purely by love. Although the family relationship of the Rivers might be idealized, as Mary Fair Burks points out in her critical review of the novel (*Negro American Literature Forum*, 10 [Fall, 1976], 83–87, 95), the idealization is understandable. If the family is to become the unit of ultimate salvation, imperfections cannot be tolerated. If the people are indeed to become godlike, the only source of their hope in this world, they must be everything to each other; they cannot afford to fail each other.

Baldwin has denuded his plot of the encumbrances that created problems for his characters in his earlier works. The major characters in *If Beale Street Could Talk* are not fanatically committed to organized religion and church affiliation. They are not subject to the torment of interracial sex/love relationships. They are not immobilized by involvement in homosexual affairs. They are just folks who love each other and who are committed to the welfare of those whom they love. They are universally and basically human; however, it is the intensity of their concern for each other and the intense way in which Tish presents the story that makes it special. By allowing Tish, with her central involvement in the story, to relate it in her own creative, though unsophisticated way, Baldwin has made graceful simplicity the force of art. He has thereby moved his own creativity to a new level.

I Hear Music in the Air: James Baldwin's *Just Above My Head*

Eleanor Traylor°

> They began playing something very slow and more like the blues than a hymn.
>
> —Another Country

Just Above My Head is a gospel tale told in the blues mode. Its beauty is achieved by an opposition of contraries arranged not merely by an eloquence of words, but of moods, of scenes, of chords, and of mighty beats. The tale begins with a death but celebrates a life. It laments a loss, yet it sings a love song. It is both a dirge and a hymn. It is simultaneously a blues moan and a gospel shout. Its scheme of ironies evokes the sublimity of the songs of the elders, lines of which begin each of the five sections of *Just Above My Head:* "I hope my wings gonna fit me well / I tried them on at the gates of Hell."

The heights and depths of Arthur Montana, a gospel singer, as his life is seen by his older brother, Hall, is the story told in *Just Above My Head.* The story is both dreadful and beautiful, but it is not new. It summons, once again, a tale told consistently for twenty-six years by a narrator whose features are clearly etched among the splendid in twentieth century global literature. Both in his folly and in his greatness that narrator, the Baldwin Witness, in works as formally different as *Go Tell It on the Mountain* (a novel), "Sonny's Blues" (a story), *The Amen Corner,* (a play), *The Fire Next Time* (two epistles), *Notes of A Native Son (a history of thought), Nobody Knows My Name* (literary and cultural criticism), *Little Man* (a children's book), *One Day When I Was Lost* (a documentary scenario), *The Devil Finds Work* (an anatomy), essentially sketches one tale or one theme. That Witness has, himself, told us as much: "For while the tale of how we suffer and how we are delighted, and how we may triumph is never new, it always must be heard. There isn't any other tale to tell, it's the only light we've got in all this darkness. . . . And this tale, according to that face, that body, those strong hands an those strings, has another aspect in every country, and a new depth in every generation" ("Sonny's Blues").

The Baldwin narrator-witness had dramatized that tale in now six novels and one collection of stories, and has staged it in two plays. Its theme of the perilous journey of love which, if not risked, denies

°Reprinted from *First World* 2, no. 3 (1979):40–43, by permission of the author and the journal.

all possibility of the glorious in human life; which, if risked, insures the depths of sorrow but the ecstasy of joy; which, if betrayed, leads to madness and death; and which, if ignored or avoided, is directly responsible for the human misery that afflicts the creature man, is once again and powerfully the theme of *Just Above My Head.* The tale of the terrifying journey of the possibilities and failures of love is the dramatic center of the blues-gospel narrative mode of James Baldwin.

The older brother of Arthur Montana, gospel singer-star, like the older brother of Sonny, the blues-jazz pianist of "Sonny's Blues," tells the story of his younger brother as Arthur attempts the discovery of his song, his love, and himself. This story forms the baseline, the unparaphrasable drama of the novel. We have met Arthur before if we know John of *Go Tell It on the Mountain,* the David of *The Amen Corner,* Rufus Scott of *Another Country,* Fonny of *If Beale Street Could Talk,* and, of course, Sonny, of "Sonny's Blues." These young men in the world of Baldwin's fiction are all of like sensibility—they share the possibilities of a distinct heroic mode. They are blues boys; they must become blues men. The struggle to achieve blues manhood engages the union of the sacred and the secular, of mind and feeling, of lore and fact, of the technical and the spiritual, of boogie and strut, of street and manor, of bed and bread. The struggle demands the abyss; the achievement commands the mountain.

Arthur's tale spans 39 years of his life. That is the longest history of the blues life that the Baldwin narrator-witness has attempted. The events of the life of the John of *Go Tell It on the Mountain,* as seen in retrospective glimpses, occur on the day of his fourteenth birthday. He is "on his way," "coming through." We know that he is, for he has experienced a blues epiphany. On "the threshing floor" of a ritual in his passage, he has a vision, the sacred and secular vitality of which begin to shape his consciousness. The details of the life of the David of *The Amen Corner* are seen in the span of a church service and in a glance into the kitchen and bedroom of his estranged but finally spiritually reunited parents' flat just before the death of his father, Luke. As David leaves his dying father's bedside, discerning where the music of a man really comes from, we know that he is on his way to the marriage within himself of the poles of his preacher-mamma/blues-pappa's experience of the world. When Rufus Scott poises his arched body on the George Washington Bridge, "giving himself to the air," we have clearly seen one year of his life while glimpsing and understanding the years which have brought him to the water—and not to be baptized. Rufus, possessing so much in him that we love, has nevertheless, cooperated with hideous external circumstance and, finally, betrayed his song. The death of a budding but unachieved blues-manhood is the most anguished human experience (and perhaps the most sublime) that modern literature has achieved. On the other hand, Fonny of *If Beale Street Could Talk* is the young stuff of blues heroism. And Tish, his young love, is a portrait of girl/blues womanhood. Fonny will "keep his appointment with his baby," for he has already done it in his will. Sonny of "Sonny's Blues" is glimpsed by his brother and us on a set in a nightclub. We have seen, as in a capsule, the formative years of his life. We have read a letter that he has written from jail. We have heard him answer his brother's question: "Sonny, what have you been?" We have heard his answer, "more than I thought possible." Then we see Sonny offer the performance for which his life has prepared him. What we see is the portrait of a young blues hero. But Arthur's rite of passage in *Just Above My Head* is the longest journey that we have taken with the Baldwin gospel-blues man. Its junctures are the compelling experience of the book.

The story of Arthur's life is told us by his older brother, Hall, whose memory arranges its details two years after Arthur dies at 39 in a London pub where "the damn'd blood burst, first through his nostrils, then pounded through the veins of his neck, the scarlet torrent exploded through his mouth, it reached his eyes and blinded him, and brought Arthur down, down, down, down, down." The death of Arthur has triggered his brother's memory of those years when Arthur, who had become a gospel star, had first sung in public: "Beams of heaven as I go through this wilderness below." In those years, Julia, the child evangelist, whose life story parallels and comments upons Arthur's, is 11; her brother Jimmy, whose life mirrors Arthur's, is nine. In those years, the Trumpets of Zion gospel quartet is soon to form, and the lives of each member—Peanut, Red, Crunch and Arthur—in relation and in opposition to each other are to map Arthur's journey from church to pub where "the steps rise up, striking him in the chest . . . pounding between his shoulder blades, throwing him down on his back, staring down at him from the ceiling, just above his head."

Hall's need to tell the story of his brother's life arises at a moment, two years after Arthur's death, when he realizes that "I was so busy getting my brother into the ground right that I've hardly had time to cry, much less talk." The death of Arthur has caused Hall to confront transition. He has been Arthur's manager, producer, and protector, and despite both his illustration and statement that his wife Ruth "makes me happy, simply" and despite even his fascination with his children, it is Arthur who has occupied center stage in Hall's life. Arthur's death has left a void the nature of which surfaces to consciousness in Hall's dreams: "A thunder rolled inside my head, a stunning thunder, and I woke up. My white washed ceiling, with the heavy, exposed, unpainted beams, had dropped to crush me-was not more than two inches, just above my head. This weight crushed, stifled, the howl in my chest, I closed my eyes: a reflex. Then I opened my eyes. The ceiling had lifted itself, and was where it had always been. I blinked. The ceiling did not move, neither up nor down. It looked like it was fixed there, forever . . . fixed, forever, just above my head." Moreover, he dreams of trying to rescue a five-year old Arthur on a landscape which conspires against him in the attempt; he dreams of a descent underground: running through subway cars in search of Arthur; he dreams of kicking open a door to a subway car and "all of a sudden the door just flew open, on the sky. I couldn't catch my balance. I arched myself back but my feet began slipping off the edge, into space." Hall Montana dreams of the abyss. But he not only dreams. He consciously realizes himself as a dweller therein: "By and by, I sat sipping coffee in the kitchen windows at the exiled trees which lined the sad streets of a despairing void. It's better than the City—that's what we say; it's good for the children—my royal black ass. It's one of the blood-soaked outposts of hell. The day is coming, swiftly, when we will be forced to pack our things, and go. Nothing can live here, life has abandoned this place. The immensely calculated existence of this place reveals a total betrayal of life."

Hall, now a suburban dweller, has grown up in Harlem on "streets where life itself—life itself—depends on timing more infinitesimal than the split second where apprehension must be swifter than the speed of light." He is a man of many parts whose ability to see one thing and understand two or more offers us the drama of oppositions on which his story turns. Through his eyes we see the personal histories of the people of *Just Above My Head* whose lives adumbrate Arthur's and his own. We see how the attitudes and values of Paul and Florence Montana, blues-parents of Arthur and Hall, counter those of Amy and Joel Miller tainted—gospel parents of Julia and Jimmy. Paul Montana is a blues-jazz pianist whose wife and sons thrive upon his music; Joel Miller is parent-pimp-assaulter of the child-evangelist, Julia, whose younger brother, Jimmy, suffers his father's neglect and contempt. While Florence Montana is the vital center of her home, serene but competent, Amy Miller, ailing and agitated, is peripheral in her house.

Through Hall's eyes, we see the disintegration of the child-preacher, Julia, and her slow recreation of herself. First, with the aid of her Southern grandmother's tutelage, then from the succor of a love affair with Hall himself, and then by a perception she receives from her journey to Abidjan, Julia "had begun to create herself."

By contrast, we see through the eyes of Hall the slow dissolution of Arthur, "his heart," his younger brother whose attempt to harmonize his sacred song with the cacophony of his secular life finally breaks his willing but unequal heart. With Hall's ears, we hear Arthur say, "When you sing . . . you can't sing *outside* the song. You've got to *be* the song you sing. You've got to make a confession." And it is with Hall's sensibility that we come to understand the song and the relationshop of the man to the song: "Time attacked my brother's face . . . Time could not attack the song. Time was allied with the song, amen'd in the amen corner with the song, inconceivably filled Arthur as Arthur sang, bringing Arthur and many thousands, over. Time was proud of Arthur, so I dared whisper to myself, in the deepest and deadliest of the midnight hours; a mighty work was being worked, in time, through the vessel of my brother, who, then, was no longer my brother, belonging to me no longer, and who was yet, and more than ever, forever, my brother, my brother still." Hall understands that "[N]o one knows very much about the life of another. This ignorance becomes vivid, if you love another. Love sets the imagination on fire, and also, eventually, chars the imagination into a harder element: imagination cannot match love, cannot plunge so deep, or range so wide." Yet only an imagination fired by love and charred into "a harder element" could envision the portraits and hear the inner music of a Peanut who meets hooded death cloaked hideously in a monstrous robe called Klan; of a Red who brings death home from a Korean battlefield whose mud has splattered "America the Beautiful;" of a Crunch who does not know his incredible beauty, who betrays "his heart," becomes profligate, and wastes himself. Hall's imagination, despite a certain myopia which blinds him to manifest ambiguities within himself, is embracive. It is epic in its scope and lyric in its formulations. But most of all, it is musical in its presentation of the reality which it perceives. Therefore, as memory takes over the shape and rhythms of his brother's life, he is not only able to envision fragments of that life and shape them as an act of recreation, but he is able also to *hear* Arthur's life as well; for he has heard the music of which Arthur has been vessel. He hears his brother's life as one melodic theme off which he riffs the personal history of those whose rhythms lend that theme both assonance and dissonance. Off the melody of Arthur's life, he also riffs the history of an era as the details of that history affect the interiority of a cultural community so splendid as the people who arise from within it, so dreadful as the abyss. That community is Harlem: the central physical and spiritual location of the travelling, and, therfore, global people of *Just Above My Head.* It is that community where "[E]verything is happening and nothing is happening, and everything is still, like thunder. . . . And always, the echo of music, the presence

of voices, as constant and compelling as the movement of the sea."
(Tell Me How Long the Train's Been Gone.)

Hall's ability to see *out* blurs, sometimes, his ability to see *within*.
For really, it is Hall's story, via Arthur, that we witness. He thinks
that he has "come out the wilderness," that Ruth (so obviously,
"whither thou goest, I will go'), his wife, "makes me so happy,
simply." But it is not Ruth who has fired his imagination to a mighty
act of poetry. It is the sublime—the terrifying and the glorious—
life of Arthur at one pole and Julia at the other which had inspired
the music of *Just Above My Head.* And because the vital presence
of Arthur has fallen "down, down, down, down, down," in a London
toilet and because the streets between his house and Julia's are
"terrifying," Hall is able to hear that music which translates the
moans of anguish and the shouts of triumph—the blues/gospel mode—
of Afro-American experience of the world. The absence of Arthur
and the de-fused position of Julia in the physical center of Hall's life
(for he has persuaded us that love finds its power not only in spiritual
but in physical assertion—action) has led him to "a stage of transition
. . .

> The metaphysical abyss both of god and man . . . nothing rescues
> man (ancestral, living, or unborn) from loss of self within this abyss
> but a titanic resolution of the will whose ritual summons, response,
> and expression is the strong alien sound to which we give the name
> of music. On the arena of the living, when man is stripped of
> excrescences, when disaster and conflicts (the material of drama)
> have crushed and robbed him of self-consciousness and pretensions,
> he stands in present reality at the spiritual edge of the gulf, he has
> nothing left in physical existence which successfully impresses upon
> his spiritual or psychic perception. It is at such moments that tran-
> sitional memory takes over and intimations rack him of that intense
> parallel of his progress through the gulf of transition, of the disso-
> lution of his self and his struggle and triumph over subsumation
> through the agency of will. (Wole Soyinka, *Myth, Literature, and
> the African World.*)

This will of the Baldwin narrator-witness to report the abyss, to
marry the sublime music to sublime word, and, therefore, to attempt
the mythopoeic rendering of a great people in their and his disintegration in the abyss and by "a titanic resolution" reassume the
shape of things beautiful, is his mighty strength. He "recreates through
the medium of physical contemporary action, reflecting emotions of
the first active battle of the will through the abyss of dissolution"
(*ibid.*). He who is able to report the abyss while, at the same time,
encouraging us in celebration of our possibilities is a blues hero. (See
A. Murray, "Stomping the Blues.")

And yet, it is not only the *will* of the narrator-witness, Hall, which propels his story. It is also, his *need* to answer the question put by his son, Tony: "What was my uncle—Arthur—like?" that provides him final urgency to tell his tale: "Nobody can really talk about it until I can talk about it." Arthur's life, as seen by Hall, is a blues life. Arthur, a vessel of music, has invested his sacred gospel song with the secular nuances of his experience of life. That life has known anguish, but it has also created joy. In telling the story of that life, Hall Montana, the narrator, has offered his children, Tony and Odessa, a gift. The importance of that gift has been stated by the creating author, James Baldwin: "I am using them [the blues] as metaphor . . . they contain the toughness that manages to make . . . this experience of life or the state of being . . . out of which the blues come articulate. . . . I want to suggest that the acceptance of this anguish one finds in the blues, and the expression of it, create also, however odd this may sound, a kind of joy" (*Playboy Magazine*, 1963). Perhaps a kind of joy, realized even in our struggle through the abyss of dread reality, is the best that an art form can offer us.

Just Above My Head inspires a vision: in a mighty city, just beyond its borders, fields of cotton, corn, and cabins, stands a tabernacle called the House of Tales. Inside the tabernacle down the middle aisle, stands a great welcome table. On the right aisle of the table, there are many pews in which a host of elders sit—singing. On the left aisle of the table, there are many pews in which sit a host of their children's children. From the right aisle comes a song. Its strains seem to root in the cotton fields, reverberate throughout the city, and fill the tabernacle. "The songs of my brethren in bonds," sings a voice. From the left aisle comes a chorus, its contrapuntal echoes resound from the fields: its chant, "Solomon done flew, Solomon done fly away, Solomon gone Home," fills the tabernacle. At the head of the welcome table stand three figures. One, on the left, is suffused in light; he stares fixedly as at the horns of a star which he has ridden. The other, on the right, stands solid, visibly beautiful, stating a silent affirmation: "I am what I am." The one in the middle, gesturing first to left and then to right, steps slightly forward; looks straight ahead, cries out in a soft but resonant voice as to a congregation waiting at the door: "Come on in the Lord's house its gonna rain."

The vision fades: its meaning clear. The tabernacle is a structure built by tale tellers since the real and mythical sea voyage of Equiano. The tale is the welcome table. On its right sit the ancient tellers of the tale; on the left, the new. The three figures at the head stand like three hosts: Richard Wright on one end, Ralph Ellison on the other. James Baldwin stands in the center between the two. We are in the congregation invited to the feast. This member "bows on my knees crying' Holy!"

Essays on Nonfiction

From Harlem to Paris

Langston Hughes*

I think that one definition of the great artist might be the creator who projects the biggest dream in terms of the least person. There is something in Cervantes or Shakespeare, Beethoven or Rembrandt or Louis Armstrong that millions can understand. The American native son who signs his name James Baldwin is quite a ways off from fitting such a definition of a great artist in writing, but he is not as far off as many another writer who deals in picture captions or journalese in the hope of capturing and retaining a wide public. James Baldwin writes down to nobody, and he is trying very hard to write up to himself. As an essayist he is thought-provoking, tantalizing, irritating, abusing and amusing. And he uses words as the sea uses waves, to flow and beat, advance and retreat, rise and take a bow in disappearing.

In *Notes of a Native Son,* James Baldwin surveys in pungent commentary certain phases of the contemporary scene as they relate to the citizenry of the United States, particularly Negroes. Harlem, the protest novel, bigoted religion, the Negro press and the student milieu of Paris are all examined in black and white, with alternate shutters clicking, for hours of reading interest. When the young man who wrote this book comes to a point where he can look at life purely as himself, and for himself, the color of his skin mattering not at all, when, as in his own words, he finds "his birthright as a man no less than his birthright as a black man," America and the world might well have a major contemporary commentator.

Few American writers handle words more effectively in the essay form than James Baldwin. To my way of thinking, he is much better at provoking thought in the essay than he is in arousing emotion in fiction. I much prefer *Notes of a Native Son* to his novel, *Go Tell*

*Reprinted from the *New York Times Book Review,* 26 February 1956, 26, by permission of the journal.

It on the Mountain, where the surface excellence and poetry of his writing did not seem to me to suit the earthiness of his subject-matter. In his essays, words and material suit each other. The thought becomes poetry, and the poetry illuminates the thought.

What James Baldwin thinks of the protest novel from *Uncle Tom's Cabin* to Richard Wright, of the motion picture *Carmen Jones,* of the relationships between Jews and Negroes, and of the problems of American minorities in general is herein graphically and rhythmically set forth. And the title chapter concerning his father's burial the day after the Harlem riots, heading for the cemetery through broken streets—"To smash something is the ghetto's chronic need"—is superb. That Baldwin's viewpoints are half American, half Afro-American, incompletely fused, is a hurdle which Baldwin himself realizes he still has to surmount. When he does, there will be a straight-from-the-shoulder writer, writing about the troubled problems of this troubled earth with an illuminating intensity that should influence for the better all who ponder on the things books say.

A Love Affair with the United States

Julian Mayfield°

With two novels, one of them the remarkable *Go Tell It on the Mountain,* and a book of essays, James Baldwin has already made his mark on American literature. In this second collection of his writing [*Nobody Knows My Name*] he confirms that he is among the most penetrating and perceptive of American thinkers.

Baldwin is a man possessed by the necessity of coming to grips with himself and his country. He is also concerned with forcing our nation—with which he has had a turbulent love affair—to come to grips with itself. Because he is a gifted black man in an environment controlled by whites, his view of life is especially illuminating. He is, as he said in a recent radio discussion, "the maid" in the American house. He is the outsider within, the agonized repository of the family's most intimate secrets.

Most of the pieces in the new book grapple with American race relations. But the range of Baldwin's interest is wide, though his view is always intensely personal. For example, in "The Northern Prot-

°Reprinted from the *New Republic* 145 (1965):25, by permission of the author and the journal.

estant" he attempts to convey the essence of the Swedish cinema artist, Ingmar Bergman, but he only succeeds in revealing more about James Baldwin. In "The Male Prison" he sheds new light on Andre Gide and homosexuality.

One essay, "East River, Downtown," which deals with the Negro demonstration in the UN Security Council precipitated by the assassination of Patrice Lumumba, should be must reading. Baldwin had intended (like me) to be among the demonstrators himself. Most Americans quickly assumed that the demonstration was Communist-inspired. Only James Reston of *The New York Times,* among the major journalists, perceived that the riot meant that something was seriously wrong in the Negro community.

"What I find appalling," Baldwin writes, ". . . is the American assumption that the Negro is so contented with his lot here that only the cynical agents of a foreign power can rouse him to protest." And later, in the same piece: "What is demanded now, and at once, is not that Negroes continue to adjust themselves to the cruel racial pressures of life in the United States, but that the United States readjust itself to the facts of life in the present world."

This is not the strident voice of a flaming radical. It is an eloquent plea from a native artist seriously concerned with the fate of the country to which he has finally returned after a long and anguished exile.

The title essay originally appeared in *Partisan Review* as "A Letter from The South." It is a poignant, enduring document of a northern Negro's first exposure to Dixie. In Atlanta, bitterly aware of the segregated bus he was about to board, Baldwin looked into the eyes of an old black man: "His eyes seemed to say that what I was feeling he had been feeling, at much higher pressure, all his life. But my eyes would never see the hell his eyes had seen. And this hell was, simply, that he had never in his life owned anything, not his wife, not his house, not his child, which could not, at any instant, be taken from him by the power of white people. This is what paternalism means. And for the rest of the time I was in the South I watched the eyes of old black men."

A collection of pieces, written over a period of years, is bound to be uneven. One wonders why Baldwin and his editors chose to include "A Fly in the Buttermilk" and "Princess and Power," two articles as close to the pedestrian as the author is likely to get. And occasionally Baldwin wades into waters over his head. W. E. B. DuBois is not, as Baldwin states, in "East River, Down-town," disillusioned. Dr. DuBois is the progenitor of all black American intellectuals, including Baldwin. At the great age of ninety-three, he is a socialist whose work is known and respected in nearly every country except his own.

I do not mean to suggest that James Baldwin is ever less than honest. Honesty and irreverence are his most maddening qualities as a writer and a human being. In this book he might have let Richard Wright rest in peace, but in "Alas, Poor Richard," Baldwin uncovers again, like an old sore, the long hostility between him and Wright. Each had fled American racism and sought refuge in Paris; neither had found a hiding place. Later Baldwin would force himself to return while Wright would continue to create novels about an America that had disappeared. In "Alas, Poor Richard," as with his "love letter" on Norman Mailer ("A Black Boy Looks at The White Boy"), Baldwin reveals so much about himself that the embarrassed reader cannot help feeling he has stumbled upon a person performing a private act. certainly no writer since Gide has written with such naked honesty.

James Baldwin: Voice of a Revolution   Stephen Spender°

It is on the whole encouraging that James Baldwin should have become the voice of American Negroes, because he is also the voice of an American consciousness (conscience) which is not Negro. The word "home" occurs frequently in his writing, sometimes bitterly, sometimes quite ordinarily: and by it he means America, in spite of his being acutely aware that the white men of his country have never shared their home with the Negroes. James Baldwin is an American writer, regarded and criticized as such, one of the outstanding living writers in the English language. His very faults as a writer and a person—given the fact of his immense distinction as both—strengthen his position, because he can be criticized and argued with as a man who is neither black nor white, but who uses, and exists, within the English language. As a writer, he has no color, but only mind and feelings as they are realized in words. One can quarrel, for example, with his misuse of words like "precisely" and "strictly" (usually introduced at a place where his argument is most blurred). James Baldwin is neither the golden-voiced god who sometimes descends on us from a black cloud—like those Negro athletes or Paul Robeson in his prime—nor is he a poet from another race and sphere of life— like Langston Hughes—for whom allowances have to be made. He

°Reprinted from *Partisan Review* 30 (1963):256–60, by permission of the author and the journal.

is simply a writer in English who has had imposed on him by circumstances a point of view made tragic by those very circumstances. All his writings are speeches out of the play which is the tragedy of his race.

Baldwin's power is his ability to express situations—the situation of being Negro, and of being white, and of being human. Beyond this, he is perhaps too impatient to be a good novelist, and although he is a powerful essayist, his experiences are so colored with feelings that he seems unable to relate the thoughts which arise from his feelings to parallel situations that have given rise to other men's thoughts. Thus it seems important to him in his feelings about American Negroes that he should write as though there were no other Negroes, no other oppressed peoples anywhere in the world. He states [in *The Fire Next Time:*] "Negroes do not, strictly, or legally speaking, exist in any other" country but the United States where "they are taught really to despise themselves from the moment their eyes open on the world." One suspects that for Mr. Baldwin it is sacrilege to suggest that there are Negroes outside America; and from this there follows the implication that the Negro problem is *his* problem that can only be discussed on *his* terms. Hence too his contempt for most people who, in the main, agree with him, especially for poor despised American Liberals. He has, as a Negro, a right, of course, to despise liberals, but he exploits his moral advantage too much.

Sometimes by Negro Mr. Baldwin means people with black skins originating in Africa, bur sometimes he defines them by their situation—that of being oppressed. And indeed if the Negro problem is resolvable, the only useful way of discussing it is to consider American Negroes in a situation which is comparable with that of workers and of Negroes elsewhere. To write as though Negroes do not exist anywhere except in America is to induce despair, to suggest that in America white and black cannot become integrated to the (rather limited) extent to which they have been, for example, in Brazil. It is in fact playing into the hands of the Black Muslims whose position is that America—and the world even—has to choose between having nothing but black or nothing but white people—by which it is meant that it would be "democratic" to have nothing but the black majority.

Mr. Baldwin would admit, I think, that when (and this is quite often) he is guided by his emotions he finds himself in a position not far from that of the Black Muslims. He quite rightly resents the claims of whites that they are superior to colored people. But in fact he thinks that the colored are superior. True, they have, like the antifascists, been made, almost involuntarily, better as a result of the crimes perpetrated against them, for which they are in no way responsible. Few independent witnesses would dispute this. But Mr. Baldwin also makes Henry-Miller-like generalizations about the emasculation, joylessness, lack of sensuality, etc., of white Americans to prove their inferiority to the joyous, spiritual, good, warm Negroes.

I agree that in certain ways, and not only in America, the so-called backward, primitive, oppressed, and—for the most part—colored people are "better" than us whites who form a world class of "haves" and rulers. The quality of this superiority James Baldwin admirably conveys by the word *sensual:* "To be sensual, I think, is to respect and rejoice in the force of life, of life itself, and to be present in all that one does, from the effort of loving to the breaking of bread." Negroes—and one might add (although Mr. Baldwin does not do so) a large number of other people in the world who are "have-nots"—are forced back onto personal values. It is by no means clear, though, whether the oppressed if they were set over their oppressors—the blacks over the whites—would not lose their "sensuality" and become as bad as the present white ruling class. Lack of sensuality is the result of running and deriving benefits from an industrial society. The "sensual" are simply the outcasts.

When he discusses white Americans and Christians, he tends to attribute to them generalized qualities. Indeed, for him, white Americans seem hardly to be people; they are an abstraction, "America." When he discusses Negroes he tends to attribute to them particularized, personal qualities. "White Americans do not believe in death, and this is why the darkness of my skin intimidates them. And this is also why the presence of the Negro in this country can bring about its destruction. It is the responsibility of free men to trust and to celebrate what is constant—birth, struggle and death are constant, and so is love, although we may not always think so—and to apprehend the nature of change, to be able and willing to change."

Mr. Baldwin asserts that the white American does not recognize death because he does not recognize life. He does not recognize the "constants" of life in himself, and therefore he does not recognize them in the Negro. If he recognized the Negro as a being like himself, then he would recognize in himself those constants which he acknowledges in the Negro. Thus the black can "save" the white by making the white conscious of his humanity.

This position is summarized in his letter to his nephew: "*Integration* means that we, with love, shall force our brothers to see themselves as they are, to cease fleeing from reality and begin to change it."

Much the same message is contained in the most quoted poem of Auden: "We must love one another or die." It is worth noting, however, that Auden in later editions dropped the stanza containing this line. When I asked him why he had done this, he replied, "Because we're going to die anyway." He might have added that if our living depended on our loving one another then we would all be doomed instantly. And to this he could have added that when we assert that we can all love one another, we cannot be sure that what we are saying is true.

Although Mr. Baldwin considers love is the only answer to the American race problem, it is not all evident from his book that he loves white Americans, and at times it is even doubtful whether he loves his own people. Not that I blame him for this. What I do criticize him for is postulating a quite impossible demand as the only way of dealing with a problem that has to be solved.

Mr. Baldwin's bias towards discussing the American Negro as though he had no characteristics in common with Negroes elsewhere or other oppressed people and classes contributes to his tendency to think that the problem can only be met by all Negroes and all white Americans being seized at the same moment by the same wave of love. My argument is that the relationship of Negro to white exists within a situation comparable to other situations. It is partly a situation of color, partly one of class. The American Negro is in effect a world proletarian who suffers under the disadvantage that he appears to be indelibly branded as such by the blackness of his skin. People used to talk about the European proletariat as Baldwin does about Negroes, as though their status was inbred and could only be changed by love (which meant it could not be changed at all). But if you change the circumstances of the workers, so long as they are white they simply become like other white people who are not workers. What is menacing about the color problem is that even if you change the status of the Negro his color remains the same. Color prejudice is extremely deep, and far more widespread than Mr. Baldwin seems to realize, since it exists all over the world, where similar circumstances (such as that of there being a majority of Negro proletarians among a minority of whites) produce similar results. Moreover, color prejudice is not confined to white Americans and Europeans. It exists between colored people themselves.

This last point is rather important, because while disapproving of the Black Muslims, Mr. Baldwin seems to accept their view that the world is divided into blacks and whites, of which the blacks are the majority. As a matter of fact, if the white races disappeared from the face of the earth, there would be perhaps worse color problems than there are today; for whereas white men are (though not fast enough) beginning to be ashamed of their attitude towards colored people, many Asians have little tolerance for other Asians of slightly different shades of color, and none at all for Negroes.

It seems best then to consider the color problem in America as the problem of a proletariat, with the special difficulty attaching to it that Negroes are labelled by their color as proletarians. Mr. Baldwin himself sometimes states the situation of the Negroes as if it were that of the industrialized and unorganized working class in Europe in the nineteenth century. He writes:

> Even the most doltish and servile Negro could scarcely fail to be impressed by the disparity between his situation and that of the people for whom he worked; Negroes who were neither doltish nor servile did not feel that they were doing anything wrong when they robbed the white people. In spite of the Puritan-Yankee equation of virtue with well-being, Negroes had excellent reasons for doubting that money was made or kept by any very striking adherence to the Christian virtues; it certainly did not work that way for black Christians. In any case, white people, who had robbed black people of their liberty and who profited by this theft every hour that they lived, had no moral ground on which to stand. They had the judges, the juries, the shot-guns, the law—in a word, power. But it was a criminal power, to be feared but not respected, and to be outwitted in any way whatever. And those virtues preached but not practiced by the white world were merely another means of holding Negroes in subjection.

Substitute "worker" for Negro, and "capitalist" or "imperialist" for "white people," and this reads like a Marxist writing in 1860 about the German or the British working class.

So-called capitalists have on the whole learned to legislate away the social problems which logically seemed to lead to irreconcileable positions ending in revolution. The color problem is the twentieth-century version of what in the nineteenth century was the problem of the proletariat. In theory at least it should today be soluble without revolution. What Mr. Baldwin calls "love"—at any rate all generous feeling—is required to support the legislation and anticipate the very dangerous situation which will arise unless a great deal is done very quickly. The great contribution of Mr. Baldwin is that he finds words to express what one knows to be true: how it feels to be an American Negro. Within his own works he has solved the problem of integration: not by love, but by imagination using words which know no class nor color bars.

The Fire Next Time This Time   Mel Watkins°

"If we . . . do not falter in our duty now, we may be able . . . to end the racial nightmare," James Baldwin said nine years ago in

°Reprinted from the *New York Times Book Review*, 28 May 1972, 17–18, by permission of the author and the journal.

The Fire Next Time, warning that, if we did not, violent and vengeful racial clashes were inevitable. His caveat was clamorously hailed, but insufficiently heeded. Riots, assassinations, the emergence of black power and the intensification of white blacklash have attested to Baldwin's powers of divination. Yet those same events may have rendered him an anachronism. Reading his latest book, *No Name in the Street*—a two-part, extended essay that is a memoir, a chronicle of and commentary on America's abortive civil-rights movement—that suspicion is nearly substantiated.

When Baldwin emerged as an essayist in 1955 the civil-rights movement was barely ambulatory. And in literature, Ralph Ellison's *Invisible Man* was still harmlessly ensconced in a cellar listening to Louis Armstrong wail "What did I do to be so black and blue," while Richard Wright's Bigger Thomas, whose pathological and decidedly unrevolutionary violence was so vividly portrayed in *Native Son,* was rare enough to be primarily a literary phenomenon. It was in this climate of superficial racial serenity that Baldwin published his first collection of essays, *Notes of a Native Son,* to instant acclaim. Alfred Kazin called it "one of the one or two best books written about the Negro in America," and said that Baldwin operated "with as much power in the essay form as I've ever seen." Baldwin's nest two essay-volumes (*Nobody Knows My Name* in 1961 and *The Fire Next Time* in 1963) elicited even more enthusiastic praise. Perhaps more important, Baldwin became the most widely read black author in American history.

Baldwin's passion, honesty and persuasiveness did much to free the impasse in racial discourse and helped create what now seems the fleeting illusion that nonblack Americans could actually empathize with blacks and seriously confront the racial problem. Along with Martin Luther King Jr. he helped shape the idealism upon which the sixties civil-rights protest was based.

But Baldwin and King, while demonstrating that blacks were "the conscience of the nation," exposed the depth of American intransigence regarding the racial issue. They were instrumental in exhausting the dream of an effective moral appeal to Americans, and, in effect, set the stage for Malcolm X, and the emergence of Stokely Carmichael, "Rap" Brown, Huey Newton, Eldridge Cleaver and George Jackson— figures who reacted in a purely pragmatic (and therefore quintes-sentially American) manner to the blighted expectations of the sixties' failed idealism.

Since he was a political leader, King's influence on the events of the sixties is readily understandable. The source of Baldwin's influence as a writer is less apparent, particularly since the ideological content of his essays was rarely new—among others, Frederick Doug-lass, W. E. B. DuBois and Richard Wright had previously dealt with many of the ideas that he presented. Aside from the accident of timing, it was the uniquely personal perspective and style in which Baldwin couched his ideas that set him apart.

His essay style, in fact, set a literary precedent that would later develop into the "New Journalism"; *Notes,* for instance, predated and probably influenced the style of *Advertisements for Myself* and Norman Mailer's later forays into egocentric reportage—though Baldwin writes from the consciousness of an American victim, while Mailer enjoys the luxury and expansiveness of self-imposed alienation. Alfred Kazin's insights were again particularly incisive when he commented on the personal nature of Baldwin's essays: "More than any other Negro writer whom I, at least, have ever read [Baldwin] wants to describe the exact place where private chaos and social outrage meet . . . the 'I,' the 'James Baldwin' who is so sassy and despairing and bright, manages, without losing his authority as the central speaker, to show us all the different people in him, all the voices for whom the 'I' alone can speak."

Moreover, as Kazin intimated, Baldwin did not write solely as a black advocate. In his essays, the multiple voices of the "I" spoke as passionately for the American heritage as they did for the Afro heritage. As a writer, then, he is part of the tradition of black-American polemical essayists that include David Walker, Henry Highland Garnet, Frederick Douglass, Booker T. Washington and W. E. B. DuBois. But he is just as much a part of the tradition of American romantic-moralists such as Ralph Waldo Emerson, Henry Thoreau and John Jay Chapman.

He became, as Albert Murray pointed out in *The Omni-Americans,* a hero of "the Negro revolution, a citizen spokesman, as eloquent . . . as was citizen polemicist Tom Paine in the Revolution of '76," but he did not as Murray asserts, "write about the economic and social conditions of Harlem." Eldridge Cleaver was more accurate when, in his otherwise outrageous attack, *Notes on a Native Son,* he asserted that Baldwin's work "is void of a political, economic, or even a social reference." For Baldwin's technique was to write through events, focusing upon the enigma that plagued his own psyche. His influence and popularity depended upon the extent to which his psyche corresponded to the mass American psyche.

Reading Baldwin's latest work, one is initially struck by its familiar elements—his style, the recurring symbols that he favors (his father and family, the Manichean terminology that permeates his writing), and, of course, the cataclysmic social events of the past two decades. But early in the book, Baldwin shifts one's attention: "Since Martin's death . . . something has altered me, something has gone away. Perhaps even more than the death itself, the manner of his death has forced me into a judgment concerning human life and human beings which I have always been reluctant to make." And perhaps because Baldwin and the civil-rights movement had demanded from Americans "a generosity, a clarity, and a nobility which they did not dream of demanding from themselves" or perhaps because of his promise of an apocalypse in *The Fire Next Time* or because of Mailer's admonition that Baldwin "seems incapable of saying—you," it is the explication of that presumably harsher "judgment" for which one looks throughout the remainder of the book.

Part One is primarily a series of personal anecdotes upon which are imposed summary political analyses. The Algerian War and the Parisians' reaction to it, Camus's equivocation on the question of liberty for Algerians, Franco, and McCarthyism are some of the subjects that Baldwin strings together in this rhetorical web of damnation of European and American politics. The moral rectitude that informs the exposition is unquestioned, yet for the most part the ideological discourse is either too abstract and facile or too obvious to impress.

The best sections of Part One are those in which he makes a brief excursion into his personal reaction to King's death and when he reports on his visit to the South in the mid-fifties. Here, as in previous essays, Baldwin invests his account with both historical resonance and a vivid sense of the people and feeling that shaped those events.

There are also passages that provide an implicit sense of his shift in perspective, the impending judgment that he has promised. He had said in an earlier book, speaking of the parents of black children involved in the school desegregation crisis: "They are doing it because they want the child to receive the education which will allow him to defeat, possibly escape, and not impossibly help one abolish the stifling environment in which they see, daily, so many children perish. But in this essay Baldwin states: "They [the children] were attempting to get an education, in a country in which education is a synonym for indoctrination, if you are white, and subjugation, if you are black. It was rather as though small Jewish boys and girls, in Hitler's Germany, insisted on getting a German education in order to overthrow the Third Reich. . . . They paid a dreadful price, those children, for their missionary work among the heathen."

After a rhetorical flurry in which Western humanism is damned as a lie, Part Two gives an account of Baldwin's experiences with and feelings about the prime movers of the civil-rights and black-power movements of the past decade. Interspersed with this is the story of a personal friend and former bodyguard who was accused of murder. Baldwin comments on his relationships with King, Malcolm X, Huey Newton, Bobby Seale and Eldridge Cleaver, as well as the 1963 march on Washington, his abortive attempt to complete the screenplay for Malcolm's autobiography, Hollywood's coterie of civil-rights patrons and the "flower children."

This is the stronger section of the book, although it still does not provide any reasoned political assessment of the events and people discussed. There are references to politics and to America's domestic policies, but they function merely as lenses to better focus on the American psyche and the moral impasse with which Baldwin is ultimately concerned.

Baldwin's most vivid writing characterizes some of the black leaders that he has encountered. "Malcolm X," he says, "was not a racist, not even when he thought he was. His intelligence was more complex than that. . . . What made him unfamiliar and dangerous was not his hatred for white people but his love for blacks, his apprehension of the horror of the black condition, and the reasons for it, and his determination to work on their hearts and minds so that they would be enabled to see their condition and change it themselves."

On Cleaver and the inherent danger of the revolutionary's view-point, he says: "I think that it is just as well to remember that the people are one mystery and that the person is another. Though I know what a very bitter and delicate and dangerous conundrum this is, it yet seems to me that a failure to respect the person so dangerously limits one's perception of the people that one risks betraying them and oneself, either by sinking to apathy of cynical disappointment, or rising to the rage of knowing, better than the people do, what the people want."

But nowhere in the essay is the judgment that Baldwin indicated he was "forced into" defined. He finally evades this crucial question. Instead, Baldwin as "I" disappears and, as the omnipotent black, he concludes: "To be an Afro-American, or an American black, is to be in the situation, intolerably exaggerated, of all those who ever found themselves part of a civilization which they could in no way honorably defend—which they were compelled, indeed, endlessly to attack and condemn—and who yet spoke out of the most passionate love, hoping to make the kingdom new, to make it honorable and worthy of life."

The reader is left, then, precisely where he was at the conclusion of *The Fire Next Time*. Instead of the threat of a holocaust, we are told "it is terrible to watch people cling to their captivity and insist on their own destruction" and warned of "the shape of the wrath to come." Baldwin has taken us full circle: He initially exposes the "irreducible" error of the sixties idealism (for which his writing was partially responsible) and, after examining the political and sociological forces that rendered that idealism unworkable and the tragedy that ensued, he concludes by taking a moral stance that is not significantly different from the position he took in his previous essays.

For black political activists like Cleaver, his voice is, no doubt, the echo of a bygone time when black men could, as did Rufus in *Another Country,* go down singing "you took the best, why not take the rest."

But in an equally important sense Baldwin's is the timeless voice of a unique black-American tradition. Baldwin's essay style is a literary parallel of the black preacher's style. It is not just that his essays are sermonic or that *No Name in the Street,* like its predecessors, is filled with terms like "redemption," "damnation," "sinner," "soul" and "redeemed." Baldwin's experience as a Baptist minister in a storefront church is so vigorously applied to his prose style that it seems a demonstration of the "stylistic features" that Henry H. Mitchell enumerates in his book, *Black Preaching.* (As such, it should also serve as a partial source of objective standards for a black esthetic.)

Aside from oral intonation and physical gesture, according to Mitchell, rhythm, repetition for intensity, role playing, folk-story-telling techniques, personal involvement and rhetorical flair are the chief elements in the black preacher's style. Admittedly these features are general enough so that the presence of one or another of them may be seen in any writer's style; but in Baldwin's prose *all of them* are found in abundance.

Nearly every critic cites rhythm as an attribute of Baldwin's writing, and closely associated with this is his frequent use of repetition for emphasis—"much, much, much has been blotted out" or "a terrible thing to happen to a man . . . and I am always terribly humiliated for the man to whom it happens." Kazin's remarks concerning Baldwin's ability to "show us all the different people hidden in him" affirm his use of multiple voices, and almost every page of a Baldwin essay demonstrates his use of folk-storytelling techniques such as elaborate and melodramatic anecdotes.

If Baldwin's prose is a consummate literary adaptation of the stylistic features of black preaching, then that style imposes limitations on content. Black preaching adapts mythic scripture to the mimetic needs of black congregations—making the tenets of Christianity relevant to the reality of black experience. The style is contrary to rationalistic conception; instead, it seeks to communicate known religious truth through the emotions and senses. Baldwin uses the same style for secular purposes. Instead of redemption in the eyes of God, he is concerned with redemption in the eyes of man. God is replaced by morality and love. His message is finally as basic as it is undeniable: If we do not love one another, we will destroy one another.

When his essays are subjected to rigorous analysis, as by Marcus Klein in *After Alienation,* it is not surprising that the conclusion is that they are "evasive," lacking in "ideational development," and only accomplish a prophetic posture and an "indulgence of Edenic fantasies." But such conclusions are irrelevant since Baldwin's intent is not to explicate but to dramatize. What is important about Baldwin's essays is the style and eloquence with which he evokes the torment and human devastation of American racism and his ability to make us feel, if only momentarily, that redemption is possible.

In *No Name in the Street*, Baldwin's prose is often mesmerizing and, though they seem less shocking and disturbing now, there are passages that are as candid, insightful and moving as any in his previous essays. That the book may seem at this time less germane is not necessarily an indication of failure. It may very well be a more serious indictment against ourselves, a palpable indication of our own moral degeneration. Only if an eloquent appeal for morality is irrelevant in the seventies, is James Baldwin anachronistic.

The Devil Finds Work   Orde Coombs°

A decade ago, as an undergraduate, my colleagues and I spent hours pouring over the works of James Baldwin. He seemed so sure-footed, then, so certain in his vision of this country, that his lacerating words were like balm to the black students who were on a whirligig in search of their identities. Because he existed we felt that the racial miasma that swirled around us would not consume us, and it is not too much to say that this man saved our lives, or at least, gave us the necessary ammunition to face what we knew would continue to be a hostile and condescending world.

Even today, one of the group, a man employed by a large Wall Street firm, and making his way with assurance up the greasy pole, returns to *The Fire Next Time* after some special corporate praise, in order to cleanse his mind of superficial cant and to anchor himself, again, in what he calls "the real reality of America."

Now Baldwin has published a long essay, *The Devil Finds Work*, the 17th book bearing his name, but the event does not call for rejoicing. In fact it brings forth not a little pain, for this work teems with a passion that is all reflex, and an anger that is unfocused and almost cynical. It is as if Baldwin were wound up and then let loose to attack the hypocritical core of this nation. And to what avail? None that I can see, for although the book purports to be an examination of the way American films distort reality, its eclecticism is so pervasive,

°Reprinted from the *New York Times Book Review*, 2 May 1976, 6–7, by permission of the author and the journal.

that all we are left with are peregrinations of the mind and ideas that jump around and contradict each other. And this from a man who was, for my money, the best essayist in this country—a man whose power has always been in his reasoned, biting sarcasm; his insistence on removing layer by layer, the hardened skin with which Americans shield themselves from their country.

In this slim volume we are taken on a three-part retrospective voyage with Baldwin at the helm, and made to stop at "Congo Square," "Who Saw Him Die? I said The Fly" and "Where the Grapes of Wrath Are Stored." These stops, vaguely chronological ones, allow Baldwin to reminisce about his experiences as a 10-year-old who is denounced as "strange" by his neighbors and "ugly" by his father. He is rescued by a young, white, female schoolteacher called Bill Miller who takes him to the movies and exposes him to a world of fantasy and awe. It is because of her that he makes the "first entrance into the cinema of [his] mind." He becomes enchanted with what the screen tells him about society, and even though he abandons the cinema, temporarily, in order to join the church, he must return, clear-eyed, to examine the myths that the movies helped to perpetuate. As he looks around him he sees the wreckage that these myths bring. And since he knows that for Americans "the language of the camera is the language of our dreams," he must force us away from those dreams and into the reality of our country. He details the bewilderment of a child seeing Bette Davis for the first time on the screen and noticing that she was not beautiful but had pop-eyes like his own. We are lectured about the myth of brotherhood in *The Defiant Ones* and the differing reactions to it. Uptown the crowd shouts at Sidney Poitier as he jumps off the train to be with his buddy Tony Curtis: "Get back on the train, you fool." Downtown the audience benignly applauds Poitier's magnanimity.

Finally Baldwin discusses his screenplay for *The Autobiography of Malcolm X.* Suffice it to say that once Baldwin accepted the proferred "technical" assistance, he found out that his script would degenerate into a series of "action" lines with little real concern for the stature and integrity of Malcolm. But he is certainly not the first writer to find this out, and he will, without doubt, not be the last. Why then the tortured speculations? Did Baldwin really expect the Hollywood clique to honor Malcolm's memory when there were cash registers to be filled? He surely must have known that every writer, even the most powerful, strikes a bargain with Celluloid City, and that is why I find his pique to be more posture than pain.

But in a discussion of *Lady Sings the Blues,* Baldwin finds that old, hortatory, rhythmic voice; that style that overwhelmed us not so long ago. He notes that the movie is related to the black American experience in about the same way, and to the same extent that Princess

Grace Kelly is related to the Irish potato famine: by courtesy. . . . It has absolutely nothing to do with Billie, or with jazz, or any other kind of music, or the risks of an artist, or American life, or black life, or narcotics, or the narcotics laws, or clubs, or managers, or policemen, or despair, or love. The script is as empty as a banana peel, and as treacherous." And so we come to the main thrust of the book, which is that the American way with cameras merely serves to perpetuate our dreams or just slightly tarnish our Edens. Our perceptions of the American reality, then, remain unchanged, and it is because we refuse to see the short, nasty, brutish side of life, that we continue to see around us examples of Yeats's "sixty-year-old smiling public man."

Baldwin has said all this before. And better. And one must be dismayed, finally, by the style of this book, which seems to be a rococo parody of his own work: "Every trial, every beating, every drop of blood, every tear were meant to be used by us for a day that was coming—for a day that was certainly coming, absolutely certainly, certainly coming."

Well, what has happened to the finely honed delivery, the sense of assurance, the rootedness of this writer? I think that Baldwin, in love and at war with his society, suffers from the distance that he has put between himself and his beloved. And because a man who loves or fights as intensely as he does must constantly be replenished by contact with the object of his imagination, I wonder about the pleasures of his exile. For they seem to be, at best, quixotic, since America rides Baldwin and will not let him go. And so, *The Devil Finds Work* is disappointing because the author must repeat, from a distance, what he has been telling us for a long time, and what he knows we know that he knows. The possible force, then, is scattered, willy-nilly, to the winds, and all that vision and moral weight that fortified a generation, become as disturbing as the memory of a hurricane on a placid summer's afternoon.

The Writer and the Preacher   Jonathan Yardley[*]

When James Baldwin was a high-school student in Harlem, he had a brief conversation with his father that he later recalled as "the

[*]Reprinted from the *Washington Post Book World,* 27 October 1985, 3–4, by permission of the author and the journal.

one time in all our life together when we had really spoken to each other." His father was a preacher, a stern and forbidding man who had encouraged his son's own apprenticeship in the pulpit but now sensed that the prodigy was becoming prodigal. "You'd rather write than preach, wouldn't you?" his father asked, to which the astonished youth replied honestly, "Yes."

This encounter, which Baldwin reports in his brilliant essay "Notes of a Native Son," is significant not merely because it marks the moment when he committed himself to the writing that eventually made him famous, but because it reminds us that he has always been as much preacher as writer. He forsook the church long ago and ever since has been a skeptic so far as matters ecclesiastical are concerned, but his upbringing in a pious household and his training as boy revivalist left marks that no amount of apostasy could erase. His prose has the rhythm, the rolling and irresistible cadences, of hellfire and brimstone; his expository method is that of the homily, a mixture of logic and passion that is both rational and emotive.

The subject of his sermons is almost always the life that black Americans live, but his real audience—his congregation, if you will— is white America. This is not to say that he has an insubstantial black readership—to the contrary, his following among black Americans is large and deservedly loyal—but that he has chosen to be the messenger of the downtrodden, and that in this role his words are directed principally to those whom he perceives as their oppressors. Depending on his mood and the aims he hopes to accomplish, these words can be angry, cajoling, contemptuous, witty, sarcastic, apocalyptic, compassionate; but they are always urgent, always intended to force the reader into a heightened awareness of the black situation and its potential ramifications for all America.

The more than four dozen essays collected in *The Price of the Ticket* display Baldwin in all his guises. They also, though quite unwittingly, provide painful evidence that since his great success in 1963 with *The Fire Next Time*—originally published the previous year in *The New Yorker* as "Letter From a Region in My Mind"— Baldwin's skills have steadily deteriorated; this conclusion is most unhappily confirmed by *The Evidence of Things Not Seen,* an excruciatingly slipshod meditation on the Atlanta child murders. What has happened to Baldwin quite simply is that since he moved to a prominent position on the public stage, the preacher has taken over from the writer; for two decades his rhetoric has grown steadily more bombastic, grandiloquent and predictable, while the humor, sensitivity and self-mockery of the early essays have virtually disappeared.

So much has been written about Baldwin's work that it seems rather pointless to provide further exegesis of it here. Suffice it to say that reading his essays from the 1950s and early '60s for the first time in many years, I was struck as forcibly as ever not merely by their power and passion, which can be quite overwhelming, but also by their civility and restraint. The Baldwin of those years—the Baldwin whose essays were collected in *Notes of a Native Son* and *Nobody Knows My Name*—was a startling voice from a land called black America that white America scarcely knew, but he was a voice that sought to reason with us even as he exposed our hypocrisies and cruelties. He was angry, with ample reason, but he appealed to the decent and humane in us; he tried to make us understand that we were all in this business together, and that a genuinely egalitarian society served the self-interest of white America as well as black.

In the best of these essays—"Many Thousands Gone," "The Harlem Ghetto," "Fifth Avenue, Uptown," the title pieces of the two aforementioned collections—Baldwin wanted to submerge us in the squalor and despair of the ghetto, but he also wanted to interest us in the people who lived there and to make us realize that they were just like us, only with different skin color. He spared us almost nothing—the fury of "Letter From a Region in My Mind" is breathtaking—yet he reached out to us. Toward the end of *Notes of a Native Son*, contemplating the death of his father, he wrote: "This was his legacy: nothing is ever escaped. That bleakly memorable morning I hated the unbelievable streets and the Negroes and whites who had, equally, made them that way. But I knew that it was folly, as my father would have said, this bitterness was folly. It was necessary to hold on to the things that mattered; blackness and whiteness did not matter; to believe that they did was to acquiesce in one's own destruction. Hatred, which could destroy so much, never failed to destroy the man who hated and this was an immutable law."

Unfortunately, though, it is a law whose effects Baldwin himself seems to have felt. When in the '60s he became one of the most prominent "spokesman" for black America, he seems to have felt it necessary to move with the crowd rather than maintain the distance he had theretofore kept from it—and the crowd was moving in the very directions Baldwin himself had deplored. During the '60s and '70s he came into contact not merely with Martin Luther King Jr., whom he revered, but also with Muslims and Panthers, whose more racist and apocalyptic messages he absorbed into his own. More and more frequently he issued insupportable blanket condemnations of whites: "Blacks are often confronted in American life, with such devastating examples of the white descent from dignity; devastating not only because of the enormity of the white pretensions, but because this swift and graceless descent would seem to indicate that white people have no principles whatever."

That was published in 1976, in a pointless and discursive piece—a short book, actually—called *The Devil Finds Work.* Now, in his introduction to *The Price of the Ticket,* Baldwin goes further. "There was not, then," he writes, "nor is there, now, a single American institution which is not a racist institution." In three decades have we made any progress toward a more egalitarian society? Of course we have. But Baldwin writes: "Spare me, for Christ's *and* His Father's sake, any further examples of American white progress. When one examines the use of this word in this most particular context, it translates as meaning that those people who have opted for being white congratulate themselves on their generous ability to return to the slave that freedom which they never had any right to endanger, much less take away."

Not merely is this twaddle, it is badly written twaddle: gassy, inflated, seat-of-the-pants rhetoric that has far less to say than its orotund phraseology at first leads one to believe. The same is true, though even more so, of the prose in *The Evidence of Things Not Seen.* This slender book, which was written on commission for *Playboy,* is a piece of nonsense in the literal meaning of the word: it makes no sense at all. It is a tortured effort to squeeze out the required number of words, an effort that leads Baldwin into wild, and wildly irrelevant, speculations on everything from emasculation to "the European horror," which is to say white culture. The book is riddled with exclamation points and italics, names are dropped in every direction—as, alas, they also are in the later essays in *The Price of the Ticket*—and self-congratulation is everywhere.

For a writer of Baldwin's gifts, *The Evidence of Things Not Seen* is a pathetic embarrassment; certainly it is embarrassing to read. That he should have gone into so great a decline is a mystery, though the burdens and distractions of fame may well have had something to do with it. Whatever the case, the writer who gave us *Notes of a Native Son* is nowhere to be found in *The Evidence of Things Not Seen;* and if the writer who once warned us against hatred has not transformed himself into a racist, he is certainly putting on a good imitation of one.

Some Tickets Are Better: The Mixed Achievement of James Baldwin

Julius Lester°

With the publication of *The Price of the Ticket,* James Baldwin presents the work on which he wants to be judged and by which he would like to be remembered. The volume contains fifty-one essays, twenty-five of them previously uncollected. The remaining twenty-six represent the entire contents of five previously published books: *The Devil Finds Work, No Name in the Street, Notes of a Native Son, Nobody Knows My Name,* and *The Fire Next Time.*

Arranged chronologically from February 1948 to January 1985, the essays are overpowering in their intensity and brilliance. Particularly in the essays from 1948 to *The Fire Next Time* (1963), Baldwin reveals himself to be a tremendously eloquent humanist.

His is not a romantic humanism, however, but a hard-edged, uninviting, and terrifying one. "But our humanity is our burden, our life; we need not battle for it; we need only to do what is infinitely more difficult—that is, accept it. The failure of the protest novel lies in its rejection of life, the human being, the denial of his beauty, dread, power, in its insistence that it is his categorization alone which is real and which cannot be transcended" ("Everybody's Protest Novel").

In the essays of the first fifteen years Baldwin writes not only as a black writer pleading the cause of blacks, but as a black pleading the cause of humanity. Baldwin startles one by his use of "we," because sometimes he speaks not as a black but as an American. "Our dehumanization of the Negro then is indivisible from our dehumanization of ourselves: the loss of our own identity is the price we pay for our annulment of his" ("Many Thousands Gone").

Baldwin's power as a writer lies in his ability to weave the deeply autobiographical with the political and social. There is no separation between Jimmy Baldwin, black child of Harlem, and James Baldwin, American. For him, the personal is never just personal, and the political never just political. Because he perceives himself not only as the individual James Baldwin but also as the black Everyman, his writing has a moral authority that would be dismissed as arrogant if so many had not affirmed what he wrote.

°Reprinted from *Dissent* 33 (1986):189–92, 214, by permission of the author and the journal.

To call Baldwin a black writer, then, is not only to relegate him to a literary ghetto, it is to dismiss his testimony. In these early essays no writer is more American than this tiny black man who first saw light in Harlem in 1924. Despite all he has seen, despite all that has been done to him, his response is not a literature delineating the emptiness and alienation in which so many Americans live. His response is not a literature of smug ridicule or clever satire. He responds with that most intangible, bothersome and intrusive of emotions—love. And the object of his love is not only blacks; its object is the republic itself. If words alone could redeem, Baldwin's would have placed us all in that "shining city on a hill" to which the current occupant of the White House deludes himself into thinking his presidency shows the way.

From 1948 to 1963 Baldwin's message was more spiritual than political, more psychological than ideological, and it had two central elements: (1) The necessity for blacks to free themselves from white-imposed definitions; and (2) The necessity for whites to free themselves from their own definitions. As long as this mutual interdependence is unrecognized, blacks and whites will be unable to be human to themselves. And if one cannot be human to oneself, it is impossible to be human to another.

By 1960 Baldwin had honed this theme into one well-crafted sentence: "It is a terrible, and inexorable, law that one cannot deny the humanity of another without diminishing one's own: in the face of one's victim, one sees oneself" ("Fifth Avenue Uptown").

Witness. That is how James Baldwin describes himself. Not many writers would be comfortable with that self-definition, or understand it, even. Elie Wiesel is the only one who comes to mind, and perhaps that is not coincidence. Both have dedicated—or is it sacrificed?—themselves to the sacred act of giving testimony to what they have seen. Yet, they write, not as prosecutors of those who inflicted the horrors, but as prophets praying to God to be merciful, a God neither is sure is really there, and if He is, whether He is listening or really cares. But they pray, nonetheless, for humanity to transform itself before God metes out His terrible justice.

Once when I pressed Baldwin to define witness, he said:

> I am a witness to whence I came, where I am, witness to what I've seen and the possibilities that I think I see. I began using the word when I began to be called a spokesman. I'm certainly not a spokesman and the only word I could find is that I'm trying to be a witness. A spokesman assumes that he is speaking for others. I never assumed that I could. What I tried to do, or to interpret and make clear was that what the republic was doing to black people it was doing to itself. No society can smash the social contract and be exempt from the consequences and the consequences are chaos for everybody in

the society. In the church in which I was raised you were supposed to bear witness to the truth. Now, of course, later on you wonder what in the world the truth is, but you do know what a lie is.

It is this need to "bear witness" that gives Baldwin's writing its urgency and passion, its rhetoric the all-emcompassing generalization and the long and, sometimes, too-complex sentences. Baldwin's prophetic voice is a melding of those of the preacher he once was and of the King James version of the Old Testament. The reader is left wondering if he or she is in the presence of a person putting words to paper, or of a force unleashed by history that howls outside our windows.

The publication of *The Fire Next Time* in 1963 was an important event in the history of the civil rights movement and of America. It was the year when Bull Connor unleashed police dogs and fire hoses on blacks demonstrating in Birmingham, Alabama: images that were seen on the nightly news and horrified the nation. *The Fire Next Time* was Baldwin's warning of the black violence that would inevitably come if white America did not confront its racism.

The book became a best-seller and made Baldwin a celebrity, because he was able to combine anger and humanism in such a way that whites could receive the anger, not as an unqualified condemnation of themselves, but as angry tears of righteousness for us all. ". . . if the word *integration* means anything, this is what it means: that we, with love, shall force our brothers to see themselves as they are, to cease fleeing from reality and begin to change it. . . . We cannot be free until they are free."

Yet, in *The Fire Next Time* there is a small, but perceptible shift in Baldwin's humanism that becomes more pronounced and obvious in many of the essays after 1963. "I could not share the white man's vision of himself for the very good reason that white men in America do not behave toward black men the way they behave toward each other" (*The Fire Next Time*).

But is that really true? "One cannot deny the humanity of another without diminishing one's own," Baldwin had written a few years earlier. If that is so (and I believe that it is), then white men in America do "behave toward each other" in the same way they behave toward blacks, but perhaps the ways are not so evident. Baldwin does not make the effort to get at what is not apparent.

The sweeping generalization has always been a hallmark of Baldwin's essays. He never questions or doubts that what he is witness to represents more than subjective experience. While this is the source of his power in *The Fire Next Time*, it is also the source of a weakness that will become more evident, a weakness wherein

Baldwin will see, more and more, only what he wishes to see, and less and less make the effort to see what is.

In *The Fire Next Time* the humanistic Baldwin wrote of his concern for the "dignity" of blacks and for the "health" of their souls, and declared that he "must oppose any attempt that Negroes may make to do to others what has been done to them. . . . It is so simple a fact and one that is so hard, apparently, to grasp: *Whoever debases others is debasing himself.* This is not a mystical statement but a realistic one, which is proved by the eyes of any Alabama sheriff—and I would not like to see Negroes ever arrive at so wretched a condition." Many of the later essays of *The Price of the Ticket* are evidence that Baldwin has not been a voice of opposition—at least not publicly—when blacks have sought to do to others what has been done to them.

He did not oppose publicly the rhetorical excesses of the Black Power movement in the late 1960s. Nor has he sought to examine the meaning of Louis Farrakhan, the glint of whose eyes bears no small resemblance to those "of any Alabama sheriff."

Baldwin is more than eloquent when articulating that the sole salvation for whites is to take responsibility for the evil they have wrought: "It has always been much easier (because it has always seemed much safer) to give a name to the evil without than to locate the terror within. And yet, the terror within is far truer and far more powerful than any of our labels: the labels change, the terror is constant" ("Nothing Personal"). Yet, he does not take the next step and say that blacks, too, must take responsibility, not only for the evil they have wrought, but even for the evil they have endured.

What has happened to James Baldwin since *The Fire Next Time* is that a black vision of the world has slowly gained precedence over his humanistic one. The roots of this lie, perhaps, in Baldwin's definition of himself as a witness and the responsibilities of a witness.

In a taped conversation I had with him a year and a half ago, I asked if Richard Wright had had a responsibility to him and did he have a responsibility to younger black writers.

> I never felt that Richard had a responsibility for me, and if he had, he'd discharged it. What I was thinking about, though, was the early fifties when the world was breaking up, when the world of white supremacy was breaking up. I'm talking about the revolutions all over the world, specifically since we were in Paris—Tunisia, Algeria, the ferment in Senegal, the French loss of their Indo-Chinese empire. A whole lot of people—darker people for the most part—came from all kinds of places to Richard's door as they do now to my door. And in that sense he had a responsibility which he didn't know— well, who can blame him? A boy from Ethiopia, a boy from Senegal—

they all claimed him. They had the right to claim him like they have the right to claim me.

What is that right? I asked. Why did they have a right to claim him? Why do they have the right to claim you?

> Well, right or not, there he was to be claimed. He was the most articulate black witness of his moment. . . . Richard was known in Paris and they had a right to claim him, much more right than those who did claim him—Sartre, de Beauvoir, etcetera. . . . I was in a very funny position. The people who knocked on his door ended up sleeping on my floor. I knew something about it which Richard didn't know . . . someone who is not white and has managed to survive somehow and attempts to be in some way responsible—of course you're going to be claimed by multitudes of black kids. There's no way around it.

But can one be claimed without eventually being enslaved? It would be presumptuous of me to maintain that this is what has happened to Baldwin. Yet, reading *No Name in the Street* (1972) one is stunned by his lack of insight into the dangers represented by the Black Panther party as well as his sycophantic attitude toward Huey Newton and Eldridge Cleaver. In many of the essays of the 1970s and 1980s, it is not only what Baldwin says that is distressing, but, equally, that he fails to demand that blacks risk the terror and burden of being human as he demands it of whites.

His review of Alex Haley's *Roots* could have been written by any black writer beating the drum of blackness. It is not James Baldwin in fearful pursuit of truth but Baldwin imitating himself poorly. At the end of the review one sees the philosophical consequences of allowing one's self to be claimed: "It [*Roots*] suggests, with great power, how each of us, however unconsciously, can't but be the vehicle of the history which has produced us." This kind of historical determinism is damaging, because it denies human responsibility, not for history itself but for what we do with history.

The most disturbing of the later essays is "An Open Letter to the Born Again." Published in the *Nation* (September 29, 1979), it was written in the bitter aftermath of Andrew Young's resignation as U.N. ambassador, when black leaders excoriated Jews for their perceived role in that resignation. Throughout his career Baldwin has written thoughtfully and insightfully about black-Jewish relations. While he has sometimes come close to what some consider anti-Semitic statements, one always gave him the benefit of the doubt because he was James Baldwin. With "An Open Letter to the Born Again" one can do so no longer. "But the State of Israel was not created for the salvation of the Jews; it was created for the salvation of the Western interest. This is what is becoming clear (I must say that it was always clear to me). The Palestinians have been paying for the British colonial policy of "divide and rule" and for Europe's guilty Christian conscience for more than thirty years." Regardless of one's views on Israel, Baldwin's assertions have the uninformed certainty of barbershop opinion. His propensity for cosmic generalizations leads him to conclude that: "The Jew, in America, is a white man. He has to be, since I am a black man, and, as he supposes, his only protection against the fate which drove him to America. But he is still doing the Christian's dirty work, and black men know it."

Yet, in Baldwin's earlier essays there are noble statements which argue against defining others solely on the basis of one's own experience, which challenge us to live on the razor's edge of risk and vulnerability.

As one follows the journey of James Baldwin over the past thirty-seven years, one must wonder if the terror within has worn him down, if he no longer has the strength to throw himself into the abyss to find the tiny nuggets of truth which only he was able to find.

Or, is it that, having permitted himself to be claimed by black people, he has abdicated the lonely responsibility of the artist and intellectual to be claimed by nothing but that futile and beautiful quest for Truth?

It was Baldwin himself who wrote in 1962 that ". . . the truth, in spite of appearances and all our hopes, is that everything is always changing and the measure of our maturity as nations and as men is how well prepared we are to meet these changes and, further, to use them for our health" ("The Creative Process").

It is not easy to be so critical of Baldwin. That his writings have made a significant difference in the way many of us, black and white, view ourselves and each other is indisputable. Read as a body, the essays of James Baldwin are a sustaining act of love and faith of which America has not been worthy.

Perhaps it is too much to ask that any one writer sustain love and faith throughout a life of terror. Perhaps it is too much to ask him to return again and again to the abyss. The price of such excursions is high and one pays in one's soul and body. Perhaps, then, no one asks another to do more than he or she can, and instead lovingly laments the absence of the growth that we would want for that person—and ourselves.

In the last essay of *The Price of the Ticket* there are these words: "The object of one's hatred is never, alas, conveniently outside but is seated in one's lap, stirring in one's bowels and dictating the beat of one's heart. And if one does not know this, one risks becoming an imitation—and, therefore, a continuation—of principles one imagines oneself to despise."

If *The Price of the Ticket* is to be the summation of Baldwin's career, then we must be grateful for the wisdom contained in its early essays and take as a warning the latter ones which are, all too often, "an imitation" and "a continuation of principles" Baldwin taught us to despise.

The Problem of Identity in Selected Early Essays of James Baldwin
Jocelyn Whitehead Jackson*

James Baldwin's major non-fictional works, including the ten essays comprising *Notes of a Native Son* (1955), show an increasing and painful awareness of the problems inherent in the quest for personal and artistic identity. The crises in Baldwin's life, most often communicated in his works as artistic, religious, and sexual, have given rise to a single-minded dedication to the search for discovery of the self, even to the present day with his recent return to America. Perceiving that one's identity must be created in one's experience. Baldwin continually demonstrates his knowledge of the triple burden of Black, artist, and bisexual in an American cultural environment inimical to each, and thereby informs his writing with an irony that intensifies his search. Each of his major works at bottom attests to the quest for identity which most Baldwin critics either have ignored, in the attempt to place him in the stream of Black protest literature, on the one hand, or minimized, on the other hand, because of their antagonism toward the duality which they find associated with the identity search.

Robert Bone was one of the first to point out the twin emotions of shame and rage in Baldwin's works, and to note that: "The flight from self, the quest for identity, and the sophisticated acceptance of one's 'blackness' are the themes that flow from this emotion."[1] Several Black scholars and other students of contemporary Black literature have pointed to a duality in Baldwin's work. Stephen Spender[2] and Edward Margolies[3] are chief among these critics who see that the quest for public acclaim and personal selfhood obscures Baldwin's

*Reprinted from the *Journal of the Interdenominational Theological Center* 6 (1978):1–15, by permission of the author and the journal.

search for artistic identity. These critics speak of a split between Baldwin the artist and Baldwin the propagandist—the transmitter of social messages and object lessons. Other critics like George Kent,[4] Howard N. Harper, Jr.,[5] Calvin C. Hernton,[6] and Charles Newman[7] see as significant the unmistakably strong influence on Baldwin's work of certain French existentialists whose vision of the human condition and how to deal with it transcends the traditional literary/sociological categories of artist and propagandist. Still others like Harper, Granville Hicks,[8] Julian Mayfield,[9] and Mike Thelwell[10] insist correctly, I believe, that Baldwin's "is not the strident voice of a flaming radical [but] . . . an eloquent plea from a native artist seriously concerned with the fate of [his] country."[11] Further, he is seen by this group of critics as a writer concerned with defining "the nature of the writer's responsibility"[12] and "the functions and the problems of the name of letters in contemporary society."[13] This approach, taken by too few critics since the period following the publication of *Nobody Knows My Name* (1961), has been followed by those who perceive Baldwin's work primarily as an engagement of inner self with outer world.

Mayfield, elsewhere a harsh critic of Baldwin's fiction, writes persuasively in the *New Republic* review of *Nobody Knows My Name* that Baldwin is "a man possessed by the necessity of coming to grips with himself and his country,"[14] a possession which suggests a seeking after wholeness rather than the duality or split asserted by critics. According to Baldwin in his most recent collection of serious essays, *No Name in the Street,* his primary aim is, and always has been, "to achieve . . . a viable, organic connection between [his] public stance and [his] private life,"[15] an aim which he claims has eluded most Americans. The attempted integration of the self, then, is the characteristic, pervasive, and crucial act resisting at every turn efforts to polarize Baldwin.

With respect to the emphasis of this paper, the essays will serve as focal points through which are refracted the issues about which Baldwin writes, and his treatment of seemingly disparate views of the human condition. Any attempt to study Baldwin's early essays in the terms already defined must concentrate on establishing certain identity patterns or themes which are introduced in the earliest and recur throughout the collected works. Likewise, undergirding and uniting these emphases is the belief that James Baldwin has been, is now, and will continue to be intent, above all, on communicating artistically his felt perception of himself, his culture, and his fellow human beings. It will be shown that Baldwin's "self" is emerging and ever-changing, and that he is, at the present moment, "making himself up."

The earliest essays in *Notes of a Native Son* seem to provide the form and style in which questions of identity are best discussed. The style of these essays is obviously more self-revelatory, more intensely personal, than that of the novels. In choosing the nonfictional form as his major genre of expression, Baldwin writes and reveals himself at the same time, thus meeting at once his artistic and therapeutic needs. As a result, the essays are not academic, since he cannot, as an artist or a Black man, afford the luxury of engaging in mere academic, impersonal exercise. I believe that Colin MacInnes' assessment of the strength of Baldwin's essay voice is correct: ". . . because I see—or hear—James Baldwin as a voice, a presence, a singer almost, that I feel the mode of direct address—to us in his own person, and not through invented 'characters'—expresses his talent and his message best."[16] For Baldwin then, the essays are a "working out" of his identity crisis in ways that are unavailable to him in the novels.

Baldwin's earliest expressed desire to be an honest man and a good writer[17] is, in David Levin's view, "the central metaphor through which to express, in his autobiographical writings, his spiritual quest and his evangelical plea to our society."[18] In these terms, Baldwin's journey has led down two roads simultaneously—the personal and the public. Likewise, Harper amplifies Levin's view in referring to the "dual personality" that Baldwin has become; he is, explains Harper, ". . . both a fiery prophet of the racial apocalypse and a sensitive explorer of man's inmost nature. In his role as Negro spokesman he has been forced into an activism in which he does not deeply believe. In his role as artist he is concerned with a problem more basic, more complex, and perhaps even more urgent than the problem of civil rights, a problem of which civil rights is only a part."[19] Levin and Harper offer a promising perspective which I shall explore by a detailed examination of the personal-artistic quest as treated in Baldwin's autobiographical essays in the first volume.

What is striking about Baldwin's essays is the pervasiveness of considerable personal experience in a literary genre that generally is impersonal. Newman argues convincingly that Baldwin, like his stylistic mentor Henry James, "has used the essay not as exposition in lieu of a work of larger intent, but as a testing ground for his fiction."[20] The first essays are concerned with identity and may be seen to establish the direction in which all of Baldwin's subsequent essays point. Stated broadly, the essays are grouped thematically under questions of artistic, personal, and national identity. In each group, Baldwin is half Negro, half American, an incomplete fusion. The very pre-supposition of human identity—the autobiographical "I" which he establishes and with which he speaks—often is ironically called into question by the overwhelming inhumanity or dehumanization pervading and dominating the American cultural environment. Considered from the triple perspective, then, each essay emphasizes some aspect of the Black man's struggle for identity and analyzes the misconceptions and hatreds separating the Black and White races. Most of these essays in some way record the difficulties not only in recognizing, understanding, or accepting one's identity, but more crucially, in *being*. In a sense, the essays are therapeutic vehicles for Baldwin, by which he can work through to his own concept of himself.

The essays of Part One in which Baldwin carefully examines the role of the literary artist and his own relationship to art as a Black man reveal some of these difficulties. If the two important essays in this section, "Everybody's Protest Novel" and "Many Thousands Gone"—widely and, surprisingly, misinterpreted—are measured in relation to Baldwin's clearly-stated assumption in the "Autobiographical Notes," then it becomes apparent that he did, very early in his literary career, lay out for himself a psycho-ideological construct on which he has been building ever since. This construct or pattern encompasses all the identity elements outlined by Erik Erikson and Abraham Maslow.[21]

Simply stated, the "Autobiographical Notes" is Baldwin's *Credo;* the two "artistic" essays are his *Apologia.* In the initial piece, he establishes his identity first as a human being, born in Harlem, and, in the second sentence, as a writer. The order to identity here is very important, for Baldwin seems to insist in this *Credo* on being confronted as an artist, on artistic terms. He claims as paramount the relationship between the experience of one's life and one's creation of art. In much the same way that Ralph Ellison articulates his artistic vision,[22] Baldwin announces: "One writes out of one thing only— one's own experiences. Everything depends on how relentlessly one forces from this experience the last drop, sweet or bitter, it can possibly give. *This is the only real concern of the artist,* to recreate out of the disorder of life that order which is art."[23] About the meaning of Baldwin's vision there should be no confusion. He determines to examine closely his own experience through his art. Furthermore, he is forthright in his statements regarding himself as a Black artist. *This* Black artist, he explains, believes as do some other artists—Black and White—that ". . . social affairs are not generally speaking the writer's concern, whether they ought to be or not; it is absolutely necessary that he establish between himself and these affairs a distance which will allow, at least, for clarity, so that before he can look forward in any meaningful sense, he must first be allowed to take a long look back."[24]

Baldwin nowhere attempts in this essay to ignore his Blackness. Certainly he does reveal a certain ambivalence regarding his relationship as Negro man to the stream of Western culture,[25] but at the same time he gives credence to and affirms the "sweet and bitter" influences that have shaped his life and art—Dickens, Stowe, Mather, Mayor LaGuardia, his father, storefront churches, a Saxton Fellowship, Richard Wright, the King James Bible. Neither does he base his artistic motivation upon the desire, as Irving Howe claims,[26] to escape his Blackness. Rather, he resembles the existentialist Outsider in wanting to transcend or obliterate any and all structures, constructs, categories, whether these are imposed on his art by White men or set up, defensively, by Blacks.[27] Although Baldwin's professional hatred and fear of the world includes Black people, this confession that "he despised them, possibly because they failed to produce Rembrandt"[28] *cannot*, must not be construed as blanket ethnic self-hatred. In the context of the "Autobiographical Notes," it is a painful admission of a limitation and an inability, thus far, fully to affirm the self or to accept his Being. This admitted hatred of Black men is now an avowal; the statement, coming as it does at the beginning of Baldwin's journey, is a tentative point on the continuum, a position that, as Lerone Bennett contends, could easily be taken by "any Negro who has not emancipated himself, as Baldwin was doing."[29] The implication is that once the Black searcher is emancipated, the position no longer is defensible or necessary.

Evidently, Baldwin wishes to reduce the importance of his Negroness, not because of the shame which he certainly has been forced to feel but rather because in maximizing the essential fact, he is that much further removed from his perceived identity as human being and artist. Perhaps he sees that being a Black man in America tends to prevent the achievement of "that psychological and emotional distance necessary to artistic creation."[30] Or perhaps he wants to work through it to his *own* concept of Black artist. Erikson suggests that, in their growing awareness of the relation of positive and negative identity elements, Black writers like Baldwin and Ellison question seriously the possibility of the usable past *or* the present cultural environment to overcome the negative image imposed on Black men. As creative individuals, these writers "must accept the negative identity as the very base line of recovery. . . . But [they] continue to write and write strongly for [literature] even in acknowledging the depth of nothingness can contribute to something akin to a collective recovery."[31]

Baldwin announces early in his career, "I am speaking as a writer."[32] He has "chosen" to become an artist. His vehicles for self-actualization are the essay and the novel, not the sociological polemic or the psychological study or the political platform. This distinction is made clearly in the "Autobiographical Notes"; once made, transition from *Credo* to *Apologia* is natural and inevitable.

Only after defining his Being in terms of a general artistic vision does Baldwin begin to examine the deeper questions inherent in a

Black vision of art. This "progression" of thought from the "Auto-biographical Notes" to the two essays on Black art is crucial to any objective assessment of James Baldwin's identity quest. What Howe and others find so unconscionable in Baldwin's rejection of Black protest literature championed by Wright's school is precisely what I find so just and necessary in the maintenance of his particular artistic vision.

The questions posed in "Everybody's Protest Novel" and "Many Thousands Gone" are: What do I wish to make of myself? and what do I have to work with?[33] What can I be? What is *my* particular mission as a Black writer? How does my mission differ from that of Black writers who have preceded me? Since I am a Black man with Black experiences gained in a Black/White world, what values emanating from my experience can I affirm in my art? Which ones must I negate or reject? In light of these burning issues, it should be apparent that Baldwin's revolt against Wright and the protest school is as much the result of his emerging personal vision of Black aesthetic identity as it is a repudiation of the literature produced by this school.

Baldwin's primary objection to protest literature is that it confines the Black man within his own skin. Whereas the aim of the American protest novel is "to bring greater freedom to the oppressed,"[34] Baldwin finds that the aim fails because such novels reject human Being and human life, deny its beauty, and insist on an existence for their heroes that is impossible for them to transcend.[35] The "novels of Negro oppression," written by Blacks and Whites alike, fail furthermore because they ignore the fact that oppressor and oppressed are bound inextricably in American culture.[36] This linking together in cultural reality, for which Baldwin employs the metaphor of a cage, *can* lead simultaneously to the discovery of identity for the oppressed and a recognition, by the oppressor, of the Black man's humanity. However, in Baldwin's view, the cage of reality of the American cultural environment is locked more securely with each appearance of that kind of novel which articulates an essentially naturalistic, behavioristic, sometimes Marxian, vision of men like Uncle Tom and Bigger Thomas. That the Black man is merely or only the product of his socio-political predicament, that literary art should seek to publish this news, is anathematic to James Baldwin.

In short, Baldwin argues in "Everybody's Protest Novel" that the American novel should have properly little to do with social experience *per se.* On the contrary, it has much to do with

> . . . something resolutely indefinable, unpredictable. In overlooking, denying, evading this complexity—which is nothing more than the disquieting complexity of ourselves—we are diminished and we perish; only within this web of ambiguity, paradox, this hunger,

darkness, danger, can we find at once ourselves and the power that will free us from ourselves. It is *this power of revelation which is the business of the novelist,* this journey toward a more vast reality which must take precedence over all other claims.[37]

As in the "Autobiographical Notes," so Baldwin repeats here the burden of Black humanity in America, which he knows cannot be ignored or escaped. So also does he fix his concern, irrevocably, with Black and White humanity which encompasses the complexities of human experience. In the context of this essay, moreover, Baldwin admits the difficulties but states emphatically that the burden of the past must be accepted nonetheless.[38] Certainly, if his *Credo* is to be considered as a statement of artistic belief and artistic intent, then the subsequent rejection of the traditional protest genre is consistent.[39] The Truth he seeks lies elsewhere, to be uncovered and proclaimed. One begins to suspect that the content and referrent of Baldwin's emerging vision of Truth is moral rather than social.

Those portions of "Many Thousands Gone" dealing with his conscious revolt against protest literature are extensions of the thought presented in "Everybody's Protest Novel," which is antedated by two years. The charges herein are far more explicit; Baldwin has become more confident in the rightness of his own vision and in his ability to refuse the mantle of Wright's tutelage. The essay, then, defines more fully than "Everybody's Protest Novel," Baldwin's position, in contradiction to Wright's. What is new—though perhaps not so much new as more carefully thought through, more forthrightly articulated—is his relating of *Notes of a Native Son* to the traditional depiction in American fiction of "an unremarkable youth in battle with the force of circumstance. . . . In this case the force of circumstance which cannnot be overcome, . . ."[40] Noting that Bigger Thomas is only *one* part of an infinitely more complex reality than Wright is willing, or able, to perceive, Baldwin points to a fundamental deficiency in Wright's vision: "What is missing in Bigger's situation and in the representation of his psychology—which makes his situation false and his psychology incapable to development—is any revelatory apprehension of Bigger as one of the Negro's realities or as one of the Negro's roles. This failure is part of the previously noted failure to convey any sense of Negro life as a continuing and complex group reality."[41] So Baldwin finds both Bigger Thomas and his novel trapped, not in the cage of reality, but in a distorted American image of Black life of which the question of Blacks' basic humanity, the depth of their relationships to each other, and their complex relationships to White Americans, is moot or not even perceived.[42]

A further contention that Baldwin presents in this essay is particularly germane to the problem of identity. Using Wright and Bigger as a framework—again for purposes of contradiction—Baldwin distinguishes between his life as a human being and his life as a Black man. The one, he believes, is his real life; the other a social and mythical life, imposed or projected. There is always a conflict between the two lives, Baldwin insists, but while the conflict never can be resolved, one must make perpetually that "paradoxical adjustment . . . [to] the dark and dangerous and unloved stranger [that] is part of himself forever."[43] In other words, one has not only to recognize but also accept "his private Bigger Thomas living in the skull, . . ."[44] Unless this is done, no Black man can begin to be free. By making these distinctions, Baldwin further defines his identity and distances himself from Wright whose naturalistic assumptions do not lead toward the same goal, artistically, that Baldwin has begun to seek. Exactly what workable formulas will serve him best are not yet apparent to him; what is clear at this juncture, however, is that Baldwin's conception of the relationship between one's social experience and literary art is markedly different from his mentor's. If Wright's failure as an artist was indeed the failure to examine the roots of the "gratuitous and compulsive" violence with which he suffused his work, then Baldwin has already determined to avoid failing in that way.

Judging the content and emphases of the essays in Part One of *Notes of a Native Son,* we note Baldwin's resolute determination to share in the panorama of common humanity through his art. He does not yet go as far as Ellison's "willed affirmation" of his Being,[45] but he does show signs in these first essays of engaging the question of human-ness (humanity). His is an inclusive vision of human beings and of literary art, excluding nothing which would bear on the spectrum of humanity. The ambivalent attitudes that Baldwin holds— Black protest literature versus personal art, Black versus White— seem to form some kind of motif of tension or conflict. It is necessary to establish this tensional pattern in the other essays and to determine what significance it has for James Baldwin's total identity quest.

Those essays of Part Two in which Baldwin exposes his youth further illustrate, in an intensely painful fashion, his difficulties in recognizing, understanding, and accepting his own identity. Although written in a language more subjective than the essays on artistic identity, they reinforce nonetheless the growing impression that Baldwin's pilgrimage is directed consciously toward every aspect of his Being. These essays reveal what Newman calls Baldwin's obsession with dualities and paradox.[46] "The Harlem Ghetto" establishes in fairly objective, dispassionate terms, the Black world into which the title piece, "Notes of a Native Son," shows Baldwin to have been born. This world assures that Negro boys and girls "by the age of puberty, [are] irreparably scarred by the conditions of . . . life. All

over Harlem, they [are] growing into stunted maturity, trying desperately to find a place to stand . . ."[47] Existence in the explosive
Harlem ghetto is marked by an aura of waiting, of bitter expectancy
which never achieves positive or meaningful fruition for its young.[48]
Baldwin introduces the motif of waiting—for tenement repairs, for
better jobs, for welfare payments, for death—in terms of the familiar
metaphor of Winter,[49] noting the stoic resignation of older, tired
Blacks that "it is coming and it will be hard; there is nothing anyone
can do about it."[50] But for the young who find daily identification
with Jewish merchants and Judeo-Christian religion unavoidable and
who share "a furious, bewildered rage, the rage of people who cannot
find solid ground beneath their feet,"[51] the bitter resignation often
is transformed into self- or other-directed destruction.

In "The Harlem Ghetto," Baldwin is unequivocal in stating his
convictions regarding the totally negative results on Black lives of
the oppressive cultural environment, touching at points the same
nerve that the psychologists and social scientists touch. He explains:
"I am not one of the people who believe that oppression imbues
people with wisdom or insight or sweet charity, though the survival
of the Negro in this country would simply not have been all he felt.
. . . the wonder is not that so many are ruined but that so many
survive. The Negro's outlets are desperately constructed. In his dilemma he turns first upon himself and then upon whatever most
represents to him his own emasculation."[52] Similarly in "Many Thousands Gone" which deals as much with the Black man's human identity
as it does with the artistic limitations of this humanity in Wright,
Baldwin analyzes the predicament in strikingly psychosocial terms.
Employing the first person plural to fix his shared humanity in American culture—in which the Black American also is part of the national
"we"—Baldwin details the problem in the following passages: "The
ways in which the Negro has affected the American psychology are
betrayed in our popular culture and in our mortality; in our estrangement from him in the depth of our estrangement from ourselves."[53] Introducing imagery of light-shadow-darkness which is developed early and recurs in clusters throughout the essay, he sees
"The Negro in America, gloomingly referred to as that shadow which
lies athwart our national life, who is far more than that. He is a series
of shadows, self-created, intertwining, which now we helplessly battle.
One may say that the Negro in America does not really exist except
in the darkness of our minds."[54] Baldwin's idea of the American Black
man as a series of self-created shadows gains import when we consider
our own personal identity search as Black man and artist in terms of
creating and "remaking" the self.[55] Again, Baldwin insists on placing
the problem in its human contexts when he observes the Blacks'
dehumanization at the hands of American Whites, or, finally, "The

American image of the Negro which lives also in the Negro's heart; and when he has surrendered to this image life has no other possible reality. Then he, like the white enemy with whom he will be locked one day in mortal struggle, has no means save this of asserting his identity."[56] It would seem from these quotations that James Baldwin claims that the Negro is like everyone else in America. This charge is levelled, wrongly I believe, by several critics, including Dachine Rainer and Marcus Klein.[57] If it is so, then the claim denies Baldwin's Negroness as a personal reality. It appears, however, that instead of psychologically repudiating his Blackness in this essay, he rather *affirms* his own existential condition and that of his Black fellows. The problems of Black identity for Baldwin go far beyond the facile matter of one's nationality; they concern deeply the collective Black impression of alienation from the human condition.

Several of Baldwin's recurrent themes are introduced in this essay, including the negative influence of the Black man's past in America, the dehumanizing effects of an oppressive culture, and the loss of and search for identity by the Black and White American alike. Baldwin views identity in the earliest essays as something to be achieved, created, or shaped, but the initial, positive statement in "Autobiographical Notes" of his own identity recognition *and* acceptance of himself as Black man, "a kind of bastard of the West,"[58] is both explicit and crucial. This realization is expressed in the same kind of language used by DuBois, J. Saunders Redding,[59] and Malcolm X. Although, he admits, "the most difficult (and most rewarding) thing in my life has been the fact that I was born a Negro and forced, therefore, to effect some kind of truce with this reality,"[60] nevertheless he affirms his Black being within the context of the fabric of American culture. Thus, the *fact* of his Blackness precedes all other considerations of human or American identity; this fact even relegates to secondary and even tertiary position what Newman calls Baldwin's "love-hate affair with religion, sex, color, America"[61] in all the essays and novels predating *Another Country*.

The title essay centers as much in Baldwin's examination of the paternal pattern and its impact upon his life as in his discovery of his relationship as Black man first to an essentially White social environment and second to himself. The "truce" with the reality of his Blackness is effected in this essay in terms which both parallel and illuminate the four-part identity-crisis event, namely, recognition, understanding or perception, acceptance, and identification or authentic relationship.

The death of David Baldwin with which the title essay begins and through which James Baldwin orders the entire piece, marks the culmination of his young manhood. It has not been sufficiently noted that the dominant motif of the essay is disease. Physical and psychic sickness infuse the Harlem ghetto of Baldwin's childhood and eats away the life of David Baldwin. The relative dispassion with which Baldwin details the effects of oppressive ghetto life in "The Harlem Ghetto" becomes in this intensely personal and probing essay a passionate, yet ordered, autobiographical case history. He manages to maintain throughout a psychic distance from his father's growing sickness—a kind of objectivity that permits him first to describe, then to analyze, and finally to empathize and reconcile for himself the terrors of the "dread, chronic disease"[62] that annihilates once and for all his father's identity but has only begun to obscure his own. However, the paternal pattern is firmly established, by Baldwin's own admission; this pattern provides, on the one hand, the framework for the painful, finally rewarding probe of his own emerging identity, and it signals the escape from this pattern on the other.

David Baldwin, a man "locked up in his terrors,"[63] was to his children "ingrown, like a toe-nail."[64] By employing this image, Baldwin manages to convey both the inward movement of a frustrated existence on itself and the potential poisoning of such an existence, for if the toe-nail is not cut out and the poison to the bloodstream is not checked, the foot withers and dies. A corollary of the disease imagery likewise is provided early in Baldwin's description of his father as "the most bitter man I have ever met."[65] The bitterness pre-existent in the ghetto infected David Baldwin, turning him slowly into a frightening Black figure, gripped by "an intolerable bitterness of spirit"[66] which Baldwin admits, at age nineteen, overflowed and became his own. In much the same way that Marlow perceives Kurtz initially as a voice, a presence,[67] so Baldwin characterizes his father in terms of a thundering voice full of rage, often issuing "bitter warnings [out] of proudly pursed lips. . . ."[68]

David Baldwin was driven to remoteness from which he never returned. Baldwin particularizes his father's decline by extending carefully the disease imagery from him to the cultural environment that bred him. Ironically, he establishes the condition of bitterness and suppressed rage in which his father lived as paradigmatic of the ghetto's constant condition; that condition is imposed, often unwittingly, on the Black man by the White world. The impression of waiting, of bitter expectancy that characterizes "The Harlem Ghetto" here is confirmed in an ingenious extension of the disease motif: Harlem "seemed to be infected by waiting."[69] The waiting characteristic of the ghetto prefigures the family's waiting at the bedside for David Baldwin's death, precipitated, according to Baldwin, because "the disease of his mind allowed the disease of his body [tuberculosis] to destroy him."[70]

The funeral more than the other events—even more than the Harlem riot of 1943 that followed—provides the testing of the son's identity in relation to it. Sitting in the crowded church, Baldwin alternates between dream digressions, in which he remembers his father, and analyses of the real impact of his father upon his own life. One reminiscence is especially significant as the only point in the entire essay that healing, or the possibility of it, is allowed. In Baldwin's mind, the existence of Harlem "testified to the potency of the poison [of hatred and oppression] while remaining silent as to the efficacy of whatever antidote, irresistibly raising the question of whether or not an antidote was desirable."[71] But the remembrance of a time in childhood when his father was not so cruel but anxious to "heal" is recounted in terms of his "[soothing] my crying and [applying] the stinging iodine."[72] Immediately following this remembrance is the famous scene, briefly presented, on the son's break from the father's vocation and way of life; this was, according to Baldwin, the only time the two ever actually *spoke* to each other: "My father asked me abruptly, 'You'd rather write than preach, wouldn't you?' I was astonished at this question—because it was a real question. I answered 'Yes.' That was all we said."[73]

Toward the end of the essay, Baldwin again makes firm the connection between Harlem's sickness and his father's by employing the imagery of disease—this time in terms of amputation and gangrene. Because "Harlem had needed something to smash. To smash something is the ghetto's chronic need,"[74] the 1943 riots were precipitated. This assertion leads the reader to recall the eighteen-year-old youth in a segregated Trenton cafeteria, driven to the point of smashing, crushing rage.[75] It also reminds one that David Baldwin did not enjoy the "luxury" of such rage; his revolt against the conditions of his existence was almost always self-directed and hence destructive.[76] But the assertion also points forward to Baldwin's own conviction of the necessity of *all* Blacks to make perpetual decisions, not between a disease and a cure, but rather between two aspects of the same disease. The ingrown toe-nail of the opening—taken then as a description of the father—now is expanded and used as the cause of all Black misery. Gangrene is pre-existent in the ghetto, while amputation—the cut—really is symbolic of it. It is explained that his father died of gangrene; however, the perpetual choice is an empty one since the "idea" of going through life as a cripple is [as] unbearable [as] the risk of swelling up slowly, in agony, with poison.[77]

It seems that precisely because Baldwin allows (invents, perhaps) for himself an alternative *other* than the two he claims for Black men generally, he is able to begin to order his own existence and to take the first step in his identity-pilgrimage. In this crucial autobiographical essay, he clearly establishes and defines his existence in opposition to his father, but that is not to say that his own emerging identity

is achieved at the expense of the annihilation of his father's. At one
point in the essay, Baldwin proudly associates his African heritage
with his father;[78] the passage reveals, however, both the father's and
son's ambivalence toward the real worth of their heritage. Again,
Baldwin analyzes the legacy left to him by his father, dwelling not
so much on the aspects of shame, rage, and hatred as on the newly-
interpreted meaning of his father's "texts and songs" which reveal
to him that "nothing is ever escaped."[79] Indeed, David Baldwin's
legacy of hatred is supplanted by the more powerful admonition. In
Baldwin's view, the two overriding ideas, seemingly opposed, of total
acceptance and total refusal to accept any injustice of life and men
which either life or men impose on one's life, signal not the break
with his father but rather Baldwin's symbolic linking in understanding
between dead father and newly-born son. Unless one doubts his
concluding insistence on the folly of holding onto anything that does
not matter, there seems to be no other possible interpretation of the
words, "The dead man mattered, the new life mattered; blackness
and whiteness did not matter. . . ."[80]

As has been shown, in "Notes of a Native Son" and in the other
essays in the "personal identity" group, Baldwin touches on certain
aspects of the "Negro's real relation to the white American";[81] but
the focus of the title essay is on the relationship to his father and
his own emerging identity. Baldwin's exploration of relationships—
to himself, his father and family, fellow Blacks, White men, Europeans
abroad—continues as central emphases throughout the volume, in
the essays that are largely personal as well as in those that are more
outwardly focused. The essays grouped under the rubric of "national
identity" speak to the issue of Baldwin's place as Black American in
the European social fabric. Two of these, "Stranger in the Village"
(1953) and "A Question of Identity" (1954) provide him with perspectives with which to interpret further the American racial problem
in terms of identity. In the first of these two essays, Baldwin demonstrates his ability to move from the personal situation—the fact of
his being a visitor in a small Swiss village—to the universal condition
of men. The "small" experience of innocent racism in this foreign
Catholic village serves as the base on which Baldwin erects a large,
sturdy, pyramidal structure; thematically, one point of the inverted
pyramid is the rage of the "disesteemed" around the world, and the
other is the search for and maintenance of one's own identity, once
discovered.

Baldwin's first visit to the tiny village of Loeche-les-Bains was in
the Fall of 1951, after he "had run away from his native land to
escape not only the Negro condition, but the condition of being
Negro."[82] Here he had completed *Go Tell It on the Mountain;* then
he returned in 1953, broke, starving, and feeling himself to be on

the verge of a breakdown. He completed "Stranger in the Village" in virtual isolation and depressive melancholy. In spite of his former residence, he still was regarded as an oddity, a non-person; he was the first and only Black man that most of these natives had seen. Thus, Baldwin early in the essay establishes his identity as a stranger in relation to the inhabitants of the "white wilderness," alienated from them because of his color in a way that no other foreign stranger could be. The remote alpine village, then, is paradigmatic of the White West "onto which," Baldwin says, "I have been so strangely grafted."[83] Employing a strategic pose of self-examination, the Black "bastard of the West" distances himself, as Black man, from the glories of Chartres, Shakespeare, Rembrandt, and the Empire State Building, all of which—for purposes for Baldwin's dialectic here—he neither feels nor wants to share any part of.[84] His presence in the village also illuminates for him the meaning of the Black/White situation in his native land.

Baldwin's conclusion in "A Question of Identity" that only from the Europe of present reality can the American discover his own country and thereby his identity signals the end of his alienation from himself. In talking with Harold Isaacs in 1959 concerning his emerging convictions regarding national identity, he insisted that the protracted and painful process brought him anew to the old conclusion: You have to go far away to find out that you never do get far away. . . . I couldn't get to *know* France. The key to my experience was *here*, in America. Everything I could deal with was here."[85] The terms with which Baldwin expresses this insight are reminiscent of the Biblical admonition that one must lose his life in order to find it.[86] Inherent in his first expatriate experience was the *necessity* almost simultaneously of losing and finding his own identity. What became ineluctably clear to him, as the result of European exile, was the unalterable fact of his Negro-ness and his Americanness. More important, acceptance of both these identities formed the basis for his next collection of essays, *Nobody Knows My Name*.

Thus, an examination of the content, style, and preoccupations of the essays in *Notes of a Native Son* establishes the direction in which the young essayist is moving, at the same time at which it reveals Baldwin's continuing journey or pilgrimage. The continual "process of rejection and negation" that Theodore Gross sees as occupying Baldwin's thought and writing to the present day[87] might be seen more accurately in the earliest essays as his conscious development of a tensional motif of acceptance and negation, resulting often in ambivalence or vacillation. By examining the later essays chronologically and thematically, it will be possible to determine if this pattern obtains.

Notes

1. Robert A. Bone, *The Negro Novel in America* (Revised ed.; New Haven: Yale University Press, 1965), p. 218.

2. Stephen Spender, "James Baldwin: Voice of a Revolution," *Partisan Review,* XXX (1963), 256–60.

3. Edward Margolies, *Native Sons: A Critical Study of Twentieth-Century Negro American Authors* (Philadelphia: J. B. Lippincott Company, 1968).

4. George Kent, *Blackness and the Adventure of Western Culture* (Chicago: Third World Press, 1972).

5. Howard N. Harper, Jr. *Desperate Faith: A Study of Bellow, Salinger, Mailer, Baldwin and Updike* (Chapel Hill: The University of North Carolina Press, 1967).

6. Calvin C. Hernton, "Blood of the Lamb: The Ordeal of James Baldwin," in *White Papers for White Americans* (Garden City: Doubleday and Company, Inc., 1966), 105–47.

7. Charles Newman, "The Lesson of the Master: Henry James and James Baldwin," *Yale Review,* LVI, 1 (October, 1966), 45–59.

8. Granville Hicks, "Commmitment Without Compromise," review of *Nobody Knows My Name,* by James Baldwin, in the *Saturday Review,* July 1, 1961, p. 9.

9. Julian Mayfield, "A Love Affair With the United States," review of *Nobody Knows My Name,* by James Baldwin, in *The New Republic,* August 7, 1961, p. 25.

10. Mike Thelwell, "*Another Country:* Baldwin's New York Novel," in *The Black American Writer: Fiction,* Vol. I, ed. by C. W. E. Bigsby (Baltimore: Penguin Books, Inc., 1969), pp. 181–98.

11. Mayfield, "A Love Affair," p. 25.

12. Hicks, "Commitment Without Compromise," p. 9.

13. Ibid.

14. Mayfield, "A Love Affair," p. 25.

15. James Baldwin, *No Name in the Street* (New York: The Dial Press, 1972), pp. 53–54. (Baldwin's most recent nonfictional work, which he calls "an essay," is *The Devil Finds Work,* published in 1976. It deals with the condition of the modern American film.)

16. Colin MacInnes, "Dark Angel: The Writing of James Baldwin," in *Five Black Writers: Essays on Wright, Ellison, Baldwin, Hughes and LeRoi Jones,"* ed. by Donald F. Gibson (New York: New York University Press, 1970), p. 121.

17. James Baldwin, "Autobiographical Notes," in *Notes of a Native Son* (New York: The Dial Press, 1955), p. 12.

18. David Levin, "Baldwin's Autobiographical Essays: The Problem of Negro Identity," in *Black and White in American Culture: An Anthology from the Massachusetts Review,* ed. by Jules Chametsky and Sidney Kaplan (New York: The Viking Press, 1971), p. 373.

19. Harper, *Desperate Faith,* pp. 137–38.

20. Newman, "The Lesson of the Master," p. 59. [Newman is particularly instructive with respect to their dialectical art, their relationship to their respective cultures, and the psychological and literary consequences of their 'mysterious' childhoods—self-imposed exile on the one hand, and the novels or dramas of 'manners' on the other. Both men as essayists wrestle with the problem of their opaque culture and their identity within it. (Ibid., pp. 45–71).]

21. See Erik H. Erikson. "The Problem of Ego Identity." *JAPA* Volume 4, Number

1 (January, 1956), 67; "Psychosocial Identity," in *International Encyclopaedia of the Social Sciences*. Volume 7, ed. by David L. Sills (New York: The Macmillan Company and The Free Press, 1968), 61; "Race and the Wider Identity," in *Identity: Youth and Crisis* (New York: W. W. Norton and Company, Inc., 1968), 296–97; also see Abraham Maslow, *Motivation and Personality*, Second ed. (New York: Harper and Row Publishers, 1968). [Other researchers who provide insights into the problem of Black identity are Abram Kardiner and Lionel Ovesey, Kenneth B. Clark, Joseph White, and Alvin Poussaint.]

22. See Ralph W. Ellison, "Hidden Name and Complex Fate," in *For Our Time: Twenty-Four Essays by Eight Contemporary Americans*, ed. by Barry Gross (New York: Dodd, Mead and Company, 1970), pp. 45–46; see also Ellison's "The World and the Jug." Ibid., pp. 63–71, 79–81.

23. Baldwin, "Autobiographical Notes," p. 11. (Italics mine)

24. Ibid., p. 10.

25. Baldwin discusses this theme more fully in one essay from *Nobody Knows My Name*, his second published volume of essays—"The Discovery of What It Means to Be an American."

26. In a bristling essay on Baldwin and Ellison, Howe charges Baldwin with "transcending the sterile categories of 'Negro-ness' " in his avowed attempt to go further than Wright's vision of the Black artist. [See Irving Howe, *A World More Attractive: A View of Modern Literature and Politics* (New York: Horizon Press, 1963), p. 99.]

27. In this connection, Howe poses the question, "What, then, was the experience of a man with a black skin, what could it be in this country? How could a Negro put pen to paper, how could he so much as think or breathe, without some impulsion to protest, . . ." [Ibid., pp. 99–100]. Obviously, Baldwin had anticipated this line of critical attack in the "Autobiographical Notes" when he stated that he would allow neither the "tremendous demands or the very real dangers" of his social situation to prevent the ordering and examining of his experience in his own ways. [Baldwin, "Autobiographical Notes," p. 11.]

28. Ibid.

29. Lerone Bennett, Jr. *Confrontation: Black and White* (Chicago: Johnson Publishing Company, Inc., 1965), p. 210.

30. Ellison, "The World and the Jug," p. 65.

31. Erikson, "Race and the Wider Identity," p. 25.

32. Baldwin, "Autobiographical Notes," p. 9.

33. Erikson suggests that this phrasing is more precise and pertinent than the generally facile phrasing, "Who am I?" Erikson, "Race and the Wider Identity," p. 314.

34. Baldwin, "Everybody's Protest Novel," in *Notes of a Native Son*, p. 18.

35. Ibid., p. 22.

36. Note the interesting similarities here in Baldwin's position on the relationship between oppressor and oppressed and Malcolm X's, and the fact that Baldwin began his literary embracing this belief while Malcolm ended his political career holding to it. Another parallel is to Frantz Fanon's observations in *Black Skin, White Masks: The Experiences of a Black Man in a White World*. Translated by Charles Lam Markmann (New York: Grove Press, Inc., 1967), pp. 150–88.

37. Baldwin, "Everybody's Protest Novel," p. 15. (Italics mine)

38. Baldwin, "Autobiographical Notes," p. 22.

39. What might not be consistent, and for what later critics have taken Baldwin

seriously to task, is his *apparent* gradual assumption in the essays and novels, of the role of Black protestor and spokesman. This "inconsistency" seems to me to be confronted and resolved by Baldwin in his 1972 collection, *No Name in the Street*.

40. Baldwin, "Many Thousands Gone," in *Notes of a Native Son*, p. 30.

41. Ibid., p. 37.

42. Ibid., p. 40.

43. Ibid., p. 33.

44. Ibid.

45. See Ellison, "The World and the Jug," p. 80.

46. Newman, "Lesson of the Master," p. 45.

47. Baldwin, "The Harlem Ghetto," in *Notes of a Native Son*, p. 64.

48. Ibid., p. 51.

49. In "Notes of a Native Son," the motif of waiting, as characteristic of the Harlem ghetto, is linked effectively to the family's waiting for David Baldwin's death and to the people's waiting for the inevitable explosion of the August 1943 riots.

50. Baldwin, "The Harlem Ghetto," p. 64.

51. Ibid.

52. Ibid.

53. Baldwin, "Many Thousands Gone," p. 23.

54. Ibid., pp. 23–24.

55. A later and fuller discussion of this idea is found in the 1961 essay from *Nobody Knows My Name*, "The Black Boy Looks at the White Boy," p. 232.

56. Baldwin, "Many Thousands Gone," p. 27.

57. See Dachine Rainer, "Rage Into Order," *Commonweal*, Volume LXIII, No. 15 (January 13, 1956), 385; and Marcus Klein, *After Alienation: American Novels in Mid-Century* (Cleveland: Meridian Books, 1962).

58. Baldwin, "Autobiographical Notes," p. 10.

59. See Redding's depiction of the problem of Black identity in terms of physical and psychological alienation in *On Being a Negro in America* (New York: Bantam Books, 1964).

60. Baldwin, "Autobiographical Notes," p. 9.

61. Newman, "Lesson of the Master," p. 53.

62. Baldwin, "Notes of a Native Son," in *Notes of a Native Son*, p. 64.

63. Ibid., p. 80.

64. Ibid., p. 78.

65. Ibid.

66. Ibid., p. 79.

67. Joseph Conrad, "Heart of Darkness," in *The Portable Conrad*, ed. by Morton D. Zabel (New York: The Viking Press, 1968), pp. 557–59, 579.

68. Baldwin, "Notes of a Native Son," p. 79.

69. Ibid., p. 88.

70. Ibid., p. 80.

71. Ibid., p. 95.

72. Ibid., p. 96.

73. Ibid., p. 97.

74. Ibid., p. 100.

75. Ibid., pp. 77–78.

76. The only exception that one might take to this point is the harsh and irrational treatment of his family, which can se seen as other-directed rage, albeit misplaced.

77. Ibid., p. 101.

78. Ibid., pp. 86–87.

79. Ibid., p. 101.

80. Ibid., p. 102.

81. Ibid., p. 100.

82. Fern Eckman, *The Furious Passage of James Baldwin* (New York: M. Evans and Company, 1967), p. 119.

83. Baldwin, "Stranger in the Village," in *Notes of a Native Son,* pp. 147–48.

84. Note the use of the same strategy in the "Autobiographical Notes." [Supra, pp. 18–19, n. 58]. The problem of his place in American and human culture that Baldwin introduces here is not resolved in this essay, although it is analyzed at length. Seemingly a resolution is arrived at in a few of the essays in *Nobody Knows My Name,* and in several published interviews following its publication. It will be interesting to trace Baldwin's thought regarding this question of his place in the stream of culture (human *and* American) from *No Name in the Street* to the present return to New York.

85. Harold R. Isaacs, *The New World of Negro Americans* (New York: The John Day Company, 1963), pp. 268–69.

86. The Gospel of Matthew, 10:39.

87. Theodore L. Gross, *The Heroic Ideal in American Literature* (New York: The Free Press, 1971), p. 168.

The Political Significance of James Baldwin's Early Criticism   Louis H. Pratt°

During the early years of James Baldwin's literary career, he published twenty-nine book reviews, nearly all of which appeared in various periodicals between 1947 and 1949. Although "Eight Men" and "The Male Prison" have been reprinted in *Nobody Knows My Name,* very little critical attention has been given to the remaining essays. These discussions provide a link between Baldwin the young critic and Baldwin the mature writer, and they reflect Baldwin's philosophy of criticism at this stage of his literary career.

As a critic of literature, Baldwin perceives an intrinsic bond between the literature of a culture and the society of that culture. Consequently, the literary significance of a creative work is directly

°Reprinted from *Middle Atlantic Writers Association Review* 1, nos. 2–3 (1982):46–49, by permission of the author and the journal.

proportionate to the cultural value assigned to it by society. And since cultural value is shaped by time, history, and politics, literary value also reflects these social elements. For Baldwin, then, literature is a political vehicle whose analysis and evaluation should be based upon the overt and covert assumptions which it makes about society. In *The Politics of Literary Expression,* Donald Gibson succinctly advances this point of view: "The literary critics' job . . . is to describe and evaluate the value system informing literary works, and they do this by means of analysis of its social dimensions. In so doing they will make explicit what is implicit in varying degrees in literature, the value system inherent in it that seeks to influence individuals and the society at large."[1] Like Gibson, Baldwin realizes that literature does not exist in a vacuum: rather it is identified with the multi-faceted social and political forces which shape its character and inform its content. Therefore, there are two salient considerations, aside from the content of the work itself, which must be taken into account in the analysis of a literary work: (1) The writer's canons of judgment reflect his social and cultural orientation. As a representative of his age, more or less, he makes a personal statement in estimation of the society, the culture, and the universe of which he is a part. (2) The writer's canons of judgment are communicated, implicitly or explicitly, to segments of the society and the culture. This ideological transmission has the effect of affirming or denying the values of these segments, and thereby impacts on the society and the culture as a whole to a greater or lesser degree.

These considerations make us aware that the critical analysis of a literary work is surrounded by problems of relativity: "Good" raises the questions of "in terms of what?" and "for whom?" and affirms the fact that the writer and society each exercise a mutual influence within the cultural arena. This raises two crucial issues which Baldwin addresses in his analysis of literary compositions at the beginning of his career: What is the picture presented by the writer? and What is the relationship of this picture to the social reality of the culture from which the writer has emerged?

As a critic, Baldwin is subject to the same social and political forces which influence the writer. Consequently, his analysis of the value system supporting the literary works under consideration reveals several assumptions which inform his critical evaluations. The first of these is that LITERATURE HAS ITS ROOTS IN THE LIVES OF HUMAN BEINGS. This concept is evident in Baldwin's book review, "Battle Hymn," which analyzes Maxim Gorki's novel, *Mother.* Baldwin argues that this book represents Gorki's *magnum opus,* but he takes issue with Gorki's concept that "art is the weapon of the working class."[2] Baldwin refuses to view art as a vehicle for accomplishing the purposes of a segment of society. Rather, he argues for the democratization of art.

Because of the political dimensions of art, and because its significance arises from cultural rather than class origins, it belongs to minority and majority alike. As a functional component of art, therefore, literature also reflects a political reality which grows out of our laws and traditions and belongs no less to the powerful than to the powerless. And because of the political dimensions of literature, it depicts the frailty, the vigor, and the folly of the human condition, without regard for the power of beggars or kings.

Baldwin praises Gorki's characterization of those individuals who have both the vision of a better world and the courage to bring it about, and he calls our attention to their struggle for truth and justice by emphasizing Gorki's conclusion that "there are only comrades and foes."[3] However, this deduction suggests an oversimplification of reality. These opposing forces are engaged in a perpetual warfare, but the battle lines are not so clearly drawn. The complexity of the contest, Baldwin observes, is intensified because ". . . the distinction between comrades and foes has become so faint as to reduce us all to a state of incipient schizophrenia."[4] Therefore, literature must record the conflict involved in man's search for peace and harmony.

This battle takes on a racial dimension in "History as Nightmare," as Baldwin analyzes Chester Himes' novel, *Lonely Crusade*. He criticizes Himes for his lumbering prose, his awkward story structure, and his ambition to pursue so comprehensive a theme. However, Baldwin is impressed with Himes' "desperate, implacable determination to find out the truth . . . to understand the psychology of oppressed and oppressor in their relation to each other."[5] Himes' story is, in part, a story of Black Americans in their efforts to survive in a hostile, white-oriented society. But it is also the story of white Americans in their attempts to come to grips with their own guilt, inadequacies, and fears. It is the story, both individual and collective, of the American dilemma. And it is this dilemma to which Baldwin refers in the closing lines of his review of five books, appropriately entitled, "Too Late, Too Late":

> . . . the full story of white and black in this country is more vast and shattering than we would like be believe and, like an unhindered infection of the body, it has the power to make our whole organism sick.
>
> We are sick now and relations between the races is only one of our symptoms. What is happening to Negroes in this country has been happening for a long time and it is something quite logical, inevitable, and deadly: they are becoming more American every day.[6]

This review, particularly the title, conveys a characteristic pessimism which is frequently reflected in early Baldwin criticism. But more importantly, it introduces a theme which becomes a thesis for Baldwin in his later essays: racism is a fatal disease which affects perpetrator and victim alike in a battle which promises to leave no survivors.

Not only does literature record the perpetual warfare of "comrades and foes," but it also has the capacity for resolving these conflicts. This brings us to Baldwin's second critical assumption: LITERATURE HAS THE POWER TO UNITE AN AMORPHOUS PEOPLE. In a 1948 review of Ross Lockridge's *Raintree County*, Baldwin discusses the fact that cultural heterogeneity in America has led us to view the American Dream in many different (and often conflicting) ways. This disparity, Baldwin subtly suggests, arises not so much from the diverse cultural backgrounds of the people as it does from the American tradition of blatant, pervasive racism. And this leads him to the question, "Which America will you have?" as he elaborates on this point: ". . . There is America for the Indians . . . There is America for the people who settled the country. . . . There is America for the laborer, for the financier, America of the North and South, America for the hillbilly, the urbanite, the farmer. And there is America for the protestant, the Catholic, the Jew, the Mexican, the Oriental and that arid sector which we have reserved for the Negro."[7] But even more significantly, what does the writer, the prophet, make of these divergences? Baldwin takes Lockridge to task for his unsuccessful efforts to make sense of these points of view, and he tells us in a later statement of his craft that ". . . the truth about us is always at variance with what we wish to be. The human effort is to bring these two realities into a relationship resembling reconciliation."[8] Not only is there a variance between reality and desire, but there is also a discrepancy between reality and the perception of that reality. And it is the writer who must help us to reconcile these ideological paths.

The third assumption which is implicit in Baldwin's early criticism is that LITERATURE MUST BE OBJECTIVE IN ITS EFFORTS TO REPRESENT SOCIAL REALITY. Therefore, the writer must be honest. In the celebrated volume of essays, *Notes of a Native Son*, Baldwin ends the introduction, "Autobiographical Notes," with a terse statement of his philosophy: "I want to be an honest man and a good writer."[9] As a Literary critic, Baldwin uses the same criterion to judge the work of other writers. However, this goal of honesty presupposes that several artistic requirements have been met. First, the writer must be able to establish an artistic distance from the people of the culture. Secondly, the writer must help us to examine our past, our history. Third, the writer must help us to explain our present selves by leading us into a recognition, analysis, and acceptance of those forces which shaped us and gave us life. And finally, the writer must help us to come to grips with our anxieties and ambivalences and see ourselves for what we really are. Essentially, then, Baldwin argues for verisi-militude, the appearance or semblance of truth, the representation of reality.

In "The Image of the Negro," a review of five novels, Baldwin clarifies his critical stance by demanding that literature be examined in political terms with reference to the value system which informs it. Consequently, he raises the following questions concerning the novels which are under consideration: "With what reality are they concerned, how is it probed, how translated, exactly what message is being brought to this amorphous public mind?"[10] In this critical review, Baldwin discusses the myth of the *white surrogate*. One of the major concerns in his quest for honesty and truth is the image of the black man which is reflected in novels written by whites. Therefore, Baldwin objects to the common, sinister presupposition of these novelists that "whiteness is a kind of salvation and that blackness is a kind of death."[11] This premise, he argues, gives rise to fair-skinned protagonists who serve as a denial of their darker brothers and advance the fallacious argument that those blacks who deserve the white reader's approbation are those whose complexions most closely resemble their own. The propagation of this myth reflects not only the failure of the individual novelists to come to terms with reality, but it also documents the failure of our society to come to terms with the truth.

In a review of Shirley Graham's biography of Frederick Douglass, *There Was Once A Slave*, Baldwin explores another myth, that of the *black superman*. Here, Baldwin's dogged, even-handed persistence in his quest for truth leads him even further into a careful, objective criticism of the white novelist. For not only must the honest writer refrain from patterning his black characters after whites, Baldwin contends, but he must also depict the black man in all of his foibles and shortcomings, as well as his virtues and successes. The good intentions of the novelist notwithstanding, the black protagonist who emerges as an unimpeachable hero and saint also flies in the face of reality and truth. This is the major criticism which Baldwin makes as he cites the basis for Graham's pattern of reverse discrimination: ". . . There is a tradition among emancipated whites and progressive Negroes to the effect that no unpleasant truth concerning Negroes is ever to be told, a tradition as insidious as that other tradition that Negroes are never to be characterized as anything more than amoral, laughing clowns."[12] This custom gives rise to Douglass' followers on the one side who, in spite of their shortcomings, emerge as high principled, uncorrupt, conscientious characters, and on the other stand those deceptive, misguided souls whose antagonistic chicanery is doomed to failure. Douglass himself is portrayed as a towering giant whose enemies cringe at the very mention of his name. These unrealistic characterizations arise from the fact that Graham becomes over-zealous in her efforts to depict Douglass as the paragon of a black man in a society dominated by whites. As a result, Baldwin argues, she "has reduced a significant, passionate human being to the obscene level of a hollywood caricature . . . and robbed him of dignity and humanity alike."[13]

There is a two-fold danger operating here. The reader who is not black, perhaps sensitive to the prejudices suffered by blacks, and eager to strike a blow for justice and equality, is liable to allow his "emancipation" to lead him along the easy path of credulity without assuming his responsibility to subject Graham's work to the critical light of logic. Moreover, there is the black reader, "progressive," as Baldwin describes him, who rejects the negative images of his people and becomes an easy victim who quickly accepts such a flattering description of the hero. And it is precisely these manifestations of emotionalism which cloud the truth and widen the gap between the reader and reality. Thus, in Baldwin's view, the writer has failed in his solemn responsibility to objectify and clarify the social realities of his times; he has become an accomplice in justifying the lies which support our society and our culture.

This position, however, must be viewed in perspective. In spite of Baldwin's insistence on objectivity in representing social reality, clearly, he realizes the limitations in this point of view. He is aware that total objectivity results in the detachment of the writer from his characters and in the reduction of literature to the reportorial level. In his review of Gorki's short stories, "Maxim Gorki as Artist," Baldwin demonstrates an awareness of the subjective dimension, a distinction which separates literature from journalism: "If literature is not to drop completely to the intellectual and moral level of the daily papers we must recognize the need for further and honest exploration of those provinces, the human heart and mind, which have operated, historically and now, as the no man's land betwen us and our salvation."[14] The mere presentation of fact must not be mistaken for literature. Therefore, the writer must penetrate beyond the objective detail to reveal the strivings and yearnings of the soul. This criterion urges a recognition and portrayal of the human spirit and suggests a fourth critical assumption: LITERATURE MUST PROBE THE RECESSES OF THE HUMAN HEART AND MIND.

Baldwin praises Gorki's concern with the human condition, his insistence on the noble destiny of mankind, and his exhortation for men to resist enslavement by their own materialistic creations and rise to retrieve their individuality. But he argues that Gorki's writing fails to transcend the objectivity of "a disquieting and honest report." Gorki remains a detached observer who cannot identify with the cold character symbols which he presents because his position is far too distant to maintain contact with humanity, to delve into the mysteries of human experience. Therefore, Gorki's sympathy for his characters ". . . did not lead him to that peculiar position of being at once identified with and detached from the humans that he studied. He is never criminal, judge, and hangman simultaneously. . . . His failure was that he did not speak *as a criminal* but spoke *for them:* and operated, consciously or not, not as an artist and a prophet but as a reporter and a judge."[15] The role of artist/prophet involves a unique duality. Not only must he identify with and detach himself from his society, but he must accept isolation. Though a product of the people, he must nevertheless maintain a certain remoteness without losing contact with the people. He and the people, though separate and distinct, are one and indivisible. Gorki's shortcoming, then, is not due to his artistic vision; it results from his inability to maintain the precise balance between involvement and detachment.

Inevitably it follows that Gorki's detachment results in the problem of using characters as vehicles of communication with the reader. The reader never views the plight of the characters in relation to himself; consequently, the aloofness of the writer is transferred to the reader as the mere accumulation of detail weighs upon him and brutalizes him without providing insight into human needs and aspirations.

The fifth critical assumption is revealed in "Dead Hand of Caldwell," a review of Erskine Caldwell's novel, *The Sure Hand of God,* for it is here that Baldwin asserts that LITERATURE MUST GRAPPLE WITH THE PERPLEXITIES OF THE HUMAN PREDICAMENT. Although he believes that Caldwell was never a great writer, Baldwin remembers that his earlier writings were concerned with the seamier sides of Southern life, and he cites *God's Little Acre, Kneel to the Rising Sun,* and *You Have Seen Their Faces* as evidence that Caldwell was once "far more concerned with human beings and the terrible circumstances of their lives."[16] Thus, he calls for a return to a more humanitarian concern for the individual who is caught up in the struggle for survival against the overwhelming odds.

This idea is also revealed in Baldwin's review of Jacques Maritan's philosophical treatise, *The Person and the Good.* Baldwin acknowledges the validity and profundity of the tenets which form the foundation of philosophy, but he focuses his assessment on what appears to be the tremendous gap between idea and reality. Philosophy, he argues, must not only postulate and theorize, but it must somehow evolve into a utilitarian prospect for improving the quality of people's lives. It must shed light on the darkness, the mysteries of the human condition; it must give hope that man will, finally, triumph over the complexities of his existence. As Baldwin advances his argument, he finds himself caught up in Maritan's philosophical circles: It is a crime to kill an innocent man, but society has the right to send its citizens to war to kill in combat "as an act of virtue." But where is the guilt, and who is to judge the guilty? Maritan does not suggest answers to these problems: instead, he assures us that these inequities will be resolved in the hereafter. Baldwin summarizes his review in characteristic laconic terms which reject the relevance and validity of Maritan's point of view: "It is unhelpful indeed to be assured of future angels when the mysteries of the present flesh are so far from being solved."[17]

If we accept the premise that literary expression is political, then we acknowledge the fact that literature is inextricably bound to a writer's experiential background as well as to the cultural and the social mores of the time. But literature also has the power to transcend the particular facts of the here and the now and achieve the universal. Hence, we approach Baldwin's sixth critical assumption: LITERATURE MUST ANALYZE THE PERSONAL, TEMPORAL EXPERIENCES OF A CULTURE IN ORDER TO LINK THAT CULTURE TO OTHER CULTURES. Since the concept of "universality has been viewed with general disapprobation among critics of Afro-American literature, and since it has taken on negative connotations, let me clarify my use of the term. The basic objection to the application of the term "universal" to the literature of black Americans, it seems to me, is that the concept is tied to the values of the dominant racial group. And because this group controls the political and economic power, the values of Black America are either negated or compromised so that they conform to the values of the majority. Thus, the values of the dominant group are accepted by both minority and majority as "universal," and they become the standards by which humanity is judged. In the September 1981 issue of the *College Language Association Journal,* Arnold Rampersad affirms his point of view:

> . . . the identification and propagation of the universal belong to the governing mechanism of the colonizer, who determines the nature and scope of universal truths, the appropriate subject matter of art, and corresponding standards of evaluation for all creative enterprise. . . . These truths become the primary texts in all appeals to liberty and justice: they are presented to the master class—and to the artists themselves—as the major evidence that the colonized artist and race are indeed human, indeed universal.[18]

I certainly concur with Professor Rampersad whose argument, I believe, is typical of the position of the critics of universality in Black writing. However, I do not use the term to explain the conscious or subconscious efforts of a writer to identify with the value system of another race in order to make a literary work "acceptable" to that race, because this perpetuates universality in colonial terms. On the other hand, as Rampersad also acknowledges, there is an ethnic universality which he refers to as "true universality," and he defines this as the process by which the artist ". . . divests himself or herself of any obsessive attachment to the universal that deprives art of its primary sources of material and inspiration . . . [and] links black life and history to all life and history through intellectually consistent and vivid metaphors and allusions that dignify the collective, universal experience of humanity without any sacrifice of the primary intention . . . which is to celebrate the dignity and the historicity of black people."[19] This process results in a literary composition which is intellectually genuine and which links the particulars of the Black experience with the universal experiences of mankind. Literature, then, not only analyzes a specific cultural experience, but it also pushes that experience beyond the centrality of the personal and the temporal to the outer periphery where it moves to the general and touches the fringes of the universal dimension of experience. In "Eight Men," Baldwin effectively captures this point of view as he recalls two of Richard Wright's short stories, "The Man Who Was Almost A Man" and "The Man Who Saw the Flood," which are set in the South during the depression. For Baldwin, these stories ". . . do not seem dated. Perhaps it is odd, but they did not make me think of the 1930's, or even, particularly, of Negroes. They made me think of human loss and helplessness. . . . It now begins to seem, for example, that Wright's unrelentingly black landscape was not merely that of the Deep South, or of Chicago, but that of the world, of the human heart."[20] Here Baldwin discusses these stories as particular ethnic expressions which capture the vitality and authenticity of life among Black Americans. But more than that, they, create ripples which move in ever-widening circles into perpetual time and space, into infinity.

If it is true, as Baldwin contends, that the writer is a prophet, a disciple *of* the people who is, albeit apart *from* the people, it follows that the writer operates within the confines of his unique sphere. His consciousness of the human condition and his sensitivity to human relationships lend greater intensity to his experiences and greater accuracy to his insights. These insights allow the writer/ prophet to give expression to the collective consciousness of his peers and reveal truths about his society and his world which are not evident to his contemporaries because of their cultivated illusions. Similarly, the critic of literature also occupies a special sphere, for it is he who must analyze the products of the imagination and assess the extent to which they serve as vehicles of truth within the social and cultural contexts. Each protects the interests of a people who are intent upon hiding from themselves. Each is in search of truth in the sense of being true to life, true to the world.

Whether we examine Baldwin the writer or Baldwin the critic, the value system which influences his analyses remains the same. Like other writers and critics, he has been shaped by his ethnic experiences within the context of the larger framework of society and culture. And it is this same ideological orientation which, in turn, impinges upon his writings and his criticism as well. For this reason, many of the issues which Baldwin raises in his early criticism have found their way into his essays, novels, and plays over the past thirty-five years. In each of these functions, Baldwin becomes the prophet whose vision penetrates beyond the facade into the hidden reality, whose analyses probe into the marrow of the complexities of our lives, and whose exhortations stimulate and challenge us to strive for the establishment of a new society founded on a genuine love of mankind, one for the other, as well as a new commitment to individual worth and human dignity.

Notes

1. Donald B. Gibson, *The Politics of Literary Expression* (Westport, Connecticut: Greenwood Press, 1981), p. ix.

2. James Baldwin, "Battle Hymn," rev. of *Mother,* by Maxim Gorki, *The New Leader,* 29 November 1947, p. 10.

3. Baldwin, "Battle Hymn," p. 10.

4. Baldwin, "Battle Hymn," p. 10.

5. James Baldwin, "History as Nightmare," rev. of *Lonely Crusade,* by Chester Himes, *The New Leader,* 25 October 1947, p. 11.

6. James Baldwin, "Too Late, Too Late," rev. of five books, *Commentary,* January 1949, pp. 98–99.

7. James Baldwin, "Lockridge: 'The American Myth'," rev. of *Raintree County,* by Ross Lockridge, *The New Leader,* 10 April 1948, p. 10.

8. James Baldwin, "The Creative Dilemma," *Saturday Review,* February 1964, p. 58.

9. James Baldwin, "Autobiographical Notes," *Notes of a Native Son* (1955; rpt. New York: Bantam Books, 1968), p. 6.

10. James Baldwin, "The Image of the Negro," rev. of five novels, *Commentary,* 5 (1948), p. 378.

11. Baldwin, "Image," p. 380.

12. James Baldwin, "Smaller Than Life," rev. of *There Was Once A Slave,* by Shirley Graham, *The Nation,* 19 July 1947, p. 78.

13. Baldwin, "Life," p. 78.

14. James Baldwin, "Maxim Gorki as Artist," rev. of *Best Short Stories,* by Maxim Gorki, *The Nation,* 12 April 1947, p. 428.

15. Baldwin, "Maxim Gorki," p. 428.

16. James Baldwin, "Dead Hand of Caldwell," rev. of *The Sure Hand of God,* by Erskine Caldwell, *The New Leader,* 6 December 1947, p. 10.

17. James Baldwin, "Present and Future," rev. of *The Person and the Good,* by Jacques Maritan, *The New Leader,* 13 March 1948, p. 11.

18. Arnold Rampersad, "The Universal and the Particular in Afro-American Poetry," *College Language Association Journal,* 25, no. 1 (September 1981), pp. 5–6 passim.

19. Rampersad, pp. 10–13 passim.

20. James Baldwin, "Alas, poor Richard," *Nobody Knows My Name* (1961; rpt. New York: Dell Publishing Company, 1970), pp. 147–149 passim.

No Name in the Street: James Baldwin's Image of the American Sixties

Yoshinobu Hakutani°

I

Whether or not one agrees with his views on race, one may be persuaded that James Baldwin is one of the most gifted essayists America has produced. Today, as an essayist writing about racial problems in American society, he has no equals. The incisiveness of his writing seems to come not so much from his eloquence, which is beyond dispute, as from his depth of feeling. As an autobiographical writer, there is no question about the authenticity of his vision. In expressing the suffering, perseverance, and aspiration of a minority, Baldwin's essays have brought out the truth about himself as Theodore Dreiser's *Dawn* and Richard Wright's *Black Boy* had done in slightly different contexts for their authors earlier.

Still, many readers are more impressed with Baldwin's eloquence than with his arguments. One critic, recognizing that Baldwin's talent is for the essay, finds a Jamesian eloquence in *Notes of a Native Son,* and "a style of flaming declamation" in such a work as *The Fire Next Time.*[1] Although elegance and declamation undoubtedly characterize Baldwin's writing, it is doubtful that his expression can generate such power without substance. What underlies his language is a desire to be "an honest man and a good writer," as he said at the beginning of his career.[2] And yet later readers, even after *No Name in the Street* had appeared, were more impressed by this manner than his matter.

Granted *Nobody Knows My Name* (1961), concerned with the

°This essay was written for this volume and appears here for the first time by permission of the author.

"love" between American blacks and whites, reflects the attitude of the liberals of the time. Similarly, *The Fire Next Time* (1963), Baldwin's revision of that concept of love,[3] reflects public sentiment on the subject at the time. With the publication of *No Name in the Street* in 1972, Benjamin DeMott went so far as to say, "Baldwin speaks of killing because the advent of a new militancy, together with disillusionment about prospects for reform, dictates still further change."[4] DeMott's argument is that Baldwin's essay is less the product of his personal philosophy than the reflection of the times in which he lived. At times, however, one is hard pressed to distinguish between a writer's personal feeling and the feeling generated by the events of society. Witness one instance in *No Name in the Street* in which Baldwin recounts a white juror's attitude toward the American system of justice:

> "As I said before, that I feel, and it is my opinion that racism, bigotry, and segregation is something that we have to wipe out of our hearts and minds, and not on the street. I have had an opinion that—and been taught never to resist a police officer, that we have courts of law in which to settle . . . that I could get justice in the courts"—And, in response to Garry's [the defense attorney's] question, "Assuming the police officer pulled a gun and shot you, what would you do about it?" the prospective juror, at length, replied, "Let me say this. I do not believe a police officer will do that."[5]

The juror's reply not only provides a "vivid and accurate example of the American piety at work," as Baldwin observes, but also demonstrates the very honesty in Baldwin that makes his feeling credible to the reader.

To reveal this kind of malady in society as Baldwin attempts to do in *No Name in the Street* requires an artist's skills. The juror's response is reminiscent of Aunt Sally's response to Huck Finn, who reports that a steamboat has just blown out a cylinder-head down the river:

> "Good gracious! Anybody hurt?"
> "No'm. Killed a nigger."
> "Well, it's lucky; because sometimes people do get hurt. . . ."[6]

What Twain and Baldwin share is the genuine feeling that an intense individualist possesses; both writers feel their own great powers and yet recognize the hopelessness of trying to change the world.

No Name in the Street is a departure from Baldwin's earlier books of essays in expressing his theory of identity and love. Baldwin does not sound like an integrationist in the book; he sounds as if he is advocating the idea of a militant separatist who has no qualm about killing a white enemy. Whatever position he finally holds here, he is dealing with the issue more deliberately and quietly than one would think. As a result, *No Name in the Street* turns out to be a far more sustained examination of the falsehood to which Americans try to cling than his previous works. Underlying the severity of his vision is a calmness and perhaps a sense of resignation. In espousing the concept of the damned human race, his voice in this book has an affinity with Twain's, and even with that of Swift toward the end of *Gulliver's Travels*. In short, *No Name in the Street* is a successful satire against man.

On the American scene the implications of Baldwin's satire are vast and prophetic. He had earlier argued that racism at home is closely related to racism abroad and the power politics of the world in particular. Once again in 1972 he reminded the reader that America had sided with wrong regimes abroad to perpetuate white supremacy at home:

> And, of course, any real commitment to black freedom in this country would have the effect of reordering all our priorities, and altering all our commitments, so that, for horrendous example, we would be supporting black freedom fighters in South Africa and Angola, and would not be allied with Portugal, would be closer to Cuba than we are to Spain, would be supporting the Arab nations instead of Israel, and would never have felt compelled to follow the French into Southeast Asia. But such a course would forever wipe the smile from the face of that friend we all rejoice to have at Chase Manhattan. (178)

His vision of the sixties is not only authentic but prophetic, for, as he insists, "The course we *are* following is bound to have the same effect, and with dreadful repercussions" (178). In *Nobody Knows My Name* he chided Richard Wright, as he did in *Notes of a Native Son* (1955), and said: "It is no longer important to be white—thank heaven—the white face is no longer invested with the power of the world."[7] Now the seventies, which seems to culminate with the Iranian crisis, bears out Baldwin's prophecy.

II

No Name in the Street employs its title as a thematic device. The title is taken from the speech by Bildad the Shuhite in the Book of Job that denounces the wicked of his generation:

> Yea, the light of the wicked shall be put out,
> And the spark of his fire shall not shine.
> His remembrance shall perish from the earth,
> And he shall have no name in the street.
> He shall be driven from light into darkness,
> And chased out of the world.[8]

Baldwin sees in Bildad's curse a warning for Americans: without a name worthy of its constitution, America will perish as a nation. "A civilized country," Baldwin ironically observes, "is, by definition, a country dominated by whites, in which the blacks clearly know their place" (177). Baldwin warns that Americans remake their country into what the Declaration of Independence *says* they wanted it to be. America without equality and freedom will not survive; a country without a morality, in Baldwin's definition, is not a viable civilization and hence it is doomed. Unless such a warning is heeded now, he forsees that a future generation of mankind, "running through the catacombs . . . and digging the grave . . . of the mighty Roman empire" (178), will also discover the ruins of another civilization called the United States.

The responsibility for Americans to rebuild their country, Baldwin hastens to point out, falls upon the blacks as heavily as upon the whites. This point echoes what he has said before, but it is stated here with a more somber and deliberate tone. It sounds comfortable indeed to hear Baldwin say in *Notes of a Native Son* that "blackness and whiteness did not matter."[9] He thought then that only through love and understanding could whites and blacks transcend their differences in color to achieve their identity as men and as a nation. In *No Name in the Street,* such euphoria has largely evaporated; the book instead alludes to the fact that American blacks are descendants of American whites. "The blacks," Baldwin insists, "are the despised and slaughtered children of the great Western house—*nameless* and *unnameable* bastards" (185; my italics). A black man in this country has no true name. Calling himself a black and a citizen of the United States is merely giving himself a label without a name worthy of his history and existence. To Baldwin, then, the race problem is not a race problem as such; it is fundamentally a problem of how the black perceives his own identity.[10]

No Name in the Street also deals with the cultural heritage of American blacks. He admonishes them that the term *Afro-American* does not simply mean the liberation of blacks in this country. The word, as it says, means the heritage of Africa and America. American blacks, he argues, should be proud of this heritage. He demands that they must at once discard the misguided notion that they are descendants of slaves brought from Africa, that inferiority complex deeply rooted in the American psyche. An Afro-American, in Baldwin's metaphysics, is considered a descendant of the two civilizations, Africa and America, both of which were "discovered" not by Americans but by European settlers.

Moreover, Baldwin's prophecy is rendered in epic proportion. "On both continents," he says, "the white and the dark gods met in combat, and it is on the outcome of this combat that the future of both continents depends" (194). Thus the true identity of an Afro-American, the very name that Baldwin finds the most elusive of all names, is given a historical light. To be granted this name, as he writes toward the end of the book, "is to be in the situation, intolerably exaggerated, of all those who have ever found themselves part of a civilization which they could in no wise honorably defend—which they were compelled, indeed, endlessly to attack and condemn—and who yet spoke out of the most passionate love, hoping to make the kingdom new, to make it honorable and worthy of life" (194). Historically, then, Baldwin is demonstrating his old contention that both blacks and whites on this continent are destined to live together and determine their own destiny.

No Name in the Street ends on a dark note, as some critics have suggested,[11] precisely because Baldwin has not yet discovered the true name for Americans. The most painful episode in the book that influences his outlook on the racial question in 1972 is his journey into the deep South. There he discovered not only a sense of alienation between blacks and whites, who had lived together over the generations, but an alienation within a white man himself. While a Southerner was conceived in Baldwin's mind as a man of honor and of human feeling like a Northern liberal, he struck Baldwin as a man necessarily wanting in "any viable, organic connection between his public stance and his private life" (53–54). Baldwin felt, in fact, that southern whites always loved their black friends, but they never admitted it. This is why Baldwin characterizes the South as "a riddle which could be read only in the light, or the darkness, of the unbelievable disasters which had overtaken the private life" (55).

In these pages, however, Baldwin's search for a national identity in the name of brotherhood and love does not seem to end; he returns to the North. In the eyes of middle-aged Baldwin, the potential for a truly American identity emerges in the North in the black and white coalition with the radical students, and even in the black and white confrontation in the cities and labor unions. Such an interaction is a rallying cry for the blacks who have seized the opportunity to make the once pejorative term *black* into what Baldwin calls "a badge of honor" (189). Though this confrontation may entail hostile and dangerous reactions, Baldwin clearly implies that it is a necessary crucible for the blacks to go through in order to achieve their identity in modern times. In the context of the late sixties, this is exactly what he meant by the experience which a person, black or white, must face and use so that he might acquire his identity. Baldwin hoped that the alienation he saw in the South could not repeat itself in the North.

Baldwin's most romantic quest in this book involves the "flower children" he saw walking up and down the Haight-Ashbury section of San Francisco in the late sixties. While he observed that the blacks then were putting their trust not in flowers but in guns, he believed that the scene brought the true identity to the threshold of its maturity. The flower children, in his view, repudiated their fathers for failing to realize that American blacks were the descendants of white fathers; they treated the black children as their denied brothers as if in defiance of their elders. "They were in the streets," he says in reference to the title of the book, "in the hope of becoming whole" (187). To him, the flower children were relying on the blacks so that they could rid themselves of the myth of white supremacy. Baldwin, however, was undeniably a realist. He did not rely upon the blacks who were putting their trust in guns, nor did he trust the flower children. In this episode he is quick to warn black listeners: "This troubled white person might suddenly decide not to be in trouble and go home—and when he went home, he would be the enemy" (188). In Baldwin's judgment, the flower children of the last decade became neither true rebels nor true lovers, either of whom would be worthy of their name in their search for a national identity. In either case, he says, perhaps to chide himself, "to mistake a fever for a passion can destroy one's life" (189).

The spectacle of the flower children thus figures as one of the saddest motifs in *No Name in the Street.* Whereas the vision of the young Baldwin was immersed in love and brotherhood, the sensibility of the older Baldwin here smacks of shrewdness and prudence. Idealism is replaced by pragmatism, and honesty and sincerity clearly mark the essential attitude he takes to the problem of identity in America. Baldwin's skeptical admiration for the flower children casts a sad note because this was the closest point to which blacks and whites had ever come in their search for understanding.

But at heart Baldwin is not a pessimist, and will never be one. These pages, filled with love and tenderness, vividly express his feeling that, through these children, American blacks have learned the truth about themselves. And this conviction, however ephemeral it may have been, contributes to his wishfulness and optimism of the early seventies. He has come to know the truth, stated before,[12] that American blacks can free themselves as they learn more about whites and that "the truth which frees black people will also free white people" (129).

III

Although *No Name in the Street* is divided into two parts, "Take Me to the Water" and "To Be Baptized," it is not a collection of individual essays. Obviously the respective titles indicate the unity of thoughts that underlies the theme of quest for a national identity.

The epigraph to the first part of the book, taken from a slave song, suggests a rationale for the author's command, "Take Me to the Water": "Great God, then, if I had-a-my way / If I had-a-my way, little children, / I'd tear this building down." Similarly, the second part of the book, "To Be Baptized" has an epigraph quoted from a "traditional": "I told Jesus it would be all right / If He changed my name." It is also obvious from the title of the entire book that this search for a viable identity for all Americans has ended in failure; despite their efforts, their true name has become as elusive as ever.

Baldwin's attitude toward the failure is also reflected in the style and method of the book. Throughout the book he persists in his belief that the failure to achieve identity was caused by the deep-seated fear Americans had in facing reality. In defending themselves against this fear, both blacks and whites deluded themselves and created all kinds of fantasies and myths about each other. Whereas his earlier books of essays, particularly *The Fire Next Time,* have demonstrated this fear and predicted its dire consequences, *No Name in the Street* focuses on how it manifests itself in contemporary American life. His voice here is less declamatory; he does not suggest the same burning mission as a spokesman for blacks as in his previous works. Rather, he goes about it quietly with the use of impressionism and imagery. He has employed such techniques before, but here with greater frequency with a larger canvas at his disposal.

He begins *No Name in the Street* with an anecdote about the rift between him and his stepfather, a well-known event in Baldwin's early life. "I am apparently in my mother's arms," he recalls, "for I am staring at my father [stepfather] over my mother's shoulder . . . and my father smiles." The narrative is abruptly interrupted with an interpolation to indicate that this is not only "a memory" but more significantly "a fantasy." Leaping in time and space, Baldwin then reveals the truth about his father, stated in the past tense: "One of the very last times I saw my father on his feet, I was staring at him over my mother's shoulder—she had come rushing into the room to separate us—and my father was not smiling and neither was I" (4). This is perhaps the strongest impression of the elder Baldwin that was ingrained in Baldwin's childhood memory. By pointing out the tendency of a mere child to delude himself, Baldwin is also directing the reader's attention to the adult world where delusion is a way of life. Such an incident accounts for Baldwin's basic argument for the achievement of identity. He demands that Americans, both white and black, must see themselves directly, not through the racial myths that have hampered their vision in the past.

Another childhood incident Baldwin remembers is conveyed as an impression he made of his grandmother (the mother of his father), who loved him and tried to protect him from his father's tyranny.

Immediately before her death Baldwin was called to her bed and presented a gift, an old metal box with a floral design. *"She* thought it was full of candy," he remembers, "and *I* thought it was full of candy, but it wasn't." After her death he discovered that it contained needles and thread, something that any child would least desire. This anecdote vividly portrays not only the child's grief over the passing away of his grandmother, but his painful apprehension of reality— the reality of her death as well as of the gift.

The impressions that derive from his personal experience thus function as effective motifs in this book. Kinship, therefore, figures as a foil against the alienation that exists between members of a race as well as between races in America. This is why Baldwin says of Richard Wright that his characterization of Bigger Thomas in *Native Son* is marred by a paucity of feeling the hero has for his fellow human beings.[13] Thus the strongest sense of kinship Baldwin felt as a young boy came from a terrifying experience he had off the Coney Island shore:

> I still remember the slimy sea water and the blinding green—it was not green; it was all the world's snot and vomit; it entered into me; when my head was abruptly lifted out of the water, when I felt my brother's [stepbrother's] arms and saw his worried face—his eyes looking steadily into mine with the intense and yet impersonal anxiety of a surgeon, the sky above me not yet in focus, my lungs failing to deliver the mighty scream I had nearly burst with in the depths, my four or five or six-year-old legs kicking—and my brother slung me over his shoulder like a piece of meat, or a much beloved child, and strode up out of the sea with me, with me! (8)

"I learned," Baldwin tells us, "something about the terror and loneliness and the depth and the height of love" (8).

Well into the middle of "Take Me to the Water," Baldwin now plunges himself into the dreary waters of mid–twentieth-century America. This part of the narrative, in contrast with the personal and family episodes preceding it, abounds with experiences that suggest impersonality and superficiality in human relationship. After a long sojourn in France, Baldwin saw his school chum, now a U.S. post-office worker, whom he had not seen since graduation. At once Baldwin felt a sense of alienation that separated the one who was tormented by America's involvement in Vietnam and the one who blindly supported it. Baldwin felt no conceivable relationship to his old friend now, for "that shy, pop-eyed thirteen year old my friend's mother had scolded and loved was no more." His friend's impression of the famous writer, described in Baldwin's own words, is equally poignant: "I was a stranger now . . . and what in the world was I by now but an aging, lonely, sexually dubious, politically outrageous, unspeakably erratic freak?" What impressed Baldwin the most about this encounter was the fact that despite the changes that had occurred in both men, nothing had touched this black man. To Baldwin, his friend was an emblem of the "white-washed" black who "had been trapped, preserved, in that moment of time" (15–18).

New York City, Baldwin's hometown, also struck him as emblematic of the impersonality and indifference that plagued American life. On his way to the South on a writing assignment he stopped by the city for rest and for the readjustment of his life spent on foreign soil for nearly a decade. But all he heard was "beneath the nearly invincible and despairing noise, the sound of many tongues, all struggling for dominance" (51). This sound reminds one of what Stephen Crane in the guise of a tramp heard at the end of "An Experiment in Misery": "The roar of the city in his ear was to him the confusion of strange tongues, babbling heedlessly; it was the clink of coin, the voice of the city's hopes, which were to him no hopes."[14]

Baldwin's travel down the Southland brought with it a sense of terror he had never known. This was at the time of the racial turmoil in Little Rock, Arkansas, in the late 1950s, when black children attempted to go to school in front of a hostile army and citizenry to face the white past, let alone the white present. On this journey Baldwin encountered one of the most powerful Southern politicians, who made himself "sweating drunk" to humiliate another human being. Baldwin distinctly recalls the abjectness of this incident: "With his wet eyes staring up at my face, and his wet hands groping for my cock, we were both, abruptly, in history's ass-pocket." To Baldwin, one who had power in the South still lived with the mentality of a slave owner. This experience convinced Baldwin that a black's identity in the South was defined by the power of such a man and that a black's humanity was placed at the service of his fantasies. "If the lives of those children," Baldwin reflects, "were in those wet, despairing hands, if their future was to be read in those wet, blind eyes, there was reason to tremble" (61–62). It is characteristic of the book's structure that the height of terror, as just described, is set against the height of love the child Baldwin felt when his life was saved by his stepbrother. The narrative in this book thus moves back and forth with greater intensity and effect between the author's feelings of abjectness and exaltation, isolation, and affinity.

Baldwin's style becomes even more effective as his tendency toward rhetorical fastenings and outbursts is replaced by his use of brief, tense images that indicates a control of the narrative voice. For instance, one summer night in Birmingham, Alabama, Baldwin met in a motel room Rev. Shuttlesworth, a marked man as Martin

Luther King, Jr., was. Gravely concerned with Shuttlesworth's safety for fear that his car might be set with a bomb, Baldwin wanted to bring it to his attention as Shuttlesworth was about to leave the room. But the minister would not let him. At first, there was only a smile on Shuttlesworth's face; upon a closer observation, Baldwin detected that "a shade of sorrow crossed his face, deep, impatient, dark; then it was gone. It was the most impersonal anguish I had ever seen on a man's face." Only later did Baldwin come to realize that the minister then was "wrestling with the mighty fact that the danger in which he stood was as nothing compared to the spiritual horror which drove those who were trying to destroy him" (67). A few pages later, this shade of dark and sorrow is compensated for by that of light and happiness. Baldwin now reminisces about his Paris days—how little he had missed ice cream, hot dogs, Coney Island, the Statue of Liberty, the Empire State Building, but how much he had missed his brothers, sisters, and mother: "I missed the way the dark face closes, the way dark eyes watch, and the way, when a dark face opens, a light seems to go on everywhere . . ." (70–71).

By far the most penetrating image occurs when Baldwin is confronted with the time-worn racial segregation in the deep South. One pleasant evening in Montgomery, Alabama, he found a restaurant on the corner only a block away from the black residential section of the town. Although the restaurant entrance for white patrons was not clearly marked as in the North, it was apparently recognized by all residents, but not by a stranger like Baldwin. So he went into the restaurant through the wrong entrance: "I will never forget it. I don't know if I can describe it. Everything abruptly froze into what, even at that moment, struck me as a kind of Marx Brothers parody of horror. Every white face turned to stone: the arrival of the messenger of death could not have had a more devastating effect than the appearance in the restaurant doorway of a small, unarmed, utterly astounded black man. I had realized my error as soon as I opened the door: but the absolute terror on all these white faces—I swear that not a soul moved—paralyzed me. They stared at me, I stared at them (71–72).

In Baldwin's description of the scene, the terror he witnessed on the white faces evokes a most poignant sense of isolation blacks ever feel. Then, he reports, one of the waitresses "rushed at me as though to club me down, and she barked—for it was not a human sound: 'What you want, boy? What you want in here?' And then, a decontaminating gesture, 'Right around there, boy. Right around there.' " Baldwin clinches the image of this woman: she had "a face like a rusty hatchet, and eyes like two rusty nails—nails left over from the Crucifixion" (72).

IV

The theme of estrangement dealt with the first part of the book continues in the second part, but greater emphasis is given to the author's references to contemporary events in American society. Although "To Be Baptized" anticipates America's rebirth, the narrative here consists of scenes that indicate a gloomier outlook than in "Take Me to the Water." This is why Baldwin appears obsessed with his memories of black martyrs such as Martin Luther King, Jr., and Malcolm X. But underneath this gloom and disillusionment, there is a sign of renewed hope that says: "these dead . . . shall not have died in vain" (89).

Despite the idea of creation sugggested by the title "To Be Baptized," Baldwin's motifs in the latter portion of the book are derived from bitter personal experience. For example, the case of Tony Maynard, his former bodyguard, imprisoned on a murder charge arising from a mistaken identity, provides the narrative with a sense of immediacy and attests to Baldwin's personal involvement with contemporary affairs.[15] The length and recurrence of the episode throughout this part of the book further demonstrate that Baldwin refuses to remain a purely observant artist and becomes a passionate participant for a cause. Since Tony Maynard is treated as a victim of the indifference and hatred that exists in society, this episode also becomes a structural thread to other episodes that otherwise appear fragmentary.[16]

The question still remains whether or not Baldwin had come away from the sixties as a disillusioned American. Throughout *No Name in the Street* he has fluctuated between his feelings of love and hatred as shown by the episodes. From the perspective of his hatred and resignation, the book clearly bodes ill; from the perspective of his love and understanding, though avowedly less frequent, it nevertheless demonstrates that its author remains hopeful.

Only the person who had faith in America could assert at the end of his book: "A person does not lightly elect to oppose his society. One would much rather be at home among one's compatriots than be mocked and detested by them" (194–95). The reader also learns in *No Name in the Street* that Baldwin was in sympathy with black militants such as Huey Newton and black separatists such as Malcolm X. Even from the vantage point of hatred and estrangement that Malcolm X seemed to have advocated, Baldwin persists in his usual doctrine of love and brotherhood. "What made him unfamiliar and dangerous," Baldwin writes, "was not his hatred for white people but his love for blacks" (97). When Baldwin declares in the epilogue that "the Western party is over, and the white man's sun has set. Period" (197), one can be puzzled, but at the same time one cannot rule out the possibility of Baldwin's meaning that the sun might also rise in America, this time for blacks as well as for whites.

Notes

1. See Irving Howe, "James Baldwin: At Ease in Apocalypse," *Harper's Magazine* 237 (1968):92, 95–100.

2. James Baldwin, *Notes of a Native Son* (Boston: Beacon, 1955), 9.

3. Baldwin writes: "If we—and now I mean the relatively conscious whites and the relatively conscious blacks, who must, like lovers, visit on, or create, the consciousness of the others—do not falter in our duty now, we may be able, handful that we are, to end the racial nightmare, and achieve our country, and change the history of the world" (*The Fire Next Time* [New York: Dial, 1963], 119).

4. See Benjamin DeMott, "James Baldwin on the Sixties: Acts and Revelations," in *James Baldwin: A Collection of Critical Essays,* ed. Keneth Kinnamon (Englewood Cliffs, N.J.: Prentice-Hall, 1974), 156.

5. James Baldwin, *No Name in the Street* (New York: Dial, 1972), 159–60; hereafter cited in the text.

6. Mark Twain, *Adventures of Huckleberry Finn,* ed. Henry Nash Smith (Boston: Houghton Mifflin, 1958), 185.

7. James Baldwin, "Alas, Poor Richard," in *Nobody Knows My Name* (New York: Dial, 1961), 215.

8. James F. Fullington, ed., *Prose and Poetry from the Old Testament* (New York: Appleton-Century-Crofts, 1950), 77.

9. Baldwin, *Notes of a Native Son,* 113.

10. In his latest volume of essays Baldwin makes a similar assertion about American blacks' somber realization of themselves: "This is why blacks can be heard to say, *I ain't got to be nothing but stay black, and die!*: which is, after all, a far more affirmative apprehension than *I'm free, white, and twenty-one*" (*The Devil Finds Work* [New York: Dial, 1976], 115).

11. Karin Möller, noting "Baldwin's mood of sombre, retrospective lucidity," writes: "The author's disillusionment with America persists throughout . . ." (*The Theme of Identity in the Essays of James Baldwin* [Göteborg, Sweden: Acta Universitatis Gothoburgensis, 1975], 131). Nick Aaron Ford writes: "It is a more hardboiled, pessimistic, disillusioned view of his country and its people" (*James Baldwin: A Critical Evaluation,* ed. Thomas B. O'Daniel [Washington, D.C.: Howard University Press, 1977], 101).

12. In 1961 Baldwin wrote in his essay "In Search of a Majority": "Whether I like it or not, or whether you like it or not, we are bound together forever. We are part of each other. What is happening to every Negro in the country at any time is also happening to you. There is no way around this. I am suggesting that these walls—these artificial walls—which have been up so long to protect us from something we fear, must come down" (*Nobody Knows My Name,* 136–37). In 1963 he wrote in "My Dungeon Shook": "Well, the black man has functioned in the white man's world as a fixed star, as an immovable pillar: and as he moves out of his place, heaven and earth are shaken to their foundations. . . . But these men are your brothers—your lost, younger brothers. And if the word *integration* means anything, this is what it means: that we, with love, shall force our brothers to see themselves as they are, to cease fleeing from reality and begin to change it" (*The Fire Next Time,* 23–24).

13. Baldwin argues that although Wright's authorial voice records the black anger as no black writer before him has ever done, it is also, unhappily, the overwhelming limitation of *Native Son*. What is sacrificed, according to Baldwin, is a necessary dimension to the novel: "the relationship that Negroes bear to one another, that depth of involvement and unspoken recognition of shared experience which creates a way of life . . . it is this climate, common to most Negro protest novels, which has led us all to believe that in Negro life there exists no tradition, no field of manners, no possibility of ritual or intercourse, such as may, for example, sustain the Jew even after he has left his father's house" (*Notes of a Native Son*, 35–36).

14. *Great Short Works of Stephen Crane* (New York: Harper, 1968), 258.

15. Benjamin DeMott regards Tony Maynard as an undeveloped character despite much space given for that purpose, but one might argue that *No Name in the Street* is not a collection of biographical portraits like Dreiser's *Twelve Men* and *A Gallery of Women*, but rather an autobiographical narrative centering upon its protagonist Baldwin. See DeMott, "James Baldwin," 158. The same argument applies to Baldwin's characterization of the black postal worker described earlier. Cf. Todd Gitlin, "Yet Will I Maintain Mine Own Ways Before Him," *Nation*, 10 April 1972, 469–70.

16. Karin Möller observes that Baldwin's various episodes are fragmentary and that his style in *No Name in the Street* is pretentiously casual (*Theme of Identity*, 129).

Essays on Drama

The Review That Was Too True to Be Published

Tom F. Driver°

The closing notice is up, and I am left to sing the blues for *Blues for Mister Charlie.*

During its brief career I went twice to see James Baldwin's play on Broadway. For one thing I wanted more of the performance by Diana Sands, the best any American actress has given all season. For another I wanted to make sure whether the plays's faults were really enough to force its closing, as some critics seem to think, or whether, as I suspected, its virtues did it in. I am now ready to maintain the latter and to see in this a phenomenon of some social importance, but before arguing the point let me pay homage to the lady.

Diana Sands first came among us some years ago in *Raisin in the Sun,* a soap opera for dark skins and light consciences not much to my liking. It required Miss Sands merely to be pert, which she was, and nothing more. My joy at seeing her unfold in the Baldwin play was great.

In the third act she had a long soliloquy, a lament for her dead lover, in which she poured over the theater a libation of anger, love and blasphemy. The sexual language of this speech is direct. It demands to be uttered without shame. Miss Sands did it with such conviction that her dignity increased with each revealing line. Furthermore, she played it at the top of the emotional register, shouting, weeping and pounding the air with her fists, an indulgence few performers could risk without disaster.

Here was acting in the grand manner. After putting it to the test of a second viewing. I can report that it lost nothing in the repetition. Honor to Miss Sands for bringing it off, to Burgess Meredith, her director, for letting her do it, and to James Baldwin for writing words to make it possible.

The play itself is based—"very distantly," as Baldwin has said—on the case of Emmett Till, murdered in 1955 by a white man who

°Reprinted from *Negro Digest* 13 (1964):34–40, by permission of the author and the journal.

was acquitted but who later confessed. In the play the murderer's guilt is clear from the start, and so is the acquittal the jury will give. A Negro youth (Al Freeman Jr.), rebellious and unstable to the point of courting death, runs afoul of a poor white (Rip Torn) with enough pride of race and insecurity of personality to pull the trigger. Baldwin is interested in these two men only as types. His portrayal of them is therefore in sketch but with absolute mastery of detail.

From these sketches our eyes are led to watch the town's reaction to the murder. The whites form an almost solid front, that abstraction called justice being less real to them than their fear. The front is broken—at any rate cracked—by Parnell, a newspaper owner (in which role Pat Hingle gave the best performance he has ever brought us). A confidant of both the victim's father and the murderer, he tries to remain friends with both while seeing that justice is done. this, of course, is impossible; and when, on the witness stand, he has to choose, it is the truth he lets go.

Among the blacks, the most important reaction we watch is that of the boy's clergyman father (Percy Rodriguez). He has long been a spokesman and a bargainer for civil rights. He becomes an agitator ready to take up arms.

The play is about the breakdown of "moderation" in the face of antagonisms that are by nature irrational and immoderate.

James Baldwin's *forte* has never been the making of plots, the structuring of fiction, nor the psychological delineation of character. He is first and last a preacher. But preaching in the theater is by no means always a fault, let alone something bad for the box office. In *The Deputy* Broadway has a sermon that is a solid hit, and the Lincoln Center Repertory has another in *After the Fall*. Neither is written half as well as *Blues for Mister Charlie*. The only trouble with sermons is that the more they are needed the less they are liked.

The terms in which James Baldwin chose to address his audience are not the terms in which they have wanted to listen. On the one hand, he alienated a large part of the liberal intelligentsia by paying scant attention to the political and economic roots of segregation. Marxist and socialist theory have not detained him. Absent also is any concern with the structure of American law and the elective process.

In other words, Baldwin stepped right outside the context in which most Americans now see the racial struggle. To them, it is a question of "civil rights," a constitutional question coupled, perhaps, with problems of unemployment, job training and other economic factors.

Instead of talking about all this, Baldwin has taken what will seem to many a reactionary step: he has described racial strife as *racial* strife, warfare between the black people and white people that is rooted in their separate ways of experiencing life, the difference symbolized in their sexuality. Baldwin thus opened himself to two attacks that critics were not slow to make: that he had swallowed "the myth of Negro sexual superiority," and that his characters were caricatures.

That is how it happened that Robert Brustein of *The New Republic* saw eye to eye with Howard Taubman of *The New York Times*, with whom he had intended strongly to disagree. They both uttered the damning judgment that the characters were stereotyped. As a matter of fact, no play about the Negro has ever been seen in America that represented small-town Southern white people more accurately than does *Blues for Mister Charlie*. (I will not judge its representation of Negroes in such a town, not having lived among them.) What the play sins against is not the reality down South but the social (hence aesthetic) myths up North.

On the other hand, Baldwin alienated the middle-class paying audience by presenting a view of the racial conflict that it fears is true. Unlike Lorraine Hansberry, who wrote the box office success *Raisin in the Sun,* he did not flatter the audience by telling it what it wanted to believe—namely, that Negroes have the same ambitions, aches and pains as other people. The moral of *that* message is that there is nothing to fear.

James Baldwin, by contrast, has been saying for some years, notably in *The Fire Next Time,* that there is plenty to fear. He tells us in *Blues for Mister Charlie* that Negroes do *not* feel and think as white people and that the assumption they do is simply a manifestation of the white's innate sense that his own values and experience are normative.

The shape of the play is not a comic one of movement from problem to solution, which would be a kind of civic reassurance. It is a movement, in the Negroes themselves, from "liberality" to warfare. As this movement is not comic, neither is it tragic. There is no catharsis in it.

Though Baldwin is no Brecht, the temper of his play is Brechtian but not Marxist. It is Brechtian in avoiding both comedy and tragedy. It is Brechtian in that it is a call to action rather than an imitation of action. It is Brechtian in that it uses what people will think are stereotypes for the deliberate purpose of challenging received ideas. It asks us to reconsider whether the "stereotypes" may not be nearer the truth than the theory that explains them away. Far from being, as some have charged, a "commercial" sort of play, this one has failed on Broadway for the same reason Brecht fails there: it frightens people by challenging the *status quo,* while at the same time it challenges their way of *seeing* the *status quo.*

The social significance of *Blues for Mister Charlie* lies in what it reveals about our fear of fear. It should be looked at side by side with the reaction many people made to the threatened "stall-in" at the World's Fair, the threat of water wastage proposed by Brooklyn CORE, and other demonstrations that go beyond attack on specific injustices in a spirit of generalized protest.

There is indeed something illogical in these actions. The public, including many white liberals, seems to see in them a threat of anarchy, and many Negro leaders have warned that riots and the temporary breakdown of law enforcement can be expected. The North is discovering its kinship with the South, and its reaction is beginning to show itself as fear. At this point some of our fixed notions display their inadequacy, and the Baldwin play becomes relevant.

Dogma has it that nothing stands in the way of racial harmony but, the ill will of benighted Southerners and other reactionaries who deny civil rights to Negroes. Ill will can be cured in due time by education, preaching and better laws. This view is so utterly rational and progressivist in character that it cannot accommodate into its understanding irrational antagonisms between racial groups. Hence it declares, contrary to much evidence, that sexual envy, which no doubt is irrational, has nothing to do with the problem. When a Baldwin says that it does, for Negro as well as white, he is said to be a purveyor of "myth."

The dogma, being designed to rule out fear, breaks down when fear becomes unavoidable. That is just where we are now. Southern "moderates" have been there a long time. Having no adequate resources to help them face that fear, having been told it was unrealistic, they became paralyzed by it and were notoriously ineffective in Southern politics. Power was exercised by the Faubuses, Barnetts and Wallaces who, however unprincipled, were realistic enough to see that fear existed, that it was inevitable and action must be predicated on it.

On the other side, Negroes became a political force in the South by virtue of the fact that they, who have lived long in fear, ceased to be afraid of it. They did not eliminate it, could not and did not try it. But they ceased to try to avoid it, and in that moment their ineffectiveness ended. I do not deny that an awakened class or racial consciousness has its importance, but class consciousness without the courage to face fear is impotent.

Impotence born of the fear of fear is what has been overcome by Negroes in the past 15 years, and it is what Baldwin is talking about in the Rev. Meridian Henry, who puts down his brief case and takes up his gun and his Bible. The message is not very sophisticated, but it is true enough; and it could hardly be more to the point at a time when the paralysis of the Southern "moderate" is creeping all over the country.

The sober citizens of the North, Midwest and West, if they do not want to be swept into the sidelines in the next five or ten years, will have to learn that some (we don't know how much) violence is unavoidable. They will have to learn that violence itself is far from the worst of evils, even in a peaceable democracy. The repression of violence by a force that perpetuates injustice is worse. The violence of terrified people is worse than the violence of brave men.

Moderates will have to know that fear is their lot. Those who cannot risk when they are afraid, who cannot cope with anything but rational progress, will be made impotent by their fear; and their impotence will bring anarchy and violence all the closer. If Baldwin's play is offensive, or even just unrealistic, to them, they will find their moment of truth arrived too late.

The Amen Corner   Harold Clurman*

James Baldwin's *The Amen Corner* (Ethel Barrymore Theatre) provides one of the very few evenings which afforded me true pleasure this season. And how surprising. For if I wished to be "real critical" (which means a little foolish) I could easily point out the play's crudities, banalities, *longueurs,* etc. Text and production are marred by many blemishes but the total effect is touching and valuable. Drama does not live by technique alone, nor is art all a matter of "mastery."

What makes *The Amen Corner* gratifying is its genuineness. I don't mean "realism." The play's locale is a "store-front church"—the kind of Harlem church which has no exact denomination or theology except for its own blasted blessedness; and I am not in the least familiar with such an establishment. The sense of genuineness the play creates comes from its sure feeling for race, place and universality of sentiment. It is folk material unadorned and undoctored. It is the stuff which has made the best in Baldwin. It has heart and reaches the heart.

Its crucial passages are beautifully written, wrought of living speech from the mouths of the people whose very clichés somehow transform themselves into poetry. A woman is described as being "full of nature." A man dies and his wife says without emphasis, "My baby. You done joined hands with the darkness." But quotations out

*Reprinted from the *Nation* 200 (1965):514–15, by permission of the author, the journal, and The Nation Co., Inc. © 1965.

of context offer only the barest hint of the sudden poignancy of some of the play's phrases and idioms which are uttered as commonplaces.

The weakest moments are the conventionally comic and the factually "satiric" ones. The play is not "propaganda": it does not insist that religiosity turns the sorry creatures of the community away from reality. There is no glib anti-clericalism here. "This way of holiness ain't no joke," says the unhappy and presumably bigoted woman minister who is the play's central character. "To love the Lord," she learns, "is to love all His children—all of them, everyone! and suffer with them and rejoice with them and never count the cost!" One believes this as one believes a spiritual. In a much simpler, a less probing way, Baldwin has used the material of his past somewhat as O'Neill used his own early youth in *Long Day's Journey Into Night.*

The Amen Corner was written before *Blues for Mr. Charlie,* which is Baldwin in an angrier, more sophisticated, less appealing but perhaps more immediately "useful" vein. But nothing in the later play is as moving as the confrontation of the derelict father and his neglected son, or the minister's "reconversion" (a reconversion to a profounder humanity) in *The Amen Corner.*

It is possible that a great part of my enthusiasm for this production is due to its acting. The play is not well staged or designed. Some of the actors are awkward, insufficiently trained. Yet nearly everything "works" because there is an organic relation between the play's essence and the company. There is little art but much "nature."

Still, Frank Silvera's Luke (the father: a moribund jazz trombonist) strikes home. He may be a trifle soft in his interpretation but there is in him a will to contact the very core of his partners' (his son's, his wife's) being which overrides every other consideration and which moves one inescapably.

Bea Richards' Sister Margaret (the minister) is glorious. Hers is certainly the outstanding achievement in acting of this past season. Again, qualifications which might be damaging in other instances— a rather thin voice and a delivery that threatens to become monotonous, an interpretation that tends to subtract some of the iron and soul-smashing drive of the character—dissolve in the truth of Miss Richards' pathos, the overwhelming fullness of her womanliness in which the sorrow of bitter experience and the abiding humor and tenderness of a total cycle of life manifest themselves effortlessly and yet with electrifying surprise.

After the first week, prices at *The Amen Corner* were lowered from a $6.90 top to maximums of $5.75 on Friday and Saturday evenings, $4.80 on Monday through Thursday and Saturday matinee, and $4 on Wednesday matinee. These are bargain prices for Broadway in 1965 and it will be good news for us all if they bring the play an audience. Show business wiseacres keep repeating that if a play is good, people will pay any price to see it. That is just not so, and the only reason that this truism is rarely contradicted is that our show folks' vision and knowledge of the world is circumscribed by the one street which is their preserve.

James Baldwin:
On the Tube at Last . . .   Martha Bayles°

James Baldwin has written 19 books and made thousands of speeches over the years, most of them thundering denunciations of white America for its constant backsliding into the sin of racism. It's a fire-and-brimstone style that in the 1950s and '60s earned him notoriety and renown, but that now reduces his stature to that of a curiosity imported to American college campuses from his adopted home in the south of France to rail against a new generation that has never heard of him and would rather watch Eddie Murphy.

Mr. Baldwin's rhetoric has simply gone on too long, berating white racism not only for the oppression of blacks, but also for every ill he has personally experienced, including the emotional devastation of having been rejected in childhood by an abusive and fanatically religious stepfather.

Yet Mr. Baldwin's voice was not always a one-note instrument. In *Go Tell It On The Mountain,* his autobiographical first novel, published in 1953, he evoked the pain of that Depression-era Harlem childhood in a cleareyed fashion that spares neither the white oppressor nor the black. Redneck rapists, Klansmen and New York police all behave brutally; but so does Gabriel Grimes, the self-styled Pentecostal preacher who vents his frustrations on his wife's illegitimate son, John.

Considered a classic for more than 30 years. *Go Tell It On The Mountain* has never been made into a movie—until now. According to Robert Geller, the producer of the remarkable film being presented tonight (9–11 p.m. EST; check local listings) on PBS's *American Playhouse,* film makers tend to avoid a novel written in very distinctive language, because too much of its effect may be "untranslatable" into a visual medium.

°Reprinted from the *Wall Street Journal,* 14 January 1985, 14, by permission of the author and the journal.

Yet I wonder whether Mr. Baldwin's rolling, biblical prose style is the main reason why this novel has never been adapted to the screen. Couldn't it also be the case that such a scorchingly truthful portrait of a downtrodden black family contains something to offend everyone? A few years ago, the media focused exclusively on the heroism of black families, not the problems. This is beginning to change, and perhaps it is easier now to put a negative black father figure on the air.

Even so, Mr. Geller admits to having "softened" Gabriel Grimes. Certainly Paul Winfield, who played the loving father in the film *Sounder*, gives the character more expression and vulnerability than even the script allows—and the script alters scene after scene to make Gabriel appear more of a victim and less of a victimizer.

Clearly, this film reworks Mr. Baldwin's novel. But not, I think, to the point of distortion. Gabriel is still pretty hateful, and Mr. Geller has a point when he says, "No audience wants to spend two hours watching a totally hard man beat up on a helpless child." It also may be necessary, in a dramatization, to display on a character's face things that, in fiction, may be shown to exist only in his heart.

Aside from some confusing flashbacks at the beginning, which don't give us a chance to accept new performers playing the youthful Gabriel and his sister Florence, the complex plot is skillfully compressed. Moreover, the flavor of Mr. Baldwin's prose is admirably preserved in the dialogue and, above all, in the music of the storefront church where the Grimes family pours out its emotions. *Go Tell It On The Mountain* is a powerful enough to lift us off the ground even before Linda Hopkins (the gospel singer who plays Sister McCandless) opens her mouth. After she does, it soars.

James Baldwin as Dramatist   Fred L. Standley°

James Baldwin's eminence as a man of letters is now well established; indeed, his books, essays, and other pieces attest to the truth of Benjamin DeMott's statement that "this author retains a place in an extremely select group: that comprised of the few genuinely indispensable American writers."[1] Within that context his reputation as a dramatist rests primarily upon two works: *Blues for Mister Charlie*

°Reprinted from *Dictionary of Literary Biography*, vol. 7, ed. John MacNicholas (© 1981 by Gale Research Co.; reprinted by permission of the publisher), Gale Research, 1981, pp. 45–49.

(1964) and *The Amen Corner* (1968), each of which has been both praised and derided by its respective admirers and detractors. Significantly, however, Baldwin is one of the few black playwrights who has had more than one production on Broadway, and he was the recipient in 1964 of the Foreign Drama Critics Award.

From the time of his initial publication, a short story on the Spanish Revolution in a church newspaper at the age of twelve, Baldwin has consciously cultivated his vocation as a writer: "I consider that I have many responsibilities but none greater than this: to last, as Hemingway says, and get my work done I want to be an honest man and a good writer."[2] The effort to implement that desire requires that the artist "cannot allow any consideration to supersede his responsibility to reveal all that he can possibly discover concerning the mystery of the human being"; for Baldwin this responsibility means that the author's role is to express the existential knowledge of human experience: "the states of birth, suffering, love and death . . . extreme states—extreme, universal and inescapable. . . . The artist is present to correct the delusions to which we fall prey in our attempts to avoid this knowledge."[3] Furthermore, the artist writes to "describe things which other people are too busy to describe," and this is a special function within any society.

Baldwin believes not only that the writer has a personal responsibility, but also that he must be "responsible to and for—the social order"[4] by developing and advocating a historical orientation and an ethical vision. Thus, in his essay "The Creative Dilemma," Baldwin views the artist as "the incorrigible disturber of the peace" who "cannot and must not take anything for granted" in the society but "must drive to the heart of every answer and expose that question the answer hides." He believes that every society and culture, especially in the United States, will determinedly endeavor to restrict the artist's vision of human experience "in which one discovers that life is tragic, and therefore unutterably beautiful." This perspective of experience presumes the validity of paradox as a model of explanation and exploration; however, America is "a country devoted to the death of paradox." For Baldwin, then, the artist's inherent duty produces a condition of warring with his society; nevertheless, "the war of an artist with his society is a lover's war, and he does, at his best, what lovers do, which is to reveal the beloved to himself and, with that revelation, to make freedom real."[5] That purpose was hauntingly reiterated just recently in an interview with Baldwin entitled "Looking Toward the Eighties" in which he said that the author's "function is very particular and so is his responsibility. After all, to write, if taken seriously, is to be subversive. To disturb the peace."[6] As an artist who has examined a multitude of subjects and themes throughout his career, Baldwin states forthrightly his conviction that only two options are available to all "writers—black or white—to be immoral and uphold the *status quo* or to be moral and try to change the world."[7]

Both *The Amen Corner* and *Blues for Mister Charlie* exhibit unmistakable parallels with and allusions to the real-life experiences of James Baldwin, although neither drama can be described as a clearly autobiographical work. By 1942 when he graduated from De Witt Clinton High School in New York City, Baldwin had been editor of the school literary magazine, had spent three years as a teenage Holy Roller preacher under the tutelage of his stepfather in the Fireside Pentecostal Assembly, and had been profoundly influenced by reading Harriet Beecher Stowe, Charles Dickens, and others. Subsequently, he worked as a porter, dishwasher, waiter, office boy, handyman, factory hand, and elevator operator while also writing book reviews and other short pieces for the *Nation* and the *New Leader*. After meeting Richard Wright and winning the Eugene F. Saxton Fellowship (1945) and a Rosenwald Fellowship (1948), he left for Paris and Europe in 1948 and remained there, except for brief visits home, for nearly a decade. With the intensification of the civil rights movement in the 1960s, Baldwin became increasingly active as a spokesman expressing in speeches and essays what it meant to be black in America—the alienation, the despair, the rage, the reality. Committed "to end the racial nightmare of our country and change the history of the world," he worked with Medgar Evers and James Meredith in Mississippi, toured on behalf of the Congress of Racial Equality, helped with voter registration in Selma, Alabama, and met with Attorney General Robert Kennedy in New York concerning the explosive nature of black-white relations.

Blues for Mister Charlie obviously reflects the author's participation in the civil rights movement, for the play is based on the case of Emmett Till, a black teenage youth from Chicago who was murdered in 1955 in Mississippi for allegedly flirting with a white woman. His two white murderers were then acquitted of the crime by an all-white jury, though one of the killers subsequently bragged about the act and recounted the details. While some critics have dismissed the play as propagandistic, bombastic, and melodramatic, others have praised the manner in which it reveals the myths and stereotypes relating to black-white relations, a thematic emphasis Baldwin had explored poignantly a year earlier in *The Fire Next Time* (1963).

Blues for Mister Charlie is a complex drama that uses its dual settings of Whitetown (the courthouse) and Blacktown (the church) to present several stories and to explore several ideas simultaneously. Whereas Richard Henry, the young black entertainer who has returned home from New York after being hooked on dope, and the black student Juanita, who is friendly with the local white liberal newspaper editor, and Lyle Britten, the white store owner who kills Richard, play central roles in the unfolding story, the two major characters are Parnell James, the editor, and Rev. Meridian Henry, local minister and father of Richard. These latter two figures embody the persistent motif of Baldwin's work at that point in his literary career, namely the need for "the relatively conscious whites and the relatively conscious blacks, who must, like lovers, insist on, or create, the consciousness of the others." Unfortunately, and rather tragically, *Blues for Mister Charlie* concludes with Parnell James, the white liberal, lacking the courage to testify at the trial that Jo Britten has lied about Richard, and with Meridian Henry, the embodiment of black moderation and nonviolence, conjoining "the Bible and the gun" in the pulpit "like the pilgrims of old." Darwin Turner has suggested in his essay "Visions of Love and Manliness in a Blackening World"[8] that *Blues for Mister Charlie* was written for a white audience and belongs in the general category of that "traditional drama" which stresses the similarities between blacks and whites, examines the dilemma of middle-class blacks, and uses black characters who challenge whites verbally but passively reject physical confrontation.

The Amen Corner, though first produced commercially in the 1960s, was written in the 1950s and performed at Howard University. The play, like Baldwin's first novel, *Go Tell It on the Mountain* (1953), draws heavily upon his earlier religious experience, especially his role as a young preacher in the Fireside Pentecostal Assembly, and also his previous attendance at Harlem's Mount Calvary of the Pentecostal Faith Church presided over by Mother Horn, "a tall, dynamic woman, the leader of a large flock, in her own way as opinionated and domineering as David Baldwin," the author's preacher stepfather. In contrast to his categorizing of *Blues for Mister Charlie,* Turner argues that *Amen Corner* is a "Black Arts" drama that ignores the relationship between blacks and whites, stresses the necessity for love in the black family and community, and rejects any doctrine of the church that emphasizes only a God of Wrath.[9] This final point is a recognition that Baldwin expresses in the play, a basic idea already expressed in *The Fire Next Time:* "If the concept of God has any validity or use, it can only be to make us larger, freer, and more loving. If God cannot do this, then it is time we got rid of Him."[10]

In act 3 of *The Amen Corner* Sister Margaret Alexander, pastor of a Harlem church, finally grasps the complete significance inherent in the realization that "it's an awful thing to think about, the way love never dies!" Having given up her rigid and legalistic religious discipline in the process of agonizingly accepting the return of her estranged, dying husband; the departure of her maturing, independent son; and the rejection by her rebellious congregation, Sister Margaret acquires compassion: "To love the Lord is to love all his children—all of them, everyone!—and suffer with them and rejoice with them and never count the cost."

In *Blues for Mister Charlie* and *Amen Corner,* as in his other literary works, Baldwin explores a variety of thematic concerns: the historical significance and the potential explosiveness in black-white relations; the necessity for developing a sexual and psychological consciousness and identity; the intertwining of love and power in the universal scheme of existence as well as in the structures of society; the misplaced priorities in the value systems in America; and the responsibility of the artist to promote the evolution of the individual and the society. The extent of Baldwin's success as a man of letters in the genre of drama remains, however, a moot question. On the one side some critics contend, as does Gerald Weales, that "despite the incidental virtues of both plays, they indicate that the dramatic form is not a congenial one for Baldwin." In contrast Carlton Molette advocates in "James Baldwin as Playwright" that the author, essentially a novelist and essayist, has demonstrated as dramatist his trust of and reliance upon many other artists; that "the ability to accomplish that collaborative working relationship may very well be the reason for Baldwin's success as a playwright where so many other novelists have failed"; and that "given the present system of producing plays professionally in the United States, we are lucky indeed to get one play per decade from the likes of James Baldwin."[11]

Notes

1. Benjamin DeMott, "James Baldwin on the Sixties: Acts and Revelations," *Saturday Review,* 27 May 1977, 66.

2. James Baldwin, "Autobiographical Notes," in *Notes of a Native Son* (New York: Dial, 1963), 6.

3. James Baldwin, "The Creative Dilemma," *Saturday Review,* 8 February 1964, 15.

4. James Baldwin, "The Black Boy Looks at the White Boy," in *Nobody Knows My Name* (New York: Dial, 1961), 188.

5. Baldwin, "Creative Dilemma," 15, 58.

6. "Interview: James Baldwin: Looking Towards the Eighties," *Black Collegian,* December–January 1979, 105.

7. Hoyt Fuller, "Reverberations From a Writer's Conference," *African Forum* 1 (1965):79.

8. Darwin Turner, "Visions of Love and Manliness in a Blackening World," *Iowa Review* 6, no. 2 (1975):82–99.

9. Turner, "Visions," 85.

10. James Baldwin, *The Fire Next Time* (New York: Dial, 1963), 61.

11. Carlton Molette, "James Baldwin as Playwright," in *James Baldwin: A Critical Evaluation,* ed. Therman B. O'Daniel (Washington, D.C.: Howard University Press, 1977), 188.

INDEX

312   Index